WORLD BALLET AND DANCE
1990–91

WORLD
BALLET AND DANCE
1990–91

An International Yearbook

Founder Editor
BENT SCHØNBERG

Editor
JANN PARRY

Associate Editor
CRISTINA SCHØNBERG

DANCE BOOKS
Cecil Court   London

First published in 1990 by Dance Books Ltd,
9 Cecil Court, London WC2N 4EZ

ISBN 1 85273 027 7

Design and production in association with
Book Production Consultants, 47 Norfolk St, Cambridge

Typeset by AsTec, Saffron Walden, Essex

Printed and bound in Great Britain by
Redwood Press, Melksham
Wiltshire

A CIP catalogue record for this book is available from the British Library.

The line drawings in the text are by Cristina Schønberg

Contents

CONTENTS

Illustrations

Acknowledgements

We wish to thank The Society for Dance Research for permission to include four of the articles in part II, *Dance Archives*. These originally appeared in the Society's journal, *Dance Research*.

Editor's Preface

When we published the first edition of *World Ballet and Dance* last year we were more than curious to know whether there was a need for the book – if we did, indeed, fill a gap. So we enclosed a questionnaire asking readers to tell us what they thought.

The answers were numerous. (Extracts from them are printed on the back cover.) Three people hated the book and a fourth wrote that it was dreadful – but he would buy the next edition anyway. The rest were more positive. We shall try to incorporate some of the suggestions they made in further editions of the book. (The prize for those who returned questionnaires was won by Miss A. Warner from London, who much enjoyed her trip to Copenhagen.)

The section giving statistical details of dance companies is clearly of value. This year we have tried to expand it by giving information on dancers' salaries around the world (well aware, of course, that dancers are generally badly paid wherever they are in relation to other professions). Would you believe it – a lot of companies hummed and hawed and talked about how impossible it would be to estimate the true value of a salary if you did not take into account the cost of living, taxation levels, social security benefits (if any), etc, etc.

To which we can only answer: trust dancers – they know a decent salary when they see it. It was so hard to get figures out of company administrators that it seemed they must be ashamed of the low rates they pay – which cannot, surely, be the case! (Our Netherlands contributor, Eva van Schaik, informs us that the energetic Dutch have commissioned an international research project into dancers' salaries around the world – see Netherlands section of dance statistics at the end of this book.)

Last year we lamented over the insane steps, jumps and tricks with which choreographers all over the world try to outdo each other – at the risk of dancers' health and seldom to the benefit of dance. The situation has not changed; and ballet's position as second-best to opera in most countries has continued to deteriorate. State support for dance companies is dwindling, with the exception of France and Germany, in western Europe. The rapid changes in eastern Europe are likely to affect state subsidies for the arts. In the Soviet Union the Bolshoi and Kirov Ballets are trying to establish a different economic footing for the companies and their dancers to lessen their dependence on the state and its agency, Gosconcert.

One consequence of *glasnost* has been the departure of a number of dancers for the west, mostly on temporary contracts which they are now able to negotiate themselves. They join the well-paid (sometimes *very* well-paid) international stars who are in demand wherever they go. Glittering names like Sylvie Guillem, Fernando Bujones, Andris Liepa and Irek Mukhamedov attract audiences to opera houses and theatres. But local dancers in the resident companies will not find their pay going up as a result; and it should be noted that the average *corps de ballet* dancer today is extremely good – at least as good as most soloists of fifty to sixty years ago.

Financial crises have closed many small dance companies in the past year and led to abrupt changes in management in larger ones. Rudolf Nureyev and the Paris Opéra administrators had a very public row which resulted in his departure as artistic director after six years. Mikhail Baryshnikov split from American Ballet Theatre, which is now being run by its executive director, Jane Hermann, together with Oliver Smith. Bitter arguments between artistic directors and administrators over which should come first, artistic growth or balanced finances, have also affected the Joffrey Ballet in the United States and English National Ballet. It seems increasingly that boards of directors, who control the money, want to control artistic policy as well – and their main concern must be to play safe and not to take risks with new work. Pity the poor dancers condemned to an endless round of *Swan Lakes*, *Coppélias*, *Nutcrackers* and *Giselles*!

Because this yearbook is published in Britain, we are particularly concerned with the state of British companies. It seems to us that English National Ballet (which should never have changed its name from London Festival Ballet, in our opinion) treated its artistic director, Peter Schaufuss, in a way that had little to do with the fair or gentlemanly behaviour upon which the English pride themselves. He was sacked in February 1990 so abruptly that he had no time to collect his belongings and then found the doors locked with security guards outside them when he returned the following day; and at the company's fortieth anniversary gala in March he was given no credit for his six years of hard work in raising the standards and the international reputation of the company. However, he was quickly snapped up by Götz Friedrich to take over the leadership of West Berlin's Opera House Ballet, where he will be able to be much more ambitious than he could be in Britain.

Meanwhile, the Royal Ballet at Covent Garden has its problems. The dancers went on strike at the beginning of the year, demanding a pay rise equal to the one the opera chorus had negotiated. They did not quite get it and discussions over a 'Dancers' Charter' have been going on for many months. Seat prices have gone up again, driving away the regulars and the young audiences of the future. Jeremy Isaacs, the Royal Opera House's general director, has enraged the powers-that-be by declaring that he is expecting a £5 million deficit. And he enraged the critics by restricting them to one complementary ticket instead of the usual two, in order to save money (a decision he later rescinded). He has not yet gone as far as the Soviet companies, which ban critics whose views they do not like.

Bad news for the Vienna Staatsoper Ballet: Dr Gerhard Brunner, who worked untiringly for years to improve the status and standards of the company, has left to head the two theatres in Graz. The seventy performances a season which he had fought for are being cut back to forty, reducing the ballet to the level 'enjoyed' by the ballet company at La Scala. The new artistic director, Elena Tchernichova (at present with American Ballet Theatre) will not take over until 1992, and then only on a part-time three-year contract, with her deputy, Susanne Kirnbauer, in charge for six months of the year.

The difficulties faced by the large companies may mean that the future lies with smaller ensembles, like the contemporary dance companies – though they are burdened with financial problems as well. As we try to look forward, all we can ask is *quo vadis?* – or perhaps better, *quo saltas?*

Bent Schønberg
Founder Editor
1990

PART I

Is Dance an International Language?

Chris de Marigny

D ance has often used the argument that it appeals to everybody, that it crosses cultural and national barriers because it does not use words (or at least it used not to). Moreover, it is said that movement is the same for everyone, something we all do. But is this really true? The production of *Giselle* which the Kirov tours around the world, is it really seen the same way in each country? Are the plotless works of Balanchine and Cunningham received in the same fashion in the United States, France and Germany? And what about those new 1980s French choreographers – why are they often less well received abroad than in their own country?

The great American critic Edwin Denby observed in his seminal article *Dancers, Buildings and People in the Streets* that the way people moved varied from country to country and that these movements were determined by all kinds of different factors. The American sense of scale and space is determined by their high buildings and vast landscapes and is entirely different from that of the Europeans. He noticed that an American 'lolling' takes up much more space than a European, and that the roll in the walk of Afro-Caribbeans was 'miraculous' when compared to the gait of the average New Yorker. These kinds of things influence our attitude to the way we see movement on the stage. What does the Kirov look like to the average African? It probably appears every bit as distorted and eccentric a form of dance as much classical Japanese theatre does to Western eyes.

Ballet is the nearest thing we have to an internationally accepted form of movement. This is due to a number of factors, one of which is status. Ballet is now recognized in many countries as an establishment art form, supported by governments and leaders of society alike. It has spread cuckoo-like around the globe, ousting indigenous forms of dance from their central position in the cultural hierarchy. Triumphantly surviving the context of its creation in seventeenth-century France, its classical impersonality, in its twentieth-century form, has permitted its migration to foreign climes. Another factor has been its steady exposure on television and video. This has reinforced the equation of dance with ballet in the minds of most people. Ballroom and disco are probably the only other forms recognized at an international level. Whilst other dance forms do appear on television, it is with nothing like the same frequency.

Making ballet an international form has many risks attached to it. The individual styles associated with the older companies, for instance, are being diluted, and the classical repertoire itself is changing more rapidly than might otherwise have been expected. The Kirov *Giselle*, for example, has been almost entirely stripped of its mimetic content. Yet one of the undoubted reasons for the success of story ballets has been the use of mime to make the plot both clear and logical. There has been a notion in recent years that story ballets can be streamlined by reducing the mime and other activity to make the action flow more easily. It is also intended, of course, that the greatest possible number of people should be able to watch and comprehend the action. However, the result is quite different. These romantic dramas lose their emotional content, and the choreographed movement which at one time conveyed meaning relating to the preceding mime, ceases to have any meaning whatsoever. Contemporary dance is not exempt from this error: Rambert Dance Company's Richard Alston has produced some singularly vapid story ballets (*Mythologies*) while Ashley Page's work *Soldat*, for the same company is similarly deficient.

The trend towards international ballet is homogenizing it into an increasingly bland form. This has been aided and abetted by major schools such as the Royal Ballet School in London changing over to Russian-style training. No doubt we will acquire some very athletic ballet dancers: the risk is, however, that they will no longer be able to dance the intricate and subtly nuanced steps and phrasing of Frederick Ashton – who represents, after all, the quintessentially British style. The likely result, in a few years time, will be that the Royal Ballet may well look like other Russian-influenced companies but will lose much of its essential Britishness, in spite of its British-based repertoire. Ballet athletics are all very well but acrobatic tricks can never be great dancing, even though they thrill a large and increasingly non-specialist public. In the long term, the danger is that the same people will watch ballet as watch athletics, but they will prefer the latter because athletes will always be able to jump higher.

Movement and gesture do not always translate. For instance, Europeans shake hands to greet each other, whereas Japanese and Indians would, in their different fashions, bow. In Europe, people shrug their shoulders to indicate that they do not know, whereas in India they wave their hands in a fluttering manner. Even non-referential movement in so-called abstract dances has great pitfalls since it allows people to try to read in to works whatever they please. Merce Cunningham, in conversation with Jacqueline Lesschaeve, related of one of his works that 'In Sweden they said it was about race riots; in Germany they thought of concentration camps; in London they spoke of bombed cities; in Tokyo they said it was the atom bomb. . . Of course it's about all of those and not about any of them, because I didn't have any of those experiences, but everybody was drawing on his experience, whereas I had simply made a piece which was involved with "falls", the idea of bodies falling.'[1]

As long as movement is related to the human body it will inevitably convey a meaning, even if it is not necessarily the same one for audiences around the world. One of the things that makes a choreographer great is his or her ability to convey meaning precisely.

1. Merce Cunningham, *The Dancer and the Dance: Merce Cunningham in Conversation with Jacqueline Lesschaeve* (New York and London: Marion Boyars, 1985), p. 105.

Meanwhile, the development of contemporary and innovative work in the 1980s has posed another set of problems. Dance has increasingly become the popular form nearly everywhere (except in England where the position seems more static). Contemporary dance, working in any number of techniques and forms, has produced a quite astonishingly broad range of work, much of which can be associated with local, regional or national characteristics – the cool, pure, unsexed work of British choreographers such as Rosemary Butcher, Siobhan Davies and Richard Alston, the violently aggressive and acrobatic work of Belgian artists Wym Vanderkeybus and Anne Teresa de Keersmaeker, the neo-expressionist work of German choreographers Susanne Linke and Pina Bausch, are only a few examples of indigenous contemporary style.

What happens when some of this work is exported? Does it travel well (as the wine industry puts it)? The work of Siobhan Davies and Rosemary Butcher, for instance, tends to bore the Latins rigid. These gentle abstractions with their lyrical effects are misread as being weak, dull and pallid. The reference to landscape, so evident in much of this work, for instance, is not even remotely understood in France. The painstaking way in which these artists try to achieve a breathtaking unity between movement, music and design is seen as chasing an aesthetic which is out of date. Contemporary French concerns are quite different. Fiona Burnside, in a recent article in *Dance Theatre Journal*, noted: 'The French art world would appear to have been convulsed by structuralism and deconstructionism. Synthesis is out, fragmentation is in. The force of these essentially language-related theories has been little felt in the dance world of this country and work which is composed according to these ideas is not likely to be understood.'[2]

When enthusiastic promoters first discovered the new French dance they were quite surprised to find that, whilst there was an initial wave of interest in this undoubtedly new form, critical opinion, in Britain at least, rapidly hardened against it. The deconstructed and fragmented storylines and choreographic strategies require the audience to find their own way through the maze. This appeals to French sensibilities, but merely irritates the British. Furthermore, French new dance has a bitter and continuous argument with the ballet world which leads many of its leading exponents to talk about 'breaking the movement' and 'chopping the action'. French choreographers' work is, in consequence, often characterized by short sequences of movement, isolated and separated from each other (Dominique Bagouet for instance) or near immobility – at least in terms of travelling across the floor (as in work by Claude Brumachon or Catherine Divérès). Innovatory dance in Britain has long since forgotten its quarrels with ballet and has got on with its own business. Here again French choreographers are misunderstood, being accused by the British of being frightened of making movement, whilst the French accuse the British of being merely dull.

Other reasons that work does not export well can relate to the cultural baggage carried by any artist abroad. For example, The Place Theatre in London recently presented a new work, *Donkey*, by the Israeli artists Nir Ben Gal and Liat Dror. This talented pair make works which concern personal relationships and patriotic duty (such as their *Two Room Apartment*, which explored their relationship as well as their experience in military service). *Donkey* takes on the problem of the migrant and the settler. This became clear as the piece developed, with its use of repetition to portray the incessant toil of the kibbutz and the repeated travelling movements of the migrant. Interposed between these sequences were others dealing with the private relationships of the adolescent and also the aged. It was only when talking to the artists after the show that I discovered the Israeli duo had drawn in themes which were Palestinian (through the use of strangely sensual, popular Arab/rock forms) alongside Jewish concerns (incorporating Israeli music artists). Furthermore, it was pointed out that the simple clothes they wore were common to both cultures. These and other references were lost on me, as they were on most of the British audience, yet these same items provoked a lot of controversy in Israel. In another section of the work the dancers exchange clothes and thereby sexual identities. The entire movement sequence is then repeated in each case by the other sex. Common-or-garden stuff in Europe, but something which again

2. Fiona Burnside, 'British spring load', *Dance Theatre Journal*, vol. 8 no. 1 (1990), p. 18.

bothered Israeli audiences no end. Nevertheless, the British audience did have a positive reaction to the work, based partly on the couple's dynamic technique and engaging personalities, and partly on the fact that the choreographic structures were extremely clear and theatrically logical.

Even in the field of experimental work there is, nevertheless, a tendency to homogenize. This happens not so much by the volition of the artists themselves but through the influence of international production systems. The audience for new work in the United Kingdom and overseas is much the same. It is young, educated broadly to the left in political terms and is often an audience which crosses over from one art form to another. (These are, of course, broad generalizations.) A generation of young promoters has grown up alongside these audiences, all closely interconnected through a series of informal networks. Over the last ten years this has led to the establishment of an orthodoxy of taste and a mutual agreement as to what is interesting and presentable from one country to another. The result is a growing uniformity of taste at many international festivals. In addition, the more these productions tour from one country to another, the more they influence the artists in those countries. Hence the possibility is increased of an international style coming into being which, as the artists become more established, will become increasingly bland and orthodox.

Dance has always been an expensive art form and in these days of budgetary restraint, co-producing, at international level, has come to be seen as the solution to giving choreographers the income they need. The price to be paid often means working to international formulae; for example, British critics increasingly refer in disparaging terms to 'Euro-length' dance works of approximately one hour. This is because most producers come from a theatrical background and this period is the average European theatre-presenter's length. Most European countries have no repertory tradition in contemporary dance allowing companies to present several short works in one evening; therefore immature European artists are attempting the impossible in trying to make full evening-length works, long before they are able to sustain such a challenge, either in terms of content or move-ment invention. The popularity of repetition, originally something only seen on the extreme edges of American avant-garde, can be partially explained by the fact that it fills in blocks of time before the next sequence begins. This is a long way from the intellectual rigour of Gertrude Stein's 'a rose is a rose is a rose' or the heady days of American minimal music in the mid-1960s.

By this time it must be becoming clear that I do not think that dance or movement can cross international frontiers with ease. But the excitement of seeing work from other countries lies precisely in the fact that, whilst it is sometimes harder to understand, at least such work promises new points of view and new ideas. The danger inherent in the belief that dance is a universal language *per se* is that it encourages artists and presenters to make lazy assumptions about the communication between artists and audiences. The converse danger of trying to make an easily digestible package for large audiences around the world must equally be guarded against, especially in Europe where the combined forces of economic union and commercial co-production could encourage a bland form of 'Eurodance'.

PART II

Dance Archives

T he dance archives described here are intended to give an idea of the very different collections held around the world. One, the dance collection of the New York Public Library (held at the Lincoln Centre), aims to provide as comprehensive a documentation of dance as possible: others represent the particular interests of the collectors who established them, such as the Derra de Moroda Archives in Salzburg. The Paris Opéra Archives are exceptionally rich and wide-ranging for a collection belonging to a single institution; and two examples are given of smaller archives kept by individual companies – the Rambert Dance Company archives in London and the Merce Cunningham Dance Company archives in New York.

The collections described here are usually accessible to scholars and researchers, but it is advisable (and sometimes essential) to make an appointment with the archivist, either by writing or telephoning in advance.

Detailed information on dance collections in different countries can be obtained from the *International Directory of Performing Arts Libraries and Museums of the World*, published by SIBMAS (Société Internationale des Bibliothèques et des Musées des Arts du Spectacle – International Association of Libraries and Museums of the Performing Arts). SIBMAS also publishes several bulletins each year giving information about exhibitions, seminars and special events.

SIBMAS Membership Secretariat:
14 Woronzow Road
London NW8 6QE
Great Britain
SIBMAS Information Bulletin:
Mrs L. Alexandrescu
Waalstraat III
1078 BN Amsterdam
The Netherlands

Archives and Collections in North America

Jane Pritchard

A ny brief survey of archival resources available for the study of dance
must necessarily appear superficial, particularly given the wealth of
material to be found in the United States and Canada. Most theatre collections include some material on dance and the American Theatre Library
Association's publications include useful guides to many such holdings,
not only in the United States but indeed internationally. The survey outlined
below indicates just a few of the collections to be found within university
and public libraries, in museums and certain specialist collections.

New York

The most widely known collection is the Dance Collection in the Performing
Arts Research Centre, New York Public Library. Located at New York's
Lincoln Centre for the Performing Arts, this is a popular collection catering
not only for the dance scholar but also welcoming the dance student or *aficio-
nado* wanting to view films and video recordings included in the Jerome
Robbins Film Archive. Today the collection houses more than 36,000
books, 6,000 prints, 1,800 original stage and costume designs, 500,000 photographs and 10,000 reels of film and videotape. Five centuries are spanned
and material covers as many forms of dance as possible. The collection has
been built up over the past forty years largely by gifts from the dance profession, thus its greatest strength is in twentieth-century material. Among
the library's specific holdings are the Ted Shawn and Ruth St Denis Collection; the Humphrey–Weidman Collection; and Hanya Holm, Agnes de Mille,
Ruth Page, Carl van Vechten, Louis Horst, Sol Hurok, George Platt Lynes,
Tatiana Chamié and Antony Tudor have all generously given records of their
work. Other special donations are the Cia Fornaroli Collection, presented
by the ballerina's husband, Walter Toscanini, which is a unique collection
on Italian ballet; the Roger Pryor Dodge Collection of Nijinsky photographs; the Isadora Duncan Collection, given by Irma Duncan; the Gabriel
Astruc Diaghilev Collection; and collections built up by Lilian Moore and
by Lincoln Kirstein. The catalogue of the Dance Collection's holdings is
now computerized and the staff willingly guide first-time visitors to material
of interest to them. No appointment is needed to use this collection but

naturally scholars undertaking major research projects are advised to contact the curators in advance.

San Francisco

The West Coast of America is building up a similarly important collection. Formerly known as the San Francisco Dance Archives, it was recently renamed the San Francisco Performing Arts Library and Museum and moved into new premises in 1989. The library, which claims a collection of more than a million items, has developed from the collection of a former dancer and designer with San Francisco Ballet, the late Russell Hartley. This library, too, has attracted important donations, particularly those documenting theatrical activity in the Bay Area. Among more recent additions have been the personal collections of the local dance teacher George Pring and the librarian Marguerite Rogers, both of which include material on Duncan, Pavlova, Theodore Kossloff and Wigman. Photographic material includes the collections of Henri McDowell and Chester Kessler. This library also houses the important archive of American pioneer ballet dancers Lew and Gisella Christensen.

University Collections

Certain university libraries in the United States are important for dance research. Princeton's William Seymour Theatre Collection has useful and developing dance holdings, with a collection on Romantic ballet (focusing on Fanny Elssler) built up by Allison Delarue; this collection also includes the Otto Kahn papers. Florida State University acquired in 1983 the Killinger collection of Denishawn costumes and memorabilia. The University of Utah's Marriot Library houses the William F. Christiansen papers and the records of Ballet West. Mills College Library in Oakland, California, includes the Jane Bourne Parton Collection of Books on Dance; the University of California, Berkeley, the Paget–Fredricks Dance Collection; the University of Denver's Martha Faure Carson Dance Library has 8,000 books and a range of dance ephemera; the Curtis Theatre Collection at the University of Pittsburg includes the Pavlova–Heinrich Collection and materials on dance in musicals; and the Walter Clinton Jackson Library at the University of North Carolina, Greensboro, has a collection specializing in physical education and dance. In Canada, the University of Waterloo, Ontario, has an important collection of rare books on European court dance and ballet from the sixteenth to the twentieth century.

However, the undoubted jewel of university theatre collections is the Harvard Theatre Collection; dance is regarded as an intrinsic part of this marvellous research centre. Established as early as 1901, the Harvard Theatre

Collection was one of the first to gather playbills, prints, programmes, artistic and administrative papers on a systematic basis. It built up important holdings on an international level long before most libraries acknowledged the importance of theatrical material. Gems in this treasure-trove include the superb collection of nineteenth-century lithographs built up by George Chaffee and more recently by Edward Binney; the famous Sergeyev papers, including his notated scores of nineteenth-century Russian classics; and the photographic collections of the British photographer Angus McBean, and of John Lindquist, who documented work at Jacob's Pillow. A few years ago the Harvard Theatre Collection purchased the scrapbooks of Lady Ripon, one of Diaghilev's British patrons; and the late historian and writer Parmenia Migel Ekstrom, of the Stravinsky–Diaghilev Foundation, has bequeathed her superb collection to this library.

The Ballets Russes are a focus of interest at the Hoblitzelle Theatre Arts Library of the University of Texas at Austin. Here there is a complete run of Ballets Russes programmes from 1909 to 1962 as well as a small collection of original costumes and designs. In the dance collection there are approximately 100 copper-plate engravings, complete with music and choreography of Contre Dances, as well as a growing collection of early primary source material and rare dance books. Although the range of material is wide, the collection is particularly strong on nineteenth- and twentieth-century productions in America and Europe. The library has acquired the Marquis de Cuevas collection of dance memorabilia (including programmes, photographs, posters, scrapbooks, manuscript material and press cuttings) and the Fred Fehl photographs of dance in New York, 1940–79.

Washington

The Library of Congress (Washington) may not be the most obvious collection for the researcher in dance, but inevitably, much can be located within their vast holdings. For example, their extensive print and photograph files include dance and dancers (with many illustrations of Duncan and St Denis), and the music collection is a rich source of information. Books on dance are housed both in the general and in the rare-book collections. The Motion Picture Division includes some dance films. Much of the non-manuscript material in this library has been acquired through copyright deposits.

A joint project of the Library of Congress and the Kennedy Centre is the Kennedy Centre Performing Arts Library. This documents performances at the Centre and provides an easily accessible performing-arts reference collection (including over 1,000 titles on dance). It also has video and record collections and growing resources in terms of ephemera. It acquired significant Ballets Russes material in the 1984 Sotheby Auction of the Lifar Collection.

13

Canada

The Metropolitan Library, Toronto, houses one of the most important theatre collections in Canada and is particularly rich in material documenting Canadian theatre. Dance material includes a comprehensive collection of reference titles and periodicals as well as extensive clipping and programme files on Canadian dancers and companies. Photographs, posters, original set and costume designs, prints, rare books and manuscript material (including the Boris Volkoff, Ralph Hicklin, Bettina Byers, Mary Wigman and John Fraser collections) are housed in the special collections room at the library.

Canada has a network of well-developed performing-arts company archives. An exhibition highlighting the range and importance of the Canadian Performing Arts Archivists, *Putting It Back Together* (Preserving the Performing Arts Heritage in Canada) was shown at Canada House in London last summer. Documenting the work of ten collections, this included items from the National Ballet of Canada's comprehensive archive, with Celia Franca's notes for that company's revival of *Jardin aux Lilas* and correspondence with Erik Bruhn concerning his staging of *Swan Lake*. The exhibition also included videos of ballets revived through *Encore*, a reconstruction project established by Dance Collection Danse.

Company Archives

In comparison with Canada, relatively few performing companies in the United States have highly organized and efficient archives. The Merce Cunningham Dance Company's Archive is a model of its kind and other dance organizations, such as the Eliot Feld Company and the Dance Theatre of Harlem, have been establishing their own collections. Some prefer to deposit much of their material with major collections; for example, many of American Ballet Theatre's administrative and artistic records are held as a special collection within the New York Public Library's Dance Collection. American companies are now being actively encouraged to establish their own archives. Collections at base are frequently richer in range and volume than the selected holdings passed on to libraries or archives. The organization Preserve, run by Leslie Hansen Kopp, is conducting workshops on how to found a dance archive and how to preserve materials.

Ballet Society in New York is a particularly useful source information on all aspects of the career of George Balanchine. In 1987 the Society published *A Reference Guide* as a supplement to *Choreography by George Balanchine: A Catalogue of Works* but also to guide researchers to other sources of material in the United States and elsewhere. It is particularly helpful in respect of photographic sources.

The Shubert Archive

Not only are the archives of small individual companies important but also those of major national theatrical organizations. The Shubert Archive, located on the upper floors of the Lyceum, a Broadway theatre, holds all the records of the Shubert brothers' activities. Producers of countless shows, plays, musicals and revues as well as the owners of a vast network of theatres throughout the United States, the Shuberts were involved in, for example, the first Pavlova–Mordkin tour of America. Particularly active during the first half of this century, the Shuberts employed many dancers and choreographers: among the correspondence and other files, the archive holds material on Charles Weidman, George Balanchine, Harriet Hoctor, Ruth Page and Gene Kelly. The Shubert Archive publishes an annual newsletter, named after one of the Shuberts' long-running successes, *The Passing Show*, which acquaints the public with its range of archival resources.

Exhibitions

Archives and libraries at times organize their own exhibitions. Some, such as the recent Lincoln Centre's exhibitions on the work of designer Rouben Ter-Arutunian, on the choreographer Antony Tudor, and a celebration of fifty years of American Ballet Theatre, draw on their own collections. Other major dance exhibitions draw selectively on several public and private collections to display a wealth of dance material. Nancy van Norman Baer, based in San Francisco, has in recent years presented a succession of informative dance exhibitions on Anna Pavlova, on the career of Bronislava Nijinska (drawing on the Nijinska archive) and on the Ballets Russes.

At Saratoga Springs, in upstate New York, there is now a National Museum of Dance. This is not intended as a repository for collections although it aims to develop links with established collections. At present, it is primarily a home for exhibitions from other sources. To date, its programme has included *Dancing from Broadway to Hollywood and Back*, *Ballet for a City and a Nation: Forty Years of New York City Ballet*, *The Fugitive Gesture* (a photographic exhibition linked to William Ewing's book of the same name), and an exhibition of Romantic ballet prints from the Parmenia Migel Ekstrom Collection. The year 1990 marks the museum's move into the international field by bringing to the United States the exhibition of *Les Ballets 1933* from Britain and, in conjunction with Eduard Nakhamkin Fine Arts, New York, *One Hundred Years of Russian Ballet 1830–1930*, a selection of treasures from the Leningrad State Theatre Museum. The museum also has a permanent display, *Shaping the American Dance Dream*, which consists primarily of photographic and video material.

Museums

Many other museums include material related to dance. New York's Museum of Modern Art still owns important designs for dance. The Metropolitan Museum of Art is currently compiling an index of all its dance-related material. The Wadsworth Atheneum in Hartford, Connecticut, is in itself resonant with dance history. Here, in the small basement theatre, Frederick Ashton's first American production *Four Saints in Three Acts* was premièred; and although Balanchine soon decided to establish his own company in New York rather than at Hartford, American Ballet's first public performances took place in that auditorium. In 1933 the Wadsworth Atheneum had the foresight to purchase the Serge Lifar collection, at a time when designs were rarely regarded as important works of art. Materials from this collection are called on whenever international Ballets Russes or general surveys of dance designs are mounted.

Ballet Society
5 West 73rd Street
New York, New York 10023

Curtis Theatre Collection
363 Hillman Library
University of Pittsburgh
Pittsburgh, PA 15260

Dance Notation Bureau Library
33 West 21st Street
New York, New York 10011

Harvard Theatre Collection
Harvard University Library
Cambridge, Massachusetts 02138

Hoblitzelle Theatre Arts Library
Humanities Research Centre
Austin, Texas 78712

Kennedy Centre Performing Arts
  Library
Washington, DC 20566

Library of Congress
Washington, DC 20540

Metropolitan Toronto Library
Theatre Department
789 Yonge Street
Toronto, Ontario M4W 2G8

Jane Bourne Parton Collection
Mills College Library
Mills College
Oakland, California 94613

Museum of Modern Art
11 West 53rd Street
New York, New York 10019

National Museum of Dance
South Broadway
Saratoga Springs, New York 12866

New York Public Library/Library
  for the Performing Arts (Dance
  Collection)
111 Amsterdam Avenue
Lincoln Centre
New York, New York 10023

San Francisco Performing Arts
  Library and Museum
Grove Street
San Francisco, California

Shubert Archives
234 West 44th Street
New York, New York 10036

Martha Faure Carson Dance Library
University of Denver
University Park
Denver, Colorado 80208

Walter Clinton Jackson Library
University of North Carolina
Greensboro, North Carolina 27412

Wadsworth Atheneum
Hartford, Connecticut

William Seymour Theatre Collec-
tion
Princeton University Library
Princeton, New Jersey 08544

Theatre Library Association
c/o New York Public Library for the
  Performing Arts
111 Amsterdam Avenue
Lincoln Centre
New York, New York 10023

Preserve
PO Box 100
391 Brooklyn
New York 11210

The Library and Archives of the Paris Opéra

Martine Kahane
Translation by Margaret M. McGowan

I nstituted by official decree (dated 15 May 1866), the Bibliothèque de l'Opéra had, nonetheless, enjoyed a kind of clandestine existence for nearly two centuries.

From the moment of the creation of the Royal Academy of Music by Louis XIV, documents about the daily life of the theatre and about performances were somehow kept, accumulated and preserved – rather according to the whims of Fortune. This very precariousness (which in no sense can be termed 'conservation') did, however, preserve this Opéra archive from the various fires which occasionally engulfed even the buildings of the Academy of Music. At each disaster the documents were happily protected, having been placed in an annexe away from the main buildings.

The first inventory date is from 1748 and it merely concerns musical material. It is only in 1875, after the construction of the Opéra Garnier and through the skills of Charles Nuitter (who systematically catalogued the documents), that the collection can be said to have found a final resting place. Just as within the theatre structure, dance and opera have always been closely linked, so it is not possible to make a selection of material from the Opéra collection which concerns ballet exclusively. Generally speaking, the archive is made up of documents which formed part of the theatrical life of the Opera House or which are officially deposited in the Library. Gifts and other acquisitions have been added to the wealth of the collection from time to time.

Those items which have been so assembled offer almost a complete, panoramic view of the activities of the Opera House since the seventeenth century, in all its variety: musical scores, libretti, stage designs, choreography, posters, drawings, pictures and photographs; all this, in addition to a general archive which is rich in literature and musical remains, on opera and on the dance. The archive is very much a going concern and is constantly being added to.

Costume and stage designs are a good example of this perpetual process of enrichment. From the founding of the Opéra, a costume designer has always been in attendance (the first was Jean Bérain); and, since the twelfth year of the Republic, designs for every performance have been pre-served. Moreover, since 1936, with the creation of the RTLN (The Union of all National Lyric Theatres), each costume and stage designer is obliged, by law, to place his final designs in the Opéra archive.

During the nineteenth century important collections of theatre and stage material were added to the archive either by sale or by transfer from national art and theatre depositaries. This regular rhythm of acquisition, which has not been interrupted either during periods of political unrest or even by the fact that certain significant artists (Picasso or Chagall, for instance) might have considered themselves exempt from legal contracts, allows scholars to trace theatrical developments over four centuries from original documents.

On the other hand, the prints and drawings section is virtually closed as a live archive in that only rare additions are made either through gift or from auctions. However, thanks to the Chasles collection, there are particu-larly rich sources for ballet, and especially for Romantic ballet. This collection is divided into several large series: portraits, stage designs, costumes, and theatres; it is organized alphabetically according to title role and work. Its principal interest is extended by an extremely rich collection of old photo-graphs. Between 1875 and 1900, for instance, the theatre management often had albums of photographs made for new opera creations in which the whole range of performers from the 'stars' to simple walk-on parts are represented. In recent years the attention that has been accorded to these old photographs has made us aware of the extraordinary value of this col-lection, which had been insufficiently appreciated before. A new catalogue of photographs is now available (listed by name of photographer) to meet the needs of researchers specializing in this field.

The Music Library, which is especially rich, was the embryo of the entire collection. Théodore de Lajarte catalogued it in 1873, and it comprises all the works ever put on in the Opéra since its inception.

Pierre Lacotte's research on the re-mounting of ballets such as *La Sylphide* or *Marco Spada* has been largely based on material housed in the Library. The Music Library has signed and autographed material from almost all the composers whose works have been staged at the Opéra: these include Rameau, Gluck, Lulli, Puccini, Grétry, Spontini, Cherubini, Hérold, Halévy, Auber, Donizetti, Meyerbeer and Rossini.

The cataloguing of documents is according to type and function: libretti, posters, programmes and musical scores. There is a general catalogue of authors, a subject catalogue and a catalogue of works. Thus, for *Giselle* (for example) one can locate musical scores, libretti, stage, decor and costume designs, performers, general information, posters and a portfolio of press cuttings. These catalogues are those which are most consulted by our readers.

The material for ballet is especially rich for the eighteenth century and for Romantic ballet, which one might consider the high points of choreographic achievement in France. The Reserve collection preserves these extremely precious documents from the earlier period; that is to say, dance manuals and treatises, volumes of choreographic notation, costume and decor designs. For the Romantic period, theatre archives, artistic material such as management records, descriptions of stage designs and of costumes are made readily available to researchers; it should be noted that all administrative documents have been deposited in the Archives Nationales.

There are a number of collections which have been bequeathed to the Library and which have direct relevance to ballet. These have been catalogued separately and in detail in order to retain their unity of interest. The more significant among them are listed here.

International Archive of the Dance
Rolf de Maré's bequest (1952) comprising works, photographs, engravings and posters; more specifically the material relates to Indo-European and tribal dances, Swedish ballets, original documents on Taglioni and on Spessivtzeva.

The Aumer Archive
(Choreographer 1744–1833)
Thirty-two portfolios contain the libretti, notes and suggestions for the decor of Aumer's ballets.

The Emilie Collomb Archive
(Dancer at the Opéra)
Twenty-nine portfolios contain letters, programmes, newspaper cuttings, and details of negotiations with theatre management from 1789 to 1811. They provide rare and important insights into the life of ballet at this difficult period, and into the social and economic conditions for artists at this time.

The Nuitter Archive
(Opéra archivist)
Bequest of 1902: 307 portfolios containing notes, correspondence, libretti and the manuscripts of several works to which Nuitter contributed either as author or adaptor of the libretto. His most celebrated work was *Coppélia*.

The Rouche Archive

(Director of the Opéra)

Bequest from Rouche's daughters in 1974. The material covers the period of his activities as Director of the Théâtre des Arts and of the Opéra, and has much to do with ballet, especially contracts with Diaghilev and the ballets of Natalia Trouhanowa. There are 413 portfolios.

The Saint-Léon Archive

(Choreographer)

One-hundred-and-seventy-nine portfolios comprising manuscript musical scores either of Saint-Léon's own work or adaptations, and many choreographic suggestions for ballets, composed for dancers at the Opéra at the beginning of their careers.

The Boris Kochno Archive

Acquired in 1975, the collection concerns the Ballets Russes. It contains Diaghilev's notebooks, articles, projects, workbooks, letters autographed by him and by his collaborators. There are also musical scores, and a large number of original photographs relating to ballets and their interpreters. The archive has been augmented by a private bequest of the same date; it includes designs and pictures originating from Boris Kochno's collection.

The Serge Lifar Archive

Bequest from 1960, includes letters, biographical material, programmes, posters, press-cuttings, books and choreographic drawings. All relate to the work of Serge Lifar at the Opéra.

The Taglioni Archive

Eighty-four portfolios from the International Archive of the Dance contain albums, souvenirs, programmes and material related to Taglioni's travels. There is a list of her performances and a number of personal documents and letters.

During the last ten years, significant developments in both the musical and choreographic arts have had a considerable effect upon the assistance which readers can now expect from the Opéra Library. Thus, our Documents Section has been improved by the creation of portfolios of press and journal material (on artists, works, companies and theatres), and by important extensions to our photographic and reproduction facilities. Opera and

21

ballet have become so much a part of the general artistic consumption of a varied public that curiosity is no longer confined to the single performance but extends beyond it to books and documents.

The address of the Paris Opéra Archives is: Bibliothèque de l'Opéra, Théâtre Nationale de l'Opéra, Place Charles Garnier, 75009 Paris.

The Paris Opéra Library and Museum is closed for restoration and rebuilding until early 1992. The enlarged premises will double the present museum space, which will be open during the day and in the evening, during performances.

The Dance Museum, Stockholm

Bengt Häger

Stockholm has the world's oldest international museum for the art of dance. It was created in 1950 by Rolf de Maré and Bengt Häger.

The Dance Museum in Stockholm has its roots in Les Archives Internationales de la Danse which Rolf de Maré opened in 1932 in Paris, as a centre for dance research. After the war the archives had grown too large for a private person to maintain. Rolf de Maré donated some 6,000 books, engravings and other items, all concerned mainly with Western dance, to the Paris Opéra Museum.

However, the museum declined to accept two substantial elements of de Maré's collection: firstly, material from his own Ballets Suédois, which was active in Paris in the 1920s; and secondly, the fruits of his expedition of exploration to Indonesia in 1936 (the first to have been undertaken with the purpose of documenting dance).

Bengt Häger made these two unwanted collections of material the nucleus of a museum devoted to the dance; and he added contributions of his own which covered especially the development of modern dance in Europe. Over many years of travelling, in Asia especially, but also in Africa and America, he acquired material relating to ethnic cultures; and he built up collections illustrating the history of the classical ballet and of European folk dance. On his death in 1964, Rolf de Maré made the Dance Museum the sole heir to his fortune; and this enabled the museum to make further acquisitions.

In 1969 the Swedish Government assumed responsibility for the Dance Museum with the normal status of a state-supported public museum, and supplied it with suitable premises and a staff (there are currently eleven employees). Its standing as an institution for scientific research was emphasized by the government's appointment of Bengt Häger as a university professor.

In the same year, the great Swedish-born ballerina Carina Ari, whose career had been in France, made a substantial capital bequest to create a separate foundation, the Carina Ari Library for dance literature, which rapidly became the most extensive library of its kind in northern Europe. Miss Ari made Häger head librarian for his lifetime, and so the library is attached to the museum.

In 1983 the UNESCO Dance Film and Video Collection was officially inaugurated by UNESCO's general director and Sweden's minister for culture, and it was committed to the museum's keeping and guaranteed safe maintenance. Climatized vaults for films and adequate machinery for all systems were installed at the same time.

The collections are constantly growing, enriched in no small part by gifts from artists who wish to have records of their achievements kept for the future. Some of these gifts form important separate collections such as the Kurt Jooss Donation and the Sakharoff Bequest.

The museum is maintained by the state in its own four-storeyed building which comprises some 2,000 square metres, half of which is used for exhibitions. This is too little to do proper justice to the wide and manifold subject of the dance. Therefore the public exhibitions are completely changed twice yearly, with exhibitions on a theme, such as 'The history of ballet in Russia', 'The Chinese dance-opera', 'Classical Indian dance', 'Dance in children's education' and 'Eighteenth-century ballet'. Over a ten-year cycle the entire content of the collections can thus be shown. A few exhibitions on more specialized subjects, sometimes with additional material on loan, are given from time to time in small exhibition rooms set aside for the purpose; for instance, 'Satie and the ballet', 'Marie Taglioni', and 'Serge Lido, master of dance photography'. Videos of dances, integrated into the display through monitors and wide screens, form an important part of all exhibitions.

The museum has frequently lent material to exhibitions in other countries, and has visited museums abroad with complete exhibitions from its collections, notably the Victoria & Albert Museum and Musée de l'Art Moderne, Paris.

Many international symposia and conferences have taken place at the museum in collaboration with UNESCO's International Council for Dance (of which Bengt Häger is president and joint-founder): such as 'Dance and the electronic media' (twice), 'Dance and the child', 'European folk dance research' (repeatedly) among others.

The museum receives and assists researchers and students, and the staff endeavours to answer the large number of postal requests for information. Scholarships for scientific research are chiefly given to Scandinavian citizens, and bursaries are awarded to assist in the costs of publishing research papers.

The address is Laboratoriegatan 10, 115 27 Stockholm, Sweden, tel. 8/67 85 12.

The Derra de Moroda Dance Archives at the University of Salzburg

Sibylle Dahms

F riderica Derra de Moroda, who died in Salzburg on 19 June 1978, devoted her life entirely to dance. As a dancer, choreographer, ballet teacher and especially as dance scholar and bibliophile, she was renowned among dance scholars all over the world. Her Dance Archives, representing more than fifty years of intensive and systematic collecting, form the most impressive testimony to her life's work.

During the 1970s Friderica Derra de Moroda stipulated that the Salzburg Institute and her Dance Archives should be given a new and permanent home at Mozartplatz 4, in one of the most beautiful buildings of Old Salzburg, which is of medieval origin. She knew about the precarious situation of the musicology department, which up to this time had been housed inadequately at Getreidegasse 9, Mozart's birthplace. She not only helped the Institute with its problems, but donated her entire collection to the Institute of Musicology of the University of Salzburg.

After her death her vast and varied collection had to be relocated in some systematic order in the newly adapted rooms of the Institute of Musicology; Derra de Moroda had developed and effortlessly mastered a special system of library arrangement, completely different from any professional system. Her catalogue slips, which she provided for most of the books, were of tremendous help in ordering items scattered throughout her house. Thus it was possible to make her dance collection accessible relatively quickly.

The *Annotated Bibliography* was finally published in 1982, the original title having been changed to *The Dance Library: A Catalogue*, since in bibliographical terms the work represents a catalogue rather than a bibliography.

The published catalogue contains only the dance-book section of the Derra de Moroda Dance Archives. It will probably be necessary to publish several more volumes for the rest of the collection, which consists of: books on dance music and practical music editions (seventeenth to twentieth centuries); dance prints, prints and books with costume designs (especially from the eighteenth and nineteenth centuries); books on theatre history, fine arts and folklore; a collection of manuscripts (mostly consisting of letters written by dancers and choreographers, nineteenth and twentieth centuries); souvenirs of dancers and a collection of photographs; periodicals concerning dance, theatre and fashion (eighteenth to twentieth centuries); a huge collection of newspaper cuttings (German, Austrian, English and American newspapers, from the 1920s onwards); programmes and posters; and the catalogues and manuscripts from Derra de Moroda's own research work.

Derra de Moroda's book collection is extensive, consisting of about 2,730 items; however there are areas of specialization which mirror the collector's interests. She had amassed numerous monographs, memoirs, diaries, biographies and autobiographies of members of the Diaghilev company (often with personal inscriptions to her).

Another area of special interest was the Free Dance movement in which she had been involved herself as a young girl. Derra de Moroda was particularly interested in the pioneers of Modern Dance so the library contains many publications on such figures as Isadora Duncan, Maud Allan, and Loïe Fuller and on such exponents of the New German Dance as Rudolf von Laban, Kurt Jooss, Mary Wigman, Niddy Impekoven, Harald Kreutzberg and Yvonne Georgi, with most of whom Derra de Moroda was on close personal terms.

The history of court and social dance, pre-Romantic and Romantic ballet are covered in great detail. The collection includes the major texts of dance history, often in more than one edition: Caroso and Negri, Menestrier, Feuillet, Rameau, Taubert, to mention only a few. Indeed, Derra de Moroda was predominantly concerned with the historical aspects of dance and she made some important contributions; notably, she discovered the original manuscript of Lambranzi's *New and Curious School of Theatrical Dancing* in 1936 in the Bavarian State Library, Munich.

She was particularly interested in the history of all types of dance notation. Her interest in the early method of notating by letters, which is used to describe the *basse danse* in various Renaissance sources, is apparent in the many primary and secondary works she collected on this subject, and also in her own article 'The "Golden MS" and some other basse danse authorities. . .', published in *The Dancing Times* in 1937. Her other special field of dance notation research was on Feuillet's system and she underlined the importance of Pierre Beauchamp, its original inventor. Several of her articles draw attention to this neglected creator of the Feuillet notation and also give some account of its further development during the eighteenth century. Many other systems of notation from descriptive methods to the most abstract forms are well represented.

The collection provides materials for musicological aspects of dance research. Derra de Moroda believed in a logical approach to tempo, rhythm and metre, accent and dynamics, deriving from the idea that dance movement and musical movement should complement one another. Stimulated by Derra de Moroda's own ideas on this subject some research work has already been started at the Salzburg Institute of Musicology. As it seems necessary to complement theory with practice, an ensemble for historical dancing has been formed at the Institute, consisting of lecturers and students from the Institute of Musicology and the Salzburg Mozarteum (conservatory). Weekly meetings of musicians and dancers and public performances are supported with increasing enthusiasm.

Ballet technique is another subject of special interest in the collection; among the books on the Cecchetti Method is *Theory and Practice of Advanced Allegro in Classical Dancing* by Margaret Craske and Derra de Moroda, who was an acknowledged authority on the technique.

As a dancer and as a collector Friderica Derra de Moroda was most interested in all aspects of folk dance, her favourite subjects being the dances of her Greek and Hungarian ancestors. An extensive collection of books on Austrian folk dances and folklore, as well as folk dance publications from many different European countries and even some significant works on ethnic dance, reflect the wide range of Derra de Moroda's interests in this area.

Friderica Derra de Moroda bequeathed her unique dance collection to the Salzburg Institute because she felt that it would stand a better chance of remaining complete there than in the world's leading museums, archives and libraries. This was in spite of various lucrative offers from many institutions around the world. She may also have wanted to establish the collection in Central Europe and in Austria, a country with a lively musical and dance tradition but in which dance now plays a lamentably secondary role (this is especially true of Salzburg and its world-famous festivals).

Derra de Moroda: *The Dance Library*, a bibliography of Derra de Moroda's collection, is published by R. Wölfle, Munich, and available in the UK from Dance Books, price £65.00.

The address of the Derra de Moroda Archives is: Getreidegasse 9/IV, A–5020 Salzburg, Austria.

Rambert Dance Company Archive

Jane Pritchard,
Company archivist

R ambert Dance Company, formerly known as Ballet Rambert, is Britain's oldest established dance company. Dating its existence from 1926, it emerged from Marie Rambert's school and developed through performances at London's Ballet Club in the 1930s into a medium-scale classical touring company in the 1940s. In 1966 it was re-formed as a smaller, more innovative ensemble with an increasingly modern repertoire. Throughout the company's history it has been noted for discovering new talent, encouraging dancers and designers, commissioning new scores, and above all giving opportunities to new choreographic talent.

The company archive was established in 1982 to ensure an accurate and complete record of the Rambert company's work and history. Its primary function is to serve the company in all its departments but it also responds to outside enquiries. It was set up with financial assistance and encouragement from the Calouste Gulbenkian Foundation.

It is a purely company-based archive. It does not hold material relating to all forms of dance but rather primary and secondary material illustrating the company's history. Whilst the focus is on the Rambert company in its various forms – The Marie Rambert Dancers, Ballet Club, Ballet Rambert and Rambert Dance Company (both as a classical ballet company and in its reformed contemporary style) – the archive also holds some material on other organizations which have directly affected the company or grown out of Ballet Rambert. These include The Camargo Ballet Society, The London Ballet, Ballet Workshop and other productions at the Mercury Theatre. It also includes a wealth of material on Marie Rambert's own career.

Material in the archive includes all forms of printed material, notes on ballets, correspondence, a few designs, costumes and a rich collection of photographs and visual material. Files are held on every work performed by the company and on the dancers, choreographers, designers, musicians and other individuals who have worked for Rambert.

The collection of programmes begins with the programme for *The Riverside Nights* (which included *A Tragedy of Fashion*) in 1926 and follows through to the most recent performances by the company. At present we have gaps in our collection of programmes and the period 1926–60 is still far from complete.

We have photographs of most of the ballets performed by the Rambert Dance Company. These are filed under the titles of the ballets and the dancers featured. There is also a collection of photographs of the company in rehearsal and off-stage.

Press cuttings cover the periods 1937–47 and from 1958 onwards in depth. At present the collection of cuttings is less complete for other periods. Press cuttings are complemented by periodicals and books containing references to the company's work and individual artists who have worked for Rambert. Posters and throwaways advertise performances by the Rambert Dance Company and announce special events, including lectures given by Marie Rambert.

The archive includes a collection of original costumes for Ballet Rambert. These include Tamara Karsavina's costume for *Mercury*, the Chief Nymph's costume for *L'Après-midi d'un faune* and Sally Gilmour's costume for *Lady into Fox*. There are the costumes for *Lilac Garden* and for *Façade* made to the original designs. Also included are more recent costumes designed by Nadine Baylis, Peter Farmer, Rouben Ter-Arutunian and Richard Smith.

The archive includes items of particular value. Ninette de Valois's notation for *Bar aux Folies-Bergère*, a score for *L'Après-midi d'un faune*, annotated by Antony Tudor when the ballet was taught to Ballet Rambert by Leon Woizikovsky, and other important documents were given to the archive by Marie Rambert.

Cataloguing of the archive is currently being undertaken. To assist with the building up of our own records we are trying to locate other material relating to Ballet Rambert's history, both to add to our collection and so that we have an index of where other material exists.

Some of the Rambert repertoire from the period 1930–66 is recorded on films made by Walter Duff at the Ballet Club, by Alan Wyn in Australia and by Edmee Wood at the Lyric Theatre, Hammersmith. Those by Duff and Wyn are amateur, but the Wood films of the early 1960s were made with the specific intention of recording the choreography. The original films are now deposited at the British Film Archive but the collection is gradually being copied on to video for the company archive. Among the films are *L'Après-midi d'un faune*, Ashton's *Foyer de danse* (1932) and his *Mars and Venus* (1931); Howard's very first choreography, *La Belle Ecuyère* (1931), as well as her *Lady into Fox* and *The Sailor's Return* (1947); and Kenneth MacMillan's *Laiderette* (1955).

Researchers might like to note that the Marie Rambert Collection of Designs is now at the Theatre Museum; the Marie Rambert/Ashley Dukes Collection of Romantic Ballet Prints is in the Department of Prints and

Drawings at the Victoria & Albert Museum and the Marie Rambert Film Collection is at the British Film Institute.

Access to the Rambert Dance Company Archive for scholars, journalists, critics and researchers is strictly by appointment only. Postal and telephone enquiries are answered when possible. Postal enquiries should always be accompanied by a stamped, self-addressed envelope for reply. Due to limited space it is preferable that appointments are made for a time when the company is on tour. Appointments may be made for between 10.30 a.m. and 5.00 p.m.

Donations

Since the establishment of the archive we have received many gifts of material for which we are most grateful. Nevertheless we still have some gaps in our records and would welcome further donations. We are willing to pay for all costs of sending items to us. If anyone has material that they are reluctant to part with we would welcome photocopies so that we can record the details. Either lend us the items to copy or we will refund expenses involved in having copies made.

All enquiries should be addressed to: Jane Pritchard, Archivist, Rambert Dance Company, 94 Chiswick High Street, London W4 1SH, tel. 081 995 4246.

Merce Cunningham Dance Company Archive

David Vaughan
Company Archivist

When I first started working as administrator for the Cunningham Studio in 1959 I began to organize the records of the company's history and to compile a chronological list of Cunningham's works, for my own interest as much as anything. Then in 1976 the National Endowment for the Arts provided a grant which enabled the Cunningham Foundation to employ me formally as company archivist, a role I have continued to fill ever since.

The Cunningham archives now contain as complete a collection of programmes of performances of his works as I have been able to assemble. The collection of press clippings goes back to the early 1940s; there is an alphabetical (by author) card file of these and of books in which Cunningham's work is discussed. Archival photographs are filed alphabetically by dance titles. There are, unfortunately, gaps in the collection of photographs – many of Cunningham's early dances were not photographed at all, owing to lack of funds. (Some early programmes, photographs and other documents were destroyed or damaged beyond repair in a flood in Cunningham's old loft on 17th Street, many years ago.) There is a chronological card file of performances; another lists dances alphabetically – on each card the dates and places of all performances of the work are listed. There are also collections of flyers and posters and other documents.

Very few original designs for Cunningham's decor and costumes exist, partly because in many cases backcloths were simply painted, or costumes dyed – or in some cases (*Summerspace*, for instance) painted directly on to the tights and leotards as the dancers wore them. There is a descriptive inventory of costumes from dances no longer in the repertory, with photographs of some of the more unusual costumes, modelled by students.

The oral history component of the archives includes taped interviews with Cunningham, John Cage, and their associates and collaborators. Cunningham himself, of course, keeps all his choreographic notes, though there are xerox copies of some of these in the archives. Video documentation of current works in the repertory is maintained – Cunningham prefers this to notation, which he finds insufficiently immediate. The tapes are stored in the Studio, under the supervision of Chris Komar, who has danced in the company since 1972 and is now Cunningham's assistant, a job that combines the functions of what in a ballet company would be the ballet master and régisseur. The Cunningham Foundation staff also includes a film/video assistant who is responsible for the marketing and distribution of the Cunningham 'Media Repertory' and also maintains the library of archival films and tapes.

In my capacity as archivist I am responsible not only for keeping the various collections of material up to date but for making them and the information they contain available to scholars, critics, editors, publicists and curators of exhibitions. Other members of the Foundation staff frequently need access to the archives when making grant proposals or arranging tours (for instance, the booking manager may need to know when last the company visited a certain city). I often give brief talks on company history to new board members, visitors, and students.

31

DANCE ARCHIVES

Access to the Cunningham Company Archive is by appointment only. Requests to consult the video archive should be made to Michael Stier: all other requests to David Vaughan, at the Cunningham Dance Foundation, 463 West Street, New York 10014, tel. 212 255 3130.

PART III

The Dancing World

Australia

Jill Sykes

With a few notable exceptions to prove the trend, the gulf is widening between mainstream dance companies and the more adventurous groups in Australia. So far, this has had little effect on their quality, but it is a worrying situation which looks like getting worse before it gets better. The only comfort is that any downward moves are starting from a high point.

A diverse selection of individual performers and small companies, most of them well established, provides audiences in the state capitals with all manner of dance styles, while the Australian Ballet, the nation's flagship company in the art form, maintains the classical tradition through new works as well as old.

Inevitably, funding is a problem for all of them. Even those who go for safety in their programming, choosing popular ballets and accessible themes for new pieces to keep up box-office returns, government support and sponsorship, are operating not much above survival level at their current standards. The more challenging approach of comparatively experimental groups, with the risk-taking that leads to choreographic development, scares potential sponsors and attracts a less affluent following, ensuring an uncertain future.

Government grants are shrinking, and with them the visibility of these small, innovative groups. In an effort to keep going they often have to cut back on their biggest expense, which is, ironically, performing for the public. So they might get together for only one or two projects in a year, extending them through touring when that is viable in this sparsely populated continent of far-flung venues, or, better still, going overseas.

Meanwhile, the legacy of the past fifteen boom years is maintaining a varied diet of dance throughout the country. Under the continuing artistic direction of Maina Gielgud, the **Australian Ballet** has built on its Béjart repertoire by presenting *Le Concours* at the end of 1989, much to the distaste of most dance critics and the apparent delectation of most subscribers. A revival of Cranko's *Onegin*, sensitively staged by Anne Woolliams, brought Gary Norman and Jonathan Kelly back to the stage in the title role with great success, as well as investing the company's leading female principal, Lisa Pavane, with a new maturity in her interpretation of Tatiana.

Laszló Seregi's *Spartacus*, revived as the company's major twentieth-century

34

work on its American tour in July 1990, made a disappointing impression in its Australian performances earlier in the year. Time, the wide-ranging achievements of the company in recent years and the more refined style of its dancers combined to emphasize the ballet's choreographic and structural weaknesses, locked into a period-piece aesthetic.

At least one Australian work was taken on tour: *Catalyst*, the first commissioned ballet by company member Stephen Baynes, which had been premièred only two months earlier. Its crisp attack and bold ensemble invention (interspersed with some cliché repetition) suggest a promising career for this young choreographer. An ambitious attempt by Timothy Gordon to encapsulate the final years of Aussie folk-hero Ned Kelly was less successful in its début season, and for the second year running the Australian Ballet simply could not find time in its packed schedule for a company choreographic workshop.

The **Queensland Ballet** continued reaping the rewards of an audience-building policy pursued by artistic director Harold Collins since his appointment in 1979. Drawing on well-known stories and remaking ballet hits of the past, he has shaped a small, classically based company which has attracted a devoted following.

Characteristic programming in the Queensland Ballet's repertoire over

Lisa Pavane, Greg Horsman, Robert Marshall and Adam Marchant of the Australian Ballet in *Catalyst* by company member Stephen Baynes.

My Name Is Edward Kelly, danced by Marilyn Jones and Stephen Heathcote of the Australian Ballet.

the past year included *Afternoon of a Faun* and a new version of *Romeo and Juliet* by Harold Collins; a season of Jacqui Carroll's *Carmina Burana* with full orchestra and chorus; and *Alice – Memories of Childhood*, for which Collins turned to Lewis Carroll and brought former ballerina Marilyn Jones back to the stage as Mrs Hargreaves, dancing to a commissioned score by Colin Brumby.

The **West Australian Ballet**, under the reaffirmed leadership of Barry Moreland, has been presenting a rather fragmented repertoire since his handsome full-length *Lady of the Camellias* earlier in 1989. Even *Earth Angels*, offered as a complete evening work out of doors in a sandstone quarry during the 1990 Perth Festival in February, was as uneven as its combined choreographic authorship might imply. Moreland shared the task with Chrissie Parrott, who is also establishing a tiny group of her own on a miniscule budget – a rare event in the current financial climate. West Australian Ballet's two major mid-year programmes of ten short works brought together choreography by Balanchine, Petipa, Moreland, Asaf Messerer and company member Edmund Stripe.

The **Australian Dance Theatre** featured a full-evening work by artistic director Leigh Warren for the 1990 Adelaide Festival, Australia's foremost arts festival, which happens to take place in the company's home city. *Beyond the Flesh* showed off the fluent strength of ADT's dancers, who have the closest stylistic affinity with modern dance of any professional group in this country, and struck a sympathetic chord with audiences in its account of reaching adulthood in Australia during the Vietnam War.

Different programmes by ADT during the year have been generous in their opportunities for company dancers to choreograph, as well as presenting works by Warren and other established creative artists, including Graeme Watson's *Bodyline* and *The Sex Life of Objects*, Douglas Wright's *A Far Cry* and Nanette Hassall's *Retort III*.

On his return to the **Sydney Dance Company** at the start of 1990, after a year's sabbatical, Graeme Murphy created a densely choreographed and intimately chronicled full-evening work called *Soft Bruising*. As an exploration of human relationships and his own choreographic intentions, it was fascinating, absorbing, yet not entirely satisfying: the beginning of a journey to be continued during the decade.

In Murphy's absence, the SDC's full programme continued in Australia and on tour to the United States. A sparkling revival of *Some Rooms* featured a star performance by Janet Vernon, and a slight but thoughtful entertainment called *Café*, by company members Paul Mercurio and Kim Walker, was so successful that it earned a return season within six months.

The **Meryl Tankard Company** has achieved a great deal in its first year. Canberra audiences have quickly learned to love the kind of dance theatre which Tankard devises, including her solo show *Two Feet*, which she toured to Japan, and the company work *Nuti*, which she choreographed for the pocket theatre in the Australian National Gallery, to coincide with the exhibition of Ancient Treasures from the British Museum.

In Melbourne, the founding director of **Danceworks**, Nanette Hassall, handed over the directorship to two interesting and contrasting choreographers, Helen Herbertson and Beth Shelton. The programme, which spanned the change of direction in mid-1989, was excitingly varied and stimulating: Herbertson's *Particular Touches*, Shelton's *Time Present* and two pieces by Hassall, *Faster than Photos* and *As The Crow Flies*.

Dance Exchange, directed by Russell Dumas, presented his most exhilarating and polished choreography in years, performed by Jo McKendry and Nick Sabel. *Blue Palm/White Lies*, in late 1989, and *Approaching Sleipner Junction*, in May 1990, both represented the pared-down style of postmodernism at its best.

Dance North, based in Townsville and directed by the enterprising Cheryl Stock, is expanding its audience reach into Asia. Always conscious of the need for accessibility in the contemporary dance works she commissions and choreographs for the company, Stock has been working individually with performers in Vietnam and making contact with dancers in Cambodia. In May 1990 she took the company to China for the Shanghai Festival with an all-Australian repertoire.

A sense of geographical place has become important to most leading Australian creative artists. It does not, mercifully, lead to slavish concentration on Australian themes, but it shows in the multicultural resonances to be found increasingly in this country's dance, informing attitudes and opening up communication with cultures much closer to Australia than Europe or the United States.

Austria

E. M. Wolf Perez

In the promotion of its cultural identity, Austria's authorities have emphasized, within certain artistic areas, the cult of the past. However, after the lifting of the Iron Curtain this glorious past has lost its exclusive character and is now also easily accessible in Prague or Budapest. Austria's role as purveyor of nostalgic reminiscences between the East and West has become obsolete. The changes in the eastern bloc countries have opened up a Middle European culture with a common past. With regard to the present, one hopes that Austria will recognize its changed position and reconsider its cultural image.

As far as dance is concerned, someone looking from the outside cannot be blamed for thinking that dance in Austria is an eternal Viennese waltz. And indeed numerous festivals seem to reaffirm that artistic developments in dance of the present and future are happening somewhere else.

Since 1982, when Gerhard Brunner, director of the ballet of the Vienna Staatsoper, started his first festival, Tanz 82, under the umbrella of the Wiener Festwochen, the number of dance festivals in Austria has been continually growing.

This biennial dance festival is, however, still the biggest of its kind and with a budget of AS 13 million is able to invite prestigious companies, for instance the Stuttgart Ballet, the Frankfurt Ballet, the Monnaie Dance Group/Mark Morris and the English National Ballet this year. Besides the big companies, Tanz 90 presented three different types of dance under the headings 'Expressionism Today', 'Indian 2' and 'New Dance'. Over a period of six weeks, twenty-one companies or soloists gave fifty-five performances. Though Tanz 82–90 is an important source of information about dance around the world, its benefit for the development of dance in Austria is always questionable. For instance, the only Austrian company represented in Tanz 90 was the Ballet of the Vienna Staatsoper with its première of *La Sylphide* in the highly acclaimed version by Peter Schaufuss. The production, with sets by David Walker together with the lighting design by Steen Bjarke, is a visual masterpiece. Schaufuss, who danced excellently as James, was partnered by Sylvia Halwax as an enchanting Effie. Brigitte Stadler as the Sylphide proved her technical ability but on the opening night had not fully mastered either style or character. The star of the evening was Niels Bjorn Larsen in his interpretation of the witch Madge. The orchestra, directed by Michel Sasson, and the technical crew should be highly praised. One might have wished for the same precision in the dancing of the *corps de ballet*.

Brigitte Stadler, Peter Schaufuss and Sylvia Halwax in Schaufuss's new production of *La Sylphide* for the Ballet of the Vienna Staatsoper.   PHOTO: AXEL ZEININGER

Another interesting task for the company was the reconstruction of choreographic works by the Austrian Expressionist dancers Gertrud Bodenwieser and Rosalia Chladek, presented in conjunction with the Kibbutz Contemporary Dance Company, which showed a piece by Gertrud Kraus.

The absence of national companies is a general problem in Austrian festivals. The *Sommerszene Salzburg*, the *Woche der Begegnung* in Klagenfurt or the *Tanztage Linz*, all festivals with an emphasis on international modern dance and the avant-garde, occasionally undertake cautious attempts to integrate one or other Austrian choreographer into their programmes. In the newly established Viennese performance festival of *International Dance Weeks*, Austrians may appear in the evening for finalists from the choreographic competition.

What are the reasons for this peculiar situation of Austrian festivals presenting almost exclusively guest artists? One of the reasons is the tendency of Austrian cultural policy to see culture as a tourist attraction, in which festivals traditionally play an important role. Most festivals in other countries, such as the Dance Umbrella in Britain or the festivals in France, are an important factor in the development of national artists, providing performance opportunities and very often financial assistance towards production costs. However, considering the absence of independent Austrian companies in festivals and, on the other hand, the indifferent official attitude towards the established ballet companies in theatres in Vienna, Linz, Graz, Salzburg, Klagenfurt or Innsbruck, the reliability of the tax-money administrators is questionable. No answer is given, for instance, to demands for the education and training of dance artists and administrative staff which would generate the skills necessary to develop and promote artistic quality of an international standard and thus create performance possibilities on a national and international level. Because of a lack of vision, the decision-making bodies within Austrian cultural politics evade their responsibility to help develop creative potential into professionalism.

Independent Companies

Tanztheater Homunculus is currently the most respected independent company in Austria. For the last five years they have been consistently working together and have now reached a level where they can not only count on their audience but also on financial support from the authorities. Manfred Aichinger, choreographer and artistic director of the group, has been given the opportunity to work with the ballet companies in Salzburg and at the Vienna Staatsoper and on both occasions had a good reception from the press. Tanztheater Homunculus employs a synthesis of theatre and dance frequently based on literary sources, as in their last production,

Elektra. All the company members are trained in the method of Rosalia Chladek; most of them studied at the conservatory of Vienna and are therefore continuing or redefining an Austrian dance tradition.

In Salzburg **Vorgänge**, a collective dance-theatre group, is well on its way to establishing the same sort of continuity. Besides producing their own shows, they occasionally invite choreographers like Laurie Booth or Wim Vandekeybus to work with them, either in workshops or towards a production.

Bernd Bienert, former dancer and occasional choreographer for the Vienna Staatsoper and now independent, is also developing an interesting line of work; but like other choreographers, for example Sebastian Prantl, Bertl Gstettner, Daniel Aschwanden, Susanne Hajdu, Peter Wissmann, Bettina Nisoli and Elio Gervasi, he has not yet been able to develop the necessary consistency. Most of the independent choreographers/companies present one production a year and have very little opportunity to perform – let alone tour. Tanztheater Homunculus holds the record, with one monthly season a year. Another unsolved problem is the lack of dancers to work with so many choreographers.

The main hope for modifying this situation lies in the initiative of young independent dancers and choreographers who, recognizing their common dilemma, have started to form pressure groups to improve their lot.

Important impulses for this solidarity come from the festivals: *Tanzsprache*, a self-help project within an alternative cultural centre; *Tanzräume*, a symposium for Austrian choreographers, which takes place each year in a different region; and *Image*, a small international festival which integrates Austrian companies.

The **Vienna Staatsoper**, Austria's largest ballet company, has appointed Elena Tchernichova as Ballet Director for 1992. The daughter of a German engineer, she was educated at the Vaganova Academy in Leningrad. Very early in her career she found her vocation in coaching dancers. With her husband, the choreographer Igor Tchernichov, she joined the ballet company in Odessa as Ballet Mistress. In 1976 she emigrated to the United States, where she became Ballet Mistress at the American Ballet Theatre under the directorship of Mikhail Baryshnikov (who left the company in 1990). Nevertheless, Tchernichova is going to continue her coaching work with ABT at the same time as directing the Viennese ballet company. Her three-year contract states that she should be at the Staatsoper for six months a year. Susanne Kirnbauer, director of the ballet of the Viennese Volksoper, has been appointed as her co-director. (Until the team takes over, the company will be headed in the interim period of 1991/2 by the present Ballet Mistress, Gerlinde Dill.)

Tchernichova is said to be a strong proponent of the Leningrad style and can rely on her experience in coaching dancers for all the big classical ballets.

Her emphasis will therefore lie in renewing the classics, which in the Viennese repertory have mostly been produced by her friend Rudolf Nureyev. Her stated aim is to improve the technical skills of the dancers and to achieve a unique image for the company. Whether she can realize her ambitions may depend on the new administration of the Vienna Staatsoper. So far, Eberhardt Waechter, currently director of the Vienna Volksoper, and Jan Holender, a former agent for opera stars, have shown little interest in the development of the ballet company. In their plans for 1992/3 they have cut ballet evenings at the opera to forty (in the last few years there were between sixty and seventy-five). On the other hand, negotiations are going on concerning a second theatre where the company would be able to mount one-act ballets. A collective agreement with the union should bring about other changes, such as better payment for the dancers. At the moment the starting salary of a *corps de ballet* dancer is AS 13,000 per month; contracts with soloists are subject to individual negotiation and payment for them lies between AS 30,000 and 50,000 per month. One of Tchernichova's concerns is to change the beginning of training sessions from 9a.m. to 10a.m.

The departing Ballet Director, Gerhard Brunner, who will take charge of both the theatre and opera in Graz, was less fortunate in his search for a ballet director there. He will direct the ballet company himself. For 1991 he has invited two guest choreographers: Ralph Lemon from the United States will choreograph Gluck's *Don Juan* and Heinz Spoerli from Switzerland *La Belle Vie* by Offenbach.

Belgium

Katie Verstockt

T wo festivals, two anniversaries and several outstanding premières made this Belgian dance season a very lively one.

Among the encouraging developments was the Flemish government's decision to double its subsidy for Anne Teresa de Keersmaeker's company, **Rosas**, so that it could be established on a regular basis. Up until now the dancers were engaged for each production and dismissed afterwards. A former member of Rosas, **Michèle Anne de Mey**, has formed her own company. Since the beginning of 1990, she has been subsidized by the French community as resident choreographer in the Théâtre Varia in Brussels. Her company performed the première of her new piece, *Sinfonia Eroica*, to Beethoven's music, at the Théâtre Varia before going on tour.

Contredance, an association that has been active for several years as an

Sinfonia Eroica, Michèle Anne De Mey's creation for her own company to music by Beethoven, Mozart and Jimi Hendrix.   PHOTO: JORGE LEON

43

information centre and as an organizer of dance workshops, has now been installed in the Maison de la Bellone in the centre of Brussels as a proper Dance Documentation Centre, with information on national and international companies. Patricia Kuypers, founder and director of Contredance, has prepared a book, *Guide de la danse de la communauté française en Belgique*, which includes dance history, information on dance training, administrative structures, companies, choreographers, etc.

Another Brussels-based association, **Danse Plus**, organizes the well-known Banc d'Essais, which offer a platform four times a year to young choreographers and helps them find an audience in a beautiful setting, the Botanique.

Belgian television (French or Flemish) has never been very dance-minded, but the music department of BRT (the Flemish channel) has begun to record a remarkable series of video dances in collaboration with several young Belgian choreographers: among them are Mark Vanrunxt, Alain Platel, Wim Vandekeybus and Nicole Mossoux.

In Antwerp, two anniversaries were celebrated: the **Royal Ballet of Flanders** was established twenty years ago and its founder and former director, Jeanne Brabants, celebrated her seventieth birthday. After her retirement from the Ballet of Flanders she started an association called Youth and Dance, another association for professional dancers and a dance group, **Danza Antiqua**, which recreates Renaissance and baroque dances. Above all, she goes on fighting for the rights of dance and dancers.

To celebrate the twentieth anniversary of the Royal Ballet of Flanders, its artistic director, Robert Denvers, commissioned an American choreographer, Stuart Sebastian, to make a new ballet for the company. Sebastian, who is artistic director of the Dayton Ballet in Ohio, created *Camelot*, based on the story of *La Mort d'Arthur*, to music by Sibelius. It is a traditional story-ballet in two acts, with a lot of mime but with plenty of dance sequences that are executed with a fresh enthusiasm by the mostly very young dancers of the Ballet of Flanders. For the première of *Camelot* the company (which has no theatre of its own) was invited to appear at the Théâtre de la Monnaie at the Cirque Royale in Brussels.

A lot of dance activities were concentrated during the two festivals: Klapstuk in Louvain and the Beweeging in Antwerp. **Klapstuk**, a biennial, international festival of contemporary dance, is now being organized by a brand-new director, Bruno Verbergt. Anne Teresa de Keersmaeker opened the 1989 festival with her magnificent trilogy *Mikrokosmos* (*Monument*, *Self Portrait* and *Bewegung*). The third section consists of dance fragments from an older work, *Bartok/Aantekeningen*, accompanied by the Mondriaan Quartet from the Netherlands. Klapstuk also co-produced a new piece by Jean-François Duroure called *Cosmo Nox*. It is a work full of a vulgar kind of sensuality, 'retrokitsch' images and absurd humour, all very reminiscent of Pina Bausch but with a typical French subtlety and elegance, and with beautifully structured dance sequences.

Besides Daniel Larrieu, Saburu Teshigawara and LaLaLa Human Steps, the festival presented work by several young Belgian choreographers. Alain Platel created *O Boom* for Klapstuk, a work inspired by Giotto's frescoes telling the apocryphal story of Joachim and Anna. The staging is dramatic and sometimes chaotic, with performers of widely differing backgrounds and ages. Roxane Huilmand, a former dancer with Rosas, danced her solo *Capricieuse* to Paganini's twenty-four *capricci* for violin; it was both an interpretation of the music and an intensely inward-looking search for her own language of moving.

The second festival that marked this season was the **Beweeging**, which took place in Antwerp in March. Every two years the director, Herbert Reymer, brings together the work of young Belgian choreographers, some of them novices, others with more experience but in need of an audience. From this year on the Beweeging has its own little theatre, seating 100 people: it is in the Vrije Val, the old warehouse where the Beweeging already has several small studios available for dancers. All this year's performances took place in the Vrije Val except one: the opening performance by Karen Vyncke had the honour of being presented in the renowned Singel.

Vyncke is a Belgian dancer who works in Paris and who was the big discovery of the Beweeging two years ago. *Mé-zon*, which was premièred a year ago at the Eurodanse Festival in Mulhouse, deals with the 'house' as an architectural structure and as a nest whose inhabitants and guests treat objects and occurrences in an almost ritualistic way.

Traditionally, the Beweeging promises a 'revelation' and this year the accolade went to Joachim Schlomer, a dancer with Mark Morris's Monnaie Dance Group. He presented five short pieces, sober and intense but without pretensions.

At the Monnaie Theatre in Brussels the director, Gerard Mortier, announced his departure in order to take on the direction of the Salzburg Festival in Austria. Mark Morris will remain at the head of the **Monnaie Dance Group** until the end of the 1990/1 season. For this season's creations he chose music of the twentieth century instead of his beloved baroque music. *Wonderland*, to music by Schoenberg, is a dark, pessimistic piece, referring to *film noir* in its images of night and shadows. It does not tell a story, it builds an atmosphere, where every detail comes to life through the sensitivity of the performers – including Morris's friend Mikhail Baryshnikov.

In April, Morris presented a programme called *Loud Music*. One of the two new pieces, *Behemoth*, was danced in silence, developing a surprising and beautiful structure; the other, *Going Away Party*, featured Morris himself as a lonesome cowboy who never quite belongs to the group of boys

Cowboys and girls in Mark Morris's *Going Away Party* for the Monnaie Dance Group/Mark Morris.   PHOTO: DANIÈLE PIERRE

Plan K company in Frédéric Flamand's *The Fall of Icarus* at the Théâtre de la Monnaie.

and girls enjoying themselves to the music of Bob Wills and his Texas Playboys.

Meanwhile, the Monnaie co-produced work by other choreographers. Frédéric Flamand created *The Fall of Icarus*, with music by Michael Nyman and huge video-sculptures by Fabrizzio Plessi. The production, though not the choreography, was spectacular.

Jan Fabre presented his latest opera, *Das Glas im Kopf wird vom Glas*, at the Antwerp Opera House in March. The music, by Eugenuisz Knapik, sounds more classical than avant-garde; Fabre, however, has really thought through the process of making an opera and has staged the piece in cool, clear images, all in his favourite Bic-blue colour. He knows how to capture and hold the audience's attention through simple movements.

Anne Teresa de Keersmaeker also premièred her new piece in Antwerp in March, at the Singel. *Stella* is dance-theatre, involving as much text as dance. It includes elements of Goethe's novel *Stella*, a novel by the Japanese writer Akutagawa, and the film of Tenessee Williams's *A Streetcar Named Desire*. The five characters created by the all-female cast are partly inspired by the texts but also by the dancers' own experiences and emotions. From their acting flow strongly structured dances, similar to those in *Bartok/ Aantekeningen*. *Stella* is a fine piece of theatre, owing much of its quality to the personality of its performers.

Brazil

Antonio José C. Faro

B razil is a country of paradoxes: great poverty amidst luxury buildings, a luxuriant forest in the south while the north-east suffers from ferocious droughts. Dance is right in the middle of such differences: while the numbers of small groups, schools and would-be dancers increase tremendously, the possibilities of survival are few, owing to the money problems that plague the fifth largest country in the world. Even the five state-run companies are suffering financially, especially after recent legislation abolishing tax concessions for private firms who sponsor the arts.

And yet, dance goes on. Audiences seem to be increasing, classrooms are as full as ever. The 1989/90 season was one of consolidation, in which no great new talent appeared on the horizon, but during which dancers, companies and choreographers somehow managed to strengthen their positions.

Of the five state-run companies, two did very little. The excellent company from Bahia, the **Ballet of the Teatro Castro Alves**, got a new director, Debby Growald, and a great hit in her *The Blue Unicorn*. But almost immediately their theatre closed for repairs, and the company vanished into rehearsal rooms. Touring in Brazil is very expensive because of the immense distances to be covered, and large companies such as the one from Bahia have considerable financial difficulties. The company from the **Clovis Salgado Foundation** in Belo Horizonte has changed direction so many times and dances so little that its existence is nearly forgotten. It is this company that has suffered the most from political entanglements.

The **Ballet of the City of São Paulo** has a new director in the critic Ruy Fontana Lopes. His first step was to revive a rich repertory of works by Oscar Araiz, Victor Navarro and other choreographers which had inexplicably been put on the shelf. Navarro contributed a new work to the repertory and the company increased the number of its performances, presenting several performances on weekends at popular prices, which were always sold out. The **Ballet of the Teatro Guaíra**, from Curitiba, is celebrating its twentieth anniversary, ten years of which have been under the directorship of Carlos Trincheiras. The company has come under a barrage of criticism because of a repertory policy which was expensive and artistically very bad. It commissioned works from popular composers, such as Edu Lobo and Sergio Ricardo, resulting in music that might have some charming melodies but no dance power. *Dance of the Half-Moon* was partly saved by the intelligent choreography of Rodrigo Pederneiras, but *Flicts*, based on a children's book by cartoonist Ziraldo, was a major disaster. Worst was Trincheiras's *The Mandala of Maria Bueno*, where a potentially good story was destroyed by a musical salad that included Mayuzumi, Mahler and Tchaikovsky, and choreography without any definite style or creativity.

The **Ballet of the Teatro Municipal** in Rio is the oldest (1936) and best of Brazil's major companies. Under Tatiana Leskova, the dancers are stylish and technically very strong. In works such as *Les Sylphides* or *Paquita* the styles of Fokine and Petipa were clearly differentiated, and in Pederneiras's strong and syncopated *Concerto* (to Prokofiev's Third), their dancing was a joy. Unfortunately, the company is in danger of becoming a museum, with a lot of classics to accommodate guest stars such as Elisabeth Platel or Jean Yves Lormeau, but no creation of its own in the last three seasons. The only new production of the year was a *Nutcracker*, with choreography by Leskova and enough left of Ivanov to guarantee some period style. Unfortunately the sets by Mauricio Sette were simply awful. Ballerinas Cecilia Kerche, Nora Esteves and Ana Botafogo danced a splendid round of *Giselle*s, and leading danseurs Francisco Timbó and Paulo Rodrigues had a splendid season throughout, showing great progress.

The **Carlton Dance Festival**, now in its fourth year, featured five foreign companies and two shared Brazilian programmes in one week, showing but a glimpse of their work. The last two festivals brought such giants as the Martha Graham Dance Company and Pina Bausch's Wuppertal Tanztheater, but also some lesser companies, like the David Gordon Pick Up Co., which had the distinction of being the first dance company to be booed at the Municipal in its 81-year history. But the philosophy of this Festival has more to do with marketing the Carlton cigarette brand than really enhancing our knowledge of what is new in the dance world.

Among the private companies, the **Vacilou Dançou** of Carlota Portella is continuing its very good transition from pure jazz to modernism with a jazz touch. The **Atores Dançarinos** of Regina Miranda continue their pursuit of a Brazilian expression of German **Tanztheater** (Regina studied with Susanne Linke in Essen). Their *Life Danger*, treating the dangerous subject of incest, was very good indeed, and extremely personal in spite of some obvious influences.

Outside Rio de Janeiro, São Paulo is the main centre for modern dance. Groups such as the **Cisne Negro** and the **Marzipan** strengthened their

Carmen Purri and Regina Advento of Grupo Corpo in Rodrigo Pederneiras's *Orphanage Mass* to music by Mozart. PHOTO: JOSE LUIZ PEDERNEIRAS

position: the Cisne Negro lacks only a good resident choreographer to give it a distinct personality. The doyen of the private companies, **Stagium**, seems to be going through some pivotal changes. The Stagium made its reputation during the dictatorship years with a series of ballets that defied censorship and raised some important banners in defence of the Indians and the oppressed. It made its name not because of the quality of its dancing but as a result of the courage of its beliefs. Its latest efforts, a homage to Villa Lobos, about the endangered species in the Matto Grosso marsh lands and another about ecology in the Amazon, were frankly demagogic and at times embarrassing. Let us hope it is just a bad phase.

The best of the private companies is now the **Grupo Corpo** from Belo Horizonte. It has, in Rodrigo Pederneiras, our best young choreographer. His musicality and invention are second to none and his steady progress is a joy to watch. His last work, *Orphanage Mass*, is a powerful and pungent account of a group of people trapped and pursued by an unseen tyrant. The marvellous sets by Fernando Velloso and costumes by Freuza Zechmeister have a 1930s look, which connects the action with the persecution of the Jews; but the greatness of the work expands its area of action into any human group suffering the persecutions of dictatorship. A year that has seen such a major creation, and the general high level of dancing, can be called vintage in spite of the serious financial problems that loom on the horizon.

Canada

Michael Crabb

B allet, like so many of the arts in Canada, is often enlivened by a self-conscious attempt to define a national identity. Where more mature nations take their independence and distinct identity for granted, Canadians are continually looking over their shoulders, wondering what others think of them and praying to the Almighty that they will not be mistaken for Americans.

There are plausible reasons for this faintly adolescent fixation. Having thrown off the shackles of two former colonial masters, the French and then the British, the people who inhabit this land must continually defend themselves against the insidious and not always benevolent influence of their southern neighbours.

Yet the truth about this country, and one that must inform any understanding of its cultural life, is that Canada is a political nation of some 26 million people, most of whom adhere more naturally to their region or city than to any abstract concept of Canadianism. It is therefore largely fruitless to look for a 'Canadian' style of ballet and it is certainly mistaken to imagine that the country's largest company, the National Ballet of Canada, holds the kind of position that for so many years was held, for example, by the Royal Ballet in Britain. The observer must look at particular instances and not hope to discover convenient generalities.

In a sense the 1989/90 season in this country belonged to its oldest professional troupe (the second oldest in North America), the **Royal Winnipeg Ballet**, celebrating its fiftieth anniversary with a packed schedule of gala programmes and ambitious tours, culminating in a Soviet visit in May and June which made it the first Canadian ballet troupe to dance at the Kirov.

It was in many respects a difficult year for the 27-dancer Royal Winnipeg Ballet. At the same time in October 1989 that it formally marked its anniversary, the company was still recovering from the devastating loss of its charismatic new director the previous April. Henny Jurriens had only been in the post for nine months when he and his wife died in a car crash. The dancers worshipped Jurriens and found it hard to accept his loss. Then in June, Senior Principal David Peregrine fatally crashed his plane into an Alaskan mountainside.

Perhaps this accounted for the uneven quality of some of the Royal Winnipeg Ballet's dancing early in its season, not helped by the disappointment of a much-promoted new Canadian ballet, *Anne of Green Gables*, based on the famous Lucy Maude Montgomery story about an impish but adorable girl in Victorian Prince Edward Island.

Jacques Lemay's choreography for this one-act exercise in sentimentality never paused for breath as it rushed from one scene to another, although, it must be conceded, had it done so the results would in all likelihood have been equally facile.

As always, the Royal Winnipeg Ballet continued to please its large audiences by the sheer verve and enthusiasm of its dancing. The RWB is a company which has always known how to sell a show, although it had been Jurriens's plan to make sure that what it had to sell was of the best quality.

This responsibility now rests with his successor, the Australian-born John Meehan. Much admired for his gifts as a dancer and patient skills as a ballet master, Meehan comes to the RWB as a first-time director. Fortunately, his genial personality has earned him everyone's good will as he rapidly learns the skills of a notoriously difficult job.

When Reid Anderson assumed his position as the **National Ballet of Canada**'s new Artistic Director in July 1989 he had the advantage of longer experience as a ballet master in Stuttgart and of a trial run at being a director

The Royal Winnipeg Ballet in Jaques Lemay's ballet based on the Canadian classic children's novel, *Anne of Green Gables*.   PHOTO: DAVID COOPER

with his two-year sojourn at Ballet British Columbia in Vancouver. His success there is credited with earning him the top job with the Toronto company.

Anderson took control of the National Ballet of Canada after it had gone through a period of vigorous artistic growth, first under the dynamic leadership of Erik Bruhn, from 1983 to 1986, and then under Bruhn's chosen successors, Valerie Wilder and Lynn Wallis. 'The two ladies', as they were quickly dubbed, did a fine job under difficult circumstances. Their wisest move was to introduce Glen Tetley as their 'Artistic Associate'. While Tetley's original works for the National Ballet, *Alice*, *La Ronde* and *Tagore*, met with a mixed critical response, they unquestionably infused the dancers with new creative energy, yielding some of the company's best performances and highlighting the talent of a younger generation of company members such as Kim Glasco, John Alleyne and Rex Harrington. With the retirement of longtime Senior Ballerina Veronica Tennant and the departure of Frank Augustyn to direct the small Ottawa Ballet, and with Karen Kain's long career inevitably reaching its final stages, the National must look to its new blood and Tetley made sure they had adequate scope to establish their artistry.

Anderson, however, without retreating from the National Ballet's commitment to commission new works, has said that he wants to strengthen the 70-dancer troupe's classical base. Given the financial resources, he

Rex Harrington in the National Ballet of Canada's production of *Sphinx* by Glen Tetley.
PHOTO: ANDREW OXENHAM

would probably like to replace several of the company's profitable staples, such as Celia Franca's age-weary *Nutcracker* from 1964 and Erik Bruhn's controversial rewriting of *Swan Lake* from 1966.

Tight money, however, means that Anderson may have to delay major restagings of the National Ballet's big classics, doing what he can instead to freshen them up. Certainly, the company has looked more awake in these productions since Anderson arrived. Meanwhile the company has continued to mix classicism with modernism with such major additions this season as Kenneth MacMillan's *Gloria*, a staging of Beethoven's Sixth Symphony by Canadian James Kudelka and a botched attempt at social comment by American modernist David Parsons called *The Need*.

Until the last few years Canada's 'Big Three', the National Ballet, Les Grands Ballets and the Royal Winnipeg, really had no competitors. Such troupes as Theatre Ballet of Canada (renamed Ottawa Ballet by Frank Augustyn) and the Alberta Ballet were at best marginal entities. Then **Ballet British Columbia** exploded onto the national scene in 1986. Although its own members joked that they were the dancers nobody else had hired, the Vancouver-based Ballet BC quickly established its reputation with invigorating programmes that mixed Ashton, Balanchine and Cranko with new works by Reid Anderson, David Allen and John Alleyne. Alleyne's work, in particular, seems to capture and exploit Ballet BC's best qualities of physical daring and theatrical expressiveness. He is, along with Kudelka, the most interesting of Canada's ballet choreographers.

All was going well as Ballet BC entered its fourth season under former Balanchine dancer Patricia Neary in August 1989. The season ended in April 1990 with Neary dismissed and the company's reputation in disarray. From the outside, Neary appeared to be doing a fine job. Her reputation as a skilled teacher proved its truth as the company's overall technical standard rapidly improved. Neary's programmes were well balanced, and for her closing show in Vancouver she broke a seven-year abstinence from choreographing by turning a set of orchestral variations by Alberto Ginastera into a dazzling display of her dancers' neo-classical talents. However, she and Ballet BC have now parted company owing to 'irreconcilable differences'.

In Montreal, **Les Grands Ballets Canadiens** went through its own change of artistic direction with the advent in August 1989 of Lawrence Rhodes to succeed longtime company stalwart Linda Stearns. Stearns had helped the company weather a difficult period during which Les Grands Ballets tried to resolve its artistic identity. Right from the start, in 1958, Les Grands Ballets had made a commitment to creating new works but by the early 1980s it had lost touch with its classical foundation and was experimenting with a dizzying range of modern and avant-garde choreography. Its classical dancing suffered, its audience began to drop and the bank manager began to worry.

The situation improved with the return of its former director-general, the tall, inscrutable but very dedicated Colin McIntyre. A new production of *Coppélia* began to win back the Montreal audience. McIntyre then oversaw impressively faithful stagings of Nijinsky's *L'Après-midi d'un faune* and later of Fokine's *Petrushka* and Balanchine's *Prodigal Son*.

Sadly, the company lacked the star dancers to make these handsome

Andrea Boardman and Rey Dizon of Les Grands Ballets Canadiens in Nacho Duato's *Na Floresta*.   PHOTO: MICHAEL SLOBODIAN

productions resonate with new life, which is perhaps why Rhodes, an American former dancer and director, is ending his first season by replacing a sizeable part of the company.

Les Grands Ballets' season was highlighted by Nacho Duato's creation of the passionate, mildly Kiliánesque *Na Floresta* and a gala tribute to one of its veteran choreographers, Fernand Nault. A new Kudelka *pas de deux*,

Romance, to Dvořák, also served to underline the potential star quality of its Chinese-born principal, Ming Hua Zhao, whose buttery lyricism is always combined with a strong masculine presence and impeccable, effortless technique.

These are but a sample of the names among a flourishing Montreal dance community that now hosts an impressive biennial international festival of new dance and from which fresh independent artists, mixing media as an artist mixes paint, seem to pop up with remarkable regularity.

Toronto seems much tamer after Montreal. Although choreographer Randy Glynn occasionally evinces his Montreal colleagues' attachment to fast, risky, almost acrobatic movement, the scene is dominated by the now almost stately **Toronto Dance Theatre**, with its adherence to a Graham-derived genre of mainstream modern dance, and by the company of **Danny Grossman**, the former Paul Taylor dancer who, since 1975, has made Canada his creative base for a series of quirky, entertaining dances that usually carry a pointed social or political sting. Typically, Grossman's newest work, *Ground Zero*, targeted humankind's environmental gangsterism by tapping a powerful language of *Angst*-ridden, tortured movement.

In Winnipeg, the zany, theatrically inclined Tedd Robinson passed **Contemporary Dancers** to American choreographer Charles Moulton, whose signature *Eighteen Person Precision Ball Passing* (it can be broken down for nine dancers too) keeps popping up everywhere.

In Vancouver, choreographer Judith Marcuse continues to purvey a very accessible, musically subtle but increasingly dated blend of balletic modern dance, while the city's longest surviving modernist, Anna Wyman, has spent the season struggling to keep afloat financially.

Perhaps because modern dance is defined internationally by its strongly individualistic traditions, Canada's modern dance scene is rarely pressured to prove its Canadianness. Choreographers are allowed to please themselves and nobody asks whether they are contributing to the national quest for a proud identity. As a result, it is perhaps here that one must look to find true artistic vitality and originality. Feeling no constraints other than those they have chosen to impose on themselves, Canada's modern and 'new' dance choreographers and companies are the ones most likely to help dispel the country's unjustified but still all too prevalent international image as a relative cultural backwater.

China

Ou Jian-ping

The year 1989 witnessed the fortieth anniversary of the founding of the People's Republic of China, with enthusiastic celebrations throughout the country by all the dance companies. By the time of the founding day, 1 October, the Second Chinese Arts Festival had spread from Beijing, the national capital, to twelve other big cities. The biennial festival highlights new creations in the past two years in almost all the performing arts, such as Peking Opera, music, dance, acrobatics, magic, puppets, shadow-play, etc., and what is more exciting to dance lovers is that dance itself has contributed ten different programmes of all kinds in Beijing alone.

The fortieth anniversary was also celebrated by a more reasonable salary system for Chinese professional dancers and choreographers, who are now paid much better according to the Central Government's new policy of different 'State Ranks'; that is 'First State Rank' dancers and choreographers receive 190 Chinese yuan, 'Second State Rank' 138, 'Third State Rank' 109.80, 'Fourth State Rank' 70.90, and apprentices with no rank yet get 67.50. Salaries are paid monthly and the basic living standard in Chinese cities generally requires 50 yuan each month. This pay system is in force throughout China, as all Chinese dance companies are wholly Government-paid; nevertheless, only the big companies in major cities are permitted to give the title of 'First State Rank' to their dancers and choreographers; one difference from Western dance companies is that dancers and choreographers get the same pay if they are on the same rank.

Central Ballet (Beijing)

The Central Ballet commemorated its thirtieth anniversary in 1989 by giving a gala season in the January of 1990, with some of the most famous world classics such as *Swan Lake*, Act II and *Don Quixote*, Act III, etc., and newly commissioned works like the Chinese-Canadian choreographer Chen Min's *Bacchanalia*, and the American choreographer Norman Wark's *Mountain Forest*.

Swan Lake has proved to be the most exciting and frequently performed production, which always meets with a full house wherever it is performed. The most fascinating scene for the audience to watch during the

57

The Shanghai Ballet's *Don Quixote*, with Yang Xin-Hua as Basil and Wang Qi-feng as Kitri.

celebration season was five ballerinas from three generations successively appearing on the stage in just Act II: Bai Shu-xiang, the first Chinese Swan Queen, then Zhong Ren-liang, Zhang Dan-dan, Li Ying and Wang Shan, who represent the company's thirty-year history from national to international level.

By contrast with the purely white Act II of *Swan Lake*, the hot and hot-red scene in Act III of *Don Quixote* is extremely stimulating, with Wang Shan and Xu Gang respectively as Kitri and Basil, and Xue Qing-hua leading the Fandango character dance. Wang Shan has just brought back a bronze medal from the Sixth Moscow International Ballet Competition, and Xu Gang got a silver medal from the Junior Division of the Thirteenth Lausanne International Ballet Competition; Xu Qing-hua was internationally well known for her heroic slave-girl's role, Wu Qing-hua, in the film of the most representative Chinese Revolutionary Model Ballet, *The Red Detachment of Women*, in 1970. The full-length version of this *Don Quixote* was staged by Rudolf Nureyev in December of 1985, and was presented at the First Chinese Arts Festival in Beijing in the autumn of 1987, always arousing cheers and bravos, with Tang Min and Zhao Ming-hua (both silver-medal winners in the Moscow Competition, and who now are with Les Grands Ballets Canadiens) in the original principal roles.

Sandwiched between these two world classics, the new and experimental choreography for *Mountain Forest* by the US choreographer Norman Wark looks fairly weak despite the same dancers and familiar Chinese music by Liu Dun-nan. Nevertheless, the three seasons are clearly depicted and fresh to the audience, and some of the ensemble dances are beautifully designed, particularly those for the male dancers.

When talking about the main problems the Central Ballet is facing, its Artistic Director Li Cheng-xiang said, 'Up till now, as many as over 130 people including the best dancers have gone abroad to dance with foreign companies or open their own schools in other countries, which casts a negative influence over the company's performance and artistic qualities.'

Shanghai Ballet (Shanghai)

The Shanghai Ballet got its present name in 1979. It was the Shanghai Dance School's production of *The White Haired Girl*, created in the mid-1960s, that paved the way for this second Chinese ballet company, and the original cast, such as Shi Zhong-qin, Ling Gui-ming and Mao Hui-fang have been the founding members of the company.

Ever since its independence from the school, the Shanghai Ballet made a surprisingly big jump on to the national and international stages with its productions of world classics such as *Swan Lake, Giselle, La Fille mal gardée, Don Quixote*, etc., and highlights from other master works such as *Coppélia, Romeo and Juliet, Nutcracker, Carmen* and *Le Corsaire*. They should also be proud of their own choreographers, who made new ballets on Chinese themes and music like *The Thunderstorm, Roses, Soul, Ah Q, Legend of the White Snake, Butterfly Lovers* and *The Deep Pool*. Inspired by the strong influence of Western modern dance since 1980, when the government began adopting the wise 'Open Door' Policy, they even made some modern numbers like *Inspirations from the Folklore, The Net, The Deer Looking Back, Deep Thought, Love for Light*, etc. All this exuberant creativity has drawn attention and praise from the national dance world.

Corresponding to this encouraging situation in choreography, the company's teachers have trained students such as Wang Qi-feng, Yang Xin-hua, Xin Li-li, Cai Li-jun, Zhang Li and Shi Hui, who have not only taken over all the leading roles in the repertoire but also won more than ten gold, silver and bronze medals in international ballet competitions in the United States, France and Japan.

The orchestra and the stage workshop of the company have employed some first-class experts who have collaborated successfully with many foreign artists. The Shanghai Ballet has always kept close contacts with world-class ballet companies as well as many famous artists, who come to teach or stage new works for the dancers. The company has so far toured Korea,

Japan, France, Singapore and Canada, as well as attended the Eleventh Asian Arts Festival in Hong Kong.

The young single dancers live in the company's dormitory, three sharing a 14m²-room – a little bit crowded but it costs them only 1 per cent of their pay. All the dancers, choreographers, teachers and other staff enjoy free medical care in the company's clinic or in an outside hospital, and the 'First State Rank' dancers and choreographers are entitled to see their doctors in two hospitals (that is, with one more choice) and also free. The company now has six studios, but no rehearsal hall or studio-theatre. They give about eighty performances each year; from the summer of 1989 to the spring of 1990, they have presented only thirty performances, including thirteen on tour.

The problems for this company's directors are, first, that they need more funds for new works – they get 450,000 yuan each year from the government, but they need at least 600,000 (last year their new production of *Don Quixote* cost 250,000 – more than half their annually allotted funds); secondly, they need young and talented dancers – Wang Qi-feng and almost all the other international prize-winners are in or nearing their thirties, with no successors in sight.

China Opera and Dance Drama Theatre (Beijing)

This original centre of Chinese Classic Dance suffered from the student riots during the spring and summer of 1989, and only presented two new, short dances: one is a group number called *Weaving the Flower Basket*, the other a *pas de deux*, *The Yellow River Lullaby*. The full-length dance drama *Sunset*, a folk-legend taken from the famous novelist Pu Song-ling's work *Liao Zhai Zhi Yi* (*The Scholars*) was scheduled for the summer before being performed at the Eleventh Asian Games in Beijing in autumn 1990.

Guangdong Experimental Modern Dance Company (Guangzhou)

This first official modern-dance company in China is entering its third year and the dancers are naturally becoming more mature after their training in technique and choreography under the guest teachers sent by Charles Reinhart, Director of the American Dance Festival.

Besides performances of their repertoire, which consists mainly of works by the US guest teachers and some by the dancers themselves, the company performed the Hong Kong choreographer Wili Cao's full-evening jazz ballet *City Romance* many times from November of 1989 to March of 1990. During these three years Wili Cao, who is Artistic Director and Resident Choreographer of Hong Kong City Contemporary Dance

Xia Li-yan and Zhang Da-Wei in *The Yellow River Lullaby pas de deux* (China Opera and Dance Drama Theatre).

Company, has been very generous in giving help to the up-and-coming company, including staging his choreography without charge. *City Romance* is made up of fifteen scenes which give an impression of not only Hong Kong or any big city's life, but also the life of all human society as a whole. This work has won a warm reception wherever it has been danced, in Guangzhou or the other locations around. It was scheduled to be taken to Beijing in the summer of 1990, together with a concert of the dancers' own choreography.

This summer the company took part in the Fifth Hong Kong International Dance Festival and in the summer of 1991 they may be invited to dance at the American Dance Festival in Durham, North Carolina, as the first Chinese Modern Dance Company (sponsored by the ADF and its Director Charles Reinhart).

Cuba

Jane King

F ive of the rehearsal studios in Havana's 150-year-old Gran Teatro are named after great dancers of world ballet: Elssler, who danced *Giselle* here in 1841; Taglioni; Pavlova, who came in 1917 and 1918; Nijinsky; and Fokine. Nicolas Yavorski, whose name appears above the sixth studio, is perhaps recorded only in the short history of Cuban ballet, but here he is of especial importance. Yavorski was Cuba's first ballet teacher, and in his classes were laid the foundations of the illustrious career of Alicia Alonso.

Alicia Alonso, creator and Prima Ballerina Assoluta of the Cuban National Ballet, is nowadays also the Director of the Gran Teatro in Havana and it is under her leadership that this superbly elegant and spacious building has been restored in the last two years to its former splendour, and has become a national centre of artistic and intellectual stimulus. The Gran Teatro encloses the García Lorca theatre, which stages the work of the major opera, ballet and theatre companies, and a vast complex of studios, concert and conference halls.

This has been a year of especially intense and successful activity for 'La Alonso': overseeing the restoration of the theatre, programming its activities, leading the company on a long and triumphant tour of Spain in the summer of 1989, and another of twelve Latin American countries in 1990, while at the same time preparing for the Twelfth International Ballet

Alicia Alonso, Prima Ballerina Assoluta of the Cuban National Ballet, in *Giselle*, Act II.
PHOTO: ALICIA SANGUINETTI

Festival of Havana. On 14 January she made one of the most historic appearances of her career when she danced, with her partner Orlando Salgado, the adagio from *Swan Lake*, Act II, at the Metropolitan Opera House in New York, on the occasion of the fiftieth anniversary of American Ballet Theatre. The audience of international ballet 'greats' gave her – the one founder-member of ABT still dancing – a standing ovation. And there was more: from Jerome Robbins came the offer of the rights of his *Interplay*, and from Herbert Ross, of his *Caprice*.

Cuba's choreographers, dancers and teachers have been in great demand this year away from home. Alberto Alonso went to Camagüey to mount his ballets *Medea* and *Grand Pas de Deux Yoruba* for the company directed by his brother Fernando. He accompanied the dancers on their tour of Greece and Cyprus. Alberto Mendez made works for Puerto Rico and Mexico, Ivan Tenorio for Colombia, and Gustavo Herrera for Uruguay. Hilda Riveros was happily able at last to return to her own country, Chile. Cuban teachers have been active in Australia, Canada, Denmark, Finland, West Germany, Italy, Spain and Switzerland. Prima Ballerina Loipa Araújo spent six months teaching and performing with Maurice Béjart's company in Lausanne; Julio Arozarena was guest artist for a season with the Ballet de l'Opéra d'Avignon. Both Loipa and Julio (who is still a member of the Cuban *corps de ballet*) danced in Paris during the bicentennial year of the French Revolution. Rosario Suarez and Jorge Esquivel, two of Cuba's most popular dancers, although no longer with the National Ballet, are still to be seen giving guest performances both at home and abroad.

Laura Alonso, Director of the newly established Centro Pro Danza, is responsible for the twice-yearly International Practical Courses in the Cuban School of Ballet (200 students in January, 300 in August). She also directs the **Joven Guardia**, a company of forty of the youngest dancers from the *corps de ballet* and outstanding students from the ballet school. The Joven Guardia gives performances of works by young choreographers in the Alejo Carpentier Hall of the Gran Teatro. The additional opportunities that this gives to the young dancers have produced a rich crop of performers with a technique and maturity of interpretation rare at such an early stage, and a record number of awards and medals won in competitions in New York, Varna, Lausanne, Brazil, Argentina and Peru. Each International course ends with a full-scale production – last year *The Three Musketeers*, this year *Coppélia* – and high-quality performances on the stage of the García Lorca – in which members of the Joven Guardia dance with the students on the course. Bursaries for study with the Cuban ballet are offered each year to students from abroad who have shown particular promise on the courses. (The next one will be 7 January to 3 February 1991.)

The **Camagüey Ballet** had a busy year, with tours of Greece and Cyprus in the autumn of 1989, of Brazil in the spring of 1990, and in July a visit to Italy to the Vignale Danza Festival in Turin. For the fifth Camagüey Biennial Festival in 1989 (8 November to 3 December) the company's choreographers produced eight new works, and the guest, Alberto Alonso, two more. The resident company was joined by members of the National Ballet, contemporary and folklore companies, the contemporary group Danza Abierta, dancers from the San Juan and Panama ballets, and the National Dance Group of Mexico.

New developments in contemporary dance, encouraged by state sponsorship, and the gradual coming together of classical and contemporary dancers and actors, have been welcome features of the artistic life of Havana during the last year. It was in 1987 that three ballerinas of the National Ballet left to set up, under the direction of Caridad Martínez, the **Ballet Teatro de La Habana**, with dancers and choreographers from the Danza Contemporánea de Cuba and actors and students from the national theatre school. Since then Marianela Boán, a leading dancer and choreographer with the Contemporánea, has created her own company, **Danza Abierta**, another mix of dancers and actors, who now share rehearsal space with the ballet, and perform, at the invitation of Alicia Alonso, at the Alejo Carpentier Hall (500 seats) of the Gran Teatro.

Another small experimental company, **Asi Somos**, may be seen performing from time to time among the sculptures in the Gran Teatro's art gallery, a particularly appropriate venue for the powerfully visual choreography of Lorna Burdsall, the company's creator. Burdsall, an American who trained with Doris Humphrey, helped to found Danza Contemporánea (then Moderna) in 1960, and was for some years its director.

The most recent development took place in Guantánamo, an hour's flight from Havana, where the city's first professional dance company was launched on 26 January 1990 in the Teatro Guaso. Elfrida Mahler directs the twenty-three dancers and seven musicians in a repertoire of Cuban folk and contemporary dance in equal proportions. Mahler, another American, is also a pioneer of Cuban Contemporary Dance, and was for some years the Director of the national dance school at Cubanacan. Her assistant director in Guantánamo is folk specialist Isaías Rojas.

This company is now giving regular seasons in Guantánamo, and has undertaken its first mountain tour – twenty-five performances in thirteen days, dancing in the streets and in the countryside, where audiences unfamiliar with contemporary dance remained fascinated and appreciative, even when it rained.

All these companies are, like the great national companies, state-funded. A thoughtful and lively search for a new dance vocabulary, to express new attitudes in a changing society, characterizes all their work. While rejecting

65

Lorna Burdsall's *Romance del Diablo* for her group Asi Somos in Havana.

PHOTO: JULIO ANTONIO RODRIGUEZ

the narrative form and accepted technical criteria, they are in no way rejecting the search for meaning. Caridad Martínez's *Test*, a full-length work mixing speech, acrobatics, ballet, 'street gesture', fantasy, grotesque comedy, and mime, is designed to shock the audience into coming to terms with their own identity. *Test* received the prize for the best production in Cuban Theatre in 1989. Marianela Boán's company's *Godot*, choreographed by Victor Varela, and inspired by Samuel Beckett's play, shared second prize with an American work at the Fourth Sai Tama International Festival in Tokyo in 1989.

There is much talk in Havana these days about 'a new aesthetic', the 'detheatricalization' of gesture, use of the spoken word, contact improvisation, minimalism. Martínez refers to Grotowsky and Peter Brook; Boán to Pina Bausch, Trisha Brown and the Alexander technique. There is a great thirst for knowledge, and visiting companies are rare in Cuba, so the Gran Teatro now has a video room, named after Luis Buñuel, where this year one could see, among other longed-for novelties, Bausch's *Rite of Spring*, a season of French and another of Post-Modern dance, and hear lectures from experts and critics on a variety of dance forms.

The **Danza Contemporánea** (DCC), celebrated its thirtieth anniversary in September 1989 with a festival in the Mella Theatre in which it was joined by the Conjunto Folklorico de Cuba, the National Dance Company of Guyana, the Experimental Dance Company of Martinique, and later, in Villa Clara, by the Grupo Espiral de Matanzas. Choreographers of the DCC contributed fifteen works, ranging from Eduardo Rivera's classic of the company's Afro-Cuban style, *Sulkary*, to works by Boán and Cardenas and a dance-theatre piece, *Uter-O*, by Guillermo Horta. DCC's founder-choreographer, the much-respected Ramiro Guerra, returned after an absence of some years to choreograph *De La Memoria Fragmentada*, which included extracts from film and some of his early works for the company.

In January 1990, **Cubadanza**, the international theoretical and practical course, which is now to be organized twice yearly by DCC (January and August), attracted fifty enthusiasts, professional and amateur, from Europe, the United States and Latin America, to their recently extended studio space at the Teatro Nacional. The course ended with a performance of works choreographed by the participants in the Nacional's studio theatre, the Covarrubias Hall.

How deeply dance is rooted in the communities in Cuba is vividly demonstrated by Rumba Saturday, held on alternate Saturday afternoons in the courtyard adjoining the studios of the National Folklore Company in Havana. Long before the performance begins, there is standing room only. The audience is ready and waiting to learn, to watch, to sing and finally to take the floor and match their own skills with those of the professionals. Rogelio Martínez Furé, Africanist scholar, singer and artist, introduces the magnificent Orishas (saints or deities) and the diverting masked diabolitos. He reveals their origins, explains the symbolism of the myth, the movement and the fantastically beautiful costumes which the dancers are about to present. He starts the singing, in Yoruba, and encourages the audience to join in – which many are able to do.

There seems to be an inexhaustible source from which the Cuban folk-dance draws its material, and there is certainly a rich creativity among the choreographers, musicians, dancers, and designers who recreate the ancient magic and present it with such freshness and power.

The **Conjunto Folklorico Nacional** also runs international courses, 'Folk Cuba', each year in February and July, for 'the serious student, professional, or enthusiast of African music, dance and culture . . . its history and development in Cuba and the Caribbean'.

Denmark

Bent Schønberg

T he Royal Theatre, Denmark's national institution representing the best in drama, opera, ballet and music, has a new director, Boel Jørgensen. Her appointment caused quite a stir, partly because she is a Swede instead of a Dane but also because she had no experience of running a theatre. Her previous job was Rector of the University of Roskilde (some 30km from Copenhagen). Yet her start as director has been promising. She listens, she listens, and when she has all the facts, she acts swiftly, efficiently, and ruthlessly when she thinks it is necessary.

She has been in many ways a good thing for the ballet. She quietly dropped the pretentious Hans Christian Andersen festival at which leading dancers and choreographers received 'The Oscar of the Ballet World' – a statuette of Andersen, who had little to do with the art of ballet. Instead, she has concentrated on building up the repertoire, in spite of the usual mini-budget that most companies around the world are trying to live with.

The 1989/90 season started with a triple bill of two new works and William Forsythe's *France/Dance* (1983). This shocked and horrified some and shocked and entertained many more. It is a ballet about things disappearing and time disappearing. It was a theatrical coup to bring in a special guest artist from France, the midget performer Sabine Rothe, to manipulate tall models of the Eiffel Tower, the Leaning Tower of Pisa, the Empire State Building and the Pyramids . . . all to music by J. S. Bach and a spoken text.

Fête galante is the second work Ib Andersen of New York City Ballet has made for his old company. To Couperin's music he has made a little ballet in the classical style, elegant and pretty but without much impact, and clearly influenced by his mentor, George Balanchine. The dances were faultlessly executed by some of the best artists in the company: Lis Jeppesen, Rose Gad, Heidi Ryom, Mette-Ida Kirk, Arne Willumsen, Peter Bo Bendixen, Nikolaj Hübbe and Alexander Kølpin. The airy designs and costumes were by Jens-Jacob Worsaae.

Anna Laerkesen, formerly one of the company's most gifted ballerinas, also premièred her second work, *Manhattan Abstraction*, to music by the Danish composer Poul Ruders – a strong, clamorous and rather frightening score. Jens-Jacob Worsaae was again responsible for the designs: no wonder he is so sought after from Los Angeles to Moscow. Dancers dressed in

Nikolaj Hübbe as the trouble-making demi-god Loke in the Danish Royal Ballet's recreation of Bournonville's *The Lay of Thrym*.   PHOTO: DAVID AMZALLAG

blue were outlined against a dark and sinister background, human beings trying to abstract themselves from the life of New York City. Most impressive was Lis Jeppesen, icy cold in her dancing until Hübbe put warmth into her with caressing movements.

The major new production this season was a recreation of Bournonville's *The Lay of Thrym*, which had not been given since 1905. The work had its première in 1868, a few years after the country's painful defeat by Bismarck's Germany. By going back to the Nordic myths, Bournonville gave the frustrated Danes an escape from the tragic realities of everyday life. The ballet was a tremendous success, and even though its elaborate machinery, many sets and hordes of costumes had been extremely expensive, the money was recouped within two months.

It is always exciting when a work by an old master can be revived after everyone thought it had been lost forever. Neither this ballet nor *Abdullah* can match up to *Napoli*, but every scrap of Bournonville gives us a fuller understanding of his genius. As a bonus, J. P. E. Hartmann's music, written a decade before *Swan Lake*, is poetic and inspiring. The Swedish former ballerina, Elsa-Marianne von Rosen, and her ballet historian husband, Allan Fridericia, had researched the ballet for years before reconstructing and recreating it for the Royal Ballet.

Fridericia pruned almost 75 per cent of the action to make the story easier for modern audiences to understand: yet it remains very convoluted – it took me three performances to follow exactly what was going on among the Nordic gods and giants. However, the ballet has proved a great success with younger members of the audience, who are familiar with the old myths through comic strips and cartoons in the press and on television.

The choreography looks typical Bournonville, although some of the steps, like the colours in the costumes, seem to be of a later date. However, von Rosen and Fridericia (who was responsible for the designs) can trace everything back to the original. The production was helped by the casting of all the leading dancers in the company, who performed their roles with great conviction. In the central role of the trouble-maker Loke, Hübbe danced with impressive attack, while Peter Bo Bendixen was more demonic and dangerous. Heidi Ryom, as Sygin, was touching in her adoration of Loke, and Rose Gad, alternating in the role, was delightful. Lloyd Riggins, a young American who joined the company only a few years ago, proved that he is a consummate Bournonville dancer.

Bournonville himself had problems in making the ballet into a unified whole. It is not easy for his descendants to bring all his ideas together and I doubt whether any foreign company could dance it – or whether foreign audiences would understand it! However, it is an interesting addition to the repertoire and it will be one of the attractions in the big Bournonville festival in 1992, when all his surviving ballets will be given.

Come to Copenhagen.
Come to Sheraton.

Location Downtown, in the heart of Copenhagen, near Tivoli Gardens, shopping, theatres and Central Station, 10 miles from airport.

Features 471 modern rooms, including a non-smoking floor and two Executive floors, all with private bath, radio, telephone, color TV with video and 8 international programs including CNN, air-conditioning, 24 hour room service. Sheraton Body Shop with sauna, jogging routes, shopping arcade. Full range of guest services.

Restaurants 3 restaurants and 3 bars, including a piano bar with international entertainment.

Meeting Facilities Our newly renovated Banquet facilities accommodating from 10 to more than 1000 persons makes Sheraton Copenhagen Hotel the place to meet with success!

Sheraton Copenhagen Hotel
The hospitality people of ITT

6 Vester Sogade, DK-1601 Copenhagen V, Denmark
TEL: +45 33 14 35 35   TELEX: (855) 27450   TELEFAX: +45 33 32 12 23
P.O. BOX 337   CABLE: SHERACO COPENHAGEN.

The teacher in the photograph is Anne Marie Vessel of the Royal (Danish) Ballet. She is principal teacher at the Royal Theatre Ballet School for pupils between nine and eighteen years old, as well as being a member of the company. She was coached by Hans Brenaa as one of his Crown Princesses to take charge of the Bournonville repertoire once he had died. She has proved a fine teacher and a zealous guardian of the heritage of the greatest name in Danish ballet. In addition to her work as teacher and performer (and mother of a three-year-old son), she is the wife of the Danish Prime Minister, Poul Schlüter, whom she married last season. He is now known to everybody at the Royal Theatre as 'son-in-law'. It is the first time in ballet history that a dancer has married a prime minister, although the Danish king Frederik VII married a former member of the Royal Ballet.

Marie-Louise Kjølbye reports on Modern Dance in Denmark

Denmark's tradition of modern dance is shorter than in most other countries. Contemporary-dance techniques were introduced in the mid-1970s, mainly by American visitors and residents. The focus of interest is Copenhagen, although the city of Aarhus is planning to have a contemporary-dance company of its own – which would be Denmark's first 'official' modern-dance group.

The lack of training for contemporary-dance students is very apparent, although ex-pupils of the founding figures and young Danes who trained abroad (at the London Contemporary Dance School, for example) work steadily to maintain professional standards. Tough competition for limited financial support and the struggle to educate an audience has limited the number of important groups to only four, or possibly six.

The most versatile and professionally run modern-dance company in Denmark is the **Nyt Dansk Danseteater** (New Danish Dance Theatre). Like most other Danish dance groups, the NDDT often uses contemporary,

71

rock-inspired music, which attracts young audiences. With popular shows touring around the country, the NDDT has shown a large public that there is more to dance than the Royal Danish Ballet. The choreography is a mix of dance and drama, drawing on techniques originally created by Martha Graham and Alvin Ailey. Themes are usually mythological or ethnic, but recently a new trend has emerged of including social dance steps – waltz, rock and roll and other popular dances – as well as modern dance or ballet movements. The company is gradually moving towards a realistic, contemporary account of society, under the powerful influence of the excellent Finnish choreographer Jorma Uotinen, among others.

The most entertaining and well-rounded of the professional companies is **Uppercut**, founded by Anne Crosset and Cher Guertze. Their choreography is inspired by the fascinating possibilities of the human body and the way that it can express relationships and human predicaments. They like to turn conventions upside down to see what happens; and their use of everyday crafts for a variety of non-practical purposes makes their school performances a great success.

Rhea Leman is not only a impressive solo dancer but also the leader and principal choreographer of the group **Teater Tango**. Her work is essentially dance theatre, using dialogue and narrative. She is less influenced by German *Tanztheater* than by American films, especially those in which crime and psychology meet. In Leman's pieces, reality is often intermingled with dreams and fantasies, so that the end result is both absurd and entertaining. She is moving increasingly away from dance towards spoken theatre.

The tragically early death of the Colombian Jorge Holguin put a stop to Danish surrealist dance. He created a magic world of illusions and witty satire, using simple but astonishing tricks, as if conceived by a wise child whose imagination was both innocent and full of horrors. His performers were not so much dancers as fantastical creators of theatre. Whether the **Jorge Holguin Dance Theatre** can survive under its new director, the talented Canadian Kathryn Ricketts, remains to be seen.

Nanna Nilson, one of the few Danish-born choreographers of contemporary dance, has herself been an eminent dancer. She trained with Merce Cunningham, whose influence is apparent in her choreography, which concentrates on movement unencumbered by false sentimentality, outworn symbols and irrelevant story lines. She often collaborates with the American composer Charlie Morrow, whose collages mix the sounds of nature with the metallic noises of civilization.

Corona Danseteater had long been known for its picturesque and exotic performances, inspired by Balinese ritual dancing and Jungian psychoanalysis: the dancers explored their inner worlds by moving through amazing sets. But in 1989 a young Danish dancer, Jorgen Carlslund, took over as director, shifting the emphasis more towards dance and 'real life' situations, while trying to keep the psychological undercurrents.

The soloist **Anita Saij** is mainly influenced by Japanese forms of theatre, especially *butoh* dance. She explores the effects of time and bodily exhaustion in fascinating and often provokingly long and slow performances. As a soloist, her influence has so far been limited but she has opened up a new avenue for Danish dance.

Charlotte Rindom and Jan Thomsen form the group **Mikado**, where speed, colour and energy are the key words. **Kompagni**, the group run by Susanne Frederiksen and Christine Meldal, perform their own works as well as some by Kim Brandstrup, the interesting young Danish choreographer who works mainly in Britain. They were all fellow students at the London Contemporary Dance School.

The Lay of Thrym.

Finland

Rebecca Libermann

The ballet season 1989/90 in Helsinki opened with John Cranko's ballet *Onegin*, performed by the Stuttgart Ballet as part of the Helsinki Festival. Minimi, a Finnish dance group and Tommi Huivinen also performed a work called *Heroes*, an interesting piece commissioned by the festival. Dance Theatre Raatikko contributed its ballet *Puerto del Puerto*, choreographed by Marja Korhola. The festival came at the end of a decade which had seen great creative development in Finnish ballet and showed Finland's readiness to look to the 1990s. This season has shown that the time is ripe for the work of new and original young choreographers: Tommi Kitti, Tiina Lindfors, Juha Vanhakartano and others have brought new life to the ballet scene and have even been given commissions from the National Ballet, which until now has liked to play safe. The use of inexperienced choreographers and new music scores is always a risk, artistically and financially, and such initiatives may not gain public support. These experiments are important, however, if dance is to progress. The Finnish Ballet proved this season that taking risks can pay off.

The **Finnish National Ballet**'s season began with an entertaining evening in October centring on the theme of jazz. Three ballets were presented which were quite different in their approach to the subject. The first, *Stairset*, was choreographed by the Finn, Tiina Lindfors, who has become known for her original and humorous social-criticism pieces for smaller modern-dance companies in Finland. For the first time, she was given the chance to work with a big classical company and she succeeded rather well. As in many of her works, stage sets were central to the ballet and here she used oblong boxes on wheels which the dancers turned into stairs, stages, bedbunks, cupboards and trolleys. On them, in them and around them, the dancers moved with cool and economical movement to Palle Mikkelborg's jazz score. The ballet, with its grotesque and humorous twists, took an ironical look at the world of American show-business.

Walter Nicks's ballet, *Spirit Blues*, dealt with the development of jazz, tracing its roots from Africa and its ritualistic beginnings through to the more sophisticated forms of South and North American jazz dance. The piece emphasized the vitality of jazz dance and presented a challenge to a company unused to this style of movement. Thanks to the extensive and patient work of the choreographer and the great flexibility of the Finnish dancers, the performance was convincing.

Unlike *Spirit Blues*, Gray Veredon's *The Ragtime Dance Company* was very lighthearted. Sheer fun, it used bicycles, roller-skates, baseball, slapstick comedy and melodrama. It was a highly entertaining piece but, unfortunately, in the end the ballet overdid the gags of the ragtime era and got stuck in its own clichés.

The National Ballet's season in January 1990 included Antony Tudor's *Gala Performance* and a world première of *Nijinsky – Divine Dancer*, to celebrate the 100th anniversary of this legendary figure. It was born out of a collaboration between the dancer-choreographer Juha Vanhakartano, the actor Hannu Huuska (both from Finland) and the German-born composer Joseph Hölderle, who now lives in Paris. Vanhakartano, who was a member of the Finnish National Ballet before he joined the Bochumer Dance Theatre, brought back with him ideas from the German Dance Theatre movement. Although he has choreographed several ballets for studio production in Helsinki, this is the first ballet he has created for a bigger company. It was a risk therefore for the Finnish National Ballet to use him; and it was a risk that paid off. The ballet is based loosely on the diaries of Nijinsky, combining elements of classical ballet, dance theatre and performance art. The character of Nijinsky was played by an actor, while his roles in *Petrushka*, *Le Spectre de la rose*, *Schéhérezade* and *L'Après-midi d'un faune*, as well as the people in his life, danced around him, born out of his memories. The ballet was divided into two acts: life and death, normality destroyed by increasing chaos. For a first large-scale piece, it was an ambitious enterprise which, apart from some moments, was surprisingly well done. *Gala Performance* on the same evening, although a beautiful piece which was formidably executed by the dancers, did not fit the bill and should have been performed on another day.

Apart from the repertory of the season – Yuri Grigorovich's *Nutcracker*, *Lady of the Camellias* by Domy Reiter-Soffer, *Ronja, the Robber's Daughter* by Marjo Kuusela, Nils Christe's *D.C.*, *Verklärte Nacht* by Jiři Kylián and *Etudes* by Harald Lander – there was a première of a work by the Australian choreographer Harold Collins, *Salome*, set to music by Peter Maxwell Davies. Without the fine performance given by the dancers, this ballet would have been unbearable. It was quite simply boring, with its interminable plot of murder and the fight between good (dressed in white) and bad (dressed in black), with Salome trapped in the middle. Choreographically as well, it was also nothing special. But one flop in an otherwise exciting season is forgivable.

Smaller dance companies also did rather well this season. In August 1989 a newcomer joined the Finnish dance theatres: **Dance Theatre Eri** (The Different Dance Theatre). Founded by five dancer-choreographers from Helsinki and Turku, Eri deals with contemporary issues and aims to find new means of expression. Their first night in December in Turku was very fresh and pleasing. They showed three works – *Eriö* by Ari Savinen, which dealt with life and relationships; *Odd Couple*, an abstract, fluently choreographed *pas de deux* based on a Lorca poem, by Sampo Kivelä and Eeva Soini, both of the Finnish National Ballet; and *Different Keeper*, by Tiina Lindfors. It is obvious that these are choreographers to look out for in the future.

Raatikko had a fairly good season under the directorship of Marja Korhola, although their work lacks innovation at the moment. Helsinki City Theatre, Aurinko Ballet, Dance Theatre Hurjaruuth and Mobita, amongst others, have had a busy season. In November there was a small festival at the Savoy Theatre in Helsinki with the theme 'Men are Dancing' and, at the end of the season, the annual **Kuopio Dance Festival** (3–10 June) was this time dedicated to Africa and the Mediterranean. It featured the Ballet Christina Hoyos from Spain, Les Ballets Africains from Guinea, Les Ballets Maliens from Mali, a dance group from Zaire, the Groupe Emile Dubois from France, the Whirling Dervishes from Turkey, Tine Rozanc from Yugoslavia and the Company Germaine Acogny from Senegal. Also contributing to this international festival were the Finns: Tommi Kitti created a new ballet called *Kilimandsharo*, Dance Theatre Raatikko again presented *The King is Coming* by Ari Numminen and Korhola's *Puerto del Puerto*, Dance Theatre Hurjaruuth showed their piece *Island*, by Arja Pettersson, a dream-like work to African music, and Dance Theatre Eri participated for the first time.

The twenty-third World Congress of ITI also took place between 27 May and 3 June 1989 in Helsinki, with the theme 'Theatre as a Cultural Bridge'.

The big news on the home front this year was the announcement of the resignation of Doris Laine as director of the Finnish National Ballet – she will leave in 1991. Jorma Uotinen, a young, internationally known choreographer, who at present heads the dance group of the Helsinki City Theatre, will take over from her. This season, Doris Laine received the state prize (30,000 FIM) for her long and active contribution to dance. A five-year state grant was also awarded to the dancer-choreographer Reijo Kela, an extremely original artist whose professional dance career began when he was already an adult. He is unique in that he always works alone and will perform wherever he finds an audience, even in a field, as in *Ilmari's Plough*.

France

Jacky Pailley

P aris can be proud to be the only capital city in the world to have a theatre dedicated solely to dance. Since October 1989, the Palais Garnier (the Paris Opéra) has been renamed the Palais de la Danse, now that the opera company has moved to the new Opéra Bastille (officially inaugurated in March 1990). The former opera house is now the home of the **Paris Opéra Ballet** company and this season, for the first time, it received five major foreign companies. The opening night was darkened by the absence of the Artistic Director of the company, Rudolf Nureyev. At that time the Russian dancer and choreographer was in the United States, playing the role of the King of Siam in the Broadway musical *The King and I*. Long-distance wrangling had started a month before between the Russian star and Pierre Bergé, the President of the Paris Opéra, over Nureyev's new contract as artistic director. His former contract ended in August 1989 and Nureyev had let it be known that he would sign the new contract only if he could continue to spend six months of the year outside France and was given absolute artistic control. Neither Pierre Bergé nor Jean-Albert Cartier, the Administrator of the Opéra, would agree on these two points. The dancers were already complaining that their director was never present and no one could make a decision without calling him in New York or somewhere else in the world. During the long negotiations, Pierre Bergé named the company's two chief Ballet Masters, Patrice Bart and Eugène Polyakov, as interim replacements for the director. Finally, in November, Nureyev resigned as Artistic Director and was named Principal Choreographer, a post created especially for him, in order 'to ensure the presence of his productions' at the Opéra. We had to wait four months to learn the name of the new director: he is Patrick Dupond, 31 years old and one of France's most celebrated dancers. His appointment seemed to satisfy everyone. It is a return home through the front door for this brilliant performer, who has only appeared a few times during the last few years on the stage of the Opéra as a guest star. In 1988 he was made director of the French Ballet of Nancy, his contract there finishing at the end of this year. His new job will start in January 1991, for eight months out of each year. His appointment has raised hopes of the return to the Opéra of two of its former *étoiles*, Eric Vu An and Sylvie Guillem (now in London), who left the company to pursue their careers elsewhere. Eric Vu An completed filming his first role in a major motion picture under the direction of Bernardo Bertolucci, and

Sylvie Guillem appeared in Paris this spring with the Kirov Ballet at the Palais des Sports but not at the Opéra, where the Russian company was also performing. Patrick Dupond has already announced a gala opening night for the next season with all the stars who have been part of the Opéra's ballets for the last forty years. Maurice Béjart, who had not set foot in the Opéra since his quarrel with Nureyev in 1986, when he named Eric Vu An an *étoile* without Nureyev's consent, was invited to the Palais Garnier with his company, the Lausanne Béjart Ballet, to present his latest work, *Around the Ring*, following its première in Berlin. With music by Wagner, of which he is terribly fond, Béjart has found new inspiration and created interesting choreography based on *The Ring*, going beyond mere illustration of the opera. After the disappointment of *1789*, last year's creation, Béjart has regained the respect of his admirers.

Bad news: the disappearance, last autumn of the GRCOP, the experimental group of the Opéra Ballet, after the death of its director, Jacques Garnier. Most of the dancers have been reintegrated into the main ballet company and some have left. Good news: an average audience capacity during the season of 98 per cent for the Opéra Ballet and 96 per cent for invited companies. At the end of its first season the Palais de la Danse will have received more than 250,000 spectators, which is an impressive figure for dance.

Paris is also proud to be the second home, after Frankfurt, of William Forsythe and the Frankfurt Ballet. Starting next season, Forsythe will spend two months of the year preparing a new piece for the Châtelet Theatre. The Frankfurt Ballet appeared there this season to show some of its most recent works. The *tout Paris* of dance was there at the opening night of this magnificent American choreographer, whom many critics have called 'the new Balanchine'. Surprised and disconcerted to begin with, the Parisian audience warmly embraced Mr Forsythe, making the Frankfurt Ballet the hottest ticket of the season.

The other showcase for dance in Paris is the Théâtre de la Ville, just opposite the Châtelet. Dedicated to the new modern-dance movement, the theatre invites Pina Bausch every year to sold-out houses, and it also gives important opportunities to new French choreographers. It is *the* place to perform. All in all, twenty-one companies were scheduled for this season.

But the centre of Paris is not the only place for dance. All around the capital, particularly in the suburbs, you can see numerous works by young companies based in outlying theatres. **Maguy Marin** is in residence in Créteil at the Maison des Arts. Her latest work, created for Avignon's festival, left many disappointed. **Angelin Preljocaj**, who is based in Champigny, has created a new piece to Stravinsky's *Les Noces*, with an orchestra and choir. **Daniel Larrieu**, who had always refused to have a permanent residence, is now settled in the *Ferme du Buisson*, a new cultural centre built on an old farm in the new city of Marne la Vallée. A brand-new theatre, with a large stage perfect for dance, has been constructed within the old structure and was inaugurated in March. Larrieu's company, Astrakan, has its own studio on the premises. Before settling in at his new home, Larrieu presented Parts I and II of his latest piece, *La Route de la soie*, in Paris: the third part was presented in Lyon in October. Some cities and *départements* around Paris are working diligently for modern dance. Val de Marne is particularly active, with an annual budget of 7 million francs allocated solely to dance, the most impressive of all the French *départements*. The **Biennale du Val de Marne** is one of the most important events in France for young choreographers. The Seine Saint Denis, another *département* in the neighbourhood of Paris, was host to the **Rencontres Internationales de Bagnolet**, an international competition for dance held every two years. In June, eighteen companies competed, representing ten countries, with a jury presided over by Merce Cunningham. The Bagnolet prize winners were as follows: Grand Prix SACD for a first work – Héla Fattoumi and Eric Lamoureux; Grand Prix de la Fondation Cointreau for a contemporary creation – Charles Cré-Ange; Grand Prix for Ballet Theatre – Aletta Collins (UK); and Grand Prix for choreography – Kilina Cremona. The New Choreography Award given by the Bonnie Bird Choreographic Fund went to Aletta Collins.

But the most important event in the region of Paris is the **Iles de Danse**. Initiated in 1988 and now in its second year, this winter it invited the participation of sixteen choreographers in residence in forty towns of the Ile de France region. It is not really a festival but more of a concentrated effort to expose dance to people in the small town suburbs who rarely get the opportunity to experience its pleasures. There are no premières: the choreographers simply present their existing work (sixty performances in all), provide workshops for the public, and work with children in schools. Trisha Brown was this year's special guest: she gave several conferences for students at one of the universities. During a one-month period, Dominique Bagouet, **Ris et Danceries**, Georges Appaix, Stéphanie Aubin, Paco Decina, Andrew Degroat, Doussaint-Dubouloz, Duroure, Preljocaj, **Roc in Lichen**, Jackie Taffanel and Elsa Wolliaston participated in this event.

Dance is becoming more and more decentralized in France. Most of the major companies are settled in regions throughout France. Fourteen are in choreographic centres subsidized jointly by the Ministry of Culture, the town and the region. The Ministry has not created any new choreographic centres recently, but it has increased its endowment to 2.5 million francs this year. It seems that the Delegation for Dance at the Ministry now prefers to promote temporary residencies. Claude Brumachon has been chosen by the city of Nantes for a residency at the opera there, after the closure of the Ballet de l'Opéra de Nantes. As a result its former Director, **Jean-Michel Gravier**, has left to head the Ballet du Rhin. Brumachon's company will be subsidized by the local communities and the Ministry of Culture but its contract is limited to several years only. This year, the Ministry has begun a new initiative, known as an 'associated choreographer residency'. This is a contract for three years between a choreographer and a venue. Two choreographers have already benefited from this arrangement: Daniel Larrieu (previously mentioned) at Marne la Vallée and **François Verret** at the National Theatre of Dance and the Moving Image at Châteauvallon. The next one will probably be **Josef Nadj** at the Production Centre in Orléans. This arrangement allows more freedom to the choreographers and greater flexibility for the partners.

At present, two choreographic centres provide independent companies with the resources and the space to create work. They are the National Centre for Contemporary Dance (CNDC) in Angers, which is also a school for professional dancers, and the Choreographic Production Centre of Orléans. Each year, the CNDC receives three or four companies in residence for a period of six or eight weeks. This year, they included Jean-François Duroure, Daniel Larrieu, Samuel Leborgne and Trisha Brown, whose company celebrated its twenty-year anniversary.

The Ministry of Culture has also funded several choreographers' residencies in theatres and cultural centres. These residencies, limited to three months, are subsidized by the Ministry on an equal basis with the local communities. The amount of this subsidy is between 150,000 and 250,000 francs. This year, the Ministry allocated a total of 1.19 million francs to these residencies. A residency is the best way for an independent company to create a work. The endowment is added to the production subsidy already allocated to the company and to the amount donated by the theatre. The company is given the best possible conditions: the theatre must provide a place for rehearsal and all the necessary technical facilities. In return, the company has to give the première of its creation at the theatre. It may also be a co-production between several theatres or cultural centres. For instance, **Michel Kéléménis** created *Vaste Ciel* this winter in Evry, a suburb of Paris, after ten weeks in residence at the Agora, Evry's cutural centre. He began in September for a ten-week period at the Maison de la Danse in Lyon. In between, he was offered work at the Choreographic Centre of Montpellier, directed by Dominique Bagouet, where he began his career as a dancer. He also received a two-week residency proposal from the Cultural Centre of Aubusson, which had agreed to present the show in advance.

Some cultural centres have built their production policy on the principle of residencies. In the far west of Brittany the **Quartz**, opened in 1988, this winter received Lanónima Imperial and Josef Nadj, who created new pro-

ductions. The companies are housed in a seventeenth-century manor sur-
rounded by a vast park, three kilometres from the centre. The dancers
work in a rehearsal studio the same size as the stage, which is open day
and night. Not all companies enjoy these good conditions, for only a few
are selected by the producers from the eighty independent subsidized
companies. The Ministry of Culture allocated a total of 11.5 million francs
this year, two million more than in the previous year. The subsidy can
range from 40,000 francs (for the *première aide*) to 370,000 francs (the maxi-
mum), for a company such as Philippe Decoufflé's DCA. Twelve new
companies received their first subsidies this year, though seven companies
which were subsidized last year did not receive any funding for 1990.

To receive subsidy is to receive a much-desired seal of approval. Without funding it is very difficult, almost impossible, for a choreographer to
mount a production. And the only way to obtain the subsidy is to show a
work which pleases the selection board, which means that the situation
remains difficult for new choreographers. Among the newly subsidized
choreographers, two have attracted particular attention: **Marceline Lartigue**
and **Héla Fattoumi**. After choreographing the highly acclaimed *Erzebet* last
year for the Eurodanse festival in Mulhouse, Marceline Lartigue, who used
to dance with Karine Saporta, created a short piece at the Mulhouse Opera,
using John Cage's music. At the same Eurodanse festival, Héla Fattoumi
and Eric Lamoureux received praise for their work. They and a few others
are the vital new blood of French contemporary dance.

Germany (East)

Dietmar Fritzsche

The season was characterized by both uncertainty and hope. Before
and after the revolutionary events in October/November 1989 –
known as the *Wende* (turnover) – many dancers left their companies in
search of new artistic fortunes in West Germany. This severely reduced
numbers within the companies, who as a consequence had to modify their
repertories and, worse still, were often not able to première their new productions. Nevertheless, the development towards freedom in the GDR primarily inspired great hope.

Opportunities for individual experimentation, which were previously
impeded by many difficulties and financial constraints, are now almost

limitless, although some hesitation remains due to lack of experience. In the regional city of Cottbus, a young and unconventional ensemble has been formed under the direction of Michael Apel. They created two innovative dance-theatre performances – *Kammer-Tanz-Theater 1* and *Kammer-Tanz-Theater 2*. In the first programme, several young choreographers presented their work, some of which had already been performed and won awards in the 1989 choreographic competition. Holger Bey, a choreographer from Berlin, was particularly remarkable for his original ideas and biting humour. The outstanding work from the second programme was *To Play or Not to Play*, in which dancers and actors joined forces in a charming play of motion.

Still in its early stages of development, the **Berlin Tanztheater/Thomas Guggi/Elke Paul** is dedicated to the exploration of the explosive nature of relationships. Their work is loaded with conflict between men and women.

An interesting world première was performed by the ballet company of the regional city of Magdeburg entitled *Berliner Antigone*, after the novel of the same title by the West German author Rolf Hochhuth. Choreographed by Peter Tornew, using music by the Berlin composer Wolfgang Hohensee, it was a courageous, if fated, deed against fascist inhumanity.

Another more cheerful piece, choreographed by Hermann Rudolph to a colourful collage of music, was premièred at Karl-Marx-Stadt. In the ballet *La Belle et la bête* (Beauty and the Beast), Rudolph displayed a rich and original fantasy, full of surprises for the audience, juxtaposing classical elegance with eccentric poses.

Major success was denied to the big companies however: the **Deutsche Staatsoper Berlin**, continuing without a resident choreographer to shape a distinctive style in the ensemble, engaged the formerly much praised dancer Peter Breuer for a production of *Don Juan/Faust* to music by Christoph Willibald Gluck and Franz Liszt. The piece only partly succeeded in portraying all the contradictory characteristics of Juan/Faust. However, the company danced excellently – particularly the soloists Oliver Matz, Torsten Händler, Steffi Scherzer and Bettina Thiel, as well as the *corps de ballet*.

The first exchange performances of the East and West Berlin companies – Deutsche Staatsoper and Deutsche Oper Berlin – were politically and artistically exciting events. Each company gave a performance at the other's theatre on the same night.

Towards the end of the season the Deutsche Staatsoper mounted a production from its repertoire, *Invitation to the Dance*, that demonstrated its classical virtues – *Les Sylphides* and *Le Spectre de la rose* by Fokine and the 'Kingdom of the Shades' from Petipa's *La Bayadère*, as well as the *grand pas* from *Paquita*. The performance took place on 5 May 1990 under the direction of Tom Schilling.

Members of the Leipzig Opera House Ballet in Enno Markwart's *Abraxas*.

PHOTO: ANDREAS BIRKIGT

The **Komische Oper Berlin** provided an opportunity for young choreographers to test themselves. In a series of performances called *Tanztheater Forum*, a former member of the company, Birgit Scherzer, presented her own piece, *Keith*, using an all-male cast. The highly talented choreographer Joachim Ahne, who is continuing to develop his own distinctive style, presented a new piece entitled *Trilogie der Sehnsucht* (Trilogy of Desire).

The **Leipzig Opera House Ballet** staged a rather dull *Kammertanz* (chamber dance). The first night showed both old and new pieces by Dietmar Seyffert and Enno Markwart. A première of a new production of *Giselle*, transferred to Leipzig by guests from Kiev, was also performed on 3 June 1990. The new Director, the Dresden-born composer Udo Zimmermann, announced, however, fine-sounding names of choreographers for the future, so I remain hopeful, if sceptical.

The **Staatsoper Dresden**, in its marvellous opera house designed by Semper, scored an unqualified success with a triple-bill evening. The programme included works by Birgit Cullberg (*Don Quixote's Dreams*), Hermann Rudolph (*La Valse*, with music by Ravel) and Emöke Pöstényi (*Bolero*), again using Ravel's music. This last work was especially fascinating. Pöstényi, the resident choreographer for the Television Ballet Company,

83

The women of the Staatsoper Dresden company in Emöke Pöstényi's new version of Ravel's *Bolero.*   PHOTO: ERWIN DÖRING

worked exclusively with female dancers who, by their excellent performance, succeeded very effectively in presenting Pöstényi's ideas. The
ensemble also continued its series of improvisation programmes within
the tradition of expressionist dance, in the vein of Gret Palucca, as well as
its series of experimental chamber dance evenings. The most recent programme was premièred under the title of *Kontraste IX* on 25 May 1990. For
dancers and audiences alike these evenings are always exciting and inspiring dance events.

There were new programmes staged at the smaller as well as the larger
theatres, mainly consisting of narrative ballets, such as *Coppélia* in Erfurt,
staged by Sigrid Trittmacher-Koch, and *The Taming of the Shrew* in Dresden-
Radebeul, with choreography by Eva Hennig, libretto by Dietmar Fritzsche
and music by Jens-Uwe Günther.

What the future will bring with the new political situation is difficult to
predict. Dancers and choreographers from Western countries are applying
for vacancies in East German companies and new fringe groups and ballet
schools are beginning to emerge. A bright start has been made and I look
forward to seeing the results.

Germany (West)

Horst Koegler

Two major decisions, long overdue, have been taken during the 1989/
90 season, both of which should have a strong influence on the development of the German dance scene. The first concerns the appointment of
Peter Schaufuss as Artistic Director of the ballet at the West Berlin German
Opera, where he is to succeed Gert Reinholm, who has been running the
company in various guises (from 1966 to 1969 as Kenneth MacMillan's
administrator) since 1961. This is to take effect from the start of the 1990/1
season. The second appointment (which will start with the 1991/2 season)
is that of Heinz Spoerli from Basle as Artistic Director of the ballet at the
Düsseldorf–Duisburg German Opera on the Rhine, where he is to succeed
Paolo Bortoluzzi, who has been in charge since 1984/5.

A major event of the 1989/90 season has been the inauguration of the
Ballet Centre Hamburg John Neumeier, a magnificent building complex
offering no fewer than nine different-sized studios and halls, all named
after famous choreographers, such as Petipa, Tudor, Nijinsky, Fokine,
Balanchine, Wigman et al. (though no Neumeier yet), for the ballet company of the Hamburg State Opera and its school. The complex includes a
boarding school and all the necessary office facilities. An architectural
landmark of the city, the former high school has been meticulously rebuilt
for its present use and was hailed at its opening ceremony on 23 September
1989 as the most beautiful ballet building in the world.

Meanwhile Neumeier has not been lazy. In December he staged as his
latest **Hamburg** première *Des Knaben Wunderhorn* (a selection of ten songs
from the famous *Lieder* cycle) and *Fünfte Sinfonie von Gustav Mahler* – a further supplement to his growing list of ballets to music by the eminent
Austrian composer, who increasingly seems to become the leitmotiv of
Neumeier's choreographic œuvre. This one, let it be said, is not a masterpiece.

A vastly more challenging Neumeier ballet was first seen on 21 January
1990 at **Stuttgart**: his full-length treatment of *Medea*, set to various music
pieces by, among others, Bartók and Schnittke. In the city where Noverre
had staged his legendary *Médée et Jason* back in 1763, it proved a shocker
through Neumeier's free-wheeling use of an immense array of different
kinds of choreography, from tribal African rituals to contemporary ballroom dancing. With a stunningly mesmeric Marcia Haydée as protagonist
– plus Wolfgang Stollwitzer's highly impressive Jason, Gigi Hyatt as

85

Kreusa, and Vladimir Klos as Kreon – the ballet completely divided the audience and critics, with some considering it a worthy successor in the true Noverre tradition, while others thought it a prime example of contemporary kitsch.

Apart from various revivals from its Cranko warehouse, Stuttgart offered a new staging of Maurice Béjart's *Wien, Wien nur du allein*, which he had created back in 1982 for his Brussels company. Haydée, who danced the lead then, now performs it with her own company, with Richard Cragun, Marion Jäger, Jean-Christophe Blavier, Randy Diamond and Mark McClain in other major roles. Haydée's latest choreographic endeavour, *Beziehungen* (Connections), featuring first a *pas de trois* group and then a *pas de deux* couple, proved as eminently forgettable as its music by Stephan Micus.

At the Munich Bavarian State Opera, the newly formed **Bavarian State Ballet** will start functioning in the 1990/1 season. Until then, its Artistic Director, Konstanze Vernon, has presented a mixed bag of revivals, among them the still thrilling *Folterungen der Beatrice Cenci* (The Torturings of Beatrice Cenci) by Gerhard Bohner, and creations, some by no means uninteresting, by Ed Wubbe, John Wisman and Ulysses Dove. The company has some promising dancers, among them the Moscow gold-medal winner Christina McDermott and the Canadian ballerina Evelyn Hart, who commutes between Winnipeg and Munich.

There is nothing very exciting to report from the company at the **West Berlin Opera**. It offered two premières. The first one suffered from taking place when all Berlin rejoiced in the tearing down of its infamous Wall, with nobody in the mood to share the despair and gloom of Anna Sokolow's *Rooms* (the other bill-fillers, José Limón's *There is a Time* and Christopher Bruce's *Land*, fared slightly better). The second was presented as *Strawinsky-Ballettabend*, with Balanchine's *Agon* followed by Béjart's *Firebird* and *Sacre du printemps*. But the major event was undoubtedly Béjart's *Ring um den Ring* (Ring Around the Ring), a collaboration between the Fondation Béjart Ballet Lausanne and the German Opera Berlin, but so far performed by the Lausanne company only, with a revival by the house's own company promised for next season. Of course it is a controversial undertaking – but then which production of Wagner's original *Ring des Nibelungen* has not been controversial? Having suffered through numerous performances of the Wagner tetralogy in all the big opera houses of the world, Bayreuth not excluded, I found it an absorbing experience watching Béjart coming to grips with this enormous task. At 4¾ hours, it must be the longest ballet ever and showed the Lausanne company in fine fettle.

Anyone interested in what ballet in the twenty-first century might look like should go to **Frankfurt**, where William Forsythe, Germany's first

Ballett-Intendant, goes from strength to strength. If his classically based high-tech choreography to the synthesized sound explosions of Thom Willems look terrifyingly overcharged in their multi-complex fragmentations, none the less they fascinate through their sustained high-energy level and daring use of space. Energy Unlimited might be a more appropriate name for Forsythe's Ballett Frankfurt, which brims with highly motivated dancers, whose technical proficiency has improved beyond recognition during the last two seasons. Forsythe's latest additions to his repertory were *Slingerland* and the three-part *Limb's Theorem*, which his spokeswomen explained as deriving from his concern with Laban and the theories of Daniel Libeskind and his school of deconstructivism – though do not ask me what that means. In spite of their bombastic intellectualizing, Forsythe's ballets thrill through their packed dance content. In Frankfurt, where he now has an ardent youthful following, Forsythe seems engaged in establishing what one feels tempted to call post-*Agon*ism.

Other ballet premières to be noted here include Pierre Wyss's *Cinderella* in **Düsseldorf**, where it ranks among the very few happier creations of the singularly depressing Bortoluzzi era; Yuri Vamos's *Spartacus* and *Coppélia of Montmartre* in **Bonn**, admired more for their dramaturgic originality and stringency than for their choreographic content; and Bernd Schindowski's highly idiosyncratic treatment of the *Coppélia* story in his *Dr Coppélius* (who emerges as a computer freak), for his small but exquisitely groomed company in **Gelsenkirchen**.

Two contemporary companies stand out: the **Cologne Tanz-Forum**, run now for almost twenty years by Jochen Ulrich, which premièred his full-length *Lulu* (adapted from Wedekind with film music by Nino Rota), a mediocre success; and **Heidelberg**, where Liz King of former Vienna Dance Theatre renown has just started her first season, offering a piece which she calls *Gegeneinladung* (Counter-invitation) – a title which not even the most fanciful of her followers has been able to explain, but which shows her group of fourteen dancers to advantage.

Dance theatre – as opposed to ballet – is now firmly established at various theatres, with numerous freelance groups (among which Rosamund Gilmore's Laokoon company is held by some in high esteem). The high priestess is still Pina Bausch at **Wuppertal** who, for the first time in three years, presented a new piece, *Palermo* (a co-production with the Teatro Biondo-Stabile di Palermo). In spite of various southern Italian overtones (the permanent chiming of bells, some processions and a succession of rituals, concerned in one way or another with water), it does not look very different from her Wuppertal-based ordeals and trials of growing up as the eternal loner and loser in hostile surroundings – as does her first feature film, called *Die Klage der Kaiserin* (Lament of the Empress), which has, of course, nothing to do with an empress of any sort at all.

The other pioneering figure of the dance theatre movement is Johann Kresnik who, after ten years at Heidelberg, has returned to **Bremen**, continuing there with what he calls his 'choreographic theatre'. His latest creation is one of his best, even if it has little to offer to the traditionally minded dance lover: *Ulrike Meinhof*, which deals with one of the central figures of the German terrorist movement, who was found dead in her cell during her trial in the notorious high-security Stuttgart-Stammheim prison. It shows her path towards doom and death in truly frightening pictures and scenes of a political revue, which add up to an acid indictment of the inhumanity of today's West German society and its consumer mentality. Kresnik does not shy away from pouring scorn over the (at present) immensely popular East–West entente and its battle cries for 'Germany, United Fatherland'.

There is nothing to report from Reinhild Hoffman, who in **Bochum** has obviously got stuck in some sort of dead end. On the solo circuit, Susanne Linke, Arila Siegert and Gerhard Bohner continue to draw their speciality audiences – with Linke and Siegert showing their very different but somehow complementary approaches in reconstructing some of the dances of the late Dore Hoyer, while Bohner's best work centres around his Schlemmer-inspired *Bauhaus-Tänze*.

But surely the thing to look forward to in Germany now is the looming unification of the Federal Republic of Germany and the German Democratic Republic and its repercussions on the ballet and dance sector – something like a marriage between New York City Ballet and Bolshoi Ballet aesthetics. One can only hope that it will not turn out a miscegenation.

Hungary

Livia Fuchs

T he political and social changes Hungary is undergoing have had no effect on the dance ensembles for the time being. The economic situation of the companies, however, has been deteriorating significantly: the number of premières is decreasing and more and more dancers are leaving to join dance companies in Western Europe.

Ildikó Pongor and Gábor Keveházi, who both have wide international experience, have taken over the management of the ballet ensemble of the Hungarian State Opera – the **Hungarian National Ballet** – under such difficult circumstances. Being at the peak of her career as a dancer, Ildikó Pongor has undertaken only the artistic direction and Gábor Keveházi, although he has not definitely left the stage, is responsible for management. On the basis of their first season we can already see in which direction they would like the company to develop: besides the main international Romantic–classical ballets (*Giselle, Swan Lake*), they want to freshen the repertoire with new and earlier works by Hungarian choreographers. Contemporary international works are very scarce, so broadening the repertoire will be an important task for the new artistic management. The Hungarian National Ballet is unusual in having three works by Béjart: *Firebird, Le Sacre du printemps* and *Opus 5*.

The most important event of the season at the Opera is related to three Hungarian choreographers: the première of László Seregi's new ballet was put off from last season to December, so that the choreographer could celebrate his sixtieth birthday with his spectacular fairy ballet entitled *A Midsummer Night's Dream*. The choreography offers real family entertainment: both dreamy adults and children spellbound by magic may enjoy it.

The production of two one-act ballets by Aurél Milloss, who died eighteen months ago in Rome, has broken the silence surrounding this internationally acknowledged choreographer in Hungary. None of his ballets had been performed in his home country for forty-eight years. Two of his works, *Estri* and *The Miraculous Mandarin*, which had been revived in Florence in 1986 on the occasion of his eightieth birthday, were taught to the Hungarian National Ballet by Marga Nativo and Giancarlo Vantaggio. The evening was not only a homage to Milloss's memory but at the same time it meant his homecoming, since the two ballets will be repertoire pieces.

The name and works of Gyula Harangozó were a hallmark of the opera ballet from the 1930s for thirty years. In the last decade, however, his works have disappeared from the repertoire, with only his *Miraculous Mandarin* (first performed in 1956) recently revived. But now one of his most ingenious ballet-comedies, *Coppélia*, has been given a new life. The three-act ballet preserves Harangozó's unique ability for caricature and his outstanding feeling for drama.

Ballet Sopianae has performed only one new programme this season. Antal Fodor, who started his career at Ballet Sopianae almost thirty years ago, taught two of his earlier works to the ensemble. *Requiem for the Living*, which was originally intended for performance in church and which had its world première two years ago in Vienna, was staged in the chamber theatre in Pécs without any alterations. Fodor confronts two worlds: the

89

Ildikó Pongor of the Hungarian National Ballet as Titania in László Seregi's *Midsummer Night's Dream.*   PHOTO: ANDRAS AGOSTON

Iván Markó's *Feast*, created for Győr Ballet's tenth anniversary.   PHOTO: ZOLTÁN MAGYAROSSY

harmonious world of dreams depicted in neo-classical dance, and the aggressive present time. His work shows a strong Pina Bausch influence but lacks a coherent dramatic structure which would unite the different dance scenes instead of changing them mechanically. Antal Fodor has choreographed Ravel's *Bolero* several times. His latest version, for a female dancer and male *corps de ballet*, is not remarkable for any special invention.

Győr Ballet celebrated its tenth anniversary at the beginning of this season. Iván Markó arranged a two-part evening from the most successful works of the past ten years with statements by the individual founder dancers between the dance mosaics. Apart from this festive programme, the ensemble performed only one new one-act ballet. In *The Feast*, Iván

91

Markó again endorses the moral force of love, using a very narrow movement vocabulary which could not be counteracted by spectacular scenery.

Szeged Ballet acquired a new artistic management this season. The contract of Roland Bokor, who re-founded the company and who was the only non-choreographer directing a ballet company in Hungary, was not renewed, and György Krámer and Zoltán Imre were appointed to replace him. György Krámer is a young artist who started his career at Györ Ballet and who has worked so far as a guest choreographer in Pécs (Ballet Sopianae) and Szeged. Zoltán Imre returned to Hungary after twenty years' absence, having forged an international career as dancer and choreographer. This season he made a three-act work for the ensemble in Szeged entitled *Plays of the Underworld*. The Orpheus story is retold in three different eras: the heroes of the ancient myth continue their lives and fates at the turn of the century as well as in the present. In addition to this evening-length ballet made in honour of Jean Cocteau, the company performed a new programme consisting of three one-act ballets on the occasion of International Dance Day. György Krámer has created with *Exodus* an immaculate neo-classical work with elements of modern dance to Kylar's captivating music. Zoltán Imre's dance drama, *The Medium*, deals with questions of power and manipulation to a music montage of ditties and songs performed by the dancers, using elements of dance theatre as well. The innovation of the evening was Matthew Hawkins's choreography for this work, based on Cunningham technique, which is so far unknown in Hungary.

Zoltán Imre's *Plays of the Underworld* for Szeged Ballet.   PHOTO: ANDRÁS AGOSTON

Israel

Giora Manor

I n spite of the turmoil and the tragic events which plagued the country during the year, the art of dance surprisingly continued to flourish. Neither the *intifada* nor the acts of extremists on both sides of the Jewish–Palestinian conflict kept audiences away from the theatres; indeed Israeli as well as foreign visiting companies attracted large audiences.

In Tel Aviv a new – or rather re-built – centre for dance and theatre was inaugurated. The Suzanne Dellal Centre, situated near Yaffa, in the buildings which once, at the beginning of the century, served as the first Jewish schools of the town, has now become the home-base for two established dance companies: **Inbal Dance Theatre**, founded in 1949 and still directed by Sara Levi-Tanai, and **Batsheva Dance Company**. Apart from studios, offices and workshops, the Inbal studio also serves as a small (230-seat) performance area. There is another proscenium-type theatre hall in the building, and across a paved courtyard (in what was once the boys' school) a well-equipped stage and auditorium, seating about 400, has been erected. Already it has become a lively venue, housing not only regular performances but also special events, such as the first ballet competition of Israel, commemorating the recently deceased ballet teacher, Mia Arbatova, and the annual Gevanim Bemahol, a three-day showcase of work by young choreographers. In the Dellal Centre, a short course for budding choreographers, directed by Robert Cohan (until recently the Artistic Adviser of Batsheva, as well as of the London Contemporary Dance Theatre) took place in the spring. The person in charge of the new centre is Yair Vardi, once a soloist with Batsheva, who later danced with the Rambert Company and directed English Dance Theatre in Newcastle before he returned to his native land a year ago.

David Dvir, the Artistic Director of Batsheva, resigned his post and Shelley Sheer took his place in tandem with Ohad Naharin, also a former dancer with the company, who has recently been active in New York and who has created many excellent works for the company. His title is Guest Artistic Director, which simply means that he needs more time to make up his mind as to whether to take on the post permanently.

For the **Israel Festival**, which takes place in Jerusalem in May–June, Naharin prepared an evening-length new work, *Kir* (*Wall* in Hebrew), with the Batsheva dancers collaborating with a rock group of musicians called The Tractor's Revenge.

Also in the framework of the Israel Festival, there were premières by the Tmu-na movement-theatre group of Nava Zuckerman (the very moving *It's Not a Movie*) and a remarkable solo performance of Schumann's *Davidsbündlertänze*, choreographed and performed by Yaron Margolin. Among the foreign companies performing at the festival, the one that created a real stir was the Frankfurt Ballet from Germany, which showed works by its Artistic Director, William Forsythe. The ballet of the Deutsche Oper of Berlin also appeared, performing a disappointing *Blue Angel* by Roland Petit and Kurt Jooss's classic *Green Table*.

Moshe Efrati and his Kol Demama company opened the festival in Jerusalem with his new choreography dealing with the 'Eternal Wandering Jew' syndrome, commemorating the 500th anniversary of the expulsion of the Jews from Spain in 1492.

The third Dance Festival in the northern town of **Karmiel** takes place in July. This three-day meeting of thousands of folk-dancers, who fill the tennis courts and parks with dance around the clock, has by now become a tradition of sorts. Several of the professional dance companies presented premières at Karmiel, among them the Tamar Dance Group from Jerusalem, with a new work by its Artistic Director Amir Kolben, dealing with the football-mania fanned by the World Cup in Rome; the Kibbutz Dance Company, with two new works by its Resident Choreographer Rami Be'er;

Kol Demama Dance Company in Moshe Efrati's *Carmina-y-torna*.   PHOTO: YARON WEINBERG

and Inbal celebrates its fortieth birthday, as the oldest professional dance company in Israel.

The opening show is devised and staged by the Artistic Director of the Karmiel Festival, Yonatan Karmon.

After a nearly total absence of relations for more than twenty years, there are again cultural ties between Israel and Russia, as well as other countries in Eastern Europe. The disintegrating Iron Curtain caused a veritable flood of visiting companies, which included the Moiseyev (more than thirty sold-out performances), the conservative but excellent ballet of the Riga Opera from Latvia, a group of 'stars' from the Bolshoi (including brilliant dancers from other companies, such as the Kirov), a young company called Moscow City Ballet, Beriozka and several others.

This influx of Russian ballet offered a rare opportunity for Israeli audiences to see full-length versions of *Swan Lake*, *Don Quixote* and other ballet staples, since the resident Israel Ballet (directed by Berta Yampolsky and Hillel Markman) does not possess the resources for such large-scale productions.

Israeli dance companies performed in Hungary (the Kibbutz Company), Poland (Batsheva as well as Bat-Dor) and Moscow and Leningrad (Bat-Dor). Rina Shenfeld danced in Prague.

The duo Liat Dror and Nir Ben Gal toured Europe in their own works, which belong to the 'minimalist' school of relentless repetition.

The political turmoil which the country experiences found expression in several choreographic works, such as Rami Be'er's *Reservist's Diary, 1989*, which the **Kibbutz Dance Company** performed not only at home but also in Budapest and Vienna. This impressive hour-long work uses poems by Zvika Sternfeld describing in terse, impressionistic, sometimes ironic verses his experiences as an Israeli soldier on reserve-duty in the occupied territories, juxtaposed with a cello sonata by J. S. Bach.

A different reflection of the situation is Amir Kolben's *Yes, Thank You, We Are Getting Used To It*, which he prepared with the **Tamar Dance Group**, of which he is Artistic Director. This dance deals with the television phenomenon familiar from the Vietnam war, when terrible events and atrocities invade one's living-room daily to the point where one becomes apathetic and uncaring.

The Israel Dance Library has finally moved to new, spacious premises at the Tel Aviv Central Municipal Library at Beit Ariela, catering for the needs of students, teachers, researchers and artists.

Italy

Freda Pitt

T he re-emergence of the Scala Ballet, in surprisingly good condition after last year's strikes and consequent cancellations, has been the most important positive factor of the 1989/90 Italian season in the classical field. The forfeit exacted for an increased number of programmes (not large by international standards, but more than in other Italian opera houses) continues to be relegation to theatres other than the Scala, usually with small stages and the acceptance of recorded accompaniment, which is now almost taken for granted.

The company seemed to demonstrate a determination to give of its best, first in the not particularly taxing polkas, waltzes, etc. devised by Micha van Hoecke for the *corps* in the big ballet set piece in the season's inaugural opera, Verdi's *I Vespri siciliani*, then in a new production of *Giselle* by Yvette Chauviré – both of these at the Scala. The dancers also showed up well in a mixed bill (without guests) on the rather poky stage of the Teatro Smeraldo. This was made up of two Balanchine ballets (one of them, *Square Dance*, unknown in Italy), Robert North's *Troy Game*, and a lyrical *pas de deux* to match Balanchine's fizzy Tchaikovsky one. They also performed a programme of choreography by a few members of the company, at yet another theatre. However, in late March the union that had fomented the protest in 1989 again complained about the profusion of guest artists (including the four Albrechts: Andris Liepa, Gheorghe Iancu, Laurent Hilaire and Robert Hill), as well as the programming and general organization. The prospects therefore seem less bright than they did.

The rest of the opera-house companies offered only somewhat sluggish activity. In **Naples**, where the company and the school are now the responsibility of Carla Fracci, a programme about Isadora Duncan and Eleonora Duse, with Carla Fracci occasionally dancing but more often gracefully seated while a small group of actors read out letters between the two great ladies of the stage, as well as assorted poems, represented an unusual venture for an opera house. Most of the choreography was by Derek Deane and Loris Gai, but an imaginative reconstruction by Millicent Hodson and Kenneth Archer of a solo of Isadora's provided the one *frisson* of the production, given at the Teatro Mercadante during the closure of the San Carlo.

Another opera house that closed for renovations is the Regio in **Turin**,

Oriella Dorella and guest artist Laurent Hilaire in La Scala's new production of *Giselle* by Yvette Chauviré.   PHOTO: LELLI AND MASOTTI

which did not offer a dance programme until May, with Fernando Bujones involved in the choreography and Paris Opéra guests in the dancing. This year's dance festival took place not in the park but in the tent which had been successfully used for the season's operas. It opened earlier than usual, on 5 June, with the European première of Maurice Béjart's recent work, *Pyramide*, performed by his own company. Companies from Sweden, France, Monte Carlo and Estonia followed, as well as the Regio group.

As in Naples, the **Rome** Opera School has acquired a favourite dancer as director – Elisabetta Terabust, who trained there herself in Attilia Radice's day. It is hoped that she will succeed in raising the standards. The opera house company urgently needs an influx of new blood, to judge from the dreary production of *Cinderella*, in Ben Stevenson's version.

Oleg Vinogradov's revised production of *Swan Lake* was presented towards the end of May, with Soviet guests for the first few performances. Julia Makhalina lacked emotional depth as Odette and looked happier as Odile, dancing with great brilliance in Act III. Andris Liepa made a truly princely Siegfried, with noble bearing and elegant style. The guest pair wore their own costumes – wisely, for those designed by Clara Centinaro were as unattractive as the scenery by Teimuraz Murvanidze. The Rome company did its best, but stylistically there is still a great deal of work to be done. The morning after the first night, a puzzling announcement was made at a press conference by the opera-house management, to the effect that during the next season the ballet company would be made independent and become an outpost of the Paris Opéra, as some kind of co-operative venture. Developments are awaited.

In the meanwhile, Terabust – who, like Fracci, is still pursuing a very active dancing career, usually as a guest of Aterballetto – staged in mid-March at the Teatro dell'Opera's subsidiary house, the Brancaccio, a programme aimed at raising funds for additional facilities at the school. Among many familiar faces, it afforded the opportunity to see Viviana Durante of the Royal Ballet dance for the first time on her home territory. She and Bruce Sansom appeared in the Balcony Scene *pas de deux* from Kenneth MacMillan's *Romeo and Juliet*. The programme also gave a Rome airing to two busy touring companies, Aterballetto and the Balletto di Toscana.

Cristina Bozzolini's Tuscan company, on the other hand, recently circulated to critics and managements a letter complaining of the excessive space given to foreign companies and staking their own claim to wider attention on account of their attempts to foster home-grown choreography (although it was Hans van Manen's *Grosse Fuge*, one of their staples, that they presented at the Brancaccio).

One of the young choreographers who has worked with the Florence-based group is Gianfranco Paoluzi, known as a dancer in England with Rambert and in the United States with Eliot Feld. He has become one of

Italy's busiest choreographers, with new works coming up in Turin and Fiesole. The Tuscan company is giving his ballet to Handel's *Water Music* at Reggio Emilia.

The influx of Soviet companies began in September, when the Bolshoi Opera paid its third visit to the Scala, bringing as one of its programmes a Rimsky-Korsakov rarity, the opera-ballet *Mlada*, the convoluted plot of which recalled in many respects that of *La Bayadère*. Nina Ananiashvili drifted ethereally round the stage, candle in hand, as the spirit of the murdered princess of the title.

It is the Latvian company, though, that is the most frequent Soviet visitor to Italy. In mid-March its familiar production of *Swan Lake* returned to Rome (Teatro Argentina) and Milan (Teatro Smeraldo), and *The Sleeping Beauty* – also edited by Alexander Lemberg – was seen for the first time in those two towns, to recorded accompaniment and, disconcertingly, shorn of the second act. It was, however, given in its entirety with orchestra at the Teatro La Fenice in **Venice** just before Christmas.

The Fenice is presenting only one more dance programme this season, Maurice Béjart's *Autour du Ring*, with his Lausanne company. A Béjart-less year is almost unthinkable in Italy; the Petruzzelli in **Bari** included the company in a dance series that opened with the Alvin Ailey company (shared with the Rome Opera, shortly before Ailey's death), and continued with Antonio Gades's *Fuego* (seen also at Reggio Emilia and elsewhere), Martha Graham, and Jiří Kylián's Nederlands Dans Theater.

Pina Bausch made a brief appearance in Palermo, at the special request of the mayor, presenting a new work based on her impressions of the city.

In **Florence**, the Teatro Comunale (opera house) continues to economize on dance while it offers sumptuous opera productions and celebrity concerts. The resident group, Maggiodanza, directed by Evgeny Polyakov (appearing outside the opera house in all but one programme), had the field to itself. Its final production of the winter season took place not in Florence but in Vicenza, where the glorious Teatro Olimpico housed *Van Gogh*, a ballet with choreography by Vicente Nebrada, to music by Mahler. The two guest artists were Santiago de la Quintana (in the title role) and Arantxa Arguelles (as Death), both from Spain. Like the company's previous production, Polyakov's version of *La Dame aux camélias*, the new work was in one act lasting just under an hour and a half – rather short measure for an evening's entertainment.

In June 1989, too late for inclusion in last year's edition of *World Ballet and Dance*, Maggiodanza gave the première of *The Overcoat*, with choreography by Flemming Flindt, as the sole dance contribution to the Maggio Musicale Fiorentino. *The Overcoat*, inspired by Gogol's famous satirical story of the same name, was the first ballet specifically made for Rudolf Nureyev with the aim of giving him a role that would be suitable for his years and his

Rudolf Nureyev as the clerk, Akaky Akakyevic, and Rachel Fabre as the tailor's wife in Flemming Flindt's *The Overcoat* for Maggiodanza.

declining strength. The role of the downtrodden clerk Akaky Akakyevic was therefore made to measure, and fitted better than the preposterously luxurious overcoat devised by Beni Montresor, whose permanent set with the St Petersburg skyline in the background dominated the work to excess.

Nureyev shuffled and shambled convincingly enough, but his hand movements – like the steps in particular of the classical-style solos – were too aristocratic for the role. Nevertheless, he performed it with insight, and with great success.

Rubens Tedeschi's choice of Shostakovich pieces for the accompaniment (which was recorded) made a faultless collage. The company of the Teatro Comunale in Florence, Maggiodanza, has frequently acted as backing for Nureyev. On this occasion a large number of dancers was employed as passers-by or guests at the ball, the only substantial solo roles being those of the tailor and his wife (Rino Pedrazzini and Rachel Fabre) and a French couple who were frequently present for no clear reason (probably to give roles to Maria Fernandez and Umberto De Luca, who danced well in rather routine choreography).

An encouraging event took place in March 1990 in the historic heart of Florence when, thanks to the persistence of Raymond Lukens and Franco de Vita, now running Brenda Hamlyn's school, the Italian branch of the Cecchetti Society was declared officially in existence, with Alicia Markova as Honorary President.

All in all, this seems a slightly better year that the previous one, but the most serious problems remain unsolved, such as the lack of co-ordination around the country and insufficient activity for the opera-house companies, caused partly by economic difficulties and partly by indifference, if not outright hostility, on the part of managements. The latter obstacle is unlikely to disappear in the foreseeable future.

Japan

Kenji Usui

The ballet scene in Japan in 1989 began with the Prix de Lausanne Competition in Tokyo. This Swiss-based competition moved to Japan in 1989 in order to gather more applicants from Asia. It was held at the Aoyama Theatre in central Tokyo.

There were seventy-six Asian applicants joined by fifteen candidates who had passed the elimination rounds held in Lausanne. The jury consisted of eleven prominent ballet teachers, including Merle Park, Jacqueline Layet, Yoko Morishita, and others, with Hans Meister as the chief of the jury.

They chose Tetsuya Kumakawa, a sixteen-year-old Japanese boy, as the gold medallist. He also received the honorary prize of Prince Takamado, cousin of the present emperor of Japan. The Prix de Lausanne scholarship was given to four dancers; the cash prize to three; the 'professional level' prize to two; and various other honours and awards were bestowed.

In February there was only one important performance, *Mandala*, by the **Matsuyama Ballet**. This historical ballet, dealing with the Japanese Middle Ages, was a rare case of a ballet based on a Japanese theme.

There were two versions of *Don Quixote* in 1989. One was based on the Moscow version brought here by Sulamith Messerer. Momoko Tani, who inherited this version, produced the ballet for members of the **Japan Ballet Association**. The leading roles were danced by guest artists Cheryl Yeager and Julio Bocca, both of American Ballet Theatre.

The other version was by Azari Plisetsky, the brother of Maya

Plisetskaya, for the **Asami Maki Ballet Company**. This production claimed to be the same Moscow version as the other, but looked completely different, and was a vast improvement on the first one. The dances were better arranged here than in the rather dull production by the Japan Ballet Association with its tortuously long *divertissement* in the Tavern Scene.

Still, the Japan Ballet Association production was successful at the box office because of the bravura technique of Julio Bocca. After the first night, word spread like wildfire, and tickets for the remaining two nights sold out instantly. In the Asami Maki production, Chan Wei Qiang, premier dancer of the Central Ballet of Peking, delivered a superb performance as Basil.

On 29 March 1989 an historical event of staggering importance for Japanese ballet occurred when Yuko Morimoto, silver medallist of the Moscow International Ballet Competition in 1985, appeared as guest artist with the Kirov Ballet in Leningrad. Miss Morimoto danced the full-length *Swan Lake* partnered by the fiery and famous Farukh Ruzimatov. Yuko Morimoto claimed the unprecedented honour of being the first Japanese ballerina to dance upon the glorious Maryinsky stage.

From 6 to 8 May the classical division of the Kobe City Dance Competition was held, with 383 applicants. The jurors chose Tomoko Kawaguchi of Kanagawa Prefecture as the first-prize winner.

On 11 May young choreographer Jun Ishii received the Education Minister's 'Art Encouragement Prize for Freshmen' for the humorous one-act ballet *François Villon, Thief Poet*. Ishii spent many years in various West German ballet companies as premier dancer, and is now regarded as one of the best choreographers in Japan. In Japan, classical ballets are so popular that it is often difficult for young choreographers to show new work. So the awarding of a governmental prize for Ishii is compelling encouragement for the younger generation of Japanese ballet.

The **Tokyo Ballet** celebrated its twenty-fifth anniversary in July in Tokyo with two performances of Balanchine's *Bugaku*, Neumeier's *Seven Haiku of the Moon*, and others. Neumeier's work was commissioned for the occasion. Haiku is a traditional form of ancient Japanese poetry consisting of seventeen syllables and four or five words. This is quintessentially Japanese, but as the company does not believe in the potential of Japanese choreographers, the work was entrusted to Mr Neumeier.

For the Moscow Ballet Competition in July, eight Japanese dancers applied and sixteen-year-old Koichi Kubo received the silver medal in the solo division, dancing the male variation from *La Bayadère* in the final round.

At the end of July the **Inoue Ballet** gave two performances of a full-length *Swan Lake* with decor by Peter Farmer and a guest appearance by Steven Heathcote of the Australian Ballet in the role of Prince Siegfried.

The Tokyo Ballet in *Seven Haiku of the Moon*, choreographed by John Neumeier for the company's twenty-fifth anniversary.

The roles of Odette and Odile were shared among the three ballerinas of the company, Sayuri Ikami, Naoko Fujii and Rieko Terada.

The Japan Ballet Association held their annual Summer Ballet Festival on 30 July. It was a big event with sections from ten classics, and seventeen creations staged by ballet masters from all over Japan. Among them, *L'Histoire du soldat* by Sachiko Goto and *The Dawn* by Kazuhiro Kaneda were the most popular.

The Annual Aoyama Festival sponsored by the Aoyama Theatre in central Tokyo was held in early August. The festival was to show the virtuoso technique of young dancers in classical *pas de deux*, but it also offered the opportunity to appreciate the work of the young choreographer Minoru Suzuki. Suzuki studied ballet at the Julliard school in New York, and is considered to be one of the most promising choreographers of the younger generation. His work *The Unknown Symphony* received very good reviews on this occasion.

For this festival, Daini Kudo, a Japanese choreographer who lives in Paris and is married to the French ballerina Noella Pontois, staged a ballet. Later in the month he held a concert to show his short works from the past ten years, with the participation of his daughter and a young member of the Paris Opéra Ballet, Miteki Kudo.

On 14 and 15 October the Matsuyama Ballet staged Tetsutaro Shimizu's version of *Romeo and Juliet* with Yoko Morishita as the ballerina. Shimizu is the husband of the internationally famous Miss Morishita, and the son of the Artistic Director of the company, Mme Matsuyama.

From 12 to 15 October the second Asian Pacific Ballet Competition organized by the Japan Ballet Association was held. This competition includes all Asian countries and Australia and New Zealand. In this competition, male power and the progress of the Korean dancers were prominent. The competition has only senior and junior divisions, not divided into male and female divisions, but all three prize-winners in the senior division were men. So Hon Wa of Hong Kong took first place, Lee Won Kuk of Korea second, and Udvalyn Bat-Erdene of Mongolia was placed third.

Even the first prize of the junior division went to a man, Masanobu Negishi. In the First Asian Pacific Competition, held in 1987, all the Korean dancers were eliminated after the second round, but this year most of them made it to the final round.

Later in September the **Tani Ballet** staged *Miss Julie*, directed by Birgit Cullberg, and the **Miyaki Ballet** staged Bournonville's *Conservatory* for the first time in Japan. Flemming Ryberg of the Royal Danish Ballet was invited to mount the production.

The Asami Maki Ballet gave two performances of Japanese ballets on 21 and 22 October. The programme consisted of four one-act ballets: *Triptych*,

Mandala, Flutist and *The Thread of the Spider*. These were the preview of its programme to be shown in Leningrad and Moscow in 1990.

On 11 November the city of Nagoya hosted a ballet festival, and *The Stone Flower* was premièred. This production was staged by Rieko Matsuoka after the Grigorovich version. On 13 November the **Homura Ballet** of Osaka staged a full-length *La Esmeralda*, following the Bourmeister production.

As in Western countries, Japan had numerous productions of *The Nutcracker* in December. The Tokyo Ballet toured the country with its Vainonen version. The Asami Maki Ballet staged the Jack Carter version, and the Inoue Ballet asked Naoki Seki to stage it with Roland Price of the Sadler's Wells Royal Ballet as guest artist. The Arima Ballet staged its own version with two guest artists from the Boston Ballet, Devon Carney and William Pizzuto. The Matsuyama Ballet, the Noriko Kobayashi Ballet and the Rieko Yamamoto Children's Ballet also mounted *Nutcrackers*.

It is imperative to realize that every Japanese classical ballet company is privately run. Ballet in Japan is a family business. Furthermore, most performances created here, regardless of their quality or potential, run only once or twice each. There are simply not enough performance opportunities to train dancers adequately for the stage. In order to promote Japanese ballet, a powerful government-sanctioned organization would need to be established.

The Netherlands

Eva van Schaik

The start of the 1990s is proving an unsettling time for Dutch dance as many familiar faces prepare to quit the dance scene. Future perspectives remain unclear, although the foundations have in the main been well established.

The largest of the state-subsidized companies, the **Dutch National Ballet**, found itself without a clear successor to Rudi van Dantzig as Artistic Director, in spite of van Dantzig's express desire not to leave a power vacuum when he retires. As far back as 1985 he warned that he intended to step down in 1991, after twenty-one years as Director of the company. First of all, he appointed the dancer Henny Jurriens as his successor – but simply forgot to get the agreement of his Board. Then, when he was supposed to be master-minding the company's move into its new home, the Music Theatre, he went away for several months in 1986, leaving Henny Jurriens in a rather awkward situation.

Jurriens made up his mind in 1986 to leave Dutch dance. He went to the Winnipeg Ballet in Canada, first as a guest dancer and then as Artistic Director: he proved the rightness of van Dantzig's insight by becoming a very talented and much-loved director. In April 1989 came the shocking news that he and his wife, Judy James, had been killed in a car accident. The effects of his death are still keenly felt in Holland as well as Canada. Han Ebbelaar, who had meanwhile been appointed as van Dantzig's successor at the Dutch National Ballet, changed his mind after reflecting on his friend's death: he decided that he preferred his personal life with his partner, Alexandra Radius. His refusal to accept the post left the National Ballet once again without a replacement for van Dantzig in 1991.

Speculation continued through 1989/90 as to who will become the next artistic conscience of the company: some fear the appointment of a foreigner who might not appreciate the Dutch dance temperament; others wonder whether a strong-willed woman might be able to make an impact on this male-dominated preserve.

The 1989/90 season saw final performances by three Dutch National Ballet members of long standing: Joanne Zimmerman, Clint Farha and Alexandra Radius. Radius ended her career as the Netherlands' most popular ballerina since the 1960s with two farewell performances in June 1990. She had previously toured Holland with her programme *Ballerina, een tijdsbeeld* – a collage of her most important roles: *La Sylphide, Isadora, The Dying Swan, Libelle, La Notte, De Maan in de trapeze*.

With the departure of Clint Farha from the stage, a famous generation of Dutch choreographers (van Dantzig, van Manen, van Schayk) will lose their dance muse. An artistic era seems to be coming to an end with the loss of so many of the personalities who embodied Dutch choreography in the 1970s and 1980s.

Netherlands Dance Theatre is also about to enter a period of change. Although its General Manager, Carel Birnie, still holds the reins firmly and intends to keep it that way until his seventieth birthday in 1993, both he and the Artistic Director, Jiří Kylián, know that they will have to seek reinforcement in the near future. After Birnie recovered from a severe illness in 1989, one of the first things he did was to appoint the former NDT dancer, Arlette van Boven (who is already Artistic Director of the junior company, NDT II), as his successor.

In the meantime, NDT's profile is changing rapidly. Last year, eleven dancers left and rumour has it that fifteen might leave at the end of this season. It is not yet known how many could follow the choreographer

Nacho Duato to Madrid, when he becomes Artistic Director of the National Ballet of Spain at the start of next season. The company has continued to be very productive, with new works by Kylián, Duato and van Manen as resident choreographers and commissioned works from Ohad Naharin, Mats Ek and Alida Chase, as well as NDT's own promising young choreographers, Phillip Taylor, Lionel Hoche and Paul Lightfoot.

Another departure has been announced in the north of Holland – that of Yoka van Brummelen, Artistic Director of the successful **Reflex** company. One of her last acts was to commission three young choreographers to make a programme called *Three Times Three*: they were Ted Bransen, Piet Rogie and Pauline Daniëls. A remarkable debut was also presented by Patrizia Tuerlings, one of Reflex's soloists.

The **Scapino Dance Company** has meanwhile been preparing itself for its move from Amsterdam to Rotterdam in 1991. Under the guidance of Nils Christe, one of the most productive freelance choreographers around, the company has worked hard to change its traditional image. Established in 1945 as a company producing work for children, Scapino now wants to be acknowledged as a grown-up company, third only to the Dutch National Ballet and Netherlands Dance Theatre. To provide a new, mature identity, the company has looked to choreographers within its ranks (Paula Vink, Tamara Roso, Kirsten Debrock) as well as to the internationally known Nils Christe and Ed Wubbe. Wubbe's contract with the Introdans company in Arnhem ended in 1990 and he was immediately asked by Christe to make at least two new works a year for the Scapino Ballet – an excellent choice, as Wubbe's *Nisi Dominus* proved convincingly in December 1989.

For **Introdans**, this was a bitter loss. Tom Wiggens, its Artistic Director, turned to two British choreographers: Christopher Bruce and Graham Lustig. Lustig made his second piece, called *Uncertain Steps* (to music by Bach), for the company. Wiggens announced that he intended giving up choreography after his April 1990 production, *Marike*.

The **Rotterdam Dance Company**, under the committed leadership of Kathy Gottschalk, has recovered from the hard financial and artistic blows of two years ago. The ten dancers have shown remarkably high standards of technique in works by Amanda Miller (of the Frankfurt Ballet), Stephen Petronio, Randy Warshaw, Shusaku Takeuchi, Ton Simons and Gosschalk herself. Amanda Miller's piece to music by J. S. Bach was particularly well received.

One of Holland's most successful modern-dance companies is directed by **Krisztina de Châtel**. The Hungarian-born choreographer revived an earlier work, *Föld* (Earth), this season: the exhausting struggle by six dancers within (and with) a wall of earth, to a repetitive score by Steve Reich, has become a modern classic. No wonder Mark Jonkers, who is responsible for the dance programme of the Holland Festival in June (in Amsterdam) and the Holland Dance Festival in September (The Hague), commissioned her third Holland Festival contribution to a collage of Purcell's operas.

Dans Produktie, under its Artistic Director Bianca van Dillen, celebrated its eleventh year by joining forces once again with Beppie Blankert. Their *Hexa-Fysica*, in autumn 1989, and *Parlando*, in spring 1990, were under the musical direction of composer Henk van der Meulen: *Parlando* used tapes of conversations between John Cage and Merce Cunningham.

Besides the state-subsidized companies mentioned above, there are many small companies which perform regularly in and outside Holland. Among them are the Bob Folz Company, Dansgroup Nan Romijn, the Nieuwe Dansgroep, Cloud Chamber, Peter Bulcaen Foundation, Zuil van Volta, Danserscollectief, Pandora and many others. These companies form a 'second circuit', providing a lively undercurrent of dance theatre. Various solo performers also belong to this second circuit, such as Truus Bronkhorst and Pauline Daniëls (who both presented brilliant solo programmes this season).

A third circuit of experimental and occasional dance groups is struggling to establish itself. With workshop facilities in Amsterdam (Danslab, Artemis, Perron II) and Rotterdam (Studio al Porto) as their starting-point, they spread like mushrooms. Their quantity is not always matched by quality; but one of the most promising is **Het Concern**, founded in 1989 by five modern-dance veterans determined to give opportunities to their younger colleagues. Among the chosen ones are Norbert Taatgens, Jan Hessels and Angela van der Weide.

The three circuits guarantee a very lively and creative dance scene in the Netherlands. During the 1988/9 season, 177 premières by Dutch companies and sixty-four premières in Holland by foreign companies were presented. Statistics for the 1989/90 season will be recorded in the fifth edition of the Dance Yearbook, published by the Netherlands Dance Institute.

Highlights of the year included a project investigating the relations between German *Ausdruckstanz, Tanztheater* and Japanese *butoh*: this brought Kazuo Ohno, Ashikawa, Carlotta Ikeda, Rosalia Chladek, Christine Brunel, Barbara Passow and Susanne Linke (among others) to the Dutch capital between October 1989 and February 1990. This year's Holland Festival was dedicated to German dance, with the participation of the Frankfurt Ballet, the Bremen Tanztheater and the Essen Folkwang Studio. The twelfth Spring Dance Festival in Rotterdam and Utrecht marked a return of familiar faces: Jean Claude Galotta, Stephen Petronio, Ping Chong and Michèle Anne de Mey were foreign guests; Truus Bronkhorst, Nan Romijn, Ton Lutgerink and Cloud Chamber were the Dutch representatives.

New Zealand

Jennifer Shennan

D ancers in New Zealand have a reputation for resilience and versatility. Given the small population and comparatively low rate of government funding for the arts, the standard and variety of dance activity is impressive. Perhaps the distance of the country from the world's centres of dance has contributed to a brand of opportunism, in the best sense of the word, in the dance profession here.

The year 1990 has been featured as a year of celebration and commemoration, marking the 150th anniversary of the arrival of Europeans in Aotearoa (New Zealand), which had been inhabited for over a thousand years by the indigenous Maori race. Dance is traditionally accorded a high value in Maori society. Ritual ceremonies of challenge and welcome and other expressions of hospitality on the *marae* (ceremonial meeting place) are frequently framed and punctuated by traditional dances for men and women.

However, the **Royal New Zealand Ballet** is the only group of professional dancers operating full-time in the country. The company was founded in 1953 by its first artistic director, Poul Gnatt, formerly of the Royal Danish Ballet (and now with the Opera Ballet in Oslo). Although Gnatt would be the first to acknowledge the dedication and work of others, it will always be recognized that founding New Zealand's national ballet company (which was awarded its 'Royal' title in 1984) was the achievement of a phenomenal man. The course of dance history in New Zealand would have run altogether differently without him.

The company gets 25 per cent of its budget in government subsidy, 10 per cent from sponsorship and 65 per cent from box office. This need to rely on high ticket sales forces the company towards a 'safe' programme policy and restricts its opportunities to tour the smaller communities in the lesser-populated South Island. The repertory system of presenting ballets is not possible on a long-term basis because the company has no home theatre and tours continuously. Triple bills of one-act ballets are usually marketed under an all-embracing title, frequently the title of just one of the ballets, around which the programme is built. The biggest successes in recent years have both been full-length ballets: *Romeo and Juliet*, to Prokofiev's music, choreographed by ex-patriate New Zealander Malcolm Burn; and Gray Veredon's *A Servant of Two Masters*, based on Carlo Goldoni's play and using music by Vivaldi.

The Royal New Zealand Ballet in *A Servant of Two Masters*, Gray Veredon's ballet based on Goldoni's play.

Veredon freely amended the material and produced a delightful and witty full-length work which amused by its inventiveness. A chorus of 'zanies' was forever upstaging the main action. Jon Trimmer and Harry Haythorne alternately sparkled and doddered through their respective Pantalone and Doctor roles, proving a comic duo without peer. This was the work the company took on its first ever European tour when forty-nine performances in twenty-five cities through six countries were given a highly acclaimed reception.

Opportunities for the RNZB to perform abroad have been very limited but there have been trips to Japan (1970), Fiji (1980), Australia (1981, 1989), Europe (1989; i.e. Netherlands, Luxembourg, Austria, Yugoslavia, Switzerland, West Germany) and there is a tour to the west coast of the United States in 1990.

Late in 1989 in *Papillon* (choreography and design by Paul Jenden, music by Offenbach, decor by Philip Markham), loopy humour and far-fetched libretto were thoroughly integrated and offered a wonderful role to a wicked witch who transformed into a butterfly. A few ageing ballerinas were discovered to be men in drag as the butterfly choreography proved too demanding for their old feet in pointe shoes. Mean but dim-witted goblins completed the retinue.

There followed a revival of Ashley Killar's *No Exit*, a stark view of hell as other people (music by Shostakovitch).

The first 1990 season celebrated Jean Batten, the famous New Zealand aviatrix who held speed and distance records in aviation for many years. She died poor and unknown in Spain several years ago, so the ballet *Jean* became a belated homage to her, more as a poetic interpretation of what may have been her dreams and ambitions rather than a direct biography (choreography by Mary Jane O'Reilly, music by Jonathan Besser, designs by Kristian Fredrikson). Houses were full and enthusiastic, responding well to the use of contemporary dancers and an actress as guest artists. A film has been made of the project.

The Southern Ballet and Dance Theatre, based in Christchurch on the South Island, is run by Russell Kerr, who has taught and choreographed in New Zealand for thirty-five years (he spent his earlier years with London Festival Ballet). He has choreographed prolifically as well as mounting such well-known ballets as *Petrushka* and *Le Tricorne*. In 1989, Southern Ballet Theatre toured the North Island with a major work by Kerr, *Inner Landscapes*, to music by Douglas Lilburn, a prominent New Zealand composer.

Limbs Dance Company, based in Auckland, founded by Chris Jannides, was a modern-dance company directed by Mary Jane O'Reilly and Susan Paterson for nine years. The company enjoyed a wide following, toured within New Zealand and abroad (Japan, New Guinea, Mexico, New York, Australia) and built up an extensive repertoire of commissioned work from New Zealand choreographers, composers and designers. Cath Cardiff became Director in 1986 and major seasons of Douglas Wright's work followed. The 1989 touring programme, *Great Leap Forward* (*Kidnapped Too*, choreographed by Sue Healey; *Off with their Heads*, choreographed by M. J. O'Reilly; *Parts Unknown*, by Brian Carbee; *Otello*, by Kai Tai Chan) was extremely successful in artistic terms. Management problems persisted, however, and the Arts Council subsidy was frozen and then withdrawn and the company closed in October 1989.

The demise of Limbs left the country without a major contracting modern-dance company. Cath Cardiff continued with an already planned season, *Dance Pacific*, for January 1990, using the programme title for a new project-based company. The two directors are herself and Taiaroa Royal, a Maori dancer of high reputation and a long-standing member of Limbs.

Douglas Wright, originally with Limbs, was with the Paul Taylor Dance Company for four years and also choreographed during this time. Two full-length works with Limbs, *Now Is the Hour* (1988) and *How on Earth* (1989), were received with critical acclaim and fixed Wright's reputation as a demanding choreographer of vision and a performer of remarkable

111

stamina. (Wright worked in London with DV8 in *Dead Dreams of Monochrome Men*.)

His most recent work, *Passion Play*, was performed by Wright and by Kilda Northcott in Wellington in February 1990 and was to have travelled to London and Edinburgh, though these plans had to be shelved.

Michael Parmenter has danced and choreographed in New Zealand since 1977. *Between Two Fires*, with composer Jack Body, was acclaimed, as have been *Insolent River, Go*, and *Gravity and Grace* (March 1990, to music by Stravinsky, Bach and Messaien). An imaginative range of dynamics and speeds characterizes Parmenter's choreography.

Another former Limbs dancer, **Shona McCullagh**, choreographed an oustanding solo for herself, *Lacrimae*, in a showcase programme, *Merchants of Venus*. American dancer **Marianne Schultz**, formerly with Laura Dean Musicians and Dancers and who now resides in New Zealand, has performed with Wright, with Limbs Dance Company and has choreographed her own solos.

Jamie Bull was Artistic Director of Impulse Dance Company, active for eight years until it closed in 1980. Bull and **Liz Davey** have since worked together on a number of collaborations.

Paul Jenden, formerly with Impulse, has choreographed and since 1981 performed in partnership with **Louis Solino**, formerly of the Limon Company. They regularly perform in New Zealand and also tour Europe (Germany, Netherlands, Austria, Switzerland). Works currently in their repertoire include *Hansel and Gretel, Dead Ballerinas, Cheek to Cheek*, and *Seven Deadly Sins*. Designs, often including masks and elaborate costume transformations, are by Jenden, who has also choreographed for Limbs, RNZB and NZSD.

Louis Solino is Contemporary Dance Tutor at the NZSD, where he has reconstructed works by José Limon (*There is a Time, The Unsung, Concerto Barocco, La Malinche*) and Humphrey (*Nightspell, The Shakers, Air*).

Susan Jordan explores choreographic themes with strong autobiographical threads, allowing the slow build-up of atmosphere to become an intrinsic part of each composition. Alternative locations to theatres are sometimes used; *Face Value* (1989) was memorably set in a once-grand, abandoned building. Other works include *Unknowing Steps, Holy Women* and *Stone the Crow*.

Shona Dunlop has for many years taught and choreographed from Dunedin. In the 1940s she was a member of the Bodenwieser Company from Austria.

Bronwyn Judge from Oamaru, near Dunedin, dances her own and Dunlop's choreographies in a style reminiscent of Bodenwieser's modern dance.

Charles Neho, a young Maori dancer and choreographer, produced in

1989 a remarkable full-length work, *Dancescape*, which explored themes from Maori mythology.

Stephen Bradshaw has directed since 1984 Taiao (formerly Te Kanikani o te Rangitahi), a Maori dance group based in Auckland. Traditional chant and oratory are used in their performances, which they have toured to remote rural areas as well as cities. Taiao is committed to 'developing dance that is of a universal language but grounded in the social, spiritual environment realities of Aotearoa'.

Te Roopu o Manutaki is a Maori cultural group which would not, for reasons of social and community orientation, think of itself as a professional dance company. It is directed by Peter Sharples, an inspiring leader whose standards of movement quality for the group, together with the significance of the themes he choreographs, make their impact second to none. Sharples, together with M. J. O'Reilly, choreographed the dance pageant for the opening ceremony of the Commonwealth Games held in January 1990 in Auckland, with a cast of 4,000.

The Philippines

Nestor O. Jardin

B y virtue of the fact that the Cultural Centre of the Philippines (CCP) is the only government institution that is devoted to the support of the arts, it plays a most important part in the development of dance in the country.

Situated in a complex of buildings on a reclaimed area along Manila Bay, the centre has seven theatres with capacities ranging from 250 to 8,000. Four of the country's leading dance companies, namely Ballet Philippines, the Bayanihan Philippine Dance Company, the Philippine Ballet Theatre and the Ramon Obusan Folkloric Group are resident companies. The CCP is often called the most worthy project of Mrs Imelda Marcos, and now that the new CCP administration, headed by Mrs Ma. Teresa Roxas, has expanded its scope and its support for artists, its value to national cultural development has become increasingly apparent.

The CCP celebrated its twentieth anniversary in 1989 with a series of big events in the various artistic disciplines. In dance, three festivals were held in Manila. *Balletfest*, a classical ballet and contemporary dance festival, was participated in by twenty-seven companies and groups from all over the country. For the first time in Philippine dance history a jazz dance festival, *Yugyugan*, was held, featuring ten of the country's leading jazz and contemporary dance groups. In folk and traditional dance, the CCP hosted a festival with the title *Pang-alay*, featuring fifteen companies from all over the Philippines. While various levels of performance quality were exhibited, these festivals nevertheless provided wonderful opportunities for communication, exchange and assessment.

The biggest dance event of the year, the CCP National Dance Festival, was held in the Visayas with the main activities concentrated in Iloilo City. Traditionally, big artistic events happen in Manila, the political, economic and cultural capital of the Philippines. With the new administration's thrust of decentralization, more and more cultural programmes are being held in provincial areas. The two-week festival included a dance convention; a series of workshops, dialogues and seminars; lecture-demonstrations and master classes; and performances by the 'Stars of Philippine Ballet', the Bayanihan Philippine Dance Company, Ballet Philippines, the Philippine Ballet Theater and various classical ballet and contemporary dance groups from the region.

The 1989/90 period was also a time for celebration for **Ballet Philippines**. Under the dynamic leadership of Alice Reyes, the company has turned twenty years old with a string of accomplishments which has made it one of south-east Asia's leading dance groups. For its CCP season, the company opened with a *divertissement* programme featuring fourteen international and local stars. The performances drew huge crowds of dance enthusiasts and received wide acclaim from the audiences and the media.

British Ballet Master William Morgan staged a full-length *Swan Lake*, the second production of the season, featuring Japanese ballerina Yoko Morishita, partnered by Nonoy Froilan; and Maniya Barredo, Prima Ballerina of the Atlanta Ballet, partnered by Rey Dizon of Les Grands Ballets Canadiens. Also alternating in the lead roles were Melissa Cuachon, Ida Beltran and Jun Mabaquiao. The third offering for the twentieth season was *Highlights*, a tribute to local and international choreographers who have made significant contributions to the company's development. The six performances which highlighted the best in Ballet Philippines' repertoire brought together the choreographers Norman Walker, Alfredo Rodriguez, Miro Zolan and William Morgan, who were joined on stage by their local colleagues, Alice Reyes, Tony Fabella, Gener Caringal, Edna Vida and Denisa Reyes, during the opening-night curtain call.

In December, Alice Reyes's acclaimed ballet *Cinderella*, choreographed to a collage of Tchaikovsky music, was restaged and once more proved to be a popular treat for the young. Featured in the lead roles were guest artist Toni Lopez Gonzalez and Nonoy Froilan, Gina Katigbak, Jun Mabaquiao,

Cecile Sicangco and Amuer Calderon. The main events of the celebration took place in February 1990, exactly twenty years after the very first concert staged by the company at the CCP. The highlight was *Festival of Dance*, a tribute to company artistic director, choreographer and co-founder Alice Reyes, with three programmes featuring her major works, including the full-length *Rama Hari, Carmina Burana, Carmen, Itim-Asu* and *Amada Company*, among others. An exhibition, a grand ball and a twentieth-anniversary publication added colour to the festivities.

The **Philippine Ballet Theatre** showed remarkable progress during its third season at the CCP under the artistic leadership of Inday Gaston Manosa. Its season-opener, *Coppélia*, was staged by Basilio and Sonia Domingo and featured Lisa Macuja and Osias Barroso, alternating with Melanie Motus and Raoul Banzon. As a tribute to the late George Balanchine, the company presented *Balanchine Remembered*, showcasing two of his best-loved ballets, *Serenade* and *Tchaikovsky pas de deux*, with a new ballet *Reflections*, by Atlanta Ballet's Artistic Director, Robert Barnett. The very successful concert featured guest artists Maiqui Manosa and Nicolas Pacana of the Atlanta Ballet, Lisa Macuja, and Rebecca Rodriguez of the Dallas Ballet.

In July the PBT presented its third production, *Encore and More*, which featured Eric Cruz's *Carmen*, Balanchine's *Serenade* and *Le Corsaire* with Lisa Macuja and Nicolas Pacana. The last concert in the season, entitled *Salute to our Choreographers*, featured new works by Basilio, Eddie Elejar, Gener Caringal and Tony Fabella.

The Philippines is blessed with a wealth of folk- and traditional dances that originate from the various regional and ethnic cultures of its 7,107 islands. At the forefront in the exhaustive process of research, documentation and theatrical presentation of these dances are the major traditional dance companies, namely the Bayanihan Philippine Dance Company, the Ramon Obusan Folkloric Group, the UP Filipiniana Dance Troupe and the Philippine Baranggay Folk Dance Company.

Under the direction of Lucrecia Reyes Urtula, the **Bayanihan Philippine Dance Company** presented two major productions in 1989 – *Paso Doble* and *Kadenilya II*, a traditional song-and-dance concert with the Philippine Madrigal Singers. The **Ramon Obusan Folkloric Group** presented two unique productions, *Unpublished Dances of the Philippines* and *Ritwal*, showing for the first time on stage many of the research works of Ramon Obusan, noted Philippine dance researcher, anthropologist and choreographer.

Under the Dance Grant Programme, several groups presented outstanding performances at the CCP. Leonor Orosa Goquingco's Ben-Lor Ballet Academy performed in a concert entitled Celebrazione '89. The Dance Theatre Philippines restaged *Mir-I-Nisa*, a full-length ballet by Julie Borromeo and

Tita Radaic, while the Philippine Baranggay Folk Dance Company, under the artistic direction of Paz Cielo Belmonte, presented *Magandang Pilipinas*.

The escalating cost of inviting international companies has limited the number of foreign dance performances. It should be noted that the CCP is presently the only entity in the country that acts as presenter for non-commercial foreign performing groups. Nevertheless, with the assistance of various embassies in Manila, six foreign companies presented outstanding concerts at the CCP. These were the Ballet Jazz de Montréal, the City Contemporary Dance Company from Hong Kong, Compagnie Bagouet from France, the National Dance Company of Korea, the Odissi Dance and Shehnai Troupe from India, and the Australian Stars of Ballet.

Five Philippine companies embarked on international tours within the 1989/90 period. Ballet Philippines performed in Japan, Korea, Taiwan and Indonesia. The Bayanihan and the Ramon Obusan Folkloric Group toured Japan. The UP Filipiniana Dance Troupe performed in France and Egypt, while the Philippine Baranggay Dance Company did an extended tour of the United States and Canada.

The drain of talent abroad is a continuing problem for folk-dance groups and classical and contemporary dance companies. The search for better opportunities and higher-paying jobs abroad sends many folk- and traditional dancers to Japan and other Asian cities where commercial dancing is a big form of entertainment in clubs, hotels and restaurants. On the other hand, the country loses its talented classical and contemporary dancers to bigger companies abroad like American Ballet Theatre, the Australian Ballet, Alvin Ailey Dance Company, Les Grands Ballets Canadiens and the Munich Opera Ballet.

There are over one hundred dance schools in the Philippines, concentrated mainly in Metro Manila, which offer dance courses ranging from classical ballet to modern dance, jazz, folk-dance, tap, Spanish dance and Polynesian dances. The CCP offered several training and education programmes during the period, namely the National Folk Dance Workshop for Teachers, the year-round Pangkat Pambata Training Program in folk-dance for children, two summer workshop programmes in classical ballet, modern dance, jazz and folk-dance, the RAD Teachers' Workshop, a seminar on dance criticism, and several lecture-demonstrations and master classes by visiting foreign groups and teachers.

The focus on training and education together with the increase in opportunities to perform has been showing positive results, as more schools and amateur groups move towards professionalism. The **Quezon City Ballet**, under the artistic direction of Shirley Cruz and Jeng Halili, was established two years ago as a fledgeling company from the Halili–Cruz School of Ballet. During the past year they have produced several shows of high artistic standard that constitute the seeds of a professional season. Ballet Philippines launched its second company, **Ballet Philippines II**, in March 1990, and since then the company of eighteen dancers under the artistic direction of Agnes Locsin has presented several concerts which have been praised by critics and audiences alike. Other emerging companies are the Leyte Kalipayan Dance Company, the Dureza Ballet of Iloilo, the Tacloban Dance Theater, the Araullo University Dance Troupe, Powerdance and the Sining Pananadem of Marawi City.

South-east Asia

Daryl Ries

S outh-east Asia enters the 1990s with an unprecedented display of performing venues from theatres to stadia, rehearsal studios to purpose-built academies. Today, there is every provision for the importation of Western arts, with grand opera, full-size orchestras and ballet companies as prime targets. Locally, the large traditional companies of Chinese opera and dance drama, Korean drummers and *kabuki* can all be fully accommodated on new stages for audiences of 1,500–3,000.

Presenting the arts in Asia has become a business by which both governments and corporations can profit in more ways than one. Geared toward fulfilling the cultural curiosity of a newly affluent and educated audience in Asia and providing a much-needed market for foreign artists, impresarios are enjoying a heyday in this former cultural desert.

The next step will be to reinforce the growth of the arts at home, a concept nurtured by the performing-arts academies in Hong Kong and Taiwan. Their graduates will be the wave of the future – barring political and economic factors that could change the course of the present artistic progress.

Hong Kong

Just prior to the eve of a new decade, Hong Kong's most recent landmark, the Hong Kong Cultural Centre, was officially opened by Prince Charles and Princess Diana. The tri-theatre structure which commands a spectacular site on Victoria Harbour cost some 600 million Hong Kong dollars, which represents a substantial investment in the territory's artistic future.

117

The 40 million dollars spent on the first month-long festival featuring opera and symphonic orchestras and crowned by the Royal Danish Ballet, reflect a popular opinion that Hong Kong is like Florence under the Medicis: a city-state where the arts have flourished under constant patronage (from the government), prodded by an increasingly affluent public (five million Chinese). The question is: can cultural developments survive the political future? Wayne Maddern, recently appointed Executive Director for Hong Kong Cultural Centres and Cultural Presentations, views the future with an equanimity shared by his colleagues: 'We'll just go on promoting the arts; I don't think we can expect another Cultural Revolution.' With international links maintained, there is confidence that Hong Kong can continue its unique identity as an East–West centre.

The Hong Kong Arts Festival, a world-class international event, continues to thrive in its eighteenth year. Focusing this year on dance, three major imports – the Stuttgart Ballet, the Paul Taylor Dance Company and the Georgian State Dance Company – appeared at the city's new theatres, with nearly 100 per cent attendance. Such a response has brought dance to the fore this year, with a record number of dance companies coming to Hong Kong, including the Kirov, the Bolshoi, the Scottish Ballet, the Royal Ballet of Flanders and the Martha Graham Company. The administration at theatre venues at the Arts Centre and Hong Kong Academy is considering a contemporary arts festival which will break through some of the conservatism that sticks to established names and shuns experimental and post-modern presentations.

Local artistic encouragement is largely the domain of the Hong Kong Academy for the Performing Arts, which hosts an annual Festival of Dance Academies along with a pan-Asian-orientated Dance Conference. This year the Conference's theme, 'Contemporary Issues in Dance: A Global View', will attract the largest international representation to the Academy's fifth summer event (which will continue to be held in other major Asian cities in the following five years). While the Hong Kong Academy prides itself as the strategic centre of the international dance conference, its shift to other sites is seen as an initiative to involve other developing arts areas in Asia.

Local dance companies are also broadening their scope by recruiting dancers and choreographers from China, Taiwan, Japan, Canada, North America and the United Kingdom, with performances bringing them to neighbouring cities and abroad.

City Contemporary Dance Company, the only professional contemporary dance company in Hong Kong, struck an essential metaphor in its East-meets-West presentation of new works by Chinese choreographers from Hong Kong, Taiwan and China for the Hong Kong Arts Festival '90. The choreographers, Hu Jia-Lu, former director of the Shanghai Dance Theat-

City Contemporary Dance Company in Daniel Maloney's *Starwatch*.

rical Company, and Cheng Wei Cheng, a noted dancer from Taiwan and Tsao, do not seek to superimpose 'Chinese culture' on to their contemporary image. The company performs periodically in China and Taiwan, and gives a subscription series each spring, sponsored by Philip Morris. The **Hong Kong Dance Company** specializes in Chinese dance-drama, and presented at the start of their 1990 season the original 1950s' version of the famed 'Dagger Society', drawing on China's noted choreographers of this pre-Cultural Revolution period. Shu Qiao, the company's Artistic Director, collaborated with her colleagues from the Shanghai Dance Drama Theatre in recreating this ornate seven-act production, accompanied by the Hong Kong Chinese Orchestra and a twenty-strong choir, with seventy dancers from the company and Academy. The highly stylized Chinese musical art is part of a legacy which is popular among more traditional audiences in Hong Kong and Taiwan, where this production will tour next.

The **Hong Kong Ballet** introduced a contemporary range of work with a new spring triple bill by Balanchine, Prokovsky and Val Caniparoli of the San Francisco Ballet. The company, which tries to maintain close relations with China's two major ballet companies, the Central Ballet in Beijing and the Shanghai Ballet, for the exchange of artists and performances, plans to take its latest works, including two ballets by Choo San Goh, to Shanghai in September for five performances at the new Shanghai Centre Theatre.

The government has selected its two representative dance companies, the Hong Kong Dance Company and the Hong Kong Ballet, to undertake a special promotional tour of Great Britain in mid-November.

Hong Kong's performance-art theatre group, **Zuni Icosehedron**, was invited to perform in the 'Turning World' Festival in London in May. Director Danny Yung created this controversial dance theatre in Hong Kong in 1982 and with its fifty non-professional participants, he has introduced avant-garde theatre concepts and a political point of view to the local performing arts.

These four companies pursue their individual objectives through the dedication of an essential core of local performers. With principal dancers still coming mainly from abroad, it is hoped that Academy students will qualify for these positions in coming years. The Academy's international staff has included well-known artists and teachers (predominantly from

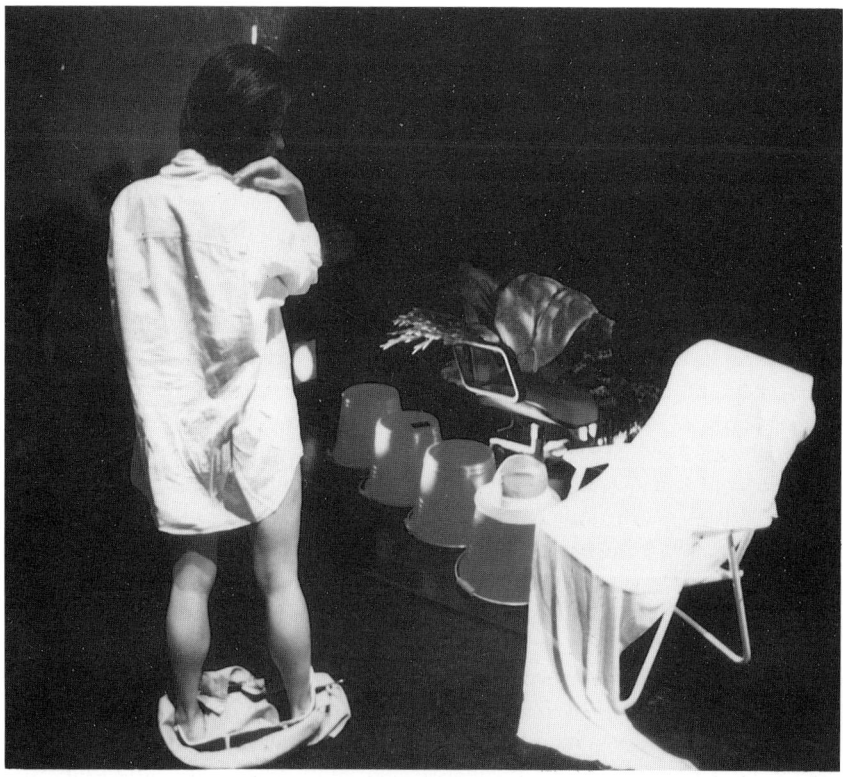

Hong Kong's avant-garde dance-theatre group, Zuni Icosehedron.

America and China) for modern dance, ballet and Chinese classical and folk-dance. The training emphasizes choreography in tandem with technique and this year's graduation concert added to the Academy's growing repertoire of original works. In addition, the annual reconstruction of a modern classic (this year, Doris Humphrey's *With my Red Fires*) makes this repertoire an invaluable corner-stone of dance development in Asia.

The concern of the Academy and the government is to make a dance career viable in Hong Kong. At present, opportunities are limited and the pay-scale is below other professions here. A standard one-year contract provides a salary range of 6,500–11,030 Hong Kong dollars per month, with increases for leading and major supporting roles. The Hong Kong Ballet is the only local company which pays principals' salaries; differences in the scale for guest artists and foreign dancers raise the budget considerably. Foreign artists have their passage home paid for annual leave, and soloists and invited personnel are accommodated free. Medical insurance and personal accident insurance are taken out for all dancers, and other benefits include end-of-contract gratuity, overtime payment, special tour allowance, dance-wear allowance, and maternity leave.

An aid to most local companies is that a high proportion of local dancers live at home and are not faced with escalating rents. However, too few are in a position to be financially independent unless they teach, work in the commercial field or find possibilities outside. These alternatives, though, are severely curtailed by lack of sufficient positions and emigration problems.

Taiwan

Taiwan will face similar problems for its graduates from the Institute of Arts in Taipei, which offers a parallel programme in dance education on a tertiary level. With the dissolution of the famed Cloudgate Dance Company last year, there is no longer a professional dance company in Taiwan and a new one will be faced with the same funding malaise that plagued the ten-year-old company. The government continues to support its vast Chiang Kai-Shek Cultural Centre as an attraction for Western companies, but it should be earmarking something towards a traditional dance company which could employ former Cloudgate members and Academy graduates.

Modern dance made an impact in this country in the 1960s, with the arrival of the Alvin Ailey, José Limón and Paul Taylor dance companies. Local dancers went to the United States to study, and Chinese dancers from the United States returned to offer workshops and form their own companies in Taiwan. All these events, in addition to the influence of Chinese opera and Taiwan's own indigenous dance history has made the dance scene in Taiwan one of the most active in Asia. Many small theatres and dance groups are experimenting with new ideas for the 1990s.

121

Singapore

Singapore has a Ballet Academy and a professional dance company, the Singapore Dance Theatre (SDT), both of which are directed by Soo Khim Goh, the sister of choreographer Choo San Goh.

By September this year the SDT should at last have a home of its own. The project, undertaken by the Parks and Recreation Department (PRD) as part of the government's efforts to rejuvenate historic Fort Canning, will see the area transformed into a cultural hub. The building which will eventually house the company has approximately 2,700m² of space, which will be taken up with studios, music rooms, a library, storerooms and offices.

The most immediate concern for the company is to raise the estimated sum of $500,000 so that the building can be properly fitted with suitable dance floors, barres, mirrors, etc. It is a formidable sum for the SDT, whose major source of income comes from the fund-raising efforts of its Funds Appeal Sub-committee, led by SDT Director Dr Geh Min.

Right now, the SDT is looking forward to more opportunities to perform within the region. For their second showing in the biennial Singapore Festival of Arts in June, marking their third anniversary, the SDT performed six ballets: *Coils of Silence*, by London Contemporary Dance Theatre choreographer Christopher Bannerman; *Gemini* and *Electric Sequences* by Ballet Nacional de Caracas's Vicente Nebrada, and three by Gray Veredon, former Artistic Director of Ballet de Lyon and Vassili Sulich of the Nevada Dance Theatre.

Singapore Dance Theatre in Graeme Murphy's *Wilderness*.

With festivals gaining momentum in Asia, cultural castles keep emerging, like the newly proposed 10,000 seat multi-complex in Singapore. With the aim of promoting the 'best in local artistic talents and providing a cosmopolitan showcase of cultural excellence', the Singapore Festival celebrates the twenty-fifth anniversary of the Republic of Singapore in 1990. In a clear demonstration of their goals, the festival presented a Singaporean musical and a Malay dance extravaganza by the Suasana Dance Company and the Singapore Dance Theatre; and an eclectic international programme of dance with Ballet du Nord, Tango from Argentina, Sankai Juku and the Alvin Ailey Dance Company.

Korea

Korea belongs to the north-east Asian cultural sphere, but throughout its 5,000-year history has developed and maintained a music and dance culture which is uniquely Korean. Today, two distinct dance cultures exist in Korea: Western and traditional.

Traditional dance comprises court-dance and folk-dance. The quiet, slow, elegant movement of the court-dances with their tranquil beauty reveals a restrained emotion disciplined by the strong influence of the Confucian ideal. The folk-dances include religious dances, mask-dances, the Farmers' Dance and other dances close to the roots of the people, in work, life and beliefs.

Han Young-Suk, a foremost exponent of traditional dance in Korea, reflects a popular conservative opinion in Asia when she says that she is 'against Western influences permeating, melting away the cultural form', although she realizes that modernization is inevitable.

Kim Maeja, the founder and Director of the contemporary Chang-Mu Dance Company, replies that there is no intention of diluting Korean dance 'in a cross-movement of the traditional and contemporary that is uninfluenced by a western style'.

Still, American modern dance has made its impact in Korea as it has in many parts of Asia, particularly Japan and Taiwan, and it is part of the dance training at many colleges throughout the country. However, like many of her colleagues, Maeja considers the universality of modern dance as a contemporary statement enhanced by and not encroaching on her traditional roots. These contemporary works are neither folk nor ethnic, but identifiably Korean and are officially known as 'New Dance'.

At the National Theatre of Korea there are two dance companies representing the traditional and the Western: The National Dance Company and the National Ballet Company.

The **National Dance Company** came into being in 1963, with the revision of the government after the Korean War and the re-emergence of the

123

National Theatre under a new Ministry of Culture. Its first objective was to restore traditional folk-dance and synthesize creative dance-drama with thirty members under the direction of Song Bom, whose pioneering New Dance has had a powerful influence on the company for the past twenty-seven years. *Chaos*, one of more than fifty of his works for the company, was performed at the official opening ceremony of the Games of the twenty-fourth Olympiad in Seoul in 1988.

Recreated traditional dance works have been toured abroad innumerable times and the 62-member company has appeared at the Olympic cultural festivals in Mexico, Munich and Los Angeles.

The **National Ballet Company** became independent of the National Dance Company in 1973; it has fifty members under the Director and founder, Lim Song-nam. The company has mounted nearly fifty major productions, including *Giselle* and *Coppélia* in 1976, and *Swan Lake* and *The Nutcracker* in 1977. More Korean ballets have emerged in recent years.

The National Theatre of Korea, which houses these two companies and four other resident performing groups, is located in Seoul and its two theatres are the principal centre for the performing arts – traditional, contemporary and foreign.

'Asian nations have always been on the receiving end', a government official says. 'At the National Theatre we want to do more than provide stages for the Western arts.' It is generally acknowledged that this should be the main objective for cultural centres throughout Asia.

The Love Story of Dalai IV, Hong Kong Dance Company.

Spain

Laura Kumin and Susan Crow

D ance in Spain today has three major strands: classical ballet, modern dance and indigenous Spanish dance. Until very recently the latter was dominant; it is only lately that classical-ballet and modern-dance companies have begun to establish themselves and build an audience. The growth and activity of the emerging Spanish dance scene is therefore all the more impressive.

Spain possesses an extraordinary variety of indigenous dance forms for a country of its size. Spanish dancing for the theatre includes not only these diverse regional dance styles and flamenco, but also *escuela bolera*, *baile español* and an increasing number of large-scale full-length choreographies where more contemporary influences are very much in evidence. The *escuela bolera* or *bolero* school developed in the eighteenth century, combining popular Spanish steps with certain elements of classical ballet technique and the use of castanets to create a truly Spanish classical dance style. Many fear that it is now in danger of disappearing due to the current concern with bringing Spanish dance up to date with contemporary international trends. *Baile español*, literally 'Spanish dance', can also refer to choreography using heelwork, castanets and traditional steps and turns to interpret Spanish classical music, such as that of Granados, Albéniz, de Falla, etc.

The large companies that popularized Spanish dance throughout the world during the 1930s, 1940s and 1950s have been greatly reduced in number, partly due to the high cost of touring such troupes. Perhaps the best-known Spanish dance company in recent years has been that of Antonio Gades, whose film collaborations with director Carlos Saura (*Blood Wedding*, *Carmen* and *Love, the Magician*) brought about a new wave of international interest in flamenco. In 1989, Gades's leading dancer for many years, Cristina Hoyos, founded her own company based in Seville, which became the first Spanish dance ensemble to perform at the Paris Opéra. Other large companies include the popular Ballet Español de María Rosa, Luisillo's Teatro de Danza Española and Paco Romero's Ballet de España. Merche Esmeralda, former special guest artist with the Ballet Nacional, has recently signed a contract to direct the Ballet de Murcia in south-east Spain.

Spanish dance companies tend to regroup and disband rather rapidly, according to available work. This makes for fluctuating company rosters that often see dancers performing with several ensembles. Outstanding flamenco artists such as Mario Maya, Carmen Cortés, El Gilito, Blanca del Rey, La Tati and Manuela Vargas do a great deal of solo work, picking up dancers to collaborate on larger productions or for special occasions. Javier Barón, Antonio Canales, Antonio Márquez and Juana Amaya are just a few of the fine young performers on the flamenco scene whose styles combine personal idiosyncrasies and knowledge of traditional structures with more contemporary elements. Flamenco choreographers José Granero and Rafael Aguilar are artists whose large-scale productions borrow from various dance styles and disciplines in an effort to create a total dance experience.

State funding for dance comes from all three levels of government: national, regional and municipal. The Spanish Ministry of Culture funds new productions, tours and scholarships for study abroad and has recently embarked on revenue funding for certain major companies. The performing arts division of the Ministry (INAEM) is divided into departments for music and drama, with dance coming under the wing of music. A fourteen-member music and dance council of experts acts as an advisory body making recommendations to the Ministry about the allocation of funds; decisions, however, rest with the Ministry, whose higher echelons are made up from political appointments.

The Ministry of Culture allocated funds for a national ballet in 1977, to consist of two parallel companies, one for Spanish dance and the other for classical ballet. The former, the **Ballet Nacional de España**, was first under the direction of Antonio Gades, followed shortly by Antonio Ruiz; the latter, the **Ballet del Teatro Lírico Nacional la Zarzuela**, headed by Victor Ullate. In 1983, both Ruiz and Ullate were replaced by the veteran and highly respected classical ballet teacher María de Avila, in charge of both companies. In 1988 direction was again split, with José Antonio, a principal of the Ballet Nacional, taking charge of that company, and Maya Plisetskaya brought in to direct the classical ensemble. Although both currently have their administrative and rehearsal base at the Teatro Real in Madrid, their home theatre for performances is the elegant Teatro Lírico de la Zarzuela. The Teatro Real is under renovation to become Madrid's opera house in 1992. Both companies will transfer their administration to new quarters but will perform at the Teatro Real.

The Ballet Nacional consists of a company of fifty-six dancers. Although an extensive repertoire has been built up of works with choreography by distinguished artists such as Mariemma, Antonio, Luisillo, Pilar López, Merche Esmeralda and Gades, the company currently performs a handful of works by José Antonio, José Granero and Alberto Lorca. To revive more of the repertoire would require more rehearsal time and longer seasons at the Zarzuela.

Angela Granados, soloist and member of Cumbre Flamenca.   PHOTO: DEE CONWAY

The company's fifty-one performances during 1989 included an extensive season in Paris in January and February, a six-week tour of Japan (where Spanish dance is much appreciated) during June and July and a brief visit to the Edinburgh Festival in August. Plans for 1990 include visits to Wiesbaden, Palermo, Athens and Verona as well as regional touring. During November, the Ballet Nacional will be visiting Moscow and Leningrad as part of a Soviet season of dance from Spain sponsored by INAEM. The major creative event of 1989 was the lavish full-length *Don Juan* with choreography by the director, music by José Nieto and a scenario adapted by the theatre director and designer Miguel Narros from José Zorrilla's *Don Juan*. This was premièred in December in Madrid and featured the guest appearance of Trinidad Sevillano as Doña Inés.

Initially a group of about twenty dancers with a repertoire of modern and neo-classical works, notably some by Béjart with whom Ullate had been a leading dancer, the Ballet del Teatro Lírico Nacional has grown to a full strength of fifty-four dancers with a more traditional repertoire. Under María de Avila, the company's classical base was emphasized and important works by overseas choreographers such as Balanchine (*Serenade, The Four Temperaments*, etc.) and Antony Tudor (*Lilac Garden*) joined the repertoire. With the arrival of Plisetskaya in 1988 came an injection of Soviet ballets and *divertissements* such as Gorsky's *Walpurgis Night*, Alberto Alonso's *Carmen Suite* as well as *Swan Lake*, Act II. Ray Barra was first given choreographic opportunities by María de Avila and subsequently appointed Assistant Director. He now holds the post of 'Director Estable', continuing to choreograph regularly for the company; his latest work, *Caín*, was premièred in May 1990.

In 1989 BTLN presented a total of seventy-six performances, including a two-week autumn season in Madrid, regional touring and overseas touring to Israel, Taiwan, Japan and the Spoleto Festival. New work included Maya Plisetskaya's choreography for the ballet sequences from Puccini's opera *Les Wilis*, performed at Perelada in a production starring Monserrat Caballé, and the mounting of the complete *La Fille mal gardée* by Plisetskaya, basing her choreography on Petipa's 1885 version and subsequent productions by Gorsky and Asaf Messerer. Alongside Ray Barra's production of *The Nutcracker* (premièred in 1986) this is the company's only full-length production. *La Fille mal gardée* was premièred at the Zarzuela in October, starring leading principal dancers, the young Arantxa Argüelles and Raúl Tino. The other programme of the Madrid season featured a revival of Béjart's *Isadora*, created in 1976 for Plisetskaya and using children from various Madrid ballet schools; Barra's *Nocturno*, a *pas de deux* set to Dvořák and danced by Hans Tino and Elena Figueroba; Nacho Duato's *Sinfonía India*; Béjart's *Bhakti*; and Balanchine's *Theme and Variations*.

From 1 June 1990 Nacho Duato, the Spanish dancer and choreographer who has spent much of his professional career hitherto with Jiři Kylián and Nederlands Dans Theater, takes over as Artistic Director. He has started work setting *Arenal* to music by María del Mar Bonet, which is projected as part of a programme of works inspired by Spanish folk-dance forms likely to be premièred during the company's planned visit to Moscow and Leningrad in November. During the Russian tour Plisetskaya will appear as a guest artist in the title role of *María Estuardo*, created round her talents in 1988, with choreography by José Granero, a dramatic score by Emilio de Diego and Victor M. Martín Rubio, and striking designs by Hugo de Ana.

Since leaving the BTLN, Victor Ullate has set up the **Ballet Victor Ullate**, now receiving state funding as a major company. Consisting of twenty-one young dancers from Ullate's Madrid studio, the company can be classified as neo-classical with a modern repertoire including works by Jan Linkens, Nils Christe, Rudi van Dantzig, Hans van Manen and Ullate himself. Plans for 1990 include Spanish touring and projected visits to Greece, Italy, Cuba and the Soviet Union during December. New additions to the repertoire include Linkens's *For a Close Friend* and Ullate's *Psicosis* (based on Hitchcock's *Psycho*), *Alma de Alba* with choroegraphy by Oliver Pérriguey, Christe's *Before Nightfall* and van Manen's *Adagio Hammerklavier*, to be premièred during the company's season at the Teatro Albéniz in Madrid.

Ballet del Teatro Lírico Nacional in José Granero's *María Estuardo*, with striking designs by Hugo de Ana.   PHOTO: PACO RUIZ

There are few other fully professional ballet companies in Spain, although the following regionally based companies should not be forgotten. Guillermina Coll founded her neo-classical Compañía de Dansa 'Dart' in Barcelona in 1986; Zaragoza and Bilbao also have their own classical companies, the former newly under the direction of Mauro Galindo, and the latter, the Ballet de Euskadi, formerly the semi-professional Joven Ballet de Bilbao, under the direction of Rafael Martí and Angeles Sautiño. The Ballet del Atlántico is a neo-classical company of ten dancers based in Las Palmas de Gran Canario and supported by the savings bank Caja de Canarias. It emerged from the school set up by the Caja in January 1985 and is under the direction of Anatol Yanowsky.

The phenomenal growth of contemporary dance in Spain, basically within the past five years, has made international programmers sit up and take notice. As if making up for lost time, choreographers have embarked on new productions at a surprising rate and ironically there are probably more contemporary dance than traditional Spanish dance companies in Spain at the present time. Barcelona is undoubtedly the cradle of Spanish contemporary dance, with the lion's share of young companies based in the Catalonian capital. The city's Institut de Teatro has established a diploma course in contemporary dance as part of the curriculum, and most of the modern dancers in Barcelona have passed through the Institut at some time in their career. The Institut also has a performing space, and programmes dance regularly.

The veteran modern dance company in Catalonia is the **Ballet Contemporani de Barcelona**, founded as a collective in 1976. Having undergone major restructuring during 1989, the company is currently directed by two of the original members, choreographer Amelia Boluda and manager Anselm García, and has been performing its latest work *Quomix*. The company tours Latin America annually and since 1985 has organized the Oscar López Iberoamerican Choreography Festival. The sixth edition of the Festival was held in April 1990 in Quito, Ecuador, and as of this year it will be held alternately in Barcelona and a Latin-American capital.

The **Compañía Gelabert/Azzopardi**, under the direction of choreographers Cesc Gelabert and Lydia Azzopardi, is one of the most established contemporary dance companies in Spain. Although the group was only founded in 1986, both Gelabert and Azzopardi have extensive professional backgrounds. Their first full-length work, *Desfigurat*, was followed in 1987 by *Requiem* (set to Verdi's *Requiem*), and in 1988 by *Belmonte*, with an original score by Carlos Santos. Gelabert is currently touring a solo programme while the company's next production is in preparation.

Lanónima Imperial, an all-male troupe, was established in 1986 by choreographer Juan Carlos García (formerly with Jean-Claude Gallotta) and composer Claudio Zulian. After creating *Eppur si muove* in 1986 and *Cástor i Pollux* in 1989, García opened the company to women for *KaiRós*, premièred in April 1990. Angels Margarit, director of **Mudances**, an all-female ensemble, has two full-length productions to her credit, *Mudances* and *Kolbebasar*, the latter winning a prize at the 1988 Choreography Competition at Bagnolet. Margarit's new production will include male dancers as well.

Metros, founded in 1985 by choreographer Ramón Oller, is currently touring his fourth full-length work, *Qué pasó con las magdalenas*, premièred in March 1990. A strong theatrical influence is evident in both this and his previous productions *De Metros i Metros*, *Nofres* and *Solos a Solas*. Sabine Dahrendorf and Alfonso Ordóñez have directed **Danat Danza** since 1984. It was the first Spanish contemporary company to perform at Paris's prestigious Théâtre de la Ville. *Herbst, Splitters* and *Bajos cantos rodados hay una salamandra* feature a very close relationship between choreography and the visual arts. The company's current production, *El cielo esta enladrillado*, was inspired by Goya's *Caprichos*. Among other choreographers of note working in Barcelona are Avelina Argüelles, María Muñoz and Pep Ramis (working as a duo under the name Mal Pelo), María Antonia Oliver, and María Rovira with her company Transit.

Contemporary dance group Lanónima Imperial in *Castor and Pollux*, by Juan Carlos García.
PHOTO: PACO RUIZ

Valencia has also become a focal point for contemporary dance, with two major companies, **Ananda Dansa**, directed by Edison Valls and Rosangeles Valls, and Gracel Meneu's **Vianants**. The regional government of Valencia's cultural council includes a theatre and dance department which organizes an annual conference/festival of contemporary dance for local and foreign programmers as well as meetings for dance professionals.

In Madrid, Carmen Senra has directed a contemporary and modern dance company since 1986. Other notable groups include 10 y 10, Ziradanza and those directed by Blanca Calvo, María José Ribot, Francesc Bravo, Pablo Ventura, Antonia Andreu, as well as solo performer Mónica Valenciano. Pamplona is the headquarters for another veteran company, Yauzkari, founded in 1979 by José Láinez and Concha Martinez. Contemporary dance is represented in Andalusia by Seville's Hydra Danza and Málaga Danza Teatro.

The presence of several national competitions has undoubtedly helped to foster dance in Spain. There are three major choreography competitions: the Ricard Moragas National Prize, organized by the Regional Government of Catalonia, the Oscar López Iberoamerican Choreography Festival, and the Certamen Coreográfico de Madrid, organized by Paso a 2. The Certamen de Danza de Monteprincipe is a dance competition for young performers working in classical ballet and Spanish dance. Organized by Maruchi Mardugán every two years, its 1990 edition will be the first to admit foreign competitors.

Until recently, Spain had no magazine specializing in dance, after the collapse of the promising *Danza 79*. For coverage of dance events and personalities it has been necessary to turn to the dance sections of music magazines such as *Monsalvat*, *Ritmo* and *Scherzo*, and occasional issues of *El Público*, the Ministry of Culture's bi-monthly performing arts periodical. However, the Asociación de Profesionales de la Danza has recently begun to publish *Por La Danza*, a bi-monthly magazine for its own members but hoping to reach a wider circulation.

Sweden

Peter Bohlin

During the autumn of 1989 the Stockholm Opera was closed for repairs. The Royal Swedish Ballet instead opened the season at the Confidence, Stockholm's second eighteenth-century theatre, with *Opportunity Makes the Thief*, a charming and witty piece choreographed in a blend of folk-dance and late-eighteenth-century ballet style by Regina Beck-Friis, which included tightrope dancing and dancing bears among the attractions. This light middle-class comedy is a valuable addition to the treasure of historical ballets of which the Royal Swedish Ballet is justly proud.

Marie Lindqvist and Johan Inger in *Opportunity Makes the Thief*, Regina Beck-Friis's eighteenth-century-style ballet for the Royal Swedish Ballet.   PHOTO: ENAR MERKEL RYDBERG

Designer David Walker managed to cram in four houses and a church on the small stage, still leaving plenty of space for dancing, and John Lanchbery arranged a fine selection of eighteenth-century music, but there were second opinions about the orchestration.

In October the Cullberg Ballet inaugurated Stockholm's new House of Dance with Mats Ek's new creation, *Old Children*, a wild mix of nursery nightmares, games and death scenes side by side. It all ends with a very different interpretation of the *Dying Swan* music.

When completed in 1991 the building will house the Dance Museum, with video show-rooms and vast exhibition areas, a fine, big stage for guest performances and a 'Black Box' for all sorts of events.

The Cullberg Ballet also introduced to Sweden the French choreographer Jean Gaudin with *The Ascetic of San Clemente and the Virgin Mary*, which seemed a risk – Swedes were never very religious. But the one-hour duet proved a triumph for the striking personalities of Monica Mengarelli and Yvan Auzely in the roles.

Later the Cullberg Ballet introduced Willliam Forsythe, with *The Vile Parody of Address*, which left most people stunned. Words, printed on three overlapping, semi-transparent frames, were whispered, in English, under

Anna Diehl in Mats Ek's *Old Children* for the Cullberg Ballet.   PHOTO: LESLEY LESLIE-SPINKS

134

parts of Bach's *Wohltemperiertes Klavier*. But there were no arguments about Forsythe's wonderfully flowing movements.

Nacho Duato's *Rassemblement* was, on the other hand, an instant success. With catchy West Indian music and hints of a black-slave story, Duato created a stirring human rights appeal which could not fit better into the company's profile.

The company's leading lady for many years, Ana Laguna, was born in Spain. She joined the company in 1974, and has acquired a solid reputation as an exceptional performer. In 1989 she was awarded the National Dance Prize from the Spanish Ministry of Culture, worth 1.5 million pesetas.

This spring Per Jonsson created, at the Royal Opera, *Heze*, for seven men in long black skirts, naked from the waist up, and logs of wood in their hands. There was also a soloist (green, purple and blue) and a short glimpse of the choreographer himself, looking like a practising priest. The effect was that of a mix betwen Eastern and Western spirituality. Later, Per Jonsson created, in Iceland, *Winds from Mercury*, for twelve women.

At the Modern Dance Theatre in Stockholm, Margaretha Åsberg premièred *Rus* (Intoxication), which started with a turn-of-the-century story about a man who killed his wife's lover and then raised the illegitimate son – the wife died. The focus then shifted over to the son and his chaotic life; by means of clouds of smoke, texts recited by an actor, superb lighting and witty stage inventions, and six dancers in ever-changing roles, the boy eventually came to terms with his past. The sense of hope, trust and humour were touching and comforting: I rank *Rus* very highly.

In Gothenburg, Jorma Uotinen created *In the Garden of Memories*, a companion piece to *The Burnt Garden* which he made for his own company in Helsinki. A man resembling one of the walking dead is looking back at his life, and memories return like glimpses from a slow-motion film. But the world is not yet destroyed, and I prefer this version for its trace of hope, after all – but the lighting design was better in Helsinki, where the opening was outright magic.

In Robert North's *Troy Game* the Gothenburg Ballet boys got a wonderful opportunity to show off the vigour and sense of humour they possess, of which they have plenty, but the full-evening *Ronja, the Robber's Daughter* proved a setback.

With *Twilight of Gods* (choreography, Gun Lund; music, Zbigniew Karkovski), the independent Gothenburg dance group Rubicon created a magic outdoor performance, evoking, on bare west-coast cliffs, both the times of the thousand-year-old local rock carvings and the lives of last century's fisher-wives.

Later, Rubicon brought nature indoors to their theatre, Unga Atalante. In *Passages* (choregraphy, Eva Ingemarsson; music, Niklas Rydén) naked, rolling tree trunks made a sound of distant drums, and in a second act the trunks stood on their ends, the dancers finally passing between them – an ode to trees in an industrialized town with such heavy air pollution that trees have their own protection organization.

The Norrköping Ballet is facing a bright future under its new Director, Vlado Juras, who, with *Poem to the Weaving Women*, created a working-class ballet and at the same time established links with the town's past: Norrköping used to be a weaving centre.

In the spring of 1990, Stockholm got two new dance stages: Efva Lilja secured one for her company and the National College of Dance has a studio stage in its new premises.

Wind Witches premièred *Fliers* (choreography, as always by Eva Lundqvist), with dancers in wide dragonfly wings and early aviators' helmets. In this production the dancers' energy seemed greater than ever.

Ex-Wind-Witch Linda Forsman has now formed a company of her own, called Korda, after Linda's first successful solo performance. This spring she created *Noder*, a dance for four. An unusual feature was the extraordinarily colourful light, which transformed the stage.

The season seemed a particularly good one for dance books: Bengt Häger's majestic book on Les Ballets Suédois in Paris 1920–5; a wholly new book on flamenco by Barbro Thiel-Cramér, a pioneer in Sweden of Spanish dance; and, among others, a yearbook series launched by the Dance Museum. This first issue points out the growing interdependence between dance and theatre: there is an interview with choreographer Birgitta Egerbladh who has created several successful productions with playwright Barbro Smeds, and another with choreographer Susanne Håkansson, who has worked with theatre director Pia Forsgren in, among other things, the first Swedish staging of Picasso's only play, *The Little Girls*. Niklas Ek, former principal with Le Ballet du XXème Siècle, created a memorable Caliban in a Stockholm staging of Shakespeare's *Tempest*.

A committee is investigating the conditions of artists outside the institutions, and is expected to bring about great improvements for freelance dancers and choreographers.

The year 1990 has been proclaimed a folk-music and -dance year: hundreds of events are taking place throughout the country, including a yearly competition at Vingåker in June of choreography based on folk-dance.

Switzerland

Richard Merz

A feeling of instability dominated the Swiss dance scene last year. The first event, bringing a long-established tradition to an end, was Heinz Spoerli's decision to leave Basle. Even more worrying was the news from Geneva, where those responsible for the Opera House seriously considered getting rid of the resident dance company, due to financial strains. This affected the stability of all large state-supported companies. Additionally, the first state-supported dance school for professional students underwent a financial crisis, as did its parent organization (Schweizerischer Dachverband für Fachkräfte des Künstlerischen Tanzes) and independent dance groups.

For these independent companies, instability is a familiar situation and not one confined to the last season alone. It has always been a struggle for these groups to survive. Indeed, it has become more obvious how hard and how discouraging that struggle is since *Flamencos en Route* showed that the difficulties may not be due to a lack of professionalism, as is often the case. Even with high professional standards, both in repertory and in performing skills (as this small group has), the threat of ruin and dissolution remains. All things considered, it is astonishing that there are always artists around who dare to go their own way with their own groups – artists such as Philippe Saire. He performed his new work, *L'Ombre du doute* in several Swiss cities during the festival 'Steps '90'. In it he created surprising scenic images and also intensely moving moments but showed difficulties in building up a dramatically clear and consistent piece. This festival was organized by Migros, one of the big foodstore chains in Switzerland, which is organized on a co-operative basis and is actively involved in widespread cultural events. Their sponsoring of national and international performing groups and their generous support of professional dance students is unique in Switzerland.

Dance education at a professional level is, in fact, something quite new to Switzerland. It has long been carried out by private teachers' personal efforts, but it has never been considered a matter for public support. Whereas students of music and theatre could benefit from state-supported schools, nothing similar existed for dance students. Then, three years ago, a professional school was founded in Zurich on a private basis, with heavy state subsidy. This first step towards an equal educational system within the arts was expected to be met with great relief and jubilation but quite the contrary happened. Everybody was angry either about the style of the school or about its director, or about its location or whatever. Anne Woolliams, who had been asked to come to Zurich to establish the new school, met with so many difficulties and was offered so little support that she resigned after two years. The board had shown no efforts to hold on to her and quickly offered a contract to Louba and Pierre Dobrievitch. This was legally done but one thing had been forgotten: the pupils. They had come to Zurich to study with Anne Woolliams and they and their parents insisted on their being able to finish their education under her tuition. As no support was offered to them, they founded, on a private basis, a new school to be run by their association under the directorship of Anne Woolliams. Maurice Béjart also joined the board. Thus, two schools are to operate in Zurich, both with financial problems and both finding difficulty in getting enough really gifted pupils.

Another institution which helped to contribute to the feeling of instability was Dachverband. There the most extraordinary and disgraceful spectacle of last season occurred. For all those not directly concerned with the argument, the intensity of the wrangling and the methods employed in the struggle seemed ridiculous. The main issue was whether the Dachverband should be responsible for administration only or if it should get involved in teaching and performing, activities already covered by its members.

All this is indicative of the general insecurity and instability of the whole Swiss dance world. Perhaps most unsettling for the public was Spoerli's decision to leave **Basle** because of the lack of support he experienced at the theatre. The audience experienced a double loss. Spoerli not only leaves Switzerland but also with his departure disappears the one instance of continuity in the Swiss dance scene, which presently seems under such threat. Many people were afraid the Basler Stadt-theater would engage a modern-dance personality to replace Spoerli and his classically based work. By appointing Youri Vamos as Ballet Director, however, the Stadt-theater clearly showed its wish to continue the line which Spoerli has so successfully followed. Meanwhile, work in the theatre was not affected by the goings-on behind the scenes and continued as before. Adding to his productions of classical ballets, Spoerli staged a version of *Don Quixote.*

The **Geneva** company, although also in real danger of dissolving, continued to work and produced a new piece by Oscar Araiz, which was more exciting for its marvellous-looking staging than for its choreography. A mixed bill with three modern works of different styles showed clever planning by the company's director, Gradimir Pankov. The dancers' performance demonstrated how great a shame it would be if this company had to dissolve because of financial reasons. The situation of the Béjart Ballet in **Lausanne** also seems less happy than in the euphoric early days.

Goran Svalberg as Siegfried in Béjart's *Autour du Ring* for the Béjart Ballet Lausanne.
PHOTO: MOATTI-KLEINEFENN

There are rumours of serious tensions between Béjart and his management, his dancers and the city of Lausanne. Nevertheless, the performances of the company in Lausanne had the same triumphant success as everywhere around the world.

The two companies in **Bern** and **Lucerne**, which started with new directors last autumn, look to be on their way to new stability. In Bern, the season started quietly, with promising choreographic and scenic work from Michael McKim and with clear, clean performances from the company. In Lucerne, however, the new season started with great excitement. Here, in one of the smallest theatres of Switzerland with an equally small company, Ben Van Cauwenbergh took over the directorship, with Galina Panova as ballerina and ballet mistress. Both danced brilliantly on the small stage and have already raised the standard of the company.

St Gallen and **Zurich** are two cities whose ballet companies benefit from a steady and unchanging directorship. However, there is no lack of problems. In St Gallen, when it became obvious that the orchestra could not manage all the work planned, it was not the opera with its numerous productions which suffered – it was, of course, the ballet which was denied orchestral accompaniment for its one and only big production of the season. Marianne Fuchs had to change plans at the last minute but nevertheless

139

succeeded in showing a well-trained company – one for which the planned and subsequently abandoned *Romeo and Juliet* would have been a worthy challenge.

In Zurich, *A Midsummer Night's Dream* by Uwe Scholz amounted to no more than a string of showy and superficial effects. However, Gulda's *Concerto for Cello* showed a brilliant capacity for choreographic parody, especially in a solo for a tired ballerina, in which Eileen Brady spectacularly proved her superb technique and acting ability.

United Kingdom

English National Ballet
Jann Parry

English National Ballet (which changed its name from London Festival Ballet in mid-1989) celebrated the company's fortieth anniversary in 1990 by sacking its Artistic Director, Peter Schaufuss, the month before the grand gala he had arranged for 27 March. His contract was abruptly terminated by a reconstituted Board under a new chairwoman, Pamela Lady Harlech.

The 'irreconcilable differences' between Board and Artistic Director centred on the company's growing deficit of £350,000 – although personality clashes seem to have been involved as well.

The company's colourful history has been marked by frequent financial crises and artistic rows. Its founder, Julian Braunsweg, wrote an entertaining account of his and Festival Ballet's temperamental coexistence, appropriately called *Ballet Scandals*. The Schaufuss scandal was only the latest in a long line of upheavals, although the Danish director's dignified silence after his dismissal did much to calm an atmosphere rife with gossip and speculation.

Schaufuss was promptly snapped up by the Deutsche Oper Ballet in West Berlin, which will inherit some of the ambitious plans he was unable to put into effect in Britain. The Berlin ballet will also acquire a number of dancers whose careers Schaufuss helped to build during his six years with ENB.

Under his leadership, ENB had been steadily consolidating its reputation at home and abroad as a stimulating ensemble of dancers from different countries, with a wide repertoire of traditional and modern classics. Its perennial problem has been to attract the near-capacity audiences that

ENB needs if it is to avoid losing money. Only the familiar handful of nine-teenth-century ballets can guarantee box-office success, although ENB has been weaning regional audiences on to Ashton's version of *Romeo and Juliet* and Cranko's *Onegin*, as well as Schaufuss's own production of *La Sylphide*.

Schaufuss had hoped that his new production of *Napoli* in June would add to the list of three-act hits. However, its première at the Dominion Theatre in London drew a lukewarm reception from audiences and out-right hostility from critics – especially those who value Bournonville's ori-ginal intentions. The production was extremely elaborate, with the stage in the third act cluttered with dogs, children and performers who had little idea how to act, let alone dance the Bournonville style. (There were, of course, honourable exceptions, including Nils Bjorn Larsen as a guest from Denmark and the company's own Matz Skoog and Patrick Armand.)

Most heinous of all, though, was Schaufuss's failure to trust the simple scenario for Act II, in which Gennaro saves Teresina from the sea demon, Golfo (with the help of the Virgin Mary). Instead, the entire act was turned into Gennaro's dream, making nonsense of the pious story and padding out the music with choreography more suited to a Petipa vision scene than Bournonville's sea nymphs. David Walker's designs were unduly ornate

Susan Hogard as Teresina and Peter Schaufuss as Gennaro, with members of English National Ballet in the second act of *Napoli*, mounted by Schaufuss.   PHOTO: BILL COOPER

141

for a fishing village and the sets could not easily be accommodated in the Dominion Theatre, which led to long delays.

Audiences stayed away from the generally uncongenial theatre, which the company had chosen for its first season under the new name, in preference to the more expensive Coliseum (whose resident company, English National Opera, had objected to the similarity in names: there is no connection between the opera and the ballet companies). The Dominion season was a financial disaster, compounded by losses on the company's American tour in July–August 1989. The deficit had tripled within a short period, much to the alarm of ENB's Board and the Arts Council.

Although the tour lost money, the company was well received in the United States on its first visit for nine years. Most of the critical plaudits went to the Ashton *Romeo and Juliet*, which Schaufuss had brought into the repertoire and which had never been seen in America. On its return to Britain, the company tried to recover its losses with frequent performances of *Coppélia, Swan Lake* and *The Nutcracker*, its regular end-of-year money-spinner. The only new work in the 1989/90 season for the main company was Christopher Bruce's *Symphony in Three Movements* to Stravinsky's music. Although the choreography is skilful in Bruce's typical mix of ballet and modern-dance styles, it will have to bear comparison with Balanchine's ballet to the same music, which is being taken into the Birmingham Royal Ballet's repertoire next season.

Christopher Bruce, who was made ENB's Associate Choreographer in 1986, resigned in despair in 1989 because his ballets were so rarely performed. The problem was the usual one of programming triple bills for resistant audiences in the regions. Bruce's works were mainly confined to short tours by the company's small ensemble, which usually performs to piano music.

Schaufuss had intended to feature Bruce's *Symphony in Three Movements* in a programme of English choreography, which would have included a revival of Tudor's *Echoing of Trumpets* and a new *Rite of Spring* by Michael Clark. Clark, who has (temporarily, it is hoped) retired from the British dance scene, withdrew his ballet until a later date, on the grounds that it needed more rehearsal time. Instead of replacing Clark's *Rite* with another British work, the management programmed Béjart's *Bolero* instead – hardly a challenging choice of choreography.

Schaufuss had also planned to commission six new works by prominent European choreographers to enter ENB's repertoire by 1992. Although this would have made it the only British company actually celebrating Europe's open frontiers, the Board feared that 'foreign' names would not attract English audiences. ENB has now dropped any plans for a European Festival – and the idea has been eagerly taken up instead by the Deutsche Oper.

142

DANCE THEATRE
TRAINING COURSES
leading to
BA (HONS)
Or
DIPLOMA in DANCE
3 YEARS FULL TIME

Training includes
CONTEMPORARY TECHNIQUE ◀
B A L L E T ◀
CHOREOGRAPHY ◀ R E P E R T O R Y ◀
PRODUCTION (COSTUME, LIGHTING, SOUND) ◀
HISTORY AND SOCIOLOGY OF DANCE ◀
▶ N O T A T I O N ◀

for more information of these and
Post Graduate courses write to
COURSE ENQUIRIES
LABAN CENTRE
LAURIE GROVE
LONDON SE14 6NH
UNITED KINGDOM

or telephone
01 - 692 4070

LABAN CENTRE
FOR MOVEMENT AND DANCE

London Studio Centre

42-50 York Way London N1 9AB Tel. (01) 837 7741 Fax (01) 837 3248

Patron: **Dame Ninette de Valois** C.H., D.B.E.
Founder: **Bridget Espinosa**
Director: **Nicholas Espinosa**

Dame Alicia Markova D.B.E., D.Mus.
will give private coaching by appointment

CURRENT TEACHING FACULTY

CLASSICAL BALLET
Wayne Aspinall
Laura Connor
Linden Currey
Conchita del Campo
Sandra Doling
Jane Elliott
Ronald Emblen
Anya Evans
Carol Grant
Sarah Hanson
Michael Ho
Barry McGrath
Donald McLennan
Ikky Maas
Herida May
Sally Mills
Michael Moor
Juan Sanchez
Anita Young

R.A.D. MAJOR EXAMS
Linden Currey
Conchita del Campo
Sandra Doling
Jane Elliott
Sarah Hanson
Michael Ho
Barry McGrath
Donald McLennan
Herida May
Sally Mills

CECCHETTI MAJOR EXAMS
Sarah Hanson
Anita Young

I.S.T.D. ASSOCIATE EXAMS
Penny Meakings

PAS DE DEUX
Barry McGrath
John Raven

SPANISH
Ana Ricarda

CONTEMPORARY
Sue Booker
Chris Carter
Ikky Maas

JAZZ
Fiona Alexanda
Nicky Bentley
Colin Charles
Bill Drysdale
Jacqui Harman
Theresa Kerr
Stephen Mear
Jacki Mitchell
Nikki Skilton
Nikki Squires

TAP
Michele Aslanoff
Janet Devenish
Sandra Doling
Bill Drysdale
Marie Fowdon
Stephen Mear
David Shelmerdine

AUDITION TECHNIQUE
Doris Barry

TV & RADIO TECHNIQUE
Norman Tozer

BODY CONTROL
Conchita del Campo
Leonie Palette

MUSICAL STAGING
Jack Gunn
Jacqui Harman
David Shelmerdine

DRAMA
Jane Atkinson
David Oliver Craik
Ian Dewar
Veronica Duffy
Gordon Fleming
Rosemary Grayson

SINGING
Jacqueline Clifton
Pam Gale
Deborah Goody
Anne Grayson
Tony Pedretti
Tina Young

STAGE FIGHTING
Philip Palmer

MIME
Wayne Pritchett

CHARACTER & NATIONAL
Sandra Doling
Sarah Hanson
John Raven

MUSICIANSHIP
John Bickley
Jacqueline Clifton
Alan Lawrence
Tony McVey

**HISTORY OF BALLET 'O' LEVEL
BENESH NOTATION ANATOMY**
Sandra Doling
Sarah Hanson

STAGE & COSTUME DESIGN
Sean Crowley
Kay Denyer

MAKE UP
Linden Currey

WEIGHT TRAINING
Barry McGrath
Donald McLennan
Michael Moor

Artist Co-Ordinator & Assistant to the Director: **Donald McLennan** Dip. RBS (TTC), AISTD, (CCB NB)   Associate Advisor: **Doris Barry**

Studio Co-ordinator & Principal of Associate School:
Sandra Doling, Dip, RBS (TTC), ARAD, AISTD, AIDTA, Inter Benesh Notation
Resident Teacher & Injury Coaching:
Sarah Hanson, Dip, RBS (TTC), ARAD, AISTD, (CB NB)
Resident Teacher & Diet Counsellor:
Linden Currey, Dip, RBS (TCPD), ARAD, AISTD
Resident Teacher & Weight Training Consultant:
Barry McGrath, ARAD, (Dip, PDTC)
Resident Teacher & Head of Body Control Studio:
Conchita del Campo, ARAD, (Dip, PDTC)

Administrator:
Francis Yeoh, LLB(Hons)
Personal Secretary to the Director:
Elsa Hughes
Secretary:
Marie Fowdon
Special Projects:
Claire Lewis

Registrar:
Sandra Johnston
**Audition Secretary &
Assistant to Studio Co-Ordinator:**
Sharon Bevins
Musical Director:
Jacqueline Clifton
Sponsorship Consultant:
Michael Rose

There are 11 architect designed dance studios, 3 music rooms, 4 drama studios, 1 body control studio and 2 rehearsal studios, with maple sprung flooring and floor to ceiling mirrors. Facilities also include a physiotherapy room, Wardrobe, canteen, modern changing rooms and showers, and a workshop theatre.

Accredited by the Council for Dance Education & Training.
The London Studio Centre gratefully acknowledges the support of Cameron Mackintosh Ltd for the sponsorship of Studio 17, and to Tom and Blackie Merrifield for the Merrifield Awards and the Reception Area exhibitions of prints.

ENB's new Artistic Director (from September 1990) is to be the former Hungarian dancer, Ivan Nagy, whose career as performer and director has been made mainly in the United States and South America. (He is, however, married to former Festival Ballet principal, Marilyn Burr.) Nagy's appointment was announced at the end of the fortieth-anniversary gala. It was a well-planned occasion, marred only by the chairwoman's failure to acknowledge Schaufuss's contribution to the company or the achievements of previous directors, such as Dame Beryl Grey and John Field. The guest artists were mainly international veterans, demonstrating that star quality lasts longer and matters more than virtuoso technique. (Their names are listed in the ENB statistics section.)

Ivan Nagy inherits a company with a fine, if sometimes erratic, reputation. He also inherits the company's inbuilt problems, including the lack of a home theatre. The company school, which Schaufuss established in 1988, continues, thanks to energetic fundraising, in the company's London headquarters.

London Contemporary Dance Theatre

Allen Robertson

This year was London Contemporary Dance Theatre's first season under its new Artistic Director, Dan Wagoner. In addition, LCDT also acquired a new Assistant Director in company dancer and choreographer Jonathan Lunn. The troupe also won the Olivier Award for Dance with its production of Kim Brandstrup's *Orfeo* and then wrapped up its season with a first-ever visit to the Soviet Union with performances in Kiev and Moscow, 28 June to 8 July.

Wagoner, at 58, is the first person other than Robert Cohan to serve as director of LCDT. He shares many of Cohan's credentials: both are Americans and both danced with Martha Graham, that veritable earth goddess of American modern dance, and both went on to other things – Cohan to London, Wagoner to Paul Taylor's company where he spent nearly a decade before founding his own troupe in 1969.

Cohan had initially suggested Wagoner as his successor several years ago, but it took until 1989 to lure him to London. After a year into the job, he has decided to return to the United States for personal reasons. He will resume runing his own New York company, which is typical of a small modern American troupe: there is only one choreographer, only a single set of artistic values to be adhered to. The LCDT approach, with three or more choreographers fitted in to each programme, has been a radical change for him.

The company hopes to announce a replacement for him before the end of 1990. The board intends to avoid the period of uncertainty which held back LCDT's artistic development while it waited for Wagoner's arrival. Yet it is already evident that a sense of freshness is sweeping through the company. Over the last year several LCDT veterans have departed. It was a gradual change rather than a mass exodus, but this season one was struck by the fact that LCDT is once again a young company, something it has not been in many a moon.

An open expectancy, burgeoning with a feeling of new beginnings, is surfacing in the works. Wagoner's first piece created for LCDT, *Turtles All the Way Down*, was a splendid kick-off for his regime in October 1989. Wagoner himself plays a central role. Wearing a stetson, he stands at the back of the stage like a lone cowpoke staring off into limitless night, atmospherically suggested by Jennifer Tipton's moody lighting. The dancers, in brownish piebald costumes, are much more reminiscent of frisky cattle than of turtles, and their zippy movements, as Wagoner herds them round the stage, are the absolute antithesis of tortoises.

The autumn season also spotlighted Wagoner's *To Comfort Ghosts*. It is danced to Shostakovich's brooding final string quartet. This work was premièred in New York in 1988 by Wagoner's own troupe, where it was hailed by several American critics as his finest work ever. Strong and clear, it has a deep underlying power that touches emotional chords without ever becoming overtly literal.

Company dancer Jonathan Lunn has been making works for LCDT and other groups for a couple of seasons now. Most of those pieces have struck me as classroom exercises, promising and competent, but nothing special. This season, in *Goes Without Saying* (24 October), Lunn produced his first fully fledged 'grown-up' choreography. This is a real breakthrough for him as an artist.

Lunn takes full advantage of a fine atmospheric score composed by Orlando Gough and John Lunn (the latter is not to be confused with the choreographer). The dance is enhanced by one of the most impressive designs that British dance has seen in a long time. Peter Mumford's set, costumes and lighting all fit together in a fresh package which gives Lunn's evocative gestural work much of its suggestive strength.

The setting is a room painted like the sky and lit through portholes and half-opened doors. It has a seascape openness about it that is in stark contrast to the dance's most striking feature – this room of sky is capped off by a full ceiling. The whole orchestra is perched up there along with a single dancer, clad in black. From the way she moves, it is clear that the whole dance down below is something she is reliving in her memory.

Kim Brandstrup's award-winning first work for the company *Orfeo* (4 October) is an ironic layering of eighteenth-century costumes, manners, music and myth. The Orpheus myth is here stylishly re-cast into a hybrid cross between classical French drama and a Peter Greenaway film. The

Tracey Fitzgerald as Euridice in *Orfeo*, Kim Brandstrup's version of the Orpheus myth.
PHOTO: CHRIS NASH

outcome is a distinct departure from the expected LCDT style and augurs well for a catholic company repertoire in the future. Both the elegant designs by Craig Givens and composer Ian Dearden's contemporary pastiche of baroque music gave strong support to Brandstrup's choreography.

Danish-born Brandstrup, 33, has run his own company, Arc Dance, since 1985 when he graduated from London Contemporary Dance School. He admits to being fascinated by the complexities and possibilities of telling stories through movement. Before he came to England in 1980 he had studied film techniques and feels that this played a strong role in developing his approach to choreography.

The resonances of myth and folk-tale obviously hold deep significance for him. On 18 April 1990, Brandstrup's *Dybbuk*, first created for Arc in 1988, was one of three works to join the LCDT repertory in the company's return to its original home stage, The Place Theatre. Here, as with *Orfeo*, Brandstrup chose to convey his story through a collage of images and

145

events rather than as a straightforward linear narrative. The story, based on Yiddish legend, is about spiritual possession from beyond the grave.

Aletta Collins, who joined LCDT as a dancer in May, also created a new work for The Place programme, *It's Gonna Rain*. As with Brandstrup, this marked her second LCDT work. It is distinguished by a frenetic sense of propulsion which has dancers dashing across the stage in rapid spurts. Both sides of the stage are filled with brightly coloured doors which the dancers fling open, crash into or frantically try to close behind the other performers. Collins has an individual approach to movement that shows much promise for the future.

The Place programme was completed with *Noon Talk on Millionth Street* by Jo Ann Fregalette Jansen, a former member of Wagoner's New York company. A mix of the urban homeless and zealous, misplaced religiosity, it proved less than a success and was dropped immediately following the April performances.

Darshan Singh Bhuller, who has been with LCDT as a dancer since 1980, created *Ace of Spades* this season. It was inspired by the Vietnam War and featured a score which mixed the music of Samuel Barber with that of a favoured LCDT composer, Barrington Pheloung. Lunn's brief duet *Doppelgänger* was also seen this season.

LCDT performed only two works from previous seasons during this year of adventuresome, forward-looking programming. One, Paul Taylor's *Arden Court*, is a masterpiece which the company dances with consummate mastery. The other, Robert Cohan's latest work for the company, *Metamorphosis*, is a solo for Singh Bhuller performed with a series of Anthony Crickmay's photos of the dancer.

The figure of death in *Orfeo*.

London City Ballet

Edward Thorpe

Perhaps the most notable aspect of London City Ballet's 1989–90 season is that, despite the ever-increasing financial squeeze that is slowly crushing all the arts in Britain, the company managed to maintain both its artistic standards and its viability. LCB survived the bitter fiscal climate entirely by its own efforts at the box office and the support it engendered from sponsors.

On the artistic level, LCB's main effort was centred on a new full-length work, *La Traviata, the Ballet,* commissioned from André Prokovsky and sponsored by the National Westminster Bank. Receiving its first performance at the Gordon Craig Theatre in Stevenage on 11 October 1989, with a gala performance a week later at the Churchill Theatre in Bromley, attended by the company's patron, HRH The Princess of Wales, *La Traviata* was also the opening work of LCB's second successful season at Sadler's Wells Theatre in March 1990. Although the ballet received somewhat mixed reviews from the London critics, the romantic drama, familiar from Alexandre Dumas fils' novel and play *La Dame aux camélias* and even more from Verdi's opera version of *La Traviata,* found great favour with audiences.

La Traviata presented both a technical and histrionic challenge to the LCB casts, with Kim Miller (who created the role) and Prima Ballerina Marian St Claire receiving considerable acclaim for their performances in the central role of Marguerite. Peter Farmer's highly atmospheric designs, achieved with a clever economy of means, made a notable contribution to the success of the ballet, as did Guy Woolfenden's effective and sensitive arrangement of Verdi's music, which included some vocal excerpts from the opera score.

The other new works in LCB's 1989–90 season were both classically based: *Aurora's Wedding,* adapted from Act III of *The Sleeping Beauty* by the company's Ballet Master, Jaakko Helkavaara, with attractive costumes by Shirley Laurenson; and *Dances from Napoli,* with choreography by August Bournonville, produced by Company Director Harold King. Revivals of ballets that had proved highly successful on previous tours included *Giacosa Variations* by Istvan Herczog, *Graduation Ball* by David Lichine, *Transfigured Night* by Frank Staff, and *Three Dances to Japanese Music* by Jack Carter. These last three works made up a well-balanced triple bill as the company's second programme during its season at Sadler's Wells. Other tours undertaken during the season included five venues in Northern Ireland and a tour of Italy during the summer of 1990.

Guest artists during the year included Derek Deane from the Royal Ballet and Matz Skoog from English National Ballet, with Kader Belarbi and Marie-Claude Pietragalla from the Paris Opéra Ballet joining the company for its highly successful summer tour of Japan in 1989.

An unexpected but welcome addition to the company's rosta of principals was Stanislav Tchassov, who decided to leave the Bolshoi Ballet after its 1989 London season to join LCB.

Northern Ballet Theatre
Bill Harpe

Northern Ballet Theatre's name is almost as well known to those who do not go to dance performances in Britain as to those who do. In the main, this is due to the company's much-publicized fight to survive, under the leadership of its Artistic Director, Christopher Gable (who took over the company in 1987). Certainly the prospect of imminent closure, due to the threatened withdrawal of its grant from the Arts Council of Great Britain, concentrated the energies of Northern Ballet Theatre and its supporters wonderfully.

The public campaign to save the company resulted in over 10,000 letters of support to the Arts Council and members of parliament. The opening press conferences had Christopher Gable flying from NBT's headquarters in Manchester to London in a helicopter donated for the occasion. He used his considerable skill as an actor to make dramatic speeches in theatres and on television. When the company's future was assured – the Arts Council agreed to guarantee funding through to 1991 – an exhausted Gable acknowledged, 'perhaps the threat of closure was the best thing that could have happened to us'.

Gable's options, however, remain limited by financial constraints. Northern Ballet Theatre, with just over thirty dancers and some twenty musicians, have slightly less than half the number of dancers and musicians of the Sadler's Wells Royal Ballet and yet receive only one-eighth of their grant. Northern Ballet Theatre are additionally under pressure from the Arts Council to produce programmes which will maximize their audiences and their income. Finally, as a company they lack the technical and financial resources to make a mid-week change of programme.

Within these constraints Christopher Gable has skilfully sought to make the company's repertoire popular, accessible, and dramatic. The anchor of this repertoire is a new production of *Giselle*, which allows full scope to Gable's aim of telling a good story – and telling it economically, cogently, and passionately. There is no doubt that Gable has put his own mark on this production – locating it in the mid-nineteenth century somewhere between Switzerland and Germany.

Triple bills are notoriously, and unfortunately, less of an attraction than full-length ballets. Gable's marketing solution has been to announce the company's latest triple bill as an evening of passion, heartbreak, spectacle and wonderful dance.

The passion is that of Parisian high society in *Liaisons amoureuses* – the champagne parties and up-market eroticism are created by choreographer Ronald Hynd and set to 'forgotten gems' from Offenbach's light operas, with a dazzling Eiffel Tower set (by Peter Docherty).

The heartbreak is that of soldier and poet Wilfred Owen in *Strange Meeting* – with the confrontation of young soldiers in a no man's land of mud and death, set by choreographer Michael Pink to original music by Philip Feeney and electronic sound by Philip Clifford. The sets are reminiscent of the trenches of World War I, illuminated by strobe lighting.

The spectacle is that of the famous white horses of the Spanish Riding School in Vienna – with choreographer Gillian Lynne setting out to create the struggle and the rapport between horse and trainer (in this case between the wild, passionate spirits of women and their male trainers). Tinidad Sevillano and Patrick Armand were guest artists for the première of *Lipizzaner* in Sheffield and for some of its London performances.

Late 1990 will see the advent of a new triple bill – intermingling *pas de deux* from *Giselle, Swan Lake* and *The Amazing Adventures of Don Quixote* with *Liaisons amoureuses* and *The Lesson*. A new full-length production of *Romeo and Juliet*, with choreography by Christopher Gable, is planned for February 1991.

The company looks set for a major and dramatic move in the near future. After over twenty years in Manchester the company is preparing to uproot itself and seek a home elsewhere in the north of England. The prospect of a new home in West Yorkshire just a mile away from the centre of Halifax offers not only the additional space which the company needs but also an escape from the urban pressures of inner-city Manchester. It offers the possibility of the Central School of Ballet in London (which is also directed by Christopher Gable) moving up to join the company, and it holds out the prospect of Northern Ballet Theatre establishing for the first time a broadly northern base – with performances and residences in Halifax, Leeds, Bradford, Manchester, Rochdale and Huddersfield – as well as maintaining its national touring commitments.

For the dancers, who have often to make financial sacrifices if they choose to work away from London, such a relocation could be like a new dawning. For Christopher Gable, it could provide the basis of sustained support from which to develop both Northern Ballet Theatre and an associated ballet school. Since becoming Artistic Director of Northern Ballet Theatre, only three short years ago, Christopher Gable has already proved that he can both inspire his company and give his audience what he knows they want. It is a tall order indeed, but if he stays as Artistic Director until the end of the 1990s, who knows but that he might also give his audiences something more than they ever dreamed of as well.

Jayne Regan and Paul Thrussell as horse and trainer in Gillian Lynne's ballet, *Lipizzaner*, inspired by Vienna's white horses. PHOTO: IAN WOOLLAMS

Rambert Dance Company

Stephanie Jordan

In the programme note to the 1990 Rambert season at the Wells, Richard Alston likened himself to the curator of a private collection, taking care of the past and putting it in fresh contexts – re-programming dances is like re-hanging paintings – as well as commissioning new work – like buying in new acquisitions. But it is well to remember that the success of any repertory-based company relies on an astute choice of pieces and on looking after them meticulously. Rambert Dance Company copes with these problems unusually well, its works chosen and choreographies commissioned on the grounds of true dance personality and clear conception, as well as to test the dancers and tease out new qualities from them. Naturally, not every piece is a winner, but Rambert programmes possess a far greater creative vitality than most. Alston continues to match progressive programming with care for his dancers – some go, others arrive, but the company's dancing identity seems to become more refined, individual dancers more individual, each year that we see them. There have been some extraordinary performances this year: in Siobhan Davies' *Embarque* and *Sounding*, Alston's own *Hymnos* and Trisha Brown's *Opal Loop*. And we have seen the company's most acute performances to date of Cunningham's *Septet*, with Gary Lambert new in the central male role.

Catherine Quinn and Glenn Wilkinson in *Sounding* by Siobhan Davies for Rambert Dance Company.

151

This year's great acquisition from the recent past was Cunningham's 1984 *Doubles*. This is the third work that this choreographer has given the company, a measure of his interest in having his work inflected differently by dancers other than his own, and his belief that Rambert can bring to it something excellent as well as individual.

Rambert's dancers approach *Doubles* with youthful, almost adolescent fervour. Their terms are already rather more abandoned and lyrically juicy than those of the Cunningham dancers. The impression is enjoyable, although in early performances there seemed to be an anxiety to make shapes clipped and stable, or a straining to achieve some of its physical awkwardness. It is a tough work, with big jumps leading directly into still more big jumps, and many unsupported sustained landings and tricky balances. It will be fascinating to see how *Doubles* develops, like *Septet* has done, as the company gets to know the piece.

Glen Tetley's *Embrace Tiger and Return to Mountain* was the in-house revival of the year, a view of the 1968 Rambert on dancers of the 1990s. This is plotless Tetley, demonstrating a sinuous lycra-clad eroticism, in the choreographer's characteristic Graham/ballet hybrid style, while celebrating the hypnotic and weighty virtues of t'ai chi. The music is by Morton Subotnick (*Silver Apples of the Moon*), the design by Nadine Baylis. People who remember have commented that the 1990 dancers do not move with the weight of the originals. Certainly, it has been interesting to watch the company striving for a state of tension and bound flow that is so alien to their usual style. They match this with their length of line and powerful stretch (which the dancers in 1968 did not have), and a determination to put drive into a work that is fundamentally slack of rhythm.

The finest new work of the year was undoubtedly *Sounding*, by the company's Associate Choreographer Siobhan Davies. Continuing to demonstrate her renewed creative vigour after her Fulbright year of study, *Sounding* is full of swift, subtle overlappings of groupings, like her *Embarque*, and emphasizes weight in great plunges and scoopings to the floor. The music is *Okanagon* by the Italian composer Giacinto Scelsi, its gong accents, wonderfully weighty impulses into reverberation ('the heartbeat of the earth' was Scelsi's description of his score), a direct inspiration for the movement.

Sounding was premièred during a short season at Sadler's Wells, Rambert's first appearance at the Almeida International Festival of Contemporary Music and Performance. Alston and his Music Director Roger Heaton remain firmly committed to using new music in Rambert programmes.

For the same Almeida Festival, Alston chose for himself a luminous gamelan-inspired score, *Pulau Dewata*, by the Canadian composer Claude

Vivier. Borrowing the music's title for his choreography, Alston integrated oriental features, the vocabulary of arm gestures and bent-kneed walks of Indonesian dance, into his own existing language.

Again for the Almeida Festival, Alston reworked his 1985 *Mythologies*, producing a much abstracted version of the earlier piece. Taking ideas from the structure of Nigel Osborne's musical score more readily than he did in 1985, Alston isolated for meditation the sensual qualities from the story that interested him.

However, the critical edge that characterized Alston's pieces of a few years back is absent from these recent works, and from the 1990 *Dealing with Shadows*. The latter is a lovely work, to Mozart's piano sonata in A, K. 331, with lots of the delicious, bouncy steps that we have enjoyed from this choreographer in the past. Alston, as always, tracks down the essential melodic and rhythmic currents in the music. Yet there is barely an image to recall from the piece. *Shadows* continues pleasantly enough, but without argument. At the moment, Alston's most brilliant creative energies are going into curatorship.

Ashley Page's *Currulao* must be his least likeable and least shaped work, the first product of the Frederick Ashton Memorial Commission, which was launched by the company in October 1989 (in association with the *Daily Telegraph*). It is prodigal in its resource, a brazen, blaring systems score by Orlando Gough (a commission) and big crazy costumes by new-wave fashion designer John Galliano. The concept juxtaposes Latin sophistication with sultry sleaze – a Columbian courtship dance that mixes Spanish and African origins is Page's explanation. Page has cobbled together a torrent of steps, rolls and predatory embraces, with legs whacking into balletic arabesque or attitude to mark each musical knife-wound. Yet, for all the theatrical paraphernalia, the effect is minimal, except perhaps some gratuitous celebration of heartless lust. Page is far better represented elsewhere in the Rambert Collection with his *Carmen Arcadiae* and *Soldat* of previous years.

The designs of fine artists have not flavoured Rambert's new works as strongly as in previous years, with the exception of Stephen Buckley's brightly coloured contribution to Mary Evelyn's short-lived *Calm*. The most exciting designs this year have come from Peter Mumford, in the form of both lighting and sets – and with Mumford, lighting often becomes set.

Who can forget his blinding icy landscape freezing the central figure at the end of *Mythologies*? Or his environment for *Sounding*, a stage space made mysterious and contained by a gauze front curtain, later crossed dramatically by orange bands of light? Mumford confirmed that he is the most brilliant lighting designer working in British dance today.

Alston was nominated for the Digital Dance Premier Award 1989 for an Outstanding Contribution to Current British Dance: he used the cheque for his nomination to support *Longevity*, Gary Lambert's first choreography for the company repertory. However, the highlight of the company year was the winning of the first Prudential Award for the Arts. With the Prudential's Award for Dance under its belt, Rambert went on to compete against four winners from other categories and to win £100,000, the richest prize for the arts in this country.

The Royal Ballet
Mary Clarke

The Royal Ballet season for 1989–90 followed very much the pattern forecast by Peter Brinson in last year's *World Ballet and Dance*. The repertory was dominated by the full-evening ballets which remain, obstinately and irrefutably, good box-office. The policy of inviting guest stars continued (and will be intensified in the year ahead), partly to please the wealthy audience conscious only of star names but also to goad and inspire young talent from within the ranks. Attendances continued to be high, averaging in the region of 91 per cent – and this despite the difficulty of selling seats for some of the triple bills. (An interesting statistic that might be added at the end of this volume is the number of bottles of champagne consumed at Covent Garden during the season.)

The season celebrated the sixtieth birthday of Sir Kenneth MacMillan and revivals of some of his finest works were among the most rewarding events of the year. A constant worry, however, was the condition of the Ashton repertory, in the absence of any controlling trust such as those which safeguard the legacies of Balanchine and Tudor.

Another concern – not entirely a new one – was the standard of orchestral playing, the pedestrian manner which is the norm being highlighted by the difference in the response of the orchestra on those occasions when Mark Ermler and, above all, Bernard Haitink took control. (There will be a change in musical direction next year.)

The season opened with Natalia Makarova's opulent staging of *La Bayadère*, which had proved popular the year before. Permanent guest artist Sylvie Guillem danced the first performance with Jonathan Cope and Fiona Chadwick. Other notable performances during the run of the ballet came from Maria Almeida, Viviana Durante and such shining guests as Julio Bocca and Altynai Asylmuratova.

The first mixed programme was made up of Balanchine's *Rubies* (in which Errol Pickford displayed an ever-growing command of technique), a new ballet by Ashley Page, *Piano*, and a fine revival of MacMillan's *Requiem*. The Page ballet, his third commissioned work for the Royal Ballet, was

154

danced to Beethoven but was chiefly notable for the fine designs by Howard Hodgkin.

Then came a run of the inescapable *Swan Lake*, together with another triple bill. This consisted of MacMillan's dark but powerful ballet *My Brother, My Sisters*; a revival of Ashton's *A Wedding Bouquet*, declared by all who knew and loved the ballet to be an absolute travesty of the original; and a revival of Wayne Eagling's *Frankenstein: the Modern Prometheus*, no longer a novelty but still pulling in the smart set. Because of a dispute over dancers' pay (they were demanding some parity with the opera), eventually amicably solved, two performances of this bill were cancelled to allow time for rehearsals of MacMillan's new full-evening work, *The Prince of the Pagodas*, which had its première on 7 December. Danced to the one score Benjamin Britten ever wrote for ballet, it was a complete re-working of the choreography and partial re-working of the libretto of the original version made by John Cranko. In superb designs by Nicholas Georgiadis, and an abundance of beautiful choreography and clever character building, it was a notable success. In Darcey Bussell MacMillan found (as he has so often before) an ideal interpreter of his central figure, Princess Rose. Her success caused her immediately to be named a principal of the company – the

Bruce Sansom as the King of the East and Darcey Bussell as Princess Rose in MacMillan's new *Prince of the Pagodas*.   PHOTO: LESLIE E. SPATT

youngest ever. As her salamander-prince, Jonathan Cope was ideally cast; so too were Fiona Chadwick as Princess Epine, Anthony Dowell as the old Emperor, and Tetsuya Kumakawa as the Fool.

Ashton's *Cinderella* came back into the repertory, for fifteen performances, over the Christmas and New Year period. Again, there was much to worry about but Sylvie Guillem made a touching début as Cinderella and some performances were made tolerable by the conducting of Mark Ermler.

On 16 January the Chaboukiani/Nureyev version of the *pas de six* from *Laurentia* was revived in an expensively unnecessary setting and costumes by Georgiadis. There was some good dancing – especially from Almeida, Bussell, Durante and Pickford – but the piece demands Russian bravura. It shared the programme with *La Fille mal gardée*, which, of all Ashton's major ballets, seems most safely preserved in the Royal repertories.

Another clutch of *Swan Lakes* brought Darcey Bussell's first Odette–Odile, tentative but glowing with promise. Then more *Pagodas* (Sylvie Guillem and Laurent Hilaire welcome guests), and some performances of Peter Wright's *Giselle* with familiar casts.

On 2 April there was to have been a new ballet by William Forsythe for Guillem but he could not finish it in time so it was replaced by Robbins's *Other Dances*, delightfully done by Guillem and Hilaire. The rest of the programme was Bintley's lively *Galanteries*, Page's gimmicky *Pursuit*, and a magnificent revival of MacMillan's *Gloria*, that poignant, angry lament for the dead of World War I.

For 17 May a new ballet by David Bintley, to Holst's *The Planets*, had been announced, but was not ready. Instead Ashton's *A Month in the Country* was given, together with MacMillan's masterpiece, *Song of the Earth*. In *A Month in the Country*, Anthony Dowell appeared with youthful conviction in his created role of the tutor Beliaev. As Natalia Petrovna, Guillem was less than ideally cast.

On 25 May Sylvie Guillem stepped into the role of Juliet in a revival of *Romeo and Juliet* which marked the culmination of the MacMillan celebrations. Carefully prepared, she gave her finest performance yet within the native Royal repertory, vastly helped by Jonathan Cope's sensitive partnering as Romeo, a fine supporting cast, and Haitink leading the orchestra through a magnificent account of Prokofiev's score. On 30 May the ballet was danced again as a tribute to Margot Fonteyn, who came from Panama for the occasion. Michael Somes returned to the stage to take his created role of Lord Capulet and Rudolf Nureyev, another of Fonteyn's famous partners, danced as Mercutio.

A hoped-for tour of North America was cancelled for lack of sponsorship so the London season ran on until August. *Romeo and Juliet* and *Swan Lake* held the fort until Bintley's *The Planets* was ready and could be given with a new work by William Tuckett called *Enclosure* on 1 August.

The sensation towards the end of the season was the announcement that Irek Mukhamedov of the Bolshoi Ballet had left to join the Royal Ballet. To celebrate the event, MacMillan made a short piece especially for him to dance with Darcey Bussell. His presence will surely be just the incentive needed by the Royal's young men – such as Pickford, Cassidy, Sansom and Trevitt – to meet such a challenge.

Sadler's Wells Royal Ballet/Birmingham Royal Ballet
Sue Merrett

Sadler's Wells Royal Ballet's performances during part of the 1989/90 season were marked with uncertainty while negotiations were in progress for the forthcoming move to Birmingham, when the company would take on the name of Birmingham Royal Ballet and be based at the Birmingham Hippodrome. Probably because of the work this entailed, the season was rather more low-key than usual for this lively company.

For the opening part of the season, Peter Wright's acclaimed production of *Swan Lake* was revived, during which time Cynthia Harvey danced some guest performances, and the company took into its repertoire George Balanchine's *Divertimento No. 15* (13 October) during its first Birmingham visit.

Three premières by company members, together with *Divertimento No. 15*, comprised the repertory intake for the year. Added to the general uncertainty as to which company members would move to Birmingham and which would not (in the event 85 per cent of the company opted to move), the industrial action taken by the two Royal Ballet companies over pay rates also dampened spirits generally. Although the dispute with the Opera House management did not result in any cancelled performances (as in the case of the Covent Garden company), Sadler's Wells Royal Ballet's Christmas season at Sadler's Wells Theatre lacked a certain sparkle. This was the first opportunity to present to London audiences the two premières from the end of the previous season, Redmon's *Auras* and Tuckett's *Those Unheard*, the first showing promise in Redmon's handling of the cast, the second suggesting that Tuckett's choice of Britten's 'Sea Interludes' from *Peter Grimes* was rather tricky music for dance.

The autumn tour had also included the first out-of-London performances of Bintley's *Hobson's Choice*, which had been such a success at its Opera House première in London the previous season. Now adapted into three acts, the ballet proved that it could accommodate individual interpretations in the very human characters of Maggie Hobson and Will Mossop, new casts of which included Marion Tait with Graham Lustig, and Bonnie Moore with Vincent Redmon.

Sadler's Wells Royal Ballet (before becoming the Birmingham Royal Ballet) in Balanchine's
Theme and Variations.   PHOTO: LESLIE E. SPATT

The first of the two London seasons marked the sixtieth birthday of
Kenneth MacMillan with a programme of *Danses Concertantes, Las Hermanas*
and *Solitaire.* Ashton's *The Two Pigeons* was revived, with guest artist
Yannick Stephant in the role of the young girl at one performance. After a
25-year career with the company, Margaret Barbieri made her farewell
performance on 30 December, for which she danced the débutante in
Façade.

Once again, following the pattern set up the previous year, a two-week
choreographic workshop rehearsal period followed the London season, a
time which also marked the company's preparation for a five-week tour of
New Zealand.

Sadler's Wells Royal Ballet's third visit to New Zealand began in
Auckland at the newly built Aotea Centre, when the company's gala per-
formance of *Swan Lake* officially inaugurated the 2,500-seat theatre. *Swan
Lake* was performed at all three venues on the tour, while Auckland and
Wellington also saw *Theme and Variations, The Dream* and *Elite Syncopations.*

By the time the company opened its second London season at Sadler's
Wells Theatre, most company members had decided whether or not they
would be moving to Birmingham. The result was that the season took off

with a sigh of relief, and with the return of the company's usual sparkle. The opening night was dedicated to the memory of Dame Peggy van Praagh, who had been director of the company formed at Sadler's Wells after the main section had moved to Covent Garden in 1946. This programme included one of Dame Peggy's favourite ballets, Ashton's *Valses nobles et sentimentales* (its only performance that season).

The two young choreographers who had presented their first company works the previous season each created a new one for London. Redmon's *Meridian of Youth* (24 April) opened with a group of young men lounging on a waterside, and followed their encounters first with a group of young girls, then with some more mature women. Redmon could almost be taking Kipling's 'the female of the species is deadlier than the male' as his theme, since the encounter with these experienced women proves fairly devastating for one young man in particular. Some people found Redmon's choice of Bartók's Second Piano Concerto over-ambitious, but there were others who perceived a skill in his handling of the complex rhythms.

For *Game* (4 May), set to Debussy's *Jeux*, Tuckett took the dictionary definitions of the word 'game' for his programme note. Some 'young things' in 1920s costume are invited by their young bespectacled host to a party, which begins to take on sinister undertones, incomprehensible to the young man. Stephen Meaha's white room and costumes for six of the cast provide a good contrast with the black costumes for a couple whose arrival turns the party sour as the white walls lose their pristine mono-colour. Kevin O'Hare gave a sensitive performance as the bewildered young man, while Tony Fabre and Bonnie Moore gave a sinister glitter to the intruding couple in black.

The last new work to enter the repertoire was Graham Lustig's *Inscape* (1 June), premièred in the last weeks of the season. For this Lustig had commissioned a score – piano and string quartet – from Peter McGowan, and from Henk Schut his first designs for a ballet in Britain. Lustig chose ten young dancers for this abstract work, the title of which is a word coined by the poet Gerard Manley Hópkins to define a formative inner essence, which composer and choreographer used for a work where ideas would develop without preconceptions.

Sadler's Wells Royal Ballet concluded its season, and its life under the 14-year-old title, by recording Bintley's *Hobson's Choice* for television. After company holidays, those involved in the move to Birmingham would re-gather at the Hippodrome in August, where rehearsals would begin for the new season. Those leaving the company, and listed as guest artists for the new season, included Petter Jacobsson, Roland Price, Graham Lustig, conductor Stephen Lade, and Tony Fabre, who joined as soloist at the beginning of the 1989/90 season.

The Scottish Ballet

Patricia Eckersley

The Scottish Ballet's origins date back to the Western Ballet Theatre Company which was founded in 1958 and which moved to Scotland in 1969, then to become the Scottish Theatre Ballet Company. Its name was changed to the Scottish Ballet in 1974.

In 1990, happily coinciding with Glasgow's year as European City of Culture, the company celebrates its twenty-first anniversary.

In the past two years, since the death of its founder, Peter Darrell, the Scottish Ballet has initiated radical changes both in its management structure and artistic output. Some of these changes have had an abrupt effect on the company, including the departure of Elaine McDonald, who for eighteen months held the post of Artistic Controller until September 1989, having been with the company since its foundation. She danced all the major principal roles in the company's repertoire to international acclaim and was in considerable demand as a guest artist with major companies in Europe and America, although her loyalty was always to Scotland.

The most notable contributions to the repertoire during the 1989/90 season have been, first, *Petrushka*, created for the company by Oleg Vinogradov of the Kirov Ballet, who was joined by his wife Yelena as Ballet Mistress, and second, the introduction of the Balanchine repertoire under the Guest Artistic Director, Nanette Glushak. The challenging disciplines and strict styles of both the New York City Ballet and the Kirov demanded a highly polished purity of technique from the dancers which, due to the intense teaching of Nanette Glushak and Yelena Vinogradov, the company achieved admirably.

Over this period, many of the company's younger dancers have been given the opportunity to excel, particularly Tristan Borrer, the first-cast Petrushka. The new ballet formed half of a Stravinsky double bill with Scottish Opera's *Oedipus Rex*, conducted by the distinguished Georgian, Vakhtang Matchavariani, also from the Kirov, who for a short season conducted the Scottish Opera's orchestra for performances of *Petrushka*.

Yelena and Oleg Vinogradov returned to the Scottish Ballet to stage four *divertissements* from the repertoire of the Kirov Ballet – *La Esmeralda, Paquita, The Fairy Doll* and *La Vivandière*, all part of the Scottish Ballet spring tour for 1990. The links formed between the Kirov Ballet and the Scottish Ballet promise new collaborative ventures for the future.

Nanette Glushak's choice of Balanchine's *Scotch Symphony* and the lively *Who Cares?*, with music by George Gershwin, is proving a valuable asset to the company's repertoire.

At the official launch of Glasgow as European City of Culture 1990, the Scottish Ballet opened an International Dance Gala with the première of Balanchine's *Scotch Symphony*. The costumes, dramatic red Highland dress,

Tristan Borrer as the sacrificed Petrushka in Oleg Vinogradov's version of the Stravinsky ballet, first mounted by the Scottish Ballet in 1989.   PHOTO: ALAN CRUMLISH

were thought especially appropriate for such an occasion and evoked a warm response from a very enthusiastic audience.

The Scottish Ballet participated in Glasgow's 1990 Mayfest Dance Festival, introducing works by three European choreographers: Amanda Miller from the Frankfurt Ballet presented *Pretty Ugly*, alongside Michel Rahn's *Aquarelle*, and there were two new works by the Rome-based Massimo Moricone, *Sun and Steel* and *Zwei Gesänge*.

Touring in large-, medium- and small-scale venues is to be greatly enhanced by the award of £250,000 from the Arts Council of Great Britain as part of the Incentive Funding Scheme, which matches money raised from sponsorship. The Incentive Funding will permit future growth in the education work of 'Steps Out/Ballet for All' by increased touring to small-scale venues and will link the educational work directly to the main company's repertoire.

The Scottish Ballet's ambitious plans for the future are to attract internationally renowned choreographers and dancers. The Board intends to appoint a longer-term Artistic Director in 1991 instead of its previous policy (since the death of Peter Darrell) of inviting a guest director for a limited period. So far, the guests have been the Vinogradovs and Nanette Glushak, with Galina Samsova invited for the 1990/1 season.

Smaller British Dance Companies

Lesley-Anne Sayers

Britain's smaller dance companies enter the new decade as strong in quality as they are rich in diversity. Artists of the calibre of Rosemary Butcher, Siobhan Davies and Ian Spink, renowned for their sustained achievement during the 1970s and 1980s, move into the 1990s alongside a new generation of acclaimed choreographers working in distinctive individual styles such as Lea Anderson, Matthew Bourne, Lloyd Newson and Yolande Snaith.

Snaith's 1990 work for herself and Kathy Crick, *Germs: Advanced Lessons and Social Skills*, extended the ideas of last year's highly successful *Lessons in Social Skills*. It is an insightful and witty exploration of puritanical values which has provided an apparently inexhaustible source for Snaith's creative ingenuity. She is particularly renowned for her attention to detail, her developed visual sense and her inventive interactions with objects. She manages to imbue her props as well as her steps with multi-layered significance and she stands out from many of her contemporaries in her ability to develop her choreographic and dramatic ideas beyond the impact of a visually satisfying image.

Lea Anderson is currently sustaining two companies: the all-female **Cholmondeleys** has so far been the domain of her more serious work, but the all-male group, **The Featherstonehaughs**, enjoys equal popularity and forms an important part of Anderson's work and her concerns with subverting stereotypical attitudes towards gender. Her latest work for The Cholmondeleys is her second full-length work to date and departs from her usual witty and humorous vein. *Flesh and Blood*, with live music by the Pointy Birds, revolves around themes of obsession and introspection. Her style proved itself well able to cope with the change of emotional range; the use of repetition and attention to minutiae take on a new and disturbing aspect. Her use of gesture and eye-movements is reminiscent of Indian dance forms, though the mechanized urbanity and dislocation of gesture from 'meaning' is a wholly Western-style preoccupation with states of alienation.

Adventures in Motion Pictures was formed in 1987 by eight graduates from the Laban Centre for Movement and Dance and has gone from strength to strength in the last couple of years. The company's main choreographers, Jacob Marley and Matthew Bourne, have enjoyed critical and popular acclaim but Bourne's recent work, *The Infernal Galop*, has been

Emma Gladstone of The Cholmondeleys in Lea Anderson's *Flesh and Blood*.

PHOTO: CHRIS NASH

an outstanding success this year. It is a humorous and witty tour of the stereotypical images of French culture and the choreography has a charm and fluidity that led one critic to compare the work to Ashton's *Façade*. Bourne has now reinforced the earlier success of *Spitfire*, which had four men in white underwear perform a delightful spoof of Perrot's *Pas de Quatre*. The company has won a Barclays Bank New Stages Award enabling the production of Bourne's first full-length work in 1991.

Far from the current fashion for the aggressively theatrical, **Rosemary Butcher** recently launched her most ambitious project to date: *d.1, d.2* and *3-D* is a triptych of work amounting to a ten-month collaborative venture involving two architects and composer Jim Fulkerson. The work is concerned with our relationship to the urban environment; *d.1*, with monochromatic line designs by architect Zaha Hadid, is described by Butcher as 'multiple-plan choreography, developing physical energy from linear forms'. Colour and an increasing lyricism is the key note of *d.2*, with paintings and light installations by architect John Lyall, designed to interact with the interior of Christ Church Spitalfields. The project plans to build in increasing complexity, culminating in the production of a 'temporary city' in Glasgow for the European City of Culture celebrations. The creation of her own locale is often an important aspect of Butcher's work, taking her out of theatre settings. This work promises to be a satisfying realization on a grand scale of some of her most central and lasting concerns.

Lloyd Newson, of **DV8 Physical Theatre**, has also been involved in a promising collaboration with an architect, Mark Foley. *If Only* is a response to the despair and loneliness evoked by DV8's previous production of *Dead Dreams of Monochrome Men*, in which the performers were slaves to their desires and the environment they inhabited. Newson had hoped to use sheets of glass to suggest the fragility, strength and danger of social and physical relationships – but the complications of touring such a set were evident at the early design stage. Foley had to come up with other ingenious ideas involving aerial devices instead of glass.

The elaborate project was made possible by an award of £30,000 – the Digital Dance Premier Award of 1989 – which was made to Val Bourne, founder director of Dance Umbrella, for her services to dance. She elected to invest the whole amount in DV8, enabling Newson to work on a much larger scale than he has ever done before. *If Only* is a co-production between Glasgow City Council and the Festival d'Eté de Seine Maritime (in collaboration with other organizations), so it has been scheduled for premières in Rouen, Glasgow and Manchester, before going on to London, Oslo, Hanover, Lisbon and Australia, all in the second half of 1990.

Siobhan Davies creates a strong sense of a special, poetic environment on stage; it is most often a serene and intimate 'landscape' resulting from Davies' concern with spatial harmonies. The relationships between her fig-

ures are understated and impersonal but resonate with emotional significance. Davies' work fits comfortably into the mainstream of contemporary
dance in Britain, and indeed it is a mainstream that her numerous works
for London Contemporary Dance Theatre and Ballet Rambert, in the 1970s
and 1980s, have gone a long way towards creating. Davies has worked consistently over many years and looks set to continue to enrich British dance
through the next decade. Her small company contains some of Britain's
best dancers and last year's success, with *White Man Sleeps* and *Wyoming*,
has been reinforced with her new works. In *Drawn Breath* and *Cover Him
With Grass*, which has a tribal theme and a 'soundscape' composed of
sounds from African life, Davies again draws her audience into the sense
of an enclosed community and its richly explored interactions in space and
time.

Davies is often called 'cerebral' for her calm, expansive harmonies; **Ian
Spink**'s intellectualism takes the form of complex structures creating lush,
visually dramatic feasts, rich in images and allusion. Spink is certainly one
of the most intellectually stimulating of present-day choreographers and
for that all-too-often missing virtue we might forgive him the lack of clarity
that marred his latest work, *Heaven Ablaze in his Breast*. The work's use of
*Doppelgänger*s, with some parts played by both singers and dancers, proved
inspiring, though it added to the complexity of this difficult deconstruction
of Hoffmann's tale *The Sandman*. Spink was primarily concerned with
Hoffmann's 'fascination with the shattered personality' and, as is becoming
usual with Spink's works, it demands more than one viewing. There is a
clear need for greater editorial control of the material and the many flashes
of Spink's genius make the presentational flaws all the more irksome,
though the work never fails to be stimulating and is excellently performed.
With Second Stride, Spink has a group of extremely versatile and first-rate
performers and he has created a vital and original new style of dance theatre
as well as contributing to the new revival of interest in the nature and role
of dance within opera.

Many smaller groups currently work in Britain without Arts Council
funding and often with very little, if anything, from other supporting
bodies. Their survival is continually under threat, though several of them,
such as the Brighton-based company **Divas**, have been acclaimed in
Europe as well as having a substantial following in the United Kingdom.
Divas, evocatively termed 'post-punk expressionists' by *Ballet International*,
is a group with a very committed and vivid style of dance theatre. The
uneasy feeling they can create with the ambiguity of their often violent,
anarchic and sometimes harrowing images may alienate many, but Liz
Aggiss has created a powerfully challenging and unnerving physical language which has no equal in terms of its visual, dramatic and emotional
power. Aggiss studied with former Mary Wigman dancer Hanya Holm,

and her style, such as in recent works *Dorothy and Klaus* and *Die Orchidee im Plastik Karton*, stems from the pre-Bausch forms of German Expressionism from the 1920s and 1930s.

Liz Aggiss was one of the choreographers chosen to represent Britain at the Twentieth International Choreographic Meeting at Bagnolet, France (June 1990). The Dance Theatre category was won by **Aletta Collins** for a 1988 work, *Gang of Five*, that she made for Phoenix Dance Company. She also won the New Choreography Award (Bonnie Bird Choreographic Fund) within the Bagnolet competition. Aletta Collins trained at the London School of Contemporary Dance and rapidly established a career as a freelance choreographer, working for large opera companies as well as small dance groups and for London Contemporary Dance Theatre (which she joined as a dancer in May 1990).

Phoenix Dance Company is a group of black dancers based in the northern city of Leeds. (Most of the original dancers came from Harehills School in Leeds.) Company members make their own choreography, under the artistic directorship of Neville Campbell, and new works are regularly commissioned from a wide range of choreographers. Phoenix, which tours middle-scale theatres, mainly in Britain, is not so much a black dance company as a group of contemporary dancers who are black. Since Easter 1990 the company has expanded its formerly all-male membership to include four women.

Last autumn's Umbrella Festival was a celebration of French dance, currently bearing the fruits of enviable government investment in the arts. Despite this year's increased funds and growing business support for dance, many of Britain's smaller dance companies face the threat of closure, with wages often below Equity minimum rates, and with the stresses and precariousness of continually having to search for business sponsorship. While the upside of this situation can produce a greater degree of professionalism, the downside can be reduced experimentation, loss of potential in developing artists who happen to have less aptitude for business, and greater difficulties for new talent to emerge. Fortunately many remain ever-inventive in the face of adversity; initiatives such as the Bonnie Bird Choreographic Awards and the Place Portfolio Scheme, run by John Ashford, have done a great deal towards supporting new choreographic talent. Among this year's winners of the Bonnie Bird Awards was Louise Richards, who is joint Artistic Director of the Midlands-based group, **Motionhouse**. They are a promising company who, like Divas, have an admirable commitment to community work as well as to their theatre productions. Their new work, *The Ticking Man*, is an interesting fusion of styles from Richard's background in new dance, including contact improvisation, to a lively use of theatre, music and speech. Richard's award is for a duet with Emma Gladstone, formerly with Adventures in Motion Pictures and currently working with The Cholmondeleys.

Finally, it is good to be able to note that **Extemporary Dance Theatre** has emerged from a difficult and uncertain period to attain funding for the next year. Sean Walsh is the new Artistic Director and his past work includes the choreography for opera productions at the Royal Opera House, for English National Opera and for Scottish Opera. In autumn 1990, Extemporary will present his first work for the company. *A Flaming Desire* is a full-length modern setting of the Faust tale with live music composed by Jeremy Sams. No doubt much will hang on it for the future of this popular touring company.

Germs: Advanced Lessons and Social Skills: Yolande Snaith and Kathy Crick.

USA

Joan Acocella

In the American dance world at this moment a primary concern is money. Rising costs, cuts in federal funding, repeal of tax benefits to private contributors: these are the causes normally cited for the financial problems facing so many dance companies. Natural causes should also be taken into account; that is, it may simply be that the dance boom of the 1960s and 1970s resulted in more growth than can now be supported either by contributions or by box office. Whatever the reasons, many companies, large and small, are suffering. Dance Theatre of Harlem, facing a projected deficit of $1.7 million, cancelled its 1990 New York season and European tour and, as of 1 April 1990, began what is projected to be a six-month lay-off of most staff. (The DTH school will continue its operations.) American Ballet Theatre, though far larger, is also facing a deficit of $1 million. The Martha Graham troupe had to put its dancers on an unusually long, two-month lay-off in early 1990: now back in rehearsal, the company has announced that in order to make money, it is going to undertake licensing and endorsement projects. (According to the *New York Times*, 'negotiations are under way to market a line of Martha Graham clothes, dancewear and accessories next year in Japan'.) The troupes of Murray Louis and Alwin Nikolais merged, partly as a cost-cutting measure. Other companies, such as San Jose/Cleveland Ballet and Cincinnati/New Orleans City Ballet, are using split bases to help shore up their finances. A split base is not a cure-all however. It was recently revealed that the **Joffrey Ballet**, which has been dividing its operations between New York and Los Angeles since 1983, has accumulated not only a deficit of $1 million, but also a debt of $800,000 in unpaid payroll withholding taxes.

Whether in the form of restraints or actual crises, these money problems have caused a great shift of power within dance companies: more and more decision-making authority is being transferred from the artistic to the administrative chiefs. The Joffrey offers a turbulent example. When, in April of 1990, the extent of the company's debt was made clear, the board of directors voted to establish a nine-member 'operating committee'. In the face of this infringement of his authority Gerald Arpino, who had been Artistic Director of the company since the death of Robert Joffrey in 1988, resigned and withdrew his and Joffrey's ballets from the company's repertory. Arpino was a co-founder of the company (with Joffrey), and in recent years his ballets have constituted about one-third of the repertory. Sentimental and danceable, they are popular with the general audience (less so with critics), and their removal would have radically altered the look of the company. By June, Arpino and the board had made peace, and Arpino returned to his post as Artistic Director, with a ten-member 'executive committee' (of which he is one member) which, according to the Joffrey press office, 'will help run the company on a day-to-day basis'. How this arrangement will prosper remains to be seen, but the power struggle at the Joffrey is simply one of many cases. In January 1990, just prior to the outbreak of the Joffrey dispute, **Pennsylvania Ballet** dismissed its Director of eight years, Robert Weiss, and his Artistic Associate, Richard Tanner, after a long period of bitter disagreement over money. Weiss has been replaced by Christopher d'Amboise – like him, a former New York City Ballet principal dancer.

American Ballet Theatre

Elsewhere, boards have simply hired administrative personnel as artistic directors. The most striking recent example is that of **American Ballet Theatre**. In June of 1989 Mikhail Baryshnikov, who had served as ABT's Artistic Director for nine years (during which time he had frequently clashed with his board over his unwillingness to take part in fund-raising functions), announced that he would leave his post in June 1990, after having seen the company through its big fiftieth-anniversary season. In other words, he was giving a year's notice. This gradual transition was not to be, however. Within three months, as a result of cost-cutting decisions on the part of the company's Executive Director, Jane Hermann, and also her decision to remove his assistant, Charles France, Baryshnikov resigned abruptly. Soon thereafter the board of trustees appointed Hermann as Director (i.e. artistic as well as executive director) of the troupe. She has a co-director, the set designer Oliver Smith, who in fact already served as co-director of the company (with Lucia Chase) from 1945 to 1980, but it appears to be Hermann, a professional administrator, who now has primary responsibility for artistic decisions at ABT.

It should be added that this growing dominance of administrative over artistic personnel is due not just to financial but also to artistic shortages. At this moment American ballet has very few artistic directors whose prestige as artists is such that their boards are reluctant to challenge them. 'Après moi, le board,' George Balanchine is reported to have said, and his prophecy, not inapplicable to his own company, New York City Ballet, has proved more true for others. The founding generation is dying off, and being replaced by middle-aged dancers who, without any pressing wish or ability to create dances, are nevertheless in need of a second career. In such a situation, it is no surprise that the boards have seized the reins.

Soviet Visitors

Aside from financial hardship, the other foremost trend in American dance, or at least American ballet, during the last year has been the continuing exchange with the Soviet Union. Five years ago the United States was effectively cut off from Soviet ballet. Stung by defections, the **Kirov** had not touched the American shore for twenty years, the **Bolshoi** for six. (During the Bolshoi's prior visit, in 1979, Alexander Godunov had defected.) Since then, thanks to *glasnost*, the Kirov has visited three times (full company in 1986 and 1989, touring company in 1987); the Bolshoi has come twice (full company in 1988, touring company in 1989) and will return in the summer of 1990. American troupes in turn have made Russian tours – Dance Theatre of Harlem in 1988, the Trisha Brown Company and the Margaret Jenkins Dance Company in 1989 – but for us the export has been minor compared with the import. Not only the large ballet troupes but also smaller ones – an ensemble from the Bolshoi Ballet Academy, a touring group led by Vladimir Vasiliev – have arrived, as have non-ballet companies such as the Alexandrov Red Army Song and Dance Ensemble, the Rustavi Company from Georgia and the Don Cossacks from Rostov.

Dancers have journeyed here by themselves as well. Andris Liepa of the Bolshoi performed with American Ballet Theatre in 1988/9. During ABT's 1990 season, Farukh Ruzimatov of the Kirov has been dancing with the company on a regular contract. As guests, ABT has had Ludmila Semenyaka for two performances of *The Sleeping Beauty* and Vladimir Vasiliev, with Ekaterina Maximova, in what he claimed would be his last performance of *Giselle*. (Despite his diminished technical powers, this was a thrilling performance.) Alexander Lunev, of the Kirov, has just been hired by Boston Ballet.

Probably more important has been the arrival of Russian teachers and coaches. Irina Kolpakova of the Kirov has spent much of the past year at ABT coaching dancers in the classical repertory. Ninel Kurgapkina, the celebrated Kirov pedagogue, spent April of 1990 at the School of American Ballet, New York City Ballet's affiliate academy, teaching variations class. Nikita Dolgushin, the great *danseur noble* of the 1960s, now Dean of the dance department at Leningrad State Conservatory, taught at Towson State University near Baltimore. The roster of Russian teachers scheduled to work in the United States during the summer of 1990 includes Sophia Golovkina, Asaf Messerer, Raisa Struchkova, Marina Kondratyeva, and Mikhail Korogodsky from the Bolshoi and Oleg Vinogradov, Kolpakova and Kurgapkina of the Kirov. One wonders whether there will be any teachers left in Russia. There have been joint ventures as well. In 1989, 150 students from the School of American Ballet spent a week working and performing with students from the Vaganova Choreographic Institute at the Holland Festival in Amsterdam.

Russian dance history, too, has made its way to the United States. In the fall of 1989, the Leningrad State Museum of Theatre and Music sent to New York City an exhibition called '100 Years of Russian Ballet, 1830–1930,' including some rare and revelatory items from the Soviet avant-garde of the 1920s. Soon thereafter, Duke University Press brought out a long-awaited translation of Elizabeth Souritz's *Soviet Choreographers in the 1920s* (originally published in Moscow in 1979); in English, this is the first book-length account of that immensely fertile period in dance history. Earlier in the year, Souritz visited the United States together with the dance historian Vera Krasovskaya and the critic Vadim Gayevsky. (For Krasovskaya and Gayevsky, this was the first trip to the United States.) The three of them spoke to audiences in New York and Miami, and an essay by Gayevsky on Balanchine's *Serenade* was published in the *New York Times*.

Repertory Exchanges

Finally, there have been exchanges of repertory. ABT performed *Elegy*, a romantic *pas de deux* by Vladimir Vasiliev; San Francisco Ballet is performing Leonid Jacobson's *Rodin*, staged for them by the choreographer's widow, Irina Jacobson, a former Kirov soloist who now teaches at SFB and at its school. Konstantin Sergeyev, with the help of Natalia Dudinskaya, set his Kirov version of *Swan Lake* on Boston Ballet, where each of the casts was led by a Russian dancer (Nina Ananiashvili, Konstantin Zaklinsky, Alexander Fadeyechev, Yulia Makhalina, Alexander Lunev and Tatiana Terekhova were the guests) paired with a Boston Ballet dancer. In turn, the Kirov had added to its repertory two Balanchine ballets: *Theme and Variations*, set on them by former New York City Ballet soloist (and current co-director of Pacific Northwest Ballet) Francia Russell, and *Scotch Symphony*, set by the great Balanchine ballerina Suzanne Farrell. This spread of the Balanchine repertory to the Kirov is particularly momentous, for it represents a home-coming: the great modernist style that Balanchine constructed on the base of Petipa's classicism returns to the home of that classicism. And in a time when there has been little new ballet choreography of real interest, this radical transfer might jolt loose some creative impulse. What the Russians could learn from Balanchine ballets, if they wished, is speed, objectivity, and musical fidelity. What the Americans might learn from the Russians – and what the Russian teachers have been stressing in their classes here – is refinement and detail in the upper body, together with co-ordination of upper and lower body. The Russians' experience of learning Balanchine, and our experience of watching them perform both Balanchine (during the 1989 Kirov tour) and their own repertory, advances us in both directions.

Regional Ballet

Outside New York, the general trend among ballet companies has been one of retrenchment. Again, this follows a period of exuberant expansion: the 'regional ballet' movement of the 1960s and 1970s. Many regional companies have been forced to cut back their staff, their repertory, and their artistic ambitions. And yet some troupes have managed this year to finance very grand projects, such as the *glasnost Swan Lake* at **Boston Ballet**, a new production of *The Sleeping Beauty* at **San Francisco Ballet**, staged by Artistic Director Helgi Tomasson, and a new *Sleeping Beauty* at **Houston Ballet** as well, in a staging by its Director, Ben Stevenson.

Perhaps the strongest trend in regional ballet repertory is the adoption of Balanchine ballets, a process hastened by the hegemony of New York City Ballet alumni over American ballet's artistic directorships. (Pennsylvania Ballet, San Francisco Ballet, Pittsburgh Ballet Theatre, Pacific North-

Altynai Asylmuratova warming up on stage before the Kirov Ballet's first performance of Balanchine's *Theme and Variations* in Leningrad.　　　PHOTO: NANCY REYNOLDS

Konstantin Sergeyev of the Kirov rehearsing the Boston Ballet in his new production of *Swan Lake* for the company.   PHOTO: J. BERNDT

west Ballet, Miami City Ballet, Atlanta Ballet, Ballet Chicago, Ballet of Los Angeles, Fort Worth Ballet, State Ballet of Missouri, Ballet Oklahoma and Dance Theatre of Harlem, not to mention New York City Ballet, are all currently directed by ex-Balanchine dancers.) According to Barbara Horgan, executrix of the Balanchine estate, approximately fifty American dance companies now have a Balanchine repertory (i.e. at least one Balanchine ballet), and that repertory is growing: the estate licenses approximately twenty new stagings and twenty restorations of earlier stagings per year.

Balanchine's greatness is now almost universally acknowledged – indeed, institutionalized, like Picasso's. A documentary entitled *Dancing for Mr B.*, by Anne Belle and Deborah Dickson, had its première at the New York Film Festival in 1989 and was later shown on public television. It shows six Balanchine dancers (Mary Ellen Moylan, Maria Tallchief, Melissa Hayden, Allegra Kent, Merrill Ashley and Darci Kistler) describing their work with him; intercut with the interviews is archival footage of these same dancers in his ballets. That the public should be deemed interested in Balanchine, not just in the usual, romantic artist/creator terms but as the patient builder of a *style* of dancing shows how far his reputation has risen since his death.

New Ballet Choreography

At the same time, the sense of depletion which beset the ballet world with the death of Balanchine – and the deaths of Ashton, Tudor and Robert Joffrey – is still strong. The most imaginative new ballet choreography produced in the United States in the last few years has been the work of **Mark Morris** and **Twyla Tharp**, both of them modern-dance choreographers (or, in Tharp's case, formerly so) and both, at this moment, officially unconnected with any major ballet company. Morris has his own modern dance troupe, currently based at the Théâtre de la Monnaie in Brussels – this move was yet another unhappy consequence of the current money troubles in American dance – and he is occupied with making work for them. He has made one ballet this year, *Ein Herz* (to J. S. Bach's Cantata BWV 134), but in France, for the Paris Opéra Ballet, not in the United States. He has made nothing for an American ballet company since his beautiful *Drink to Me Only with Thine Eyes* for ABT in 1988.

As for Tharp, she became an artistic associate of ABT under Baryshnikov in 1988, adding to its repertory several works that she had made for her own company, Twyla Tharp Dance (which she dissolved upon joining ABT), together with a number of new ballets made especially for ABT. In 1989 the company premièred a trio of new pieces by her: *Everlast*, with music by Jerome Kern and with a plot (big, sweet, stupid boxing champion, loved by artless serving girl, ignores her and courts spoiled heiress, who does not love him, etc.) based on the small-scale musicals that Kern wrote for New York's Princess Theatre in the 1910s and 1920s: *Bum's Rush*, also based on popular comedy but of the less genteel sort (vaudeville, radio shows, burlesque) and set to a piano score by Dick Hyman interlarded with howls, grunts, beer songs, animal noises and other rude sounds; and *Quartet*, a rigorous abstract piece to music by the minimalist composer Terry Riley. The programme was not, in the end, a great success: Tharp has for years been fascinated by old-style popular comedy, but she is not always able to draw the audience in with her. Still, it was a fresh and sophisticated show, with some beautifully wrought dances.

When Baryshnikov left, Tharp – along with ABT's other 'artistic associate', Kenneth MacMillan – gave up her post with the company. Nevertheless, as planned, she created a ballet for the company's fiftieth anniversary season. This was *Brief Fling* (1990), a large (cast of eighteen), long pure-dance piece to music by Michel Colombier, incorporating Percy Grainger songs. *Brief Fling* is an immensely successful work in Tharp's classic style. As in *Push Comes to Shove* (1976), her first work for ABT, the stage picture is one of tamed disorder – various troops of dancers pursuing seemingly disparate manoeuvres – and the dancing is a humorous but at the same time heroically virtuosic extension of the *danse d'école*. Between *Brief Fling* and *Sinatra Songs*, a suite of couple dances (indeed, an encyclopaedia of couple dancing) created for her own company in 1982 and first performed by ABT in 1990, Tharp's contribution to new repertory at ABT within the last year has been immensely distinguished, far more so than that of anyone else, not only at ABT but at any other major company in the United States. Yet she still has no permanent arrangement with ABT. The only associate the artistic staff has taken on so far is Natalia Makarova, whose appointment as artistic adviser was announced in June 1990.

That the most talented ballet choreographer now residing in the United States should be unmoored to any company is somehow typical of the times. Throughout the American dance world, but especially the ballet world, there is the sense that a great age has passed, with the next great age nowhere in sight.

New York City Ballet

At **New York City Ballet**, our country's most celebrated dance institution, the *Götterdämmerung* has been especially pronounced. Balanchine died in 1983. Now, after a decent interval, it seems that the foremost guardians of his art are leaving the field of action. In 1989/90 Suzanne Farrell and Patricia McBride, two great Balanchine ballerinas, retired from the stage; Robert Irving, the company's long-time music director, ceased to perform with the company; and, most momentous of all, Lincoln Kirstein, who wooed Balanchine to America and with him founded New York City Ballet and the School of American Ballet, retired as general director of the former and president of the latter. (Robert Lindgren, once a soloist at New York City Ballet, left his job as director of the North Carolina School of the Arts to take Kirstein's place at SAB). Jerome Robbins who, so different from Balanchine, had for years created with him the NYCB repertory – and who, after his death, had taken the post of co-ballet-master-in-chief with Peter Martins – also resigned. The main feature of the company's 1990 spring season was a two-week festival of his work, in honour of his departure.

With all these changes at New York City Ballet there have been corresponding changes in repertory, the most significant being the gradual reduction of Balanchine ballets. From 1978 through 1980, Balanchine's last years of healthy productivity, his ballets accounted for an average of 76 per cent of the company's performances (*Nutcracker* excluded). Since that time they have dropped to an average of 59 per cent, the difference being taken up largely by the ballets of Peter Martins, which are by no means the equal of what they are replacing. In this process, very great works are being threatened with extinction. To name two, *Agon* has been out of regular repertory now for five seasons, *La Valse* for seven. It is not known whether they can now be faithfully remounted.

But the passing of Balanchine, his people and his works is only the most monumental of our losses. **Alvin Ailey** died in late 1989, leaving a repertory that had declined sharply since Ailey's great beginnings and a company that was also weakened. (The celebrated Ailey dancer Judith Jamison has taken over as Artistic Director, and given her success with her own troupe, the Jamison Project – now melded into the Ailey – this bodes well for the company.) **Martha Graham**, in the meantime, is ninety-six years old. The new works presented by her company under her name seem pastiche at best, while her older works, including the very greatest, such as *Appalachian Spring*, are often given shoddy performances.

In this atmosphere of loss, there has been a turning toward the past. The goals of ABT's new administration offer a good example. The new directors have made it known that they plan to use guest artists (indeed, they have already done so) to stress their dancers' 'personalities', and – after Baryshnikov's emphasis on Balanchine and on younger classicists – to return to a more narrative and expressionist choreography: in old works, Tudor and de Mille revivals; in new works, people such as Glen Tetley and Jiři Kylián. (Kylián's *Sinfonietta* has already been slotted in for the 1990/1 season, and he has reportedly promised to make a new work for the company as well.) In other words, what the new administration seems to be planning is, in large measure, a return to the spirit of Lucia Chase's administration (1945–80), which preceded Baryshnikov's.

Reconstructions

Nostalgia for the past, together with the scarcity of talented young choreographers, is also reflected in the number of so-called historical reconstructions now being mounted by major American companies. Though it was hardly the first important ballet reconstruction, the version of Nijinsky's *Rite of Spring* mounted by Millicent Hodson and Kenneth Archer for the Joffrey Ballet in 1987, followed by their version of Balanchine's *Cotillon* in 1988 (also for the Joffrey), was probably the thing that kicked off the current rage for reconstructions. The major entries during the past year have been Balanchine's 1944/72 *Danses concertantes* at New York City Ballet, Bronislava Nijinska's 1952 *Rondo Capriccioso* at Dance Theatre of Harlem, Nijinska's 1924 *Le Train bleu* at Oakland Ballet, the 'Steps in the Street' section from Graham's 1936 *Chronicle* at the Graham company, and the new version of *Afternoon of a Faun* that Ann Hutchinson Guest has extracted from Nijinsky's notations of the ballet and set on the Juilliard Dance Ensemble. All of historical interest, these reconstructions vary in their theatrical power. (The Nijinska works, at least as reconstructed, proved very minor compared to *Les Noces* and *Les Biches*.)

Darci Kistler and Robert La Fosse in New York City Ballet's revival of Balanchine's *Danses concertantes*.   PHOTO: PAUL KOLNIK

177

And all were accompanied by considerable confusion on the part of the critics. Should a production be praised simply because it is said to be a replica of an historically important work? If the reconstruction is an artistic failure, is this the fault of the original or of the reconstructors? Or, to describe the situation more pointedly, if the critic is not in a position to assess the authenticity of the production, as is usually the case, should he or she then withhold judgement as to its artistic value? Finally, what *is* authenticity in a dance reconstruction? Considering how dance exists in time, altering with each performance, changing with different performers, what in fact are we looking at in most reconstructions if not an assemblage of disparate pieces culled from organically different occasions? The whole reconstruction trend, while it has raised interesting questions about the nature of dance and even resulted in some good productions, has been attended by a discouraging amount of producer ballyhoo, audience gullibility, and critical timidity.

Conservatism

Beyond reconstructions, the general conservatism of contemporary American ballet can be seen in the number of new productions of the classics – this past year, two major new *Swan Lake*s (ABT and Boston Ballet) and two *Sleeping Beauty*s (Houston Ballet and San Francisco Ballet) – despite the cost of these large court ballets, and also in the new choreography. The house choreographers of most of our major companies – Peter Martins at New York City Ballet, Helgi Tomasson at San Francisco Ballet, Robert Weiss at Pennsylvania Ballet (until recently), Ben Stevenson at Houston Ballet, Clark Tippet at ABT – have produced works that, while sometimes very attractive, discover no new grounds for expressiveness in the classical vocabulary. The premières at New York City Ballet during the last year offer a good illustration. Richard Tanner, as guest choreographer, contributed *Prague Symphony*, a tidy, finicky neo-classical ballet which was completely overshadowed by the great Mozart symphony to which it was set. Peter Martins made two works of a sleeker, more up-to-date variety, *Echo* and *Fearful Symmetries*, both to scores by the young American composer Michael Torke, who by virtue of Martins's fondness for his work has become the closest thing to a house composer since Stravinsky. But just as Tanner's work was a pale reflection of Balanchine's Mozartian mode, so whatever was eye-catching in the Martins ballets instantly recalled Balanchine's Stravinskian mode.

Modern Dance

In modern dance there is no single galvanizing young leader of the kind that Graham was for her generation. **Mark Morris**, who would be the foremost candidate for this position, has been working in Brussels since 1988. Still, he has brought some of his works here on tour. In the summer of 1989 his company had a season at Jacob's Pillow Dance Festival; on the same tour, but in Boston, they presented his *Dido and Aeneas*, a dance version of Purcell's opera in which Morris takes both the role of Dido and that of the Sorceress. This work, like the rest of Morris's ten-year *œuvre*, shows a weighted but often highly tooled dance style, a fondness for recurring motifs, a profound musicality, an obsession with history, a love of bad-boy humour, an unselfconscious humanism, and an immensely fertile dance imagination, the last quality especially evident in *Dido*'s split between two dance styles: a noble angularity for the queen and her court, a more free, maenadic, Duncanesque look for the witches' den.

Morris will be touring the United States extensively in late 1990 and will probably return here permanently when his contract with the Monnaie expires in mid-1991. Today his influence can be detected in the work of several young choreographers; it will no doubt spread. Despite his removal to Belgium, he is widely recognized as the most important modern-dance choreographer to emerge in the United States in the last decade. The controversies surrounding his Brussels seasons have merely served, in his absence, to keep his name in the papers and to encourage American critics to travel to Belgium to see his new work.

Politics and Dance

A very important trend in the last few years has been the invasion of political feeling into modern dance. Politics is of course nothing new in modern dance. It is a tide which ebbs and flows. But throughout the 1980s it flowed noticeably, and by the end of the decade two related phenomena had resulted in an extreme politicization of the field.

The first is AIDS, the fatal disease that has so stricken the homosexual community in the United States. Here as elsewhere, the dance profession is disproportionately homosexual. Therefore it has suffered disproportionately from AIDS, and anger over the government's slowness in allocating appropriate funds for AIDS research, together with renewed anger over having to occupy a widely scorned position in the society at large, has spilled into dance.

The second spur to the politicizing of dance in the past year has been a controversy over censorship. In June 1989 the Corcoran Gallery of Art in Washington, DC, cancelled a scheduled exhibition of photographs by Robert Mapplethorpe which included images of homosexual and sadomasochistic content. There were also photographs of children that could be construed as sexually provocative. This was a travelling exhibition which, prior to the Corcoran cancellation, had been seen in several cities and had elicited a certain amount of public outcry, the more so in that the show was funded in part by the National Endowment for the Arts; that is, by the taxpayers' money. After the Corcoran withdrawal, however, the controversy became extremely bitter, one side claiming that public money should not be used to support art that most of the public would consider obscene, the other side claiming that the government had no right to dictate the content of art and that to do so was a violation of the right to free expression guaranteed by the First Amendment to the United States Constitution. The fact that Mapplethorpe had died of AIDS shortly before the Corcoran cancellation fanned the controversy. Senator Jesse Helms of North Carolina proposed to Congress legislation barring the National Endowment for the Arts from funding projects considered obscene or pornographic; this legislation is still pending. Others have urged the actual dismantling of the NEA, whose charter is due to expire shortly. President Bush at first recommended that the NEA be rechartered for five years without restriction. (He later reduced his recommendation to one year.) Others have proposed restrictions of various degrees of stringency: that NEA-supported art must not be obscene, that it must not desecrate the flag, that it must reflect 'American ideals,' and so on. Conservative and liberal elements in the society have rallied hotly to the two sides of this issue.

Together with AIDS, this controversy has deeply affected dance. In the last few years, and more so in the last year, there has been a great wave of works dealing with sexual transgression and sexual heterodoxy. Bill T. Jones, Phyllis Lamhut and Jeff McMahon have presented pieces directly expressing grief and anger over AIDS. (In one of the pieces included in his 1989 season, Jones, whose longtime partner Arnie Zane had recently died of AIDS, brought onstage a member of his company – Demian Acquavella, now dead – who was so disabled by the disease that he had to crawl on the floor, a manoeuvre that some people saw as effective political theatre and others as audience manipulation.) Many choreographers and performance artists – Steve Gross, Marty Pottenger, Tim Miller, Richard Elovich, David Cale, Reno, Holly Hughes, Lisa Kron – have presented works about homosexuality. The performance artist Karen Finley has addressed sexual abuse and incest. Others will use vivid sexual material as simply one of many kinds of imagery. In all, though, the number of dance works dealing with sexual non-conformity and allied subjects (physical illness, abuse of women, social catastrophe) has been extraordinary. 'Obscenity', together with its theatrical adjuncts – nudity, cross-dressing – is a staple of today's experimental dance and performance art, at least in New York.

Multiculturalism

Another political trend in American dance is 'multiculturalism', the movement to recognize the various ethnic groups, especially the less privileged ones, which go to make up the population of the United States. As with the sexual-politics trend just described, multiculturalism is an anti-authoritarian effort, the authority in this case being white people of European descent and the kinds of dance created by them. The proponents of multiculturalism argue that funders, presenters, critics and other crucial supporters of dance pay attention only to Euroamerican forms (e.g. ballet, post-modern dance) and ignore the dancing which has risen out of other groups, such as blacks, Latinos and American Indians. In some major population centres, such as San Francisco and Los Angeles, there is no longer a white majority: the multicultural argument is that 'white' dance should therefore not command a majority of resources. The publicity attendant upon the 1989 concerts of the **American Indian Dance Theatre** which presents theatricalized versions of the traditional dances of many different American Indian tribes, was in some measure a response to this movement. So was the decision to make multiculturalism the subject of the 1990 Dance Critics Association conference, which will include many different forms of 'ethnic' dance together with symposia on how critics reared on European-derived forms should approach these other styles.

Humanism

Beyond the strictly political, there appears to be a far more humanistic emphasis in the modern dance of today. Many, many modern dance works seem to be concerned with how people should (and do) treat one another and how communities should live. An exemplary work of this order was **Susan Marshall**'s *Articles of Faith*, a forty-minute piece presented under the palm trees of the winter garden of New York City's World Financial Centre in March of 1990. It is ironic that a huge marble-and-glass office complex, a palace of commerce, should be the setting for a work in which dancers clad in white muslin draperies act out the primal dramas of social organization – dominance, co-operation, betrayal – but this is the rule of today. As our world becomes increasingly dominated by the mass media and the questionable values which govern that arena, our dance art is, at least for the moment, increasingly concerned with the values of the hearth or the town meeting. This was amply demonstrated in a series called **Manmade** at New York City's Joyce Theatre in early 1990. A large number of the choreographers in this series (Bill Young, Ralph Lemon, Doug Varone, Randy Warshaw), ostensibly linked only by the fact that they were all male, took on the great human themes: the relationship of friend to friend, of lover to lover, of the individual to the group. And they addressed them in a similar tone: tender and thoughtful. The same is true of recent concerts by Lar Lubovitch, Bebe Miller and David Dorfman. (Rocky Bornstein and Johanna Boyce have taken on the subject of motherhood.) Together with this new humanistic emphasis, there has been a return to a more fluid, sweeping, lyrical line reminiscent of José Limón and other idealistic-minded choreographers from the 1950s.

Surrealism

In other corners of contemporary dance there is a darker psychology afoot, a species of surrealism. In **Tere O'Connor**'s 1989 *Four Sister Dances* we see five people who seem to be siblings. (As in other O'Connor pieces they wear little unisex suits that look like school uniforms.) With febrile intensity, they perform a sort of barefoot ballet combined with mysterious gestures – fallings, shiverings, finger-twiddlings – which clearly mean something very dire though we never know exactly what. The collective called **Kinematic** (Tamar Kotoske, Maria Lakis, Mary Richter) makes work that, while it shows a clearer narrative line, has a similarly enigmatic tone. Their 1990 *Paradise for the Worried*, about a doctor humbled by a miracle, was a good example. **Ohad Naharin**, trained in his native Israel and then at the Martha Graham school and the Juilliard School in New York, seems now to be mining the same vein. His recent long piece, *Sinking of the Titanic*, looked like a dream that might have been dreamed by the drowned themselves, dancing under the sea.

Sarah Perron, Chrysa Parkinson and Tere O'Connor in O'Connor's *Four Sister Dances*.

As humanistic feeling has come to the forefront, the radical expressionism of German *Tanztheater* and Japanese *butoh* has lost some of the fascination that it exercised over American audiences in the mid-1980s. In 1989/90 the Brooklyn Academy of Music's influential Next Wave Festival included a series of so-called **Ruhrworks**, artworks from West Germany's industrial Ruhr Valley. Of the several dance programmes in the series, only Susanne Linke's reconstructions of the works of her teacher Dore Hoyer were truly successful. Reinhild Hoffmann's *Machandel* (Juniper Tree), a classic work of *Tanztheater* (fragmented narratives, colliding time planes, despair, regressive imagery, viscous substances being smeared on various surfaces), was coolly received, as was Min Tanaka's *butoh*-inspired *Can We Dance a Landscape?*, a collaboration with the Dutch painter Karel Appel. On the other hand, the work of **Eiko and Koma**, a Japanese-born husband-and-wife team who have been in the United States since 1976, becomes ever stronger. Their 1990 *Passage*, which they performed naked in what seemed a vast pool of gore edged in grey satin, had a ghastly glamour, and together with other aspects of the piece, this seemed to signal a transition to a kind of surrealism.

Paul Taylor

Apart from Graham, whose older repertory commands more respect than any of her recent work, the two most revered and influential people in American modern dance are Merce Cunningham and Paul Taylor. The **Taylor** company is not in its best form at this moment. Dominated for years by large, burly men, the male ranks are now peopled by smaller men, who are only slowly coming to possess a repertory made for different bodies. In 1990, furthermore, Taylor's great star, Kate Johnson, will leave the company, and she is not easily replaceable. Taylor's two new works for his 1990 thirty-fifth anniversary season, *The Sorcerer's Sofa* and *Of Bright and Blue Birds and the Gala Sun*, continue his exploration of good and evil and, in the evil department, of guilt and terror within the family. *The Sorcerer's Sofa*, a comic work set to Dukas's *Sorcerer's Apprentice*, takes place in a psychiatrist's office. *Of Bright and Blue Birds*, an evening-long (seventy-eight minutes) work incorporating the 1987 *Syzygy* and set, like *Syzygy*, to a score by Donald York, the company's music director, the setting and characters are less specific. As in other Taylor works, what we see is the human community, alternately blessed and damned, and expressing this primarily through dance means: speed, shape, rhythm, attack.

Merce Cunningham

Cunningham created three new works this past year: *August Pace* (1989), with music by Michael Pugliese and set and costumes by Afrika (Sergei

Bugaev); *Inventions* (1989), with a score by John Cage and set and costumes by Carl Kielblock: and *Polarity* (1990), with music by David Tudor,
costumes by William Anastasi and a set consisting of two greatly enlarged
nature drawings – one of a rabbit, one of two birds – by Cunningham,
adapted by Anastasi. *August Pace*, a series of duets, was probably American
dance's first *glasnost* collaboration: the 23-year-old Afrika is a Soviet
painter. *Polarity*, in which the dancers seemed at times to huddle
conspiratorially and at other times to suffer and die, is a continuation of the
tragic/elegiac strain that for the last decade has been so pronounced in the
work of this supposedly dry, cool, abstract choreographer.

As has been pointed out by so many observers, the avant-garde
choreographers of the 1960s and early 1970s, so analytic and anti-theatrical
in their early work for Judson Dance Theater and the improvizational collective Grand Union, are now far more expressionist and theatrical. **Trisha
Brown**'s 1989 *Astral Convertible* had a toughness of tone and structure
utterly foreign to her loose-look works of the 1970s and early 1980s. (It
should be added that Robert Rauschenberg's interactive set, whereby the
dancers' movements set off changes in sound and lighting, was a pure
throwback to the 1960s.) **Douglas Dunn**, like Brown one of the most
conceptual choreographers of the Judson/Grand Union period, now uses
elaborate sets and costumes, accessible music – or at least fragments

Dean Moss, Karen Graham and Scott Cunningham in David Gordon's cumulative work,
United States (1987–90), using text, dance and materials from different regions of the USA.
PHOTO: ANDREW ECCLES

thereof – and, occasionally, dancey movement, as can be seen in his recent *Sky Eye*, dressed in monk's robes and set to a collage score ranging from the liturgical chants of Abbess Hildegard of Bingen, to Debussy's *Nuages*, to the songs of rain-forest pygmies.

David Gordon spent the years 1987 to early 1990 creating a cumulative dance work called *United States*, dealing with, financed by and with materials contributed from different regions of the country: New England, Minnesota, San Francisco, New York and so forth. Though the piece contained a great deal of spoken text (on tape), it was nevertheless one of Gordon's most pure-dance pieces. In his present project, *Mysteries, and What's So Funny?*, he returns to the theme of family which has occupied him in earlier works and again, as in earlier works, sets his dancers talking. **Lucinda Childs**, whose company was forced by financial problems to cease performing for almost a year in 1988/9, came back in mid-1989 with *Mayday*, a work full of highly poetic, quasi-narrative imagery, quite different from the sleek manoeuvres of Child's classic style. Like the Childs company – indeed, like most middle-sized modern-dance companies in the United States – **Laura Dean**'s troupe has been intermittently stalled by money problems, but she too presented recently a very fully programmed New York season. Her old, minimalist works, such as *Tympani* (1981), are still her most powerful creations. Her new pieces, like those of so many of her colleagues from the 1960s and 1970s, are less austere, less intransigent, more accessible, more pretty.

USSR

Elizabeth Souritz

The new theatre season begins for most Soviet companies in September, but this season there was an important summer event. In June 1989, the sixth competition for ballet dancers was held in Moscow. The first was in 1969, so this was a jubilee, which did not prevent critics and juries in interviews and private conversations expressing their disappointment. They feel that the prestige of the Moscow competition is not as high as it used to be and this year there was less talent among the competing dancers, with few discoveries or pleasant surprises. There were hardly any representatives from such important ballet schools as those of France and

Denmark, not to mention English dancers who, as far as I know, have never taken part in the Moscow competition. Even some of the first-rate Soviet schools sent no one: Leningrad and Perm, for instance.

In the press bureau of the competition there was plenty of opportunity for all interested in ballet to meet and discuss their impressions. The magazine *Soviet Ballet* later published articles expressing different opinions, some of them unfavourable. Asaf Messerer, for instance, one of the most famous ballet teachers, criticized the training of boys. He feels their dancing is often without expression, just a display of tricks. Another topic that many brought up was the authenticity of the choreography in the classical *pas de deux* and variations. For the Moscow competition, dancers have to choose from a list of dances, most of them belonging to ballets or the Russian repertoire of the nineteenth century. There are always complaints about dancers not keeping to the original choreography. However, we now have an innovation to help competitors in the future. To coincide with the competition, *Soyuzteatr* has issued a set of descriptions of thirty variations from famous classical ballets, with music, description of the dances (in words and ballet terms, not in notation) and photographs. In Russia they are available only in Russian, but outside the country they can be purchased in English and French.

Gold medals at the Moscow competition went to Christine McDermott, a pupil of Konstanze Vernon at the Munich school and to Galina Stepanenko and Vladimir Malakhov, both from Moscow.

This season none of the big companies belonging to the local opera houses gave any premières: neither the Bolshoi nor the Kirov, the Maly in Leningrad nor the Stanislavsky in Moscow (due to show a new *Romeo and Juliet* by Vladimir Vasiliev on 22 June), the Novosibirsk, Sverdlovsk nor any other important theatre in the provinces. It seems that the situation of deep crisis or stagnation which was diagnosed last year at the conference of representatives from the music theatres has not changed for the better. If one looks at the statistics published by *Soviet Ballet* magazine each season one sees that the list of leading ballets is always the same: *Swan Lake* is inevitably first and *Giselle* second, with *Don Quixote* or *Nutcracker* coming next. New productions do not seem to last, which reflects the politics of the theatres' management and also the taste of the audience, which is generally very conservative. For anything new, one has to look to the small companies which spring up here and there, sometimes on a semi-amateur basis and independent of the Ministry of Culture. Some are commercial ventures with little artistic value, but at times one finds talented people working there. Unfortunately, very little information about smaller companies appears in the press, especially if they work outside Moscow. Our theatres do not get regular press coverage. It can happen that even a première in a big opera house gets no reviews, so small experimental

Konstantin Zaklinsky in the Kirov's production of *The Sleeping Beauty*.   PHOTO: SNOWDON

groups stand even less chance of a mention. But I can recommend at least one dance group that I have seen recently and have found interesting: it is a company called **Experiment**, based in Perm under Yevgeny Panfilov. The ballet I have seen is *On the Race*, after a famous play by Mikhail Bulgakov which deals with the tragedy of people escaping from Russia during the revolution of 1917. The choreographer has used music by Alfred

Schnittke. The style of the choreography is closer to modern dance than ballet: highly strung, sometimes convulsive and passionate.

Perm is one place where things are happening. It has been a kind of 'ballet capital' of the Ural region since the war, when the Kirov theatre moved there and the Perm ballet school was founded by Leningrad teachers. Recently Perm has realized that it was the town where Diaghilev lived as a child and youth. Enthusiasts have started to research, the art gallery has held exhibitions and conferences, a group named Arabesque prints a newspaper called *Ballet of the Ural* and an association of lovers of ballet has been organized this season. Recently Sverdlovsk (also a town in the Ural region) decided to move in the same direction. A new company called **Pirouette** has been organized there by the choreographer Edwald Smirnov, a large group of young dancers having decided to break away from the local ballet attached to the opera house. They want a repertory of works by modern Western choreographers (Jerome Robbins, José Limón's *Moor's Pavane*, etc.) along with new ballets by Smirnov.

Another event of importance was the festival in honour of the centenary of Nijinsky's birth, which was held in **Moscow** in March. Two groups of people representing two institutions were involved in it. The Bolshoi, under Grigorovich, produced a revival of *Petrushka* with Irek Mukhamedov, and invited dancers from the Paris Opéra (Charles Jude, Florence Clerc, Manuel Legris and Natalie Riqué) to dance *L'Après-midi d'un faune* and *Le Spectre de la rose*. The Association of Music Theatres of the Actors' Union (its ballet section is headed by Vladimir Vasiliev), together with the magazine *Soviet Ballet* and the society *Soyuzteatr* arranged a very ambitious programme. There was an exhibition of photographs and documents (partly from Paris) and there were a number of performances by Leningrad and Moscow companies: *Petrushka* (Leningrad Maly theatre), *Le Faune* (Leningrad Conservatory), *Le Spectre* (Moscow Classical Ballet), *Nijinsky* (choreography by Natalia Volkova from the Leningrad Ensemble of Choreographic Miniatures). There was also a meeting of researchers, including Ivor Guest and Ann Hutchinson from England, Claudia Jöschke from Germany and Lynn Garafola from the United States. Videos of revivals of *Faune* and *Sacre du printemps* were shown. And there was another performance that attracted a large audience – Jorge Donn and the Mexican actress Cecilia Linsovsky gave a new version of Béjart's *Nijinsky, Clown of God* (for two performers).

On the whole, one should note that the Association of Music Theatres of the Actors' Union, which was organized last year, has done a lot to help arrange dance events. It continued to work even after a tragedy occurred: on 15 February, a fire destroyed the greater part of the six-storey building of the Actors' Union in Gorky Street. Even now, the full extent of the calamity cannot be appreciated, for it is not known what has been salvaged.

Vladimir Vasiliev and Ekaterina Maximova in *Fragment of an Autobiography* at the jubilee celebration of Vasiliev's fiftieth birthday at the Bolshoi.   PHOTO: DMITRY KULIKOV

Many precious archives, collections of manuscripts, photographs and tapes have perished.

Apart from the Nijinsky Festival, the Association has organized an evening to commemorate the late Maris Liepa, and his daughter, Ilse Liepa, gave a performance in memory of her father. In March, the Association arranged a festival of ballet schools in Perm. In Moscow, there was a conference of teachers of history of dance. In November, *Soviet Ballet* magazine held an international conference of editors of ballet magazines and ballet critics. There were guests from many countries: USA (Anna Kisselgoff), Germany (Rolf Garske), Japan (Kehji Usui), and others.

During this season, concerts (so-called benefit performances) were given by Vadim Pisarev, Bulat Ayukhanov (from the Kazakh Republic), Kai Kyrd (Estonia). Vladimir Vasiliev, who turned fifty, had a very grand jubilee performance at the Bolshoi.

A rare première of the season on 30 April was the first showing in Russia of the **Moscow Classical Ballet**'s new production of *Swan Lake* (made with the collaboration of the Entertainment Corporation of Great Britain). The

Alla Khaniashvili as Odile in Moscow Classical Ballet's production of *Swan Lake*, which received its Russian première this season, after touring Britain and America in 1988. Designs by the British theatre designer Tim Goodchild; costumes supervised by Kim Baker.

production had already been extensively toured in Britain and America. The staging is by the company's directors, Natalia Kasatkina and Vladimir Vassilyov: the choreography seems to be based mostly on the Moscow production by Gorsky – one of his versions which includes Petipa's choreography in the first act and Ivanov's in the second. The last act is the same as the one Asaf Messerer staged in 1937, apart from its ending. Messerer's was a happy one (Odette is changed back into a woman and united with Siegfried), while in this version they die together.

The production includes a Russian dance in Act III, which featured in the Moscow productions of the nineteenth century but not in the Petipa/ Ivanov Petersburg version of 1895: until now, only Grigorovich had used it in his Bolshoi production. So it seems that Kasatkina has taken bits of choreography from many versions, without succeeding in merging them into a meaningful whole or finding a fresh approach. Nevertheless, the audience seemed interested and happy. The press, as usual, has been slow in publishing any reviews.

There were fewer tours by foreign companies than we expected because the Martha Graham Company and American Ballet Theatre were unable to come. However, the Joyce Trisler company visited from the United States, Laocoon from West Germany, the Royal Winnipeg Ballet from Canada and the Hamburg Ballet (with Neumeier's *Peer Gynt*, which was much admired). London Contemporary Dance Theatre was scheduled to visit in July 1990. There was also a festival of avant-garde Flemish companies with works by Wim Vandekeybus and Anne Teresa de Keersmaeker.

PART IV

The Statistics of
Dance Companies

Australia

Salary information: Established companies base dancers' salaries on the actors' Equity agreement: leading dancers negotiate their own rates. For state or regional contemporary dance companies the Equity minimum is $358.50 per week for those with up to one year's professional experience, rising each year as follows: $378.90; $400.30; $422.80; $447.40.

THE AUSTRALIAN BALLET

2 Kavanagh Street
South Melbourne
Victoria 3205
Tel: (03) 649 8600

Artistic director:
Maina Gielgud
Administrator:
Noel Pelly

Principal dancers:
David Ashmole, Steven Heathcote, Greg Horsman, Ulrike Lytton, Adam Marchant, David McAllister, Lisa Pavane, Colin Peasley, Fiona Tonkin

Guest artists:
Edna Edgley, Jonathan Kelly, Cecilia Kirche, Gary Norman, Christine Walsh

Senior artist:
Elizabeth Toohey
Leading soloists:
Mark Brinkley, Larry Köhne-Drube
Soloists:
6 female, 3 male
Coryphées:
5 female, 7 male
Corps de ballet:
14 female, 13 male

Premières:
The Competition (Le Concours)
Australian première, Victorian Arts Centre, Melbourne
Choreography: Maurice Béjart
Staging: Bertrand D'At
Music: Hugues le Bars and collage
Sets: Claude Tissier
Original costumes: Catherine Verneuil

Catalyst
Sydney Opera House, 4.5.90
Choreography: Stephen Baynes

Music: Poulenc
Design: Andrew Carter

My Name Is Edward Kelly
Sydney Opera House, 4.5.90
Choreography: Timothy Gordon
Music: Peter Sculthorpe
Design: Kenneth Rowell

Repertory

Birthday Offering
Choreography: Frederick Ashton
Music: Glazunov
Costumes: André Levasseur

Four Last Songs
Choreography: Maurice Béjart
Music: Richard Strauss

Graduation Ball
Choreography: David Lichine
Music: Johann Strauss, arr. Antal Dorati
Costumes: Geoffrey Guy, after original Benois designs

Onegin
Choreography: John Cranko
Music: Tchaikovsky
Designs: Jürgen Rose

Transfigured Night
Choreography: Jiři Kylián
Music: Schoenberg

La Sylphide
Choreography: Bournonville
Staging: Erik Bruhn
Music: Løvenskjold

Spartacus
Choreography: László Seregi
Music: Khatchaturian
Sets: Gábor Forray
Costumes: Tivadar Márk

The Merry Widow
Choreography: Ronald Hynd
Staging: Robert Helpmann

Music: Lehár, arr. Lanchbery
Design: Desmond Heeley

Number of performances:
188

Foreign tours:
Taiwan, Thailand, Singapore, November
1989; United States of America, July 1990

SYDNEY DANCE COMPANY

The Wharf, Pier 4
Hickson Road
Walsh Bay, NSW, 2000
Tel: (02) 221 1811

Artistic director:
Graeme Murphy
General manager:
Lynn Ralph

QUEENSLAND BALLET

129 Margaret Street
Brisbane, QLD, 4000
Tel: (07) 229-3355
Fax: (07) 221-2390

Artistic director:
Harold Collins
General manager:
Wayne McKenna

AUSTRALIAN DANCE THEATRE

120 Gouger Street
Adelaide, SA, 5000
Tel: (08) 212-2084
Fax: (08) 231-1036

Artistic director:
Leigh Warren
General manager:
Rainer Jozeps

THE WEST AUSTRALIAN BALLET COMPANY

His Majesty's Theatre
825 Hay Street
Perth, WA, 6000
Tel: (09) 481-0707

Artistic director:
Barry Moreland
General manager:
John Catlin

DANCEWORKS

2/36 Cardigan Place
Albert Park, Victoria, 3206
Tel: (03) 696-1702

Joint artistic directors:
Beth Shelton, Helen Herbertson

MERYL TANKARD COMPANY

Gorman House
Ainslie Avenue
Braddon, ACT, 2601
Tel: (06) 247-3103

Artistic director:
Meryl Tankard
Company manager:
Dick Allen

DANCE NORTH

Townsville Arts Centre
Cnr Walker and Stanley Streets
Townsville, QLD, 4810
Tel: (077) 72-2549

Artistic director:
Cheryl Stock
General manager:
Lorna Hempstead

Austria

BALLETT DER WIENER STAATSOPER

Opernring
1010 Wien
Tel: 51444-0

Director:
Dr Gerhard Brunner
Guest choreographer:
Peter Schaufuss
Principal teachers:
Gerlinde Dill, Carlos Gacio, Zoltan Nagy,
Milan Hatala

Principal dancers:
Lilly Scheuermann, Gyula Harangozó
Soloists:
Christine Gaugusch, Marialuise Jaska,
Roswitha Over, Jolantha Seyfried, Brigitte
Stadler, Heinz Heidenreich, Ludwig Karl,
Christian Tichy
Corps de ballet:
40 female, 32 male

New production:

La Sylphide, Wiener Staatsoper, 16.2.90
Choreography: Bournonville, adapted by
Peter Schaufuss
Production: Peter Schaufuss
Music: Løvenskjold
Design and costumes: David Walker
Lighting design: Steen Bjarke

Repertory:

Apollo
Choreography: Balanchine
Music: Stravinsky

A Midsummer Night's Dream
Choreography: Neumeier
Music: Mendelssohn, Ligeti
Design: Jürgen Rose

The Fairy Doll
Choreography: Hassreiter, Gaul
Music: Joseph Bayer

The Sleeping Beauty
Choreography: Petipa, Nureyev
Production: Rudolf Nureyev
Music: Tchaikovsky

Designs: Georgiadis

The Three-cornered Hat
Choreography: Massine
Music: de Falla
Designs: Picasso

Grosse Fugue
Choreography: van Manen
Music: Beethoven
Designs: Vroom, van Manen

Kettentanz
Choreography: Arpino
Music: Johann Strauss, snr.
Designs: Eula

Les Noces
Choreography: Nijinska
Music: Stravinsky
Designs: Gontcharova

Liebeslieder Walzer
Choreography: Balanchine
Music: Brahms
Designs: Langenfass, Karinska

The Nutcracker
Choreography: Grigorovich
Music: Tchaikovsky
Designs: Virsaladze

Return to the Strange Land
Choreography: Kylián
Music: Janáček

Dream Dances
Choreography: Kylián
Music: Berio
Designs: Nobbe, Kim

Symphony in D
Choreography: Kylián
Music: Haydn
Designs: Schenk

Verklärte Nacht
Choreography: Kylián
Music: Schoenberg
Designs: Kylián, Stokvis

Wiegenlied
Choreography: Kylián
Music: Berg
Designs: Macfarlane

Reconstruction of dances:
by Bodenweiser, Chladek, Wiesenthal

Number of performances:
50, including 3 in the Deutsches Theater,
Munich, in March 1990

Salary information:
Not available

**BALLETTSCHULE DER
ÖSTERREICHISCHEN BUNDESTHEATER**

Hanuschgasse I
1010 Wien
Tel: 51444-0

Director:
Michael Birkmeyer

BALLETT DER WIENER VOLKSOPER

Währingerstrasse 78
1090 Wien
Tel: 0222/51444-0

Director:
Susanne Kirnbauer

**BALLETT DER VEREINIGTEN BÜHNEN
GRAZ**

Kaiser Josefplatz 10
8010 Graz
Tel: 0316/76451

Director:
Waclaw Orlikowski

**BALLETT DES SALZBURGER
LANDESTHEATERS**

Schwarzstrasse 22
5024 Salzburg
Tel: 0662/71512-0

Director:
Fred Marteny

BALLETT DES LANDESTHEATERS LINZ

Promenade 39
4020 Linz
Tel: 0732/277651

Director:
Virgil Stanciu

**BALLETT DES STADTTHEATERS
KLAGENFURT**

Theaterplatz 4
9020 Klagenfurt
Tel: 0463/55266

Director:
Radomir Krulanovic

**BALLETT DES TIROLER
LANDESTHEATERS**

Rennweg 2
6020 Innsbruck
Tel: 05222/21771-0

Director:
Josette Gatineau

Belgium

ROYAL BALLET OF FLANDERS

Keizerstraat 14
B-2000 Antwerp
Tel: (03) 234 34 38

Director:
Robert Denvers

Guest choreographers:
Vicente Nebrada, Lynne Taylor-Corbett,
Stuart Sebastian

Principal teacher:
Robert Denvers

Principal dancers:
Dawn Fay, Vinciane Ghyssens, Lenka
Jaroskiova, Kaatje Verelst, Chris Roelandt,
Jacob Sparso, Jan Vandeloo, Christian
Poggioli

Guest artists:
Irek Mukhamedov, Jan Broeckx, Mats
Skoog, Lars van Cauwenbergh

Corps de ballet:
20 female, 20 male

Premières:

A Dance for You, Ghent, 22.9.89
Choreography: Vicente Nebrada
Music: Maria Teresa Carreno
Design: Christina Gianini

Dark Elegies (company première), 22.9.89
Choreography: Antony Tudor
Staging: Sallie Wilson
Music: Mahler
Design: after Nadia Benois

Great Galloping Gottschalk, 22.9.89
Choreography: Lynne Taylor Corbett
Music: Gottschalk
Design: Gretchen Warren

Camelot, Théâtre de la Monnaie, Brussels,
16.3.90
Choreography: Stuart Sebastian
Music: Sibelius
Designs: Roger Bernard and Joëlle Roustan

Repertory:

Capriccio
Choreography: Balanchine
Music: Stravinsky

Continuo
Choreography: Antony Tudor
Music: Pachelbel

Symphony in Three Movements
Choreography: Nils Christe
Music: Stravinsky

Symphony in D
Choreography: Jiři Kylián
Music: Haydn

Serait-ce la Mort?
Choreography: Maurice Béjart
Music: Richard Strauss

Allegro Brillante
Choreography: Balanchine
Music: Tchaikovsky

Tchaikovsky pas de deux
Choreography: Balanchine

Napoli Divertissement
Choreography: Bournonville
Music: Paulli and Helsted

Go! Said Max
Choreography: Lynne Taylor-Corbett
Music: Robert Muczynski

A Lover's Tale
Choreography: Marc Bogaerts
Music: Grieg

The Lesson
Choreography: Flemming Flindt
Music: Georges Delerue

Paquita Divertissement
Choreography: Petipa
Music: Minkus

Variations
Choreography: Violette Verdy
Music: Brahms

Danses qu'on croise
Choreography: Thierry Malandain
Music: Brahms

Don Quixote
Choreography: Rudolf Nureyev after Petipa
Music: Minkus, arr. Lanchbery
Set: Roger Bernard after drawings by Alain
Vaes
Costumes: Anna Anni

La Sylphide
Choreography: Bournonville
Staging: Flemming Flindt
Music: Løvenskjold
Sets and lighting: Roger Bernard
Costumes: Anna Anni

Salary information:
Not available

Company school:
Stedelijk Institut für Ballet

Artistic director:
Jos Brabants

**BALLET ROYAL DE WALLONIE –
COMPAGNIE JORGE LEFEBRE**

Palais des Beaux-Arts
Place du Manège
6000 Charleroi
Belgium
Tel: (071) 314420

Artistic director:
Jorge Lefebre (died 15 May 1990)

General director:
Guy Rassel

Principal choreographer:
Jorge Lefebre

Visiting choreographers:
Jacques Dombrowski, Mauricio Wainrot

Ballet master:
Serge Lefèvre

Principal teachers:
Wojciech Rybak, Ménia Martinez

Principal dancers:
Christine Klepal, Catherine Plomteux,
Caroline Jenkins; Serge Lefevre, Arpad
Kovacs, Arnold Quintane, Francis Pedros
Corps de ballet:
13 female 10 male
Number of performances:
70

Salary information:
Not available

MONNAIE DANCE GROUP/MARK MORRIS

103 rue Bara/Barastraat 103
1070 Brussels
Belgium
Tel: 523 98 08

Director and choreographer:
Mark Morris

Dancers:
Alyce Bochette, Joe Bowie, Ruth Davidson,
Tina Fehlandt, Penny Hutchinson, Dan
Joyce, Olivia Maridjan-Koop, Clarice
Marshall, Erin Matthiessen, Jon Mensinger,
Rachel Murray, June Omura, Kraig
Patterson, Mireille Radwan-Dana,
Guillermo Resto, Keith Sabado, Joachim
Schlömer, William Wagner, Jean-Guillaume
Weis, Holly Williams, Megan Williams

Guest dancers:
Mikhail Baryshnikov, Rob Besserer

Premières:

Love Song Waltzes, Théâtre Royal de la
Monnaie, 4.11.89
Choreography: Mark Morris
Music: Brahms

Wonderland, Théâtre Royal de la Monnaie,
4.11.89
Choreography: Mark Morris
Music: Schoenberg
Costumes: Martin Pakledinaz

Behemoth, Halles de Schaerbeek, 14.4.90
Choreography: Mark Morris
Danced in silence
Costumes: Christine Van Loon

Going Away Party
Choreography: Mark Morris
Music: Bob Wills and his Texas Playboys
Costumes: Christine Van Loon

Repertory (all choreography by Mark
Morris)

Ballabili
Music: Verdi

Lovey
Music: Violent Femmes

The Tamil Film Songs in Stereo pas de deux
Music: Indian pop

Dido and Aeneas
Music: Henry Purcell

L'Allegro, il Penseroso ed il Moderato
Music: Handel

Number of performances:
60

Salary information:
Not available

ROSAS

19 Werkhuizenstraat
B-1080 Brussels
Tel: 32 2 425 36 29

Director and choreographer:
Anne Teresa De Keersmaeker

Teachers:
José Besprosvany, Francine Levy,
Bernadette Dormeux
Dancers:
Fumiyo Ikeda, Johanne Saunier, Carlotta
Sagua, Nathalie Milliou, Marion Levy

Première:

Stella, Toneelschuur, Haarlem
(Netherlands), 2.3.90
Choreography: Anne Teresa De
Keersmaeker
Music: Gyorgy Ligeti
Designs: H. Sorgelaas

Tour:
March–July 1990,
Netherlands, Austria, Yugoslavia, Spain,
USSR, Scotland, Switzerland, France

Salary information:
Everyone receives 64,000 francs per month

COMPAGNIE MICHELE ANNE DE MEY

Théâtre Varia
59 Rue du Sceptre
B-1040 Brussels
Tel: 32 2 640 35 50

Director and choreographer:
Michèle Anne De Mey

Teachers:
Katharina Bader, Mischa Van Dullemen
Dancers:
Andreu Bresca, Michèle Anne De Mey,
Olga De Soto, Françoise Rognerud, Gabi
Sund, Mischa Van Dullemen, Gilles
Welinski

Première:

Sinfonia Eroica
Choreography: Michèle Anne De Mey
Music: Beethoven, Mozart, Jimi Hendrix
Costumes: Isabelle Lhoas and Claudia
Vellat
Assistant and musical adviser: Thierry De
Mey

Number of performances:
About 50

Salary information:
35,000 francs per month for performers,
administrators and technicians

COMPAGNIE AIME DE LIGNIERE

Isabellalei 83
2018 Antwerp
Belgium
Tel: 03 230 75 02

Director and choreographer:
Aimé de Lignière

Administrative director:
Martine Tack

Teachers:
Wini Jacobs, Aimé de Lignière

Guest choreographer:
Michel Bouts

Dancers:
Catherine Claereboudt, Pascale De Groote,
Majella De Roover, Claudia De Smet,
Fabienne Huygen, Ann Jehaes, Lieve
Mertens, Vjera Somers, Veronica Stalpaert,
Myriam Van den Bossche, Leontien
Wiering.

Repertory:
All choreography by Aimé de Lignière

Mauthausen
Music: Theodorakis

Afscheid
Music: Alan Stivell

Verschoven Nu
Music: Luc Van Hove
Designs: Jan Dries

Rejected Angels
Music: André Laporte
Designs: Tilly Gielen

Salle des pas perdus
Music: Frits Celis

Le Chant de l'appel
Traditional music from Guinea
Designs: John Bogaerts

Chronos
Music: Peter Sculthorpe
Designs: Jetje de Kort

Embrace Tiger, Return to Mountain
Choreography: Michel Bouts
Music: André Van Belle

Number of performances:
About 70

Salary information:
Not available

MARC VANRUNXT

c/o Furioso
54 E. de Becolaan
B-1050 Brussels
Tel: 32 2 649 01 31

Director and choreographer:
Marc Vanrunxt

Teachers:
Marc Vanrunxt, Rio de Corte, Marianne Schotte
Dancers:
Marianne Schotte, Eric Roeves, Eddi Bal, Marc Vanrunxt

Première:

Moderne Compositie, Antwerp, 25.1.90
Choreography: Marc Vanrunxt
Music: Thierry Geniooi
Set: Erik Kouwenhoven
Costumes: Eric Roeves

JOSÉ BESPROSVANY

c/o Furioso
54 E. de Becolaan
B-1050 Brussels
Tel: 32 2 649 01 31

Director and choreographer:
José Besprosvany

Dancers:
Tobias Bausch, Kitty Kortes Lynch, Ida de Vos, Marinos Tilios, Catherine Sarrelangue

Première:

Von Heute auf Morgen, Amsterdam, 14.11.89
Choreography: Besprosvany
Music: Schoenberg, Berg
Set: Manuel Herrera
Costumes: Frouke Schernau

Salary information:
Not available

Brazil

BALLET DO TEATRO MUNICIPAL DO RIO DE JANEIRO

Teatro Municipal
Rua Maestro Francisco Braga no.42/ap.701
Copacabana-CEP 22041
Rio de Janeiro
RJ Brazil
Tel: 210 2463

Director and ballet mistress:
Tatiana Leskova

Choreographer and ballet mistress:
Eugenia Feodorova
Régisseur and Choreographer's assistant:
Denis Gray
Ballet masters:
Denis Gray, Eliana Karin, Aldo Lotufo, Heliana Pantoja
Répétiteurs:
Denis Gray, José Moura, Heliana Pantoja, Berta Rosanova, Sonia Vilela

Notator:
Christina Schroeder
Principals:
Ana Botafogo, Nora Esteves, Aurea Hamerli, Cecilia Kirche, Paulo Rodrigues, Francisco Timbó
First soloists:
Silvia Barroso, Bettyna Dalcanale, Marcia Faggioni, Lourdja Mesquita, Rosane Soneghetti, Helio Bejani, Antonio Gaspar
Second soloists:
Christina Costa, Irene Orazem, Shirley Pereira, Sandra Queiroz, Paulo Arguelles, Joseny Coutinho
Coryphées:
Marcia Antunes, Elisa Baeta, Francina Borges, Lucia Guimarães, Celeste Lima, Beatriz Melucci, Paula Passos, Vilma Rocha, Ines Schlobach, Tereza Cristina Ubirajara, Sonia Vilella, Luiz Carlos Cavalcanti, Cassio Luiz, Valmir Prado, Rodolfo Rau
Corps de ballet:
22 female, 16 male

THE STATISTICS OF DANCE COMPANIES

New production:
The Nutcracker, 14 December 1989
Music: Tchaikovsky
Choreography: Ivanov, Nijinska, Leskova
Sets: Mauricio Sette
Costumes: Biza Vianna

Repertory:

Cantabile
Choreography: Araiz
Music: Samuel Barber

Giselle
Choreography: Coralli, Perrot, Petipa
Music: Adam
Staging: Peter Wright, remounted by
Dennis Bonner

Swan Lake
Choreography: Petipa/Ivanov
Music: Tchaikovsky
Staging: Eugenia Feodorova

The Nutcracker
Choreography: Tatiana Leskova
Music: Tchaikovsky

La Bayadère
Choreography: Petipa
Music: Minkus
Staging: Eugenia Feodorova

Le Corsaire
Choreography: Petipa
Music: Minkus
Staging: Tatiana Leskova

Paquita
Choreography: Petipa
Music: Drigo, Minkus
Staging: Eugenia Feodorova

Les Sylphides
Choreography: Fokine
Music: Chopin
Staging: Tatiana Leskova

L'Après-midi d'un faune
Choreography: Nijinsky
Music: Debussy
Staging: Tatiana Leskova, Nelly Laport

Concerto
Choreography: Rodrigo Pederneiras
Music: Prokofiev

Le Combat
Choreography: William Dollar
Music: Rafaello Banfield
Staging: Tatiana Leskova, Aldo Lotufo

Tango
Choreography: Luiz Arrieta
Music: Astor Piazzolla

Rhytmetron
Music: Marlos Nobre
Choreography: Arthur Mitchell

The Triumph of Aphroditis
Music: Orff
Choreography: Milko Sparemblek

Number of performances in Rio:
50

Tours:
To São Paulo and Belo Horizonte, 12
performances in 2 weeks

Salary information:
Not available

BALLET OF THE TEATRO GUAÍRA

Ballet director:
Carlos Trincheiras

Ballet mistress:
Isabel Santa Rosa
Assistant ballet mistress:
Marta Nejm
Répétiteur:
Ana Silva
Principals:
Eleonora Greca, Eunice Oliveira, Regina
Kotaka, Wanderley Lopes, Jair Moraes,
Jurandi Silva
Soloists:
Heloisa Almeida, Vania Kesikowski, Paula
Righesso, Daisi Wor, Eduardo Laranjeira,
Pedro Pires
Corps de ballet:
14 female, 10 male

New productions:

Flicts, 4.10.89
Choreography: Jurandi Silva
Music: Sergio Ricardo
Designs: Rosa Magalhães

Aurora's Wedding, 25.4.90
Choreography: Petipa and Nijinska
Music: Tchaikovsky
Designs: Nilson Penna
Produced: Tatiana Leskova

202

Presences, 25.4.90
Choreography: Luiz Arrieta
Music: Rachmaninov
Designs: Arrieta

Repertory:

Archipel 3
Choreography: Trincheiras
Music: Boucourichiliev

Exultate Jubilate
Choreography: Vasco Wellenkamp
Music: Mozart

Great Mystic Circus
Choreography: Trincheiras
Music: Edu Lobo

Inter-rupto
Choreography: Trincheiras
Music: Samuel Barber

Life and Death of a Lonely Woman
Choreography: Trincheiras
Music: Richard Strauss

The Mandala of Maria Bueno
Choreography: Trincheiras
Music: several

The Nutcracker
Choreography: Trincheiras
Music: Tchaikovsky

Pastoral
Choreography: Milko Sparemblek
Music: Beethoven

Prophecy
Choreography: Francisco Duarte
Music: Goldsmith

La Ronde
Choreography: Schindovski
Music: K. Weill and J. Françaix

Symphony 3
Choreography: Trincheiras
Music: Stravinsky

Number of performances in Curitiba:
25

Tours to Florianopolis and Cascavel:
6 performances in 2 weeks

GRUPO CORPO

Belo Horizonte

Directors:
Emilio Kalil, Paulo Pederneiras

Choreographer:
Rodrigo Pederneiras
Répétiteur:
Carmen Purri
Ballet mistress:
Graça Salles
Dancers:
Regina Advento, Paula Bonome, Ines
Bogea, Cristina Castilho, Letici Carneiro,
Alessandra Papini, Myriam Pederneiras,
Carmen Purri, Cristina Purri; Marcio Alves,
Renato Augusto, João Aur, Luiz Couto,
Bernardo Gama, Werner Glik, Rodrigo
Silva, Alexandre Vasconcellos

Première:

Orphanage Mass, Rio de Janeiro, 15.5.89
Choreography: Rodrigo Pederneiras
Music: Mozart
Sets: Fernando Velloso
Costumes: Freuza Zechmeister

Duo
Choreography: Pederneiras
Music: Villa Lobos

Preludes
Choreography: Pederneiras
Music: Chopin

Songs
Choreography: Pederneiras
Music: Richard Strauss

Uakti
Choreography: Pederneiras
Music: Marco A. Guimerães

Women
Choreography: Susanne Linke
Music: Penderecki

Number of performances:
20 in Belo Horizonte

Tour:
20 weeks in 32 cities

CISNE NEGRO CIA. DE DANCA

Rua das Tabocas, No. 55 CEP 05445
São Paulo, Brazil
Tel: (011) 212 2327

Director:
Hulda Bittencourt

Ballet mistresses:
Ivonice Satie, Lais Galvão
Dancers:
Adriana Naldoni, Beth Risoléu, Claudia
Palma, Dany Bittencourt, Fernanda
Guimarães, Liris do Vale, Mara Mesquita,
Armando Aurich, Carlos dos Santos,
Laudney Delgado, Marco Antonio Gomes,
Mario Matiazzo, Sergio Marshall, Vitório
Casarin

Guest artist:
Ana Botafogo

Premières:

Equinoxe, 14.4.89
Choreography: Gigi Caciuleanu
Music: M. Jarre

Midnight Cantata
Choreography: Caciuleanu
Music: Vivaldi

Soul in Fire, 8.11.89
Choreography: Ana Maria Mondini and
José Possi Neto
Music: several
Designs: Marco Antonio Lima

Jungle, Santos, 26.4.90
Choreography: Armando Duarte
Music: Nana Vasconcellos

Shogun, Santos, 26.4.90
Choreography: Ivonice Satie
Music: Milton Nascimento

Repertory:

Bailantas
Choreography: Ana Maria Mondini
Music: several

Keep Going
Choreography: Vasco Wellenkamp
Music: Luciano Berio

Sabía
Choreography: Vasco Wellenkamp
Music: Tom Jobin

Number of performances:
50 in São Paulo

Tour:
20 weeks in 35 cities: 60 performances

BALLET OF THE CITY OF SAO PAULO

Teatro Municipal de São Paulo
Praça Ramos de Azevedo
São Paulo SP-CEP 01037

Artistic director:
Rui Fontana Lopes
Assistant director and ballet master:
Hugo Travers

Assistant choreographers and répétiteurs:
Sergio Funari, Susana Mafra, Monica Mion
Teachers:
Ady Addor, Gustavo Molajoli, Consuelo
Rios, Ilse Wiedmann
Dancers:
Ellen Addario, Nancy Bergamim, Brasilia
Botelho, Marta Cesar, Ana Veronica
Coutinho, Claudia Decara, Mariana Grade,
Monica Kodato, Lumena Macedo, Silvia
Machado, Susana Mafra, Andrea Maia,
Monica Mion, Paula Perillo, Luciana Porta,
Lilia Shaw, José Maria Alves, Sandro
Borelli, Raymundo Costa, Maurício
Christyan, Jorge Filio, Milton Kennedy,
Osman Khelili, Rogerio Maia, Irineu
Marcovechio, Maurício Oliveira, Marcelo
Omine, Nilson Soares, Paulo Vinicius

Premières:

Voices, 10.4.89
Choreography: Victor Navarro
Music: several

Blue Land, 5.4.90
Choreography: Sergio Funari
Music: Andrew Lloyd Webber
Sets: Rodrigo Campos
Costumes: Leda Senize

Variations on a Theme by Haydn
Choreography: Rodrigo Pederneiras
Music: Brahms
Costumes: Freuza Zechmeister

Repertory:

Adagietto
Choreography: Oscar Araiz
Music: Mahler

Bolero
Choreography: Robatto
Music: Ravel, Trythall

Cantares
Choreography: Oscar Araiz
Music: Ravel

Karadá
Choreography: Susana Yamauchi, João Maurício
Music: several

Mandala
Choreography: Luiz Arrieta
Music: Ravel

Mikrokosmos
Choreography: Sergio Funari, Wilson Aguiar
Music: Bartók

Presences
Choreography: Luiz Arrieta
Music: Rachmaninov

Sacred and Profane Dances
Choreography: Victor Navarro
Music: Debussy

Trinity
Choreography: Luiz Arrieta
Music: Barber

Vivaldi
Choreography: Victor Navarro
Music: Vivaldi

Number of performances:
15 in São Paulo

Tour:
20 performances in 7 cities, 5 weeks

Salary information:
Not available

Canada

THE NATIONAL BALLET OF CANADA

157 King Street East
Toronto, Ontario M5C 1G9
Tel: (416) 362-1041
Fax: (416) 368-7443

Artistic director:
Reid Anderson
Associate director:
Valerie Wilder
General manager:
Robert Johnson

Resident choreographer (from July 1990):
John Alleyne

Conductor and music administrator:
Ermanno Florio
Musical director emeritus:
George Crum

Principal ballet mistresses:
Joanne Nisbet, Magdalena Popa
Ballet mistresses:
Lorna Geddes, Mary Jago
Ballet master:
Victor Litvinov

Guest teacher:
Joysanne Sidimus

Principal dancers:
Kimberly Glasco, Rex Harrington, Yoko Ichino, Karen Kain, Martine Lamy, Serge Lavoie, Kim Lightheart, Owen Montague, David Nixon, Kevin Pugh, Jeremy Ransom, Raymond Smith, Gizella Witkowsky
Principal character artists:
Victoria Bertram, Jacques Gorrissen, Charles Kirby, Tomas Schramek, Hazaros Surmeyan

205

Guest artists:
Frank Augustyn, Gregory Osborne

First soloists:
3 male, 1 female
Second soloists:
1 male, 3 female
Corps de ballet:
18 male, 24 female
Apprentices:
10

Premières:

Dream Dances (company première)
Choreography: Jiři Kylián
Music: Berio

Gloria (company première)
Choreography: Kenneth MacMillan
Music: Poulenc

The Need (world première)
Choreography: David Parsons
Music: Raye (commissioned score)

Repertory:

Giselle
Choreography: trad., arr. Peter Wright
Music: Adam

La Bayadère
Choreography: Natalia Makarova
Music: Minkus arr. Lanchbery

La Ronde
Choreography: Glen Tetley
Music: Korngold

Napoli
Choreography: Bournonville/staged by
Peter Schaufuss
Music: Gadde, Helsted, Paulli, Lumby, arr.
by Norlyng

*Celebrating the Tennant Magic: 25th
Anniversary Gala
The Nutcracker*
Choreography: Celia Franca
Music: Tchaikovsky

La Fille mal gardée
Choreography: Frederick Ashton
Music: Hérold, arr. Lanchbery

Concerto
Choreography: Kenneth MacMillan
Music: Shostakovich

Transfigured Night
Choreography: Jiři Kylián

Music: Schoenberg

Elite Syncopations
Choreography: Kenneth MacMillan
Music: Joplin

Serenade
Choreography: George Balanchine/staged
by Joysanne Sidimus
Music: Tchaikovsky

Swan Lake
Choreography: Erik Bruhn
Music: Tchaikovsky

Voluntaries
Choreography: Glen Tetley
Music: Poulenc

Les Sylphides
Choreography: Fokine/production by Celia
Franca and Erik Bruhn
Music: Chopin

Salary information:
$412–732 per week as per Actors' Equity
agreement

Length of Season:
July 1989 to June 1990

Number of performances:
86

Tour:
Western Canada, West Germany, USA

THE NATIONAL BALLET SCHOOL

*105 Maitland Street
Toronto, Ontario M4Y 1E4
Tel: (416) 964-3780
Fax: (416) 964-3632*

Founder and artistic advisor:
Betty Oliphant
Artistic director:
Mavis Staines
Administrative director:
Paul Le Forestier

Academic principal:
Mora Oxley
Ballet vice-principal:
Carole Chadwick

Director of development:
Maggie Wygant
Director of public relations:
Alison Galt

206

Registrar:
Gillian Bishop

Ballet staff:
Reginald Amatto, Luc Amyot, Carina
Bomers, Debbie Bowes, Rosalie Brake,
Catherine Buffie-Carter, Judy Edwards-
Gainforth, Elaine Fisher, Glenn Gilmour,
Louis Godfrey, Deborah Hess, Elizabeth
Keeble, Maisie MacPhee, Mary Ross,
Denise Schultze, Sergiu Stefanschi, Shirley
Tetreau, Laurel Toto, Jean Geddis, Tia
Zhang

ALBERTA BALLET

10645–63 Avenue
Edmonton, Alberta T6H 1P7
Tel: (403) 438-4350

Nat Christie Centre
141–18th Avenue S.W.
Calgary, Alberta T2S 0B8
Tel: (403) 245-4222

Artistic director:
Ali Pourfarrokh
General manager:
Greg Epton
Ballet mistress:
Monica Trogaru

Principal dancers:
Gregory Askins, Miguel Aviles, Nancy
Latoszewski, Daniel McLaren, Barbara
Moore

Premières/Repertory:

Donizetti Variations (company première)
Choreography: George Balanchine
Music: Donizetti
Staged: Victoria Simon
Costumes: executed by Allison Yardley-
Jones

Evening Song
Choreography: Ali Pourfarrokh
Music: Dvořák
Decor: Douglas T. McCullough
Costumes: Allison Yardley-Jones

Syrinx (company première)
Choreography: Ali Pourfarrokh
Music: Debussy
Decor: Douglas T. McCullough
Costumes: Allison Yardley-Jones

Bolero (Canadian première)
Choreography: Igal Perry
Music: Ravel
Costumes: executed by Allison Yardley-
Jones

The Nutcracker
Choreography: Brydon Paige
Music: Tchaikovsky
Decor and costumes: David L. Lovett

Aria (Canadian première)
Choreography: Ali Pourfarrokh
Music: Villa-Lobos
Costumes: executed by Carolyn Devins

Miss Julie (Canadian première)
Choreography: Birgit Cullberg
Music: Ture Rangstrom
Staged: Jeremy Leslie-Spinks
Decor: Douglas T. McCullough
Costumes: Allison Yardley-Jones

Twice upon a Time
Choreographer: Ali Pourfarrokh
Music: Moondog (Louis Hardin)
Decor: Douglas T. McCullough
Costumes: Laara Cassells

Lyric Dances
Choreography: Ali Pourfarrokh
Music: Joseph Suk
Decor: Douglas T. McCullough
Costumes: Laara Cassells

Salary information:
$365–600 per week

Length of season:
1989/90: 36 weeks; 1990/1: 38 weeks

Number of performances:
62

BALLET BRITISH COLUMBIA

Suite 502–68 Water Street
Vancouver, British Columbia
Tel: (604) 669-5954

Acting artistic director:
Barry Ingham
Ballet mistress:
Marquita Lester

General manager:
Robert J. McGifford
Company manager:
Linda Blankstein

Dancers:
Leigh-Ann Cohen, Ainslie Cyopik, Anne
Dryburgh, Charie Evans, Kirk Hansen, Patti
Hines, Nicole Lamontagne, Marc LeClerc,
Fiona Macdonald, William Marrie, Jackson
McKiee, Gwyneth Obrecht, John Ottmann,
Crystal Pite, David Mark Tice, Jay Gower
Taylor, Todd Willard

Premières:

Irish Fantasy
Choreography: Jacques d'Amboise
Music: Saint-Saëns

The Desires of Merlin
Choreography: Serge Bennathan
Music: Benjamin Britten, Ärvo Part

Variations on a Nursery Song
Choreography: László Seregi
Music: Ernst von Dohnanyi

Dvořák Serenade
Choreography: John Clifford
Music: Dvořák

Go Slow, Walter
Choreography: John Alleyne
Music: John Cage

Variations Concertantes
Choreography: Patricia Neary
Music: Alberto Ginastara

Repertory:

Flying to Paris
Choreography: John Alleyne
Music: David Wynne

Urlicht
Choreography: William Forsythe
Music: Mahler

Return to the Strange Land
Choreography: Jiři Kylián
Music: Janáček

Blood Wedding
Choreographer: Pierre Wyss
Music: Manuel de Falla

Length of season:
33 weeks

Number of performances:
26

Salary information:
$320–445 per week

LES BALLETS JAZZ DE MONTREAL

1435 Argyle Avenue,
Montreal
Quebec, Canada H3G 1V5
Tel: 875 9640

Artistic director:
Geneviève Salbaing
Administrative director:
Caroline Salbaing
Technical director:
Daniel Ranger

Administrative assistant:
Danielle Béland

Guest choreographer:
Mauricio Wainrot

Resident lighting designer:
Nicolas Cernovitch

Répétitrice:
Odette Lalonde

Dancers:
Lise Bernier, Marco Cannavo, Chantal
Dauphinais, Suzanne Holden, Carol
Horowitz, Eric May, Yvan Michaud,
Charles St-Onge, Aaron Shields, Eytan
Sivak, Kim Timbers, Hua Fang Zhang

Premières:

Dérivations, world première
Choreography: Mauricio Wainrot
Music: Morton Gould

Acelerando, world première
Choreography: Mauricio Wainrot
Music: François Bourassa

Entre dos Aguas, company première
Choreography: Robert North
Music: Paco de Lucia, Simon Rogers

Red Hot Peppers, world première
Choreography: Brian McDonald
Music: Jelly Roll Morton

Repertory:

La Perfectly Swell
Choreography: Rael Lamb
Music: musical collage

208

Les Chaises musicales
Choreography: Lynne Taylor-Corbett
Music: Andrew Lloyd-Webber

Bad Blood
Choreography: Ulysses Dove
Music: Laurie Anderson

Ebony Concerto
Choreography: John Cranko
Music: Stravinsky

La Femme aux talons hauts
Choreography: Howard Richard
Music: Tom Waits

Appearances
Choreography: Lynne Taylor-Corbett
Music: Pat Metheny, Lyle Mays

Big Band
Choreography: Brian McDonald
Music: Stan Kenton

Libertango
Choreography: Mauricio Wainrot
Music: Astor Piazzolla

After
Choreography: Mauricio Wainrot
Music: The Art of Noise

Fiesta
Choreography: Mauricio Wainrot
Music: Ravel

Percussion pour six
Choreography: Vicente Nebrada
Music: Lee Gurst

L'Oiseau de feu/Firebird
Choreography: Ferenc Barbay
Music: Stravinsky

Adieux
Choreography: Richard Levi
Music: Pat Metheny

Janis for Joplin
Choreography: Mauricio Wainrot
Music: Janis Joplin

Tour:
Spring 1990: USA, London, Paris

Number of performances:
103

Salary information:
$325–530 per week

DANCEMAKERS

927 Dupont Street
Toronto, ON M6H 1Z1
Canada
Tel: (416) 535-8880

Artistic director:
Bill James
Assistant artistic director:
Julia Sasso
Musical adviser:
Michael J. Baker

Company teacher:
Pat Miner

Technical director and lighting designer:
Patrick Matheson

Dancers:
Scott Buffett, Marie-Josée Chartier, Philip Drube, Merle Holloman, Bruce Mitchell, Julia Sasso, Carolyn Woods

Repertory:

Amorosa
Choreography: Bill James
Music: Matthew Fleming
Costumes: Serge Saintonge
Lighting: Patrick Matheson

Atlas Moves Watching
Choreography: Bill James
Music: Matthew Fleming
Decor: Bill James
Lighting: Patrick Matheson

Burning House
Choreography: Carol Anderson
Music: Kirk Elliott
Costumes: Sylvain Brochu

In the Trees, world première
Choreography: Bill James
Music: Michael J. Baker
Costumes: Denis Joffre
Decor: Aiko Suzuki

Mutual Aid
Choreography: Bill James
Music: Matthew Fleming

Predators of Light
Choreography: Bill James
Music: Rodney Sharman
Costumes: Serge Saintonge
Sets: Dereck Revington

209

Number of performances:
27

Salary information:
Between $375 and $430 per week

DANNY GROSSMAN DANCE COMPANY

511 Bloor Street West, 2nd Floor
Toronto, Ontario
Canada M5S 1Y4
Tel: (416) 531-8350

Artistic director:
Danny Grossman

General manager:
Jane Marsland

Dancers:
Trish Armstrong, Brigitte Bourbeau, France
Bruyere, Pamela Grundy, Eddie Kastrau,
Andrea Nann, Stephen Osborne, Bohdan
Romaniw, Arthur Lee Rose, Monique
Trudelle, Ivano Zappetti

Premières:
(All choreography by Danny Grossman)

The Equilibrist, world première, November
1989
Music: John Coltrane
Costume and set: Mary Kerr

Ground Zero, world première, March 1990
Music: Shostakovich
Costume and set: Mary Kerr

Repertory:

Scherzi
Music: Jean Baptiste Arban
Costumes: Mary Kerr

Bella
Choreography: Danny Grossman and Judy
Jarvis
Music: Puccini
Costume and set: Mary Kerr

Ces Plaisirs
Music: Ann Southam
Costumes: Susan Rome

Inching
Music: Dumisani Abraham Maraire
Costumes: Lola

La Valse
Music: Ravel
Costumes: Mary Kerr

Fratelli
Music: Milhaud
Costume and set: Mary Kerr

Twisted
Music: Lambert, Hendricks, Ross
Costumes: Mary Kerr
Lighting: David Morrison

Curious Schools of Theatrical Dancing: Part 1
Music: Couperin
Costumes: Mary Kerr
Lighting: David Morrison

Divine Air
Music: Gordon Phillips
Costumes: Susan Rome
Lighting: David Morrison

Magneto Dynamo
Music: Charles Mingus
Costumes: Susan Rome

Endangered Species
Music: Krysztof Penderecki
Costume: Mary Kerr

Couples
Music: Terry Riley
Costumes: Lola

Higher
Music: Ray Charles
Costume and set: Mary Kerr

Nobody's Business
Music: Jelly Roll Morton and the Red Hot
Peppers/Joe Turner with the Trumpet All
Stars
Costumes: Mary Kerr

Number of performances:
36

Salary information:
$350–500 per week

DESROSIERS DANCE THEATRE

629 Eastern Avenue
Toronto, Ontario
Canada M4M 1E4
Tel: (416) 463-5341

Artistic director:
Robert Desrosiers
Designer:
Myles Warren

Music director:
Eric Cadesky

Business manager:
Ursula Martin
Administrative assistant:
Michelle Powell

Dancers:
Sonja Delwaide, Marie-Josée Dubois,
Jennifer Dick, Robin Wilds, Jean-Aimé
Lalonde, Gaétan Gingras, Robert Glumbek,
Marq Frerichs

Repertory:

Avalanche
Choreography: Robert Desrosiers
Music: Eric Cadesky, Gordon Phillips, John
Lang
Design: Robert Desrosiers, Myles Warren

Concerto in Earth Major
Choreography: Robert Desrosiers
Choreographic assistance: The Company
All taped music composed by: Ron Allen,
John Lang
All stage music performed by: The
Company
Costume: Anna-Marie Cobbold, Jerrard
Smith

Incognito, (1988/9)
Choreography: Robert Desrosiers
Music: Eric Cadesky, John Lang
Design: Robert Desrosiers, Myles Warren
Costume: Astrid Janson

Brass Fountain
Choreography: Robert Desrosiers
Music: Ron Allen, Jean Dorais, Ahmed
Hassan, John Lang
Guitar solo: Jesse Cook
Costumes: Cheryl Cohoon
Lighting design: Robert Thomson

Number of performances:
34

Salary information:
Not available

LES GRANDS BALLETS CANADIENS

4816, rue Rivard
Montréal (Québec)
Canada H2J 2N6

Founder:
Ludmilla Chiriaeff
Director general:
Colin McIntyre
Artistic director:
Lawrence Rhodes

Artistic adviser:
Fernand Nault

Resident choreographers:
James Kudelka, Brian Macdonald, Fernand
Nault
Principal ballet mistress:
Karen Brown
Principal dancers:
Andrea Boardman, Josée Ledoux, Min
Tang, Diane Partington, Rey Dizon, Edward
Hillyer, Kenneth Larson, Min Hua Zhao
Principal character dancer:
Maurice Lemay
Soloists:
8 females, 2 males
Demi-soloists:
5 females, 3 males
Corps de ballet:
7 females, 9 males
Scholarship programme:
1 female, 1 male

Premières:

Romance, 22.2.90
Choreography: James Kudelka
Music: Dvořák
Costumes: Sylvain Labelle

Na Floresta, 22.2.90
Choreography: Nacho Duato
Music: Brasil, Matogrosso, Tiso after Villa-
Lobos
Interpretation: Ney Matogrosso
Sets: Walter Nobbe
Costumes: Nacho Duato

The Prodigal Son, company première,
27.10.89
Choreography: George Balanchine
Music: Prokofiev
Staged by: Richard Tanner
Sets and costumes: Georges Rouault

Schumann Divertissement, 27.10.89
Choreography: James Kudelka
Music: Schumann
Costumes: Michel Proulx

Schéhérazade, 27.10.89
Choreography: James Kudelka and David
Earle
Music: Rimsky-Korsakov
Sets and costumes: Peter Horne

Repertory:

L'Après-midi d'un faune
Choreography: Vaslav Nijinsky
Music: Debussy
Reconstructed and staged by: Ann
Hutchinson-Guest, Claudia Jeschke
Sets and costumes: Léon Bakst

Divertimento No. 15
Choreography: George Balanchine
Music: Mozart
Staged by: Sara Leland, Victoria Simon
Costumes: Nicole Martinet

The Nutcracker
Choreography: Fernand Nault
Music: Tchaikovsky
Sets: Peter Horne
Costumes: François Barbeau

Le Sacre du printemps
Choreography: James Kudelka
Music: Stravinsky
Costumes: Sylvain Labelle

Carmina Burana
Choreography: Fernand Nault
Music: Carl Orff
Sets: Robert Prévost
Costumes: François Barbeau

Number of performances:
90

Salary information:
Dancers operate under a collective
agreement – Union des Artistes

**ASSOCIATED SCHOOL OF LES GRANDS
BALLET CANADIENS:**

**ECOLE SUPERIEURE DE DANSE DU
QUEBEC**

4816, rue Rivard
Montréal (Québec)
Canada H2J 2N6
Tel: (514) 849-4929

Director and administrator:
Donald Fortin

Artistic director:
Ludmilla Chiriaeff

Resident choreographer:
Nicole Vachon

Professional programme:
Christine Clair
*Professional development, teachers'
programme:*
Alain Pauzé
Ballet master:
Daniel Seillier
Principal counsellor:
Annette Av Paul
Chief conservator, documentation centre:
Vincent Warren

Principal teachers:
Kathryn Biever, Denise Biggi, Barbara
Boudot, Christiane Dufort, Louise
Labrecque, Manon Montpetit, Susan
Toumine, Charmaine Turner, Vincent
Warren, Christine Williams

Guest teachers and complementary courses:
Danielle Arendasova, Natalia Borlestean,
Pierre Bourbonnais, Sonia Del Rio, Diane
Geoffrion, Stéphanie Gilbert, Oded Kafri,
Rose-Marie Lebe-Néron, Gabriella Orbach,
Diane Paquette, Thérèse Petit, Yolaine
Prévost, Wendy Wright

LE JEUNE BALLET DU QUEBEC

4816, rue Rivard
Montréal (Québec)
Canada H2J 2N6
Tel: (514) 849-4929

Director:
Donald Fortin
Artistic direction:
Ludmilla Chiriaeff, Christine Clair, Daniel
Seillier

Resident choreographer:
Nicole Vachon
Artists:
8 female, 6 male

Length of season:
October–April (30 weeks); first full
operating year 1990/1

Number of performances during season:
60

212

Repertory, 1990/1:

Charmes et fantaisies
Choreography: Nicole Vachon
Music: Saint-Saëns
Costumes: Nicole Martinet
Sets and lighting: Judith Curnew

**JUDITH MARCUSE DANCE COMPANY/
JUDITH MARCUSE DANCE PROJECTS
SOCIETY**

1128A West 15th Street
North Vancouver, BC
Canada V7P 1M9
Tel: (604) 985 6459

Artistic director:
Judith Marcuse

Dancers:
Linda Arkelian, Annemarie Cabri-Verbeke,
Robert Glumbek, Marthe Leonard, Jackie
Nel, Gilles Petit, Sylvain Senez

Premières:

Madrugada
Choreography: Judith Marcuse
Music: musical collage
Sets: Sterling McLean and Gordon Smith,
based on an original painting by Gordon
Smith
Costumes: Kimberley Bothen

Distant City (1989)
Choreography: Christopher House
Music: Claude Vivier
Costumes: Susan Berganzi, Kim Bothen

Blue Skies, Purple Haze
Choreography: Judith Marcuse
Music: Lukas Foss, Jimi Hendrix

Baby, I Love You
Choreography: Judith Marcuse
Music: Aretha Franklin
Costumes: Judith Marcuse

Bach and Blue
Choreography: Judith Marcuse
Music: Bach
Costumes: Eva Christiansen

Closed Circuit (1986)
Choreography: Judith Marcuse
Music: Louis Andriessen

Time Out
Choreography: Judith Marcuse

Music: Touré Kunda
Costumes: Phillip Clarkson

Seascape
Choreography: Judith Marcuse
Music: Bach
Costumes: Michelle Heon, Judith Marcuse

Number of performances:
32

Salary information:
$360–400 per week

ANNA WYMAN DANCE THEATRE

3rd Floor, 927 Granville Street
Vancouver, BC
Canada V6Z 1L3
Tel: (604) 662 8846

Artistic director:
Anna Wyman
General manager:
Karen Williams

Number of dancers:
8

Première:

Walls (world première)
Choreography: Anna Wyman
Music: John Adams
Costumes: David Chipman Siebert

Salary information:
$250–400 per week

O VERTIGO DANSE

3575 St-Laurent, suite 403
Quebec
Canada H2X 2T7
Tel: (514) 845-0566

Artistic director and choreographer:
Ginette Laurin
Rehearsal mistress:
France Roy
Administrative director:
Mireille Martin

Dancers:
Marc Boivin, Pierre-André Côté, Carole
Courtois, Scott Kemp, Mireille Leblanc,
Jacqueline Lemieux, Natalie Morin

Repertory:

Chagall
Choreography: Ginette Laurin
Music: Janitors Animated, Gaétan Leboeuf
Sets: Stéphane Roy
Costumes: Jean-Yves Cadieux

Don Quichotte
Choreography: Ginette Laurin
Music: Janitors Animated
Sets: Rose-Marie Goulet
Costumes: Carole Courtois

Number of performances:
30

Salary information:
$350–400 per week, starting wage $250,
top wage $450

OTTAWA BALLET (formerly Theatre
Ballet of Canada)

126 York Street
PO Box 366
Station A
Ottawa, Ontario
Canada K1N 8V3
Tel: (613) 235-7296

Artistic director:
Frank Augustyn

Ballet mistress:
Margery Lambert
Principal dancers:
Andrea Allen, Ping Feng, Stephanie
Hutchinson, Amy Lehman Baldwin,
Kataryna Kwasniewska, Carlos Rogue
Loyola, Guo Ping Lu, Rachel Wates, Jan
Zdanowicz

Première:

Come Rain, Come Shine, 24.3.90
Choreography: Francis Patrelle
Music and songs of Judy Garland

Repertory:

Bella
Choreography: Danny Grossman
Music: Puccini

Glass Houses
Choreography: Christopher House
Music: Ann Southam

Jeux-poème dansé
Choreography: Lawrence Gradus
Music: Debussy

A Toast
Choreography: Lawrence Gradus
Music: Carl Schultz

Andante
Choreography: Lawrence Gradus

Inching
Choreography: Danny Grossman

Continuo
Choreography: Antony Tudor
Music: Pachelbel

Full Moon
Choreography: Lynne Taylor-Corbett

Number of performances:
24

Salary information:
$600–1,000 per two weeks

ROYAL WINNIPEG BALLET

380 Graham Avenue
Winnipeg, Manitoba
Canada R3C 4K2
Tel: (204) 956-0183

Artistic director:
John Meehan
Music director and conductor:
Earl Stafford
Associate artistic director
Andre Lewis
Assistant to the artistic director:
Catherine Taylor

Ballet mistress:
Alla Savchenko
Artistic consultant:
David Moroni
Artistic adviser:
Arnold Spohr
Guest teacher:
Galina Yordanova
Assistant ballet mistress:
Patti Caplette

Principal dancers:
Evelyn Hart, Elizabeth Olds, Stephen
Hyde, John Kaminski

214

Soloists:
Laura Graham, Caroline Gruber, Sarah
Slipper, Vincent Boyle, Mark Godden,
Daniel Nelson
Second soloists:
Diane Buck, Tamara Hoffmann, Barry Watt
Corps de ballet:
7 female, 6 male

Premières:

Anne of Green Gables, 11.10.89
Choreography: Jacques Lemay
Music: Norman Campbell
Orchestration: Robert Farnon/Earl Stafford
Story adaptation: Janis Dunning
Decor and costumes: Mary-Robinson Kerr

L.I.F.E. (Love is for Eternity), 4.10.89
Choreography: Michael Peters
Music: Collage
Costumes: Anne Armit

Sequoia, 11.10.89
Choreography: Mark Godden
Music: Joan Tower
Sets: Paul Daigle/Mark Godden
Costumes: Paul Daigle

Seventh Symphony, 6.10.89
Choreography: Toer van Schayk
Music: Beethoven
Sets: Toer van Schayk
Costumes: Toer van Schayk

Symphony in C, 5.10.89
Choreography: George Balanchine
Music: Bizet
Costumes: Karinska

Repertory:

The Ecstasy of Rita Joe
Choreography: Norbert Vesak
Music: Anne Mortifee
Lyrics and dialogue: George Ryga
Costumes and lighting: Norbert Vesak
Film director: Don S. Williams

Three Pieces
Choreography: Hans van Manen
Music: Grazyny Bacewicz
Sets: Jan van der Wal
Costumes: Jan van der Wal

Threnody
Choreography: Judith Marcuse
Music: Monteverdi
Decor and costumes: Claude Girard

Gaité Parisienne
Choreography: Leonide Massine
Music: Jacques Offenbach
Staged by: Lorca Massine
Mounted by: Susanna Della Pietra
Scenery and costumes: Claude Girard

Concerto Barocco
Choreography: George Balanchine
Music: Bach
Staged by: Susan Hendl
Decor and costumes: Eugene Berman

5 Tangos
Choreography: Hans van Manen
Music: Astor Piazzolla
Orchestration: Earl Stafford
Decor and costumes: Jean-Paul Vroom

Paquita
Choreography: Jorge Garcia after Petipa
Music: Minkus, Deldevez
Orchestration: William McDermot, John
Lanchbery
Costumes: Doreen Macdonald

Pas d'action
Choreography: Brian Macdonald
Music: Mayerbeer, arr. von Suppe
Decor and costumes: By Chance

Symphony in D
Choreography: Jiři Kylián
Music: Haydn
Costumes: Tom Schenk

The Nutcracker
Choreography: John Neumeier
Music: Tchaikovsky
Scenery and costumes: Jürgen Rose

Romeo and Juliet
Choreography: Rudi van Dantzig
Music: Prokofiev
Scenery and costumes: Toer van Schayk

Don Quixote pas de deux
Choreography: Petipa
Music: Minkus

Le Corsaire
Choreography: Gorsky
Music: Drigo

Nuages
Choreography: Kylián
Music: Debussy

Pas de deux romantique
Choreography: Carter
Music: Rossini

Tarantella
Choreography: Balanchine
Music: Gottschalk

Tchaikovsky pas de deux
Choreography: Balanchine

Number of performances:
36 home, 94 on tour

Salary information:
$400–650 per week, as per Canadian Ballet agreement with Actors' Equity

ROYAL WINNIPEG BALLET SCHOOL, PROFESSIONAL DIVISION

380 Graham Avenue
Winnipeg, Manitoba
Canada R3C 4K2
Tel: (204) 956-0183

Principal:
David Moroni

Administrator:
Gordon Wright

Vice-principal:
Jacqueline Weber

Teaching staff:
Julia Arkos, Joanne Gingras, Petru Macra, Arlene Minkhorst, Bruce Monk, Elaine Werner-Hutchison

Guest teachers:
Galina Yordanova, Bulgaria
Jacque Lynn Bell, USA
Jacques Lemay, Canada

TORONTO DANCE THEATRE

80 Winchester Street
Toronto, Ontario
Canada M4X 1B2
Tel: (416) 967-1365

Artistic director and co-founder:
David Earle

Resident choreographer and co-founder:
Patricia Beatty
Resident choreographer:
Christopher House
Resident choreographer and co-founder:
Peter Randazzo

Administrative director:
Kenneth A. Peirson

Principal dancers:
Karen duPlessis, Christopher House, Laurence Lemieux, Michael Sean Marye, Suzette Sherman
Soloists:
4 female, 2 male
Number of dancers:
13, 2 apprentices

Repertory:
All lighting design by Ron Snippe and all costume design by Denis Joffre unless otherwise indicated.

Gaia (company première)
Choreography: Patricia Beatty
Music: Sharon Smith

Against Sleep
Choreography: Patricia Beatty
Music: Ann Southam
Costume: Susan Macpherson
Set design: Ursula Hanes

Baroque Suite
Choreography: David Earle
Music: Bach, Vivaldi, Corelli

El Amor Brujo (company première)
Choreography: David Earle
Music: de Falla

Sacra Conversazione
Choreography: David Earle
Music: Mozart

Frostwatch
Choreography: David Earle
Text: Graham Jackson

Dreamsend (world première)
Choreography: David Earle
Music: Webern

Openings & Inventions (company première)
Choreography: David Earle
Music: Bach

Sacred Garden
Choreography: David Earle
Music: Pergolesi

Scherzo (world première)
Choreography: Christopher House
Music: Schumann
Lighting: Howard Munroe

216

Island
Choreography: Christopher House
Music: Steve Reich

Green Evening Clear and Warm
Choreography: Christopher House
Music: Mozart

Artemis Madrigals
Choreography: Christopher House
Music: Stravinsky

Fjeld (world première)
Choreography: Christopher House
Music: Arvo Part

The Court of Lions
Choreography: Christopher House
Music: Hans Kotter, Francis Pilkington, Josquin de Press, Francesco Canova

Zefiro Torna (world première)
Choreography: Christopher House
Music: Monteverdi

A Simple Melody
Choreography: Peter Randazzo
Music: collage by Dave Davis
Costume: Carol Cawley

Arch
Choreography: Peter Randazzo
Music: Keith Jarrett
Visual design: Gera Dillon

Cadenzas (world première)
Choreography: Peter Randazzo
Music: Alexina Louie

Court of Miracles
Choreography: David Earle, James Kudelka, Christopher House, Peter Randazzo, Kenny Pearl, Ron Ward
Set design: Ron Ward

Quodlibet (world première)
Choreography: David Earle, Christopher House
Music: Schumann, Duke Ellington, John Cage, Bach

Number of performances:
63

Salary information:
Regular company members: $300–500 per week plus benefits; apprentices: $225 per week plus benefits

China

CENTRAL BALLET

3 Tai Ping Jie
Beijing 100500
P.R.O. China
Tel: 33 4962

Artistic director:
Li Cheng-xiang
Associate directors:
Bai Shu-xiang, Jiang Zu-hui, Yu Lei-di
Assistant directors:
Deng Yuan-sen, Zhao Ru-heng

Choreographers:
Li Cheng-xiang, Jiang Zu-hui, Wang Shi-qi, Sun Zheng-ting, Shu Jun-jun

Teachers:
Zhang Chun-zeng, Wu Zhen-rong, Yang Rong-rong, Zhang Min-chu, Cao Zhi-guang, Jiang Wei-hao, Chen Cui-zhu, Sun Xi-wen

Notators:
Wu Jing-zhu, Zhang Ling-ling

Principal dancers:
Feng Ying, Zhang Dan-dan, Bai Lan, Li Ying, Wang Shan, Wang Cai-jun, Pan Jia-bin, Xu Gang, Wei Dong-sheng
Soloists:
Chen Li-e, Yu Guo-hua, Wang Ping-ping, Xue Qing-hua, Li Song, Tang Guo-hua, Wang Quan-xing, Pei Qiang

Corps de ballet:
70

Première:

Mountain Forest, 17.1.90, Capital Theatre, Beijing
Choreography: Norman Wark (USA)
Music: Liu Dun-nan
Set design: Zheng Ri-yang
Costume design: Norman Wark

Repertory:

Swan Lake
Choreography: Pyotr A. Gusev
Music: Tchaikovsky

Don Quixote
Choreography: Rudolf Nureyev
Music: Minkus

Ballet Concert
Both classic and modern by Chinese and foreign choreographers

SHANGHAI BALLET

1674 Hong Qiao Lu
Shanghai 200335
P.R.O. China
Tel: 2759516

Director:
Hamuti
Deputy directors:
Cai Guo-ying, Shen Wei-chuan
Artistic directors:
Lin Yang-yang, Yu Qing-yun

Choreographers:
Lin Yang-yang, Lin Xin-ge, Zhang Da-wei, Dong Xi-lin, Lu Jin, Chen Yu-zhuang

Teachers:
Yu Qing-yun and four others

Principal dancers:
Wang Qi-feng, Xin Li-li, Du Hong-ling, Cai Li-jun, Zhang Li, Yang Xin-hua, Li Chun-yuan, Shi Hui
Soloists:
10
Corps de ballet:
30

Premières:

Don Quixote, 27.5.89, Shanghai Municipal Auditorium, Shanghai

The Bright Footsteps
Highlights of the company's repertoire including Ivanov's *Nutcracker pas de trois*, Balanchine's *Tchaikovsky pas de deux*, Petipa's *Don Quixote pas de deux*, Fokine's *Les Sylphides*, William Sorrell's *Isle*, Amalie Dienzero's *The Wakening Flower Goddess*, and four premières:

Flower Buds
Choreography: Lu Jin, Chen Yu-zhuang
Music: Strauss

Classical Symphony
Choreography: Lin Yang-yang, Lin Xin-ge
Music: Prokofiev

Flower Waltz
Choreography: Zhang Da-wei, Lin Yang-yang, Yu Qing-yun
Music: Tchaikovsky

Spring Waltz
Choreography: Balanchine
Music: Strauss

Touring plans:
New Zealand and Australia: autumn of 1990

CHINA OPERA AND DANCE DRAMA THEATRE

2 Nan Hua Dong Jie
Hu Fang Lu
Beijing 10052, P.R.O. China
Tel: 335215/338052

Director of the theatre:
Qiao Yu
Deputy director in charge of the Dance Drama Company:
Wang Shu-yun
Director of the Dance Drama Company:
Li Bai-cheng
Deputy directors of the DDC:
Ji Jin-wu, Luo Di-qiang

Choreographers:
Zhang Guo-yu, Sun Dai-zhang, Lan Heng, Li Jun-chen

Teachers:
Shen Di-cai, Zhang Jin-xin, Pan Jing-sheng, Qi Dong-hai, Luo Di-qiang, Zhang Ming-juan, Zhai Jie-ming

Principal dancers:
Zhao Qing, Chen Ai-lian, Ji Jin-wu, Hai Yan, Fang Bo-nian, Liu Da-xing, Yu Jian, Ye Jian-ping, Gai Yi-kun, Xia Li-rong, Bai Ling
Soloists:
Liu Fang, Yang Hong, Zhang Wei, Dai Lian-sheng, Xia Li-yan, Liu Dou-zhi, Zou Ying, Liu Kai
Corps de ballet:
50

Premières:

Weaving the Flower Basket
Choreography: Zhao Qing
Music: Chinese folk-music adaptation

The Yellow River Lullaby
Choreography: Wu Ming-qi
Music: Bao Jing-shu
Orchestration: Shi Zhi-you
Stage set: Zheng Yu-yang, Liang Hong-zhou, Liu Bi-yuan
Costume design: Dong Shu-fang, Yang Lin

GUANGDONG EXPERIMENTAL MODERN DANCE COMPANY

Guangdong Provincial Dance School
Sa Ho Ding, Shui Yum Road
Guangzhou 510075
P.R.O. China
Tel: 775237, 753522

Director:
Yang Mei-qi
Administrative director:
Lin Pai-shi

Guest choreographers:
American Dance Festival Faculty, Hu Jia-lu (originally resident choreographer of Shanghai Dance Drama Theatre, and now a student at the Martha Graham Centre for Contemporary Dance), Wili Cao (artistic director and resident choreographer of the Hong Kong City Contemporary Dance Company)

Guest teachers:
ADF Faculty
Ballet teacher:
Zhao Long

Dancers:
Zhao Long, Huang Wen-ge, Zhang Yin-zhong, Qin Li-ming, Ma Shou-ze, Su Ka, Li Peng, Shen Wei, Zhang Yan, Yan Ying, Huang Wen-chi, Yin Xiao-rong, Qiao Yang, Qu Xiao, Lin Li, Gu Wen-hao

Première:

City Romance
Choreography: Wili Cao
Music: adaptations by Wili Cao
Set design: Lin Zi-qi
Costume design: Li Hui-e

Salary information:
See article by Ou Jian-ping (p. 57)

Cuba

BALLET NACIONAL DE CUBA

Calzada No. 510, entr D y E
Vedado
C. Havana
Cuba
Tel: 32 4625

Director:
Alicia Alonso
Deputy director (technical):
Salvador Fernández
Musical director:
Marlene Urbay

Choreographers:
Alicia Alonso, Alberto Alonso, Gustavo
Herrera, Alberto Méndez, Hilda Riveros,
Iván Tenorio
Press and public relations:
Mayda Bustamente
Archivist:
Miguel Cabrera

Prima ballerina assoluta:
Alicia Alonso
Dancers:
Loipa Araujo, Aurora Bosch, Amparo Brito,
Sonia Calero, Marta García, Ofelia
González, María Elena Llorente, Josefina
Méndez, Mirta Plá, Rolando Candia, Lázaro
Carreño, Fernando Jhones, Orlando
Salgado, José Zamarano
Principal Dancers:
Dagmar Moradillo, Rodolfo Castellanos,
Pablo Moré, Rafael Padilla, Francisco
Salgado, Jorgé Vega
Number of dancers:
76 female, 52 male

Premières:

Intermezzo por L'Amore, 15.10.89
Choreography: Alberto Méndez
Music: P. Mascagni, F. Schmidt

Azor
Choreography: Alberto Méndez
Music: T. A. Vitali
Design: Salvador Fernández

Degas
Choreography: Marianela Boán
Music: José M. Vitier
Design: Salvador Fernández

Inti Raymi
Choreography: Gustavo Herrera
Music: Sergio Cortés
Design: Ricardo Reymena

Requiem por un Poeta
Choreography: Iván Tenorio
Music: Tchaikovsky, J. M. Blanco
Design: Salvador Fernández

Porgy and Bess
Choreography: Gladys González
Music: Gershwin
Costumes: Otto Chaviano
Scenario: Nelson Dorr

Foreign tours:
Spain (42 performances in 12 cities):
September/November 1989
Latin America: 1990 – Ecuador, Peru,
Argentina, Chile, Uruguay, Paraguay,
Dominican Republic, Puerto Rico,
Guatemala, Mexico, Costa Rica, Brazil

BALLET DE CAMAGÜEY

Carretera Central Este y 4
Camagüey 70300
Cuba
Tel: 96535/99215

Director:
Fernando Alonso

Maîtres de ballet:
Fernando Alonso, Hilda Martínez, Jorge
Rodríguez

Choreographers:
José A. Chávez, Francisco Lang
Guest choreographer:
Alberto Alonso

Press and public relations:
Juan Morciego

Prima ballerina:
Aïda Villoch
Principal dancers:
Osvaldo Beiro, Pedro M. Boza
Ballerinas:
Christine Ferrando, Bárbara García, Celia
Rosales
First dancers:
Pedro Beiro, Víctor Carnesoltas, Guillermo
Leyva, Orlando Lopéz
Number of dancers:
76

Premières:

Trio, Teatro Principal Ciego de Avila, 8.9.89
Choreography: Lázaro Martínez
Music: Philip Glass

Caminos, Teatro Principal Camagüey,
28.9.89
Choreography: Francisco Lang
Music: Eleni Karaindru

*Premières at the Camagüey 5th Dance
Festival:*

Conflictos, 8.10.89
Choreography: Menia Martínez
Music: Jean-Michel Jarre

De Amor y de Muerte, 14.10.89
Choreography: José A. Chávez
Music: Fidel Arango de Quesada

Formas Para Concierto, 9.10.89
Choreography: Menia Martínez
Music: J.S. Bach

Manada, 25.10.89
Choreography: Lazaro Martínez
Music: Paul Winter

Grand Pas de Deux Yoruba, 1.12.89
Choreography: Alberto Alonso
Music: Julián Blanco

Foreign tours:
Greece and Cyprus, August/September
1989; Brazil, March 1990 – Porto Alegre,
São Paulo, Brazilia; April 1990, Rio de
Janeiro

Number of performances:
60
The Camagüey Festival is biennial: the next
one will be November/December 1991

**CENTRO DE PROMOCION DE LA
DANZA LA JOVEN GUARDIA**

Calle 5ta No. 253 esq a E
Vedado
C. Habana 4
Cuba
Tel: 32-4625/32-7752

Director:
Laura Alonso
Advisers:
Miguel Gómez, Denia Hernández,
Reynaldo Muñiz

Press and public relations:
Marta Bercy, Hector Figueredo
Artistic committee:
Laura Alonso, Reynaldo Muñiz, Miguel
Gómez, Denia Hernández, Raúl Bustabad,
Lupe Calzadilla, Mercedes Reguero

Teachers and répétiteurs:
Laura Alonso, Denia Hernández, Lupe
Calzadilla, Miguel Gómez, Raúl Bustabad,
Reynaldo Muñiz, Mercedes Reguero, Isaura
Guzman, Marta Bercy, Héctor Figueredo,
Zoraida Rodriguez, Niurka Naranjo

*Principal dancers of the Joven Guardia (all
members of BNC corps de ballet):*
José Carreño, Svetlana Ballester, Lienz
Chang, Lorena Feijoo, Jesus Corrales, Julio
Arozarena, Marcela Goicochea, Yatseng
Chang

Number of dancers:
40

Repertory:
As well as a large number of *pas de deux*
from the international repertoire, the
company performs new works by members
of the Joven Guardia and their teachers
from the Centro.

Tours:
Cuba, Nicaragua and Peru

DANZA ABIERTA

Gran Teatro de La Habana
Prado Promenade
Entre San Rafael y San José
C. Habana

221

Director:
Marianela Boán
Assistant director:
Luis Ernesto Ruíz
Consultant:
Víctor Varela

Choreographers:
Marianela Boán, Víctor Varela, Jessica Llano
Ballet teacher:
Jeanette Moreno
Contemporary technique teachers:
Marianela Boán, Jessica Llano
Sound:
Alberto Pérez
Music:
Antonio Carreras

Premières:

L'Image de l'image de l'image de . . ., 9.12.89,
Teatro Principal de Camagüey, Festival de
Danza
Choreography: Jessica Llano
Music: Collage
Decor and costumes: Jessica Llano

*Antoine Marie Joseph Artaud: Mutilado por la
sociedad*, 8.12.89, Gran Teatro Sala Alejo
Carpentier
Choreography: Víctor Varela
Music: Víctor and Carlos Varela
Decor and costumes: Víctor Varela
Scenario: David Placeres

La Mas Feurte
Choreography: Marianela Boán
Music: Fragment of Schoenberg's
Transfigured Night, arr. Rául Díaz Puig
Decor and costumes: Ricardo Reymena

Sin Permiso
Choreography: Marianela Boán
Music: Philip Glass, Pergolesi, Meredith
Monk
Decor and costumes: José Franco

Un Arbol un Poco Vibratorio, 29.6.89, Teatro
Mella
Choreography: Gabri Christa (guest from
Holland)
Music: Yma Sumac
Text: Gabri Christa (poem)
Costume: Gabri Christa

Techniek, Techniek, 29.6.89
Choreography: Víctor Varela
Lighting: Fernando J. Alonso
Costume: Víctor Varela

Unidos, 29.6.89
Choreography: Lesmes Grenot
Music: Vangelis
Costumes: Lesmes Grenot

Ejes, 29.6.89
Choreography: Marianela Boán
Music: Matyas Seiber
Costumes: Marianela Boán

Godot, 29.6.89
Choreography: Víctor Varela
Music: José Antonio Leyva
Costumes: Víctor Varela

BALLET TEATRO DE LA HABANA

Teatro Nacional
Paseo y 39
Plaza de la Revolución
C. Habana
Cuba
Tel: 79-2728/79-6410

Director and principal choreographer:
Caridad Martínez

Guest choreographer:
Víctor Cuellar

Dancers:
Mirta Carcía, Caridad Martínez, Rosario
Suárez
Actor dancers:
María Elena Diardes, Raúl Durán, Cristóbal
Gonzalez, Pedro Sicard, Selma Soreghi
Guest dancer:
Rúben Rodríguez

Premières:

Test, 1989
Choreography: Caridad Martínez
Production and decor: Rubén Torres Lorca

Exilio, April 1990, Covarrubias Hall,
National Theatre, Havana
Choreography: Caridad Martínez, Miguel
Angel Sirgard, Pedro Sicard (collectively)

Dejame Que Te Cuente (Let me tell you),
April 1990, Covarrubias Hall, National
Theatre, Havana
Choreography: Caridad Martínez

Improvisación, April 1990, Covarrubias Hall,
National Theatre, Havana
Choreography: Selma Soreghi

Tour:
Mexico, September/October 1989

ASI SOMOS

Calle A No. 310 apto 7B
Entre 3ra y 5ta
Playa
C. Habana
Cuba
Tel: 2-42-76

Founder/director/choreographer:
Lorna Burdsall

Dancers:
Lourdes Cajigal, Mariela Castro, Vilma
Lara, Estela Paz, Rodolfo Hechavarría, Jan
José Rodríguez, Sergio Saiz

Lighting designer:
Israel Velasquez
Music adviser:
Jorge Berroa

Repertory:
(all pieces choreographed by Lorna
Burdsall)

Asi Somos
Music: Beethoven, Crumb, Russo

Moda del Malecón
Music: Música Popular

Tubos
Music: Ives

Duos I y II
Music: Berroa

Barril I
Music: Russo

Barril II
Music: Piazzolla

Barril III
Music: Albinoni

Vieja Maria
Music: Lavista, and poem by Ernesto Che
Guevara

Pan Integral Con Queso Crema
Music: Música Popular

Temprano
Music: Pachelbel

Manuscrito Antiguo
Music: Brouwer

Encontrado en una Botella Tela I
Music: Berio

Sabado Corto
Music: Brubeck

La Cebra
Music: Burdsall

Tardes Grises
Music: Garay

Ayer
Music: Chopin

Carnaval
Music: Música Popular

Vierte Corazon
Music: Berroa, inspired by a poem of José
Marti

**EL CONJUNTO DE DANZAS
ESPANOLAS**

El Gran Teatro de La Habana
Prado Promenade
Entre San Rafael y San José
C. Habana

Director:
Olga Bustamente

Repertory:

Mariana
Noche Española
Olé de la Curra
Sevilla
Asturias
Galicia
Pasadoble
Noche de Leucona
La Dolorosa (a Zarzuela)
Capricio Español
Estampas Andaluzas
Bernano
Excerpts from *El Sombrero de los Tres Picos*
(Three Cornered Hat) with music by
Augustin Lara, Albéniz, Leucona, De Falla,
among others

**DANZA CONTEMPORANEA DE
GUANTANAMO 1990**

Artes Escenicas
Los Maceo Guantanamo

Director:
Elfrida Mahler

Principal choreographers:
Elfrida Mahler and Isaías Rojas
Choreographers:
Tomás Guilarte, Alfred Velázquez
Guest choreographer:
Antonio Pérez, Director of Conjunto
Folclorico de Oriente

Modern-dance teachers:
Elfrida Mahler and Isaías Rojas
Folklore teachers:
Isaías Rojas, José Rojas
Folklore advisers:
Lolita Casimír and the group Los Cosía
Producer:
Herminio Daudinot

Number of dancers:
9 female, 14 male

Company debut:
26.1.90 at Teatro Guaso, Guantanamo

De Mi Bohio
Choreography: Isaías Rojas
Music: traditional Cuban folk

Zafra
Choreography: Elfrida Mahler
Music: Olavo Alén
Text: Tomás Gonzalez

Salvese Si Puede
Choreography: Elfrida Mahler
Music: Grupo Monte de Espuma

La Rebelión
Choreography: Isaías Rojas
Music: traditional Cuban

Cinco Instantes de un Junio Caliente
(dedicated to Winnie and Nelson Mandela)
Choreography: Elfrida Mahler
Music: songs sung in Zulu by Harry
Belafonte and Miriam Makeba
Poetry: anonymous Zulu, translated by
Rogelio Martínez Furé

El Pajaro de Oloro
Choreography: Antonio Pérez
Music: composed by the company's
musicians

28.1.90 at Teatro Guaso:

Propuestas a Analizar
Choreography: Tomás Guilarte

Music: Mussorgsky, electronic arrangement
by Jean-Michel Jarre

El Pensador
(Based on the Rodin sculpture)
Choreography: Alfredo Velázquez
Music: Milton do Rascimento
Poetry: Johannes R. Becher

El Amor Sonambulo
Choreography: Alfredo Velázquez
Music: Madrigal by Carlos Fariñas

Los Ultimos Juegos
Choreography: Alfredo Velázquez
Music: Scott Joplin

CONJUNTO FOLKLORICO DE CUBA

Calle 4 No. 103, entre Calzada y 5ta
Vedado
C. Habana
Cuba
Tel: 30-3060/30-3939

Director:
Teresa González
Consultant ethnologist:
Rogelio Martínez Furé

Principal choreographer:
Manolo Micler
Musical advisers:
Lázaro Ross, Margarita Ugarte, Candido
Zayas, Zenaida Armeteros, Teresa Polledo

Principal dancers:
Johannes García, George W. Dixon, Juan
Jesús Ortíz, Alfredo O'Farril, Zenaida
Armeteros, Margarita Ugarte, Silvina Fabars
Number of dancers and musicians:
100

Premières:

De La Clave Al Danzon, Mella Theatre,
7.12.89 (a history of Cuban social dance
from the 18th to the 20th century)

Ajanú
Choreography: Manolo Micler

Alafin de Oyó
Choreography: Lázaro Ross and Roberto
Espinosa

Brindis de Salas
Choreography: Leonardo Soto

Chango Bongoché
Choreography and direction: Teresa and
Tomás González

224

Revivals:
Mella Theatre, February 1990

Ciclo Yoruba (Yoruba Cycle)
Ciclo Congo (Congo Cycle)
Habanera y Apalencado (Havana Woman and Runaway Slave)
Refranes, Dicharachos y Trabalenguas (Proverbs, Spicy Remarks and Tongue Twisters)

The open-air Saturday Rumba takes place at 3 p.m. every other week in the courtyard of the Folklorico studios, and is one of the most popular of Havana's entertainments. Members of the company dance and sing; Martínez Furé comments on the origins of the works performed, and finally all are invited to join in and demonstrate their skills. International folklore workshops (15 days) take place on the third Monday in January and the first Monday in July.

Tours:
1989: Martinique, Fort de France Cultural Festival; German Democratic Republic, Berlin Festtage Festival
1989: December: Martínez Furé made a lecture tour of Mozambique, Angola, Benin, and Nigeria

CONJUNTO FOLCLORICO CUTUMBA

Enramadas 170 altos
Entre Padre Pico y Corona
Santiago de Cuba

Director:
Roberto Sánchez

Choreographers:
Ernesto Armiñán, Roberto David

Teachers:
Janilda Ruano, Idalberto Bandera, José Carrión, José Gabriel Exprest, Luís Armiñán, Rolando Ruiz
Design:
Pedro Bravo, Jorge Pozo
Costumes:
Maria L. Barnal

Principal dancers:
Juana I. Salazar, Idalberto Bandera, José Carrión
Number of dancers:
19

CONJUNTO FOLCLORICO DE ORIENTE

San Felix No. 407 esq. San Francisco
Santiago de Cuba

Director:
Antonio Pérez

The Conjunto Folclórico de Oriente, founded in 1959, recently changed its name to Compañia Folclórico and embarked on a more ambitious policy with the production of a full-length folk ballet, *Yemaya y el Pescador* (Yemaya and the Fisherman). The company continues to develop its work of rescuing African songs and dances and those of Haitian origin brought to the island in the past, whose roots are preserved in Cuban folk-traditions throughout the country.

AFROCUBA – AGRUPACION FOLKLORICA DE MATANZAS

Dirrección Provincial de Cultura
Magdalena 7705 entre Manzano y Contreras
Matanzas Cuba
Tel: 3121

Director:
Francisco Zamora

Number of dancers:
8 (7 singers also dance)

Matanzas claims to have received 75 per cent of all the slaves who were shipped from Africa and therefore to have the most characteristic dances from Angola, Benin, Congo, Dahomey and Nigeria.

DANZA CONTEMPORANEA DE CUBA
(formerly Danza Nacional)

Paseo y 39
Plaza de la Revolución
C. Habana
Cuba

Director:
Miguel Iglesias

Choreographers:
Eduardo Rivero, Manuel Vázquez, Víctor Cuéllar, Rosario Cárdenas, Isidro Rolando, Nereida Doncel, Milagros Medina, Narciso

Medina, Marianela Boán, Gerardo Lastra,
Neri Fernández
Visiting choreographer:
Gabri Christa

Musical director:
Regino Jiménez

Répétiteurs:
Manuel Vázquez e Isidro Rolando
Ballet teacher:
Zelaida Romero

Principal dancers:
Rubén Rodríguez, Dulce María Vale, Regla
Salvent, Gisela González, Luis Roblejo,
Milagros Medina, Arístides Bringuez,
Manuel Vázquez, Reinaldo Suárez,
Armando Ríos, Luis Mariano
Number of dancers:
34 female, 22 male

Premières:

Celestina
Choreography: Víctor Cuéllar
Music: Michel Wusser, Peter Margelar, José
Maria Vitier, Claica Arabe, Folklorica
Afrocubana
Designs: Eduardo Arrocha

Ninfas
Choreography: Nereida Doncell
Music: Tomás Fortín
Designs and lighting: Eduardo Arrocha

Pajaro Dorado
Choreography: Nereida Doncell
Music: Miguel Cobas
Designs: Eduardo Arrocha

Zodiaco Antillano
Choreography: Isidoro Rolando
Music: Juan Blanco
Designs and lighting: Eduardo Arrocha

Variantes
Choreography: Milagros Medina
Music: Orquestra de Percusión de Danza
Contemporánea de Cuba
Designs and lighting: Eduardo Arrocha

Uter-O (Dance Theatre)
Choreography: Guillermo Horta Betancourt
Music: Juan Piñera and others
Designs: Eduardo Arrocha from an idea by
Guillermo Horta

Encuentro
Choreography: Eddy Veitía
Music: Vangelis Espataasis
Costumes: Eduardo Arrocha

Un Grano de Oro
Choreography: Narciso Medina
Music: José Maria Vitier
Designs and lighting: Gabriel Hierrezuelo

Del Espectro Nocturno
Choreography: Rosario Cárdenas
Music: Juan Piñera
Costumes: Rosario Cárdenas

Dedalo (1989 UNEAC choreography prize)
Choreography: Rosario Cárdenas
Music: Juan Piñera
Dramatist: Salvador Lemis
Scenery: Roberto Gottardi
Masks and costumes: Eduardo Arrocha

Ofelia O El Amor
Choreography: Manuel Vasquez
Music: Rachmaninov
Designs: Eduardo Arrocha

De La Memoria Fragmentada
Choreography: Ramiro Guerra
Music: Ritual Yoruba, Eyeleo de Lucía
Huergo (Grupo Sintesis), Aleatoria de
Jorge Berroa, Popular de Carnaval,
Ausencia de Jaime Prats
Costumes: Eduardo Arrocha

Denmark

THE ROYAL DANISH BALLET

PO Box 2185
DK-1017 Copenhagen K
Tel: 33 32 20 20

Artistic director:
Frank Andersen
Director:
Boel Jørgensen
Associate artistic director:
Lise la Cour

Ballet masters:
Lise la Cour, Jens Graff, Henning
Kronstam, Arlette Weinreich

Teachers:
Fredbjørn Bjørnsson, Sorella Englund, Jens
Graff, Palle Jacobsen, Niels Kehlet,
Henning Kronstam, Margaret Mercier,
Kirsten Ralov, Flemming Ryberg, Kirsten
Simone, Ulla Skow, Anne Sonnerup, Anne
Marie Vessel, Arne Villumsen
Guest teachers:
Truman Finney, Rimma Karelskaja, Stanley
Williams

Principal dancers:
Annemarie Dybdal, Sorella Englund, Linda
Hindberg, Mette Hønningen, Lis Jeppesen,
Mette Ida Kirk, Heidi Ryom, Kirsten
Simone, Frank Andersen, Arne Bech,
Fredbjørn Bjørnsson, Johnny Eliasen (on
leave of absence), Nikolaj Hübbe, Palle
Jacobsen, Niels Kehlet, Alexander Kølpin,
Aage Poulsen, Lloyd Riggins, Flemming
Ryberg, Arne Villumsen
Guest dancers:
Oliver Matz, Gregory Osborne
Corps de ballet:
46 female, 32 male

Premières:

France Dance, 17.11.89, Royal Theatre, Old
Stage
Choreography: William Forsythe
Music: Bach
Staging: Urs Frey
Design: Cara Perlmann

Manhattan Abstraction, 17.11.89, Royal
Theatre, Old Stage
Choreography: Anna Lærkesen
Music: Poul Ruders
Staging: Anne Lærkesen and Sorella
Englund
Design: Jens-Jacob Worsaae

Fête Galante, 17.11.89, Royal Theatre, Old
Stage
Choreography: Ib Andersen
Music: Couperin
Design: Jens-Jacob Worsaae

The Lay of Thrym, 11.5.90, Royal Theatre,
Old Stage
Choreography: August Bournonville
Music: J. P. E. Hartmann
Staging: Elsa Marianne von Rosen
Design: Allan Fridericia

Revival:

Giselle
Choreography: Jean Corelli and Jules
Perrot
Music: Adolphe Adam, arr. John Lanchbery
Scenery: Desmond Heeley
Staging: Henning Kronstam, Arlette
Weinreich

Repertory:

Don Quixote
Choreography: Yuri Grigorovich after
Petipa and Gorsky
Music: Minkus
Staging: Juri Grigorovich by Rimma
Karelskaja, Anatoly Simatyov, Henning
Kronstam and Lise la Cour
Scenery and costumes: Jens-Jacob Worsaae

Apollon Musagètes
Choreography: George Balanchine
Music: Stravinsky
Staging: Henning Kronstam

Rhapsody in Blue
Choreography: Lar Lubovitch
Music: Gershwin
Staging: Lar Lubovitch, Jens Graff
Costumes: Barbara Matera

La Sylphide
Choreography: August Bournonville
Music: Løvenskjold
Staging: Henning Kronstam, Arlette
Weinreich
Scenery: Søren Frandsen
Costumes: Henrik Bloch

Napoli
Choreography: August Bournonville
Music: Gade, Helsted, Paulli and Lumbye
Staging: Kirsten Ralov
Design: Søren Frandsen

Agon
Choreography: Balanchine
Music: Stravinsky
Staging: Patricia Neary, Jens Graff

Afternoon of a Faun
Choreography: Jerome Robbins
Music: Debussy
Staging: Bart Cook, Sorella Englund
Scenery and costumes: Jean Rosenthal and
Irene Sharaff

Moon Reindeer
Choreography: Birgit Cullberg
Music: Knudåge Riisager
Staging: Birgit Cullberg, Gunilla Roempke,
Arlette Weinreich
Scenery and costumes: Per Falk

Onegin
Choreography: John Cranko
Music: Tchaikovsky
Staging: Reid Anderson, Jane Bourne,
Henning Kronstam, Jens Graff
Design: Jürgen Rose

Coppélia
Choreography: Hans Brenaa after Arthur
Saint-Leon
Music: Delibes
Staging: Anne Marie Vessel, Frank
Andersen
Design: Søren Frandsen

Salary information:
Aspirants up to 100.000 Danish Crowns a
year; other dancers up to 250.00 DKR. A
very few soloists 300.000 DKR

COMPANY SCHOOL

The Royal Theatre Ballet School
PO Box 2185
DK-1017 Copenhagen K
Tel: 33 32 20 20

Director:
Frank Andersen

Administrator/principal teacher:
Anne Marie Vessel

The Royal Theatre Archives and Library
PO Box 2185
DK-1017 Copenhagen K

The theatre archives date back to 1748 and
the ballet archives to the time of Galeotti at
the start of the 19th century.

Finland

FINNISH NATIONAL BALLET

Bulevardi 23–7
00181 Helsinki
Tel: 80–12912

Director:
Doris Laine

*Company and/or guest teachers during
season:*
Jekaterina Pavlova, Jocelyn Alizart, Tiiu
Randviir, Laura Alonso, Maria Kekesi, Tiit
Härm, Vladimir Koshelev

Ballet mistress:
Joan Blakeney

Ballet assistants:
Jocelyn Alizart, Rauno Marttinen

Notator:
Rauno Marttinen (Benesh)

Soloists:
7 female, 6 male
Artists:
55
Guest artists:
Irek Mukhamedov, Jukka Aromaa

Length of season:
Mid-August 1989 to end of May 1990

Premières: (at Finnish National Opera
House)

Stairset, 19.10.89
Choreography: Tiina Lindfors
Music: Palle Mikkelborg
Design: Carmela Wager

Spirit Blues, 19.10.89
Choreography: Walter Nicks
Music: Duke Ellington
Design: Carmela Wager

The Ragtime Dance Company, 19.10.89
Choreography: Gray Veredon
Music: Scott Joplin
Design: Carmela Wager

Nijinsky, 18.1.90
Choreography: Juha Vanhakartano
Music: Joseph Hölderle
Design: Mark Väisänen

Gala Performance, 18.1.90
Choreography: Antony Tudor
Music: Prokofiev
Design: Hugh Laing and Mark Väisänen

Salome, 29.3.90
Choreography: Harold Collins
Music: Peter Maxwell Davies
Design: Seppo Nurmimaa

Repertory:

The Nutcracker
Choreography: Yuri Grigorovich
Music: Tchaikovsky
Design: Anneli Queflander

Lady of the Camellias
Choreography: Domy Reiter-Soffer
Music: Camille Saint-Saëns
Design: Seppo Nurmimaa

Ronja, The Robber's Daughter
Choreography: Marjo Kuusela
Music: Jukka Linkola
Design: Seppo Nurmimaa

D.C.
Choreography: Nils Christe
Music: Stravinsky
Design: Keso Dekker

Verklärte Nacht
Choreography: Jiři Kylián
Music: Arnold Schönberg

Etudes
Choreography: Harald Lander
Music: Riisager, after Czerny

Number of performances:
91

Touring:
Finland, Spain

Salary information:
From 6514 FIM to 13,905 FIM per month,
depending on length of time in the
company. Extra money is paid for each
performance, with a paid vacation in June.
Pensions are 60 per cent of full salary and
may be drawn when women retire at 42
and men at 46.

**BALLET SCHOOL OF THE FINNISH
NATIONAL BALLET**

Director:
Maj-Lis Rajala

Teachers:
Seppo Koski, Ilkka Lampi, Maksim
Lukjanof, Jutta Mustakallio, Maj-Lis Rajala,
Marianna Rumjantseva, Eija Lilja, Seija
Silfverberg, Kaija Helo

Guest teachers:
Jekaterina Pavlova, Aime Herkül, Vladimir
Koshelov

DANCE THEATRE RAATIKKO

Orvokkitie 13
PL 28
01301 Vanta
Tel: 358-0-8731184, 8732306

Director:
Marja Korhola

Principal teacher:
Tulla Kjällström

Number of dancers:
6 female, 6 male

Length of season:
August 1989 to end of May 1990

New productions:

Puerto del Puerto, Helsinki, 5.9.89
Choreography: Marja Korhola
Design: Metti Nordin

The Witch Women, Helsinki, 4.12.89
Choreography: Maria Wolska

The King is Coming, Helsinki, 16.12.89
Choreography: Ari Numminen
Design: Kari Petäjä

Vino's Bride, Helsinki, 5.3.90
Choreography: Tiina Jalkanen

Number of performances:
Approximately 80

Repertory:

Fox Skin
Choreography: Marjo Kuusela
Music: Stravinsky

Toe Dance
Choreography: Marja Korhola
Design: Marja Korhola and Marja Leino

Quartet for the End of Time
Choreography: Marjo Kuusela
Music: Olivier Messiaen
Design: Soili Eriksson

Eight Caprices
Choreography: Tuomo Railo
Music: Niccolò Paganini

Ten Feet
Choreography: Marja Korhola
Music: Collage

Jolly Jumper
Choreography: Marja Korhola

Orient-Express
Choreography: Marja Korhola
Design: Reija Kirvikoski

Gala Performance
Choreography: Marja Korhola

RAATIKKO COMPANY DANCE SCHOOL

Director:
Erja Asikainen

THE DANCE GROUP OF THE HELSINKI CITY THEATRE

Eläintarhantie 5
00530 Helsinki
Tel: 3580–39401

Director:
Jorma Uotinen

Principal choreographer:
Jorma Uotinen

Number of dancers:
11 (sometimes more)

Length of season:
August 1989 to end of May 1990

New productions:
(at the City Theatre, Helsinki)

Opéra Comique, 22.9.89
Choreography: Markku Nenonen

Ballet Pathétique, 22.9.89
Choreography: Jorma Uotinen

Sleeping Beauty, 6.1.90
Choreography: Jorma Uotinen

Repertory:

Siddharta
Choreography: Maisa Savolainen

Kalevala
Choreography: Jorma Uotinen

Piaf Piaf
Choreography: Jorma Uotinen

Number of performances:
Approximately 60

Tours:
Holland and West Germany

DANCE GROUP MOBITA

Kirkkokatu 1
33100 Tampere
Tel: 358-31-130113

Dancer/choreographers:
Ester Naparstok, Päivi Järvinen, Tuula
Linnusmäki, Jari Sihvo, Mirja Tukiainen

Repertory:

How are you then?
Choreography: Tuula Linnusmäki, Jari
Sihvo

Ärviset
Choreography: Päivi Järvinen

Coin Dance
Choreography: Linnusmäki, Naparstok,
Sihvo, Väisänen

Totte and Jalmari, 25.10.89, Tampere
Choreography: Tuula Linnusmäki, Jari
Sihvo

Rooms, 26.11.89, Tampere
Choreography: Marjo Hämäläinen

If You Call Somebody, 3.12.89, Tampere
Choreography: Tuula Linnusmäki, Jari
Sihvo

Circus-Story, 24.3.90, Tampere
Choreography: Taina Väisänen

Love, 21.4.90, Tampere
Choreography: Ruth Matso

A Couple of Relationships, 21.4.90, Tampere
Choreography: Linnusmäki, Sihvo

Number of performances:
About 50

Touring:
West Germany, Estonia

AURINKO BALLET (SUN BALLET)

Arvinkatu 5
20140 Turku
Tel: 538-21-302182, 329440

Director:
Raija Lehmussaari

Productions:

Magic Flute
Choreography: Liisa Priha
Music: Mozart

Such Things Do Occur
Choreography: Elsa Sylvestersson
Music: Erkki Melartin

Pessi and Illusia, Turku, November 1989
Choreography: Raija Lehmussaari

Ballet, Turku, 22.1.90
Choreography: Boris Eifman
Music: Heikki Sarmanto

Pseudo, Turku, 22.1.90
Choreography: Raija Lehmussaari

Love, Honour and Revenge, Turku, 19.4.90
Choreography: Raija Lehmussaari

Number of performances:
100–120

DANCE THEATRE ERI

Yrjanankatu 2
20300 Turku
Tel: 35821-501032, 3580-7017267

Administrative director:
Vivica Bandler

Choreographers/dancers:
Sampo Kivelä, Tiina Lindfors, Suvi
Pohjonen, Lassi Sairela, Eeva Soini

Productions:

Essential
Choreography: Tiina Lindfors

Eri Gallery
Choreography: Tiina Lindfors

Eriö, Turku, 2.12.89
Choreography: Ari Savinen

Odd Couple, Turku, 2.12.89
Choreography: Sampo Kivelä, Eeva Soini
Music: Alikoski-Wallasvaara

Different Keeper, Turku, 2.12.89
Choreography: Tiina Lindfors
Music: David Byrne

Firework, Turku, 7.1.90

Shostakovich, Turku, 30.3.90

Passion, Espoo, 11.4.90

DANCE THEATRE HURJARUUTH

Viinenkuja 5
00370 Helsinki
Tel: 3580-555820

Director/principal choreographer:
Arja Pettersson

231

Number of dancers:
From 4 to 6

New productions:

Five plus Five, Helsinki, 25.9.89
Choreography: Mirja Tukiainen

Via, Helsinki, 26.11.89
Choreography: Sanna Tyyri
Music: Jorma Tapio

Kanteletar, Helsinki, 28.2.90
Choreography: Arja Pettersson

Repertory:

Guess What?
Choreography: Arja Pettersson

Age of the Rustling Moon
Choreography: Ulla Koivisto

Ear
Choreography: Mirja Tukiainen

Chinese Story
Choreography: Arja Pettersson

Island
Choreography: Arja Pettersson

Number of performances:
Approximately 100

Touring:
North Korea, Estonia

France

PARIS OPERA BALLET

Opéra de Paris Garnier
8, rue Scribe
75009 Paris
Tel: 40 17 35 35

Director designate:
Patrick Dupond

Principal choreographer:
Rudolf Nureyev

Guest choreographers:
Mark Morris, Roland Petit, Merce
Cunningham

*Ballet masters and assistants to the
director:*
Patrice Bart, Eugène Polyakov

Répétitrices:
Patricia Ruanne, Aleth Francillon

Teachers:
Josette Amiel, Annie Carbonnel, Attilo
Labis, Gilbert Mayer, Noëlla Pontois,
Ghislaine Thesmar

Etoiles:
Florence Clerc, Isabelle Guérin, Françoise
Legrée, Monique Loudières, Elisabeth
Maurin, Elisabeth Platel, Claude de
Vulpian, Kader Belarbi, Patrick Dupond,
Jean Guizerix, Laurent Hilaire, Charles
Jude, Manuel Legris, Jean-Yves Lormeau

Premiers danseurs:
Carole Arbo, Karin Averty, Fanny Gaïda,
Marie-Claude Pietragalla, Clotilde Vayer,
Jaques Namont, Jean-Christophe Paré,
Olivier Patey, Stéphane Prince, Wilfried
Romoli
Other dancers:
64 female, 54 male

New productions: (company premières):

Tanz-Schul
Choreography: Jiri Kylián
Music: Mauricio Kagel
Design: John MacFarlane

Sinfonietta
Choreography: Jiri Kylián
Music: Janáček
Design: Walter Nobbe

Points in Space
Choreography: Merce Cunningham
Music: John Cage
Set: William Anastasi
Costumes: Dove Bradshaw

Speaking in Tongues
Choreography: Paul Taylor
Music: Matthew Patton
Design: Santo Loquasto

Ein Herz (world première 6.6.90)
Choreography: Mark Morris
Music: J. S. Bach

Repertory:

The Sleeping Beauty
Choreography: Petipa, Nureyev
Staging: Rudolf Nureyev
Music: Tchaikovsky
Design: Nico Georgiadis

Diaghilev programme
(Le Spectre de la rose, L'Après-midi d'un faune,
Petrushka)

Roland Petit programme
(Le Jeune Homme et la mort, Carmen)

In the Night
Choreography: Jerome Robbins
Music: Chopin
Design: Antony Dowell

Serenade, Violin Concerto, Prodigal Son –
Balanchine

ASSOCIATED SCHOOL
Ecole du Ballet de l'Opéra de Paris

Director:
Claude Bessy

Comprehensive information on French
dance companies can be obtained from:

Le Centre National d'Action Musicale
(CENAM)
51 rue Vivienne
75002 Paris
Tel: 42 33 38 24

This organization publishes *La Danse en*
France – a guide to dance companies, places
and activities. It also has a Minitel service
giving computerized up-to-the-minute
dance information. From Paris, tap in 36 15
DANSE.

Théâtre Contemporain de la Danse
9 rue Geoffroy l'Asnier
75004 Paris
Tel: 42 74 44 22

This organization promotes contemporary
dance choreographers and companies,
rents out studios and supplies dance
information

Dance magazines:

Les Saisons de la danse (classically orientated
monthly)
3 rue des Petits Carreaux
75002 Paris
Tel: 42 36 12 04

Pour la danse (contemporary dance
quarterly)
39 rue du Temple
75004 Paris
Tel: 42 77 09 49

Danser: Voir et vivre la danse (classical and
contemporary monthly)
Rue du Faubourg Saint Antoine
75550 Paris
Tel: 40 02 62 62

Contemporary-dance school

Centre National de la Danse
Contemporaine
42 Bd Henri Arnaud
49021 Angers
Tel: (41) 88 71 52

A selection of contemporary dance
companies

COMPAGNIE MAGUY MARIN

Maison des Arts
Place Salvador Allende
93000 Créteil
Tel: 48 99 55 80

COMPAGNIE BAGOUET

Centre Chorégraphique de Montpellier
Languedoc-Roussillon
11 bvd Victor Hugo
34000 Montpellier
Tel: 67 60 63 73

Artistic director:
Dominique Bagouet

COMPAGNIE KARIN SAPORTA

Centre Chorégraphique National de Caen
10 rue Pasteur
BP 393
14009 Caen
Tel: 31 85 73 16

GROUPE EMILE DUBOIS

Centre Chorégraphique de Grenoble
4 rue Paul Claudel
BP 7040
38020 Grenoble
Tel: 76 25 70 56

Artistic director:
Jean Claude Gallotta

COMPAGNIE LES RIXES

131 rue de la Santé
75013 Paris
Tel: 45 88 38 30

Artistic director:
Claude Brumachon

COMPAGNIE ASTRAKAN

28 rue de la Gaieté
75014 Paris
Tel: 42 06 48 79
and Ferme du Buisson, Marne la Vallée

Artistic director:
Daniel Larrieu

COMPAGNIE ANGELIN PRELJOCAJ

CMA Jean Vilar
52 Rue Pierre et Marie Derrien
94500 Champigny
Tel: 48 86 56 31

COMPAGNIE MARCELINE LARTIGUE

18 rue Gabrielle
75108 Paris
Tel: 42 54 12 05

Artistic director:
Marceline Lartigue

COMPAGNIE HELA FATTOUMI–ERIC LAMOUREUX

142 boulevard de la Villette
75019 Paris
Tel: 42 39 13 39

Germany (East)

DEUTSCHE STAATSOPER BERLIN

Unter den Linden 5-7
DDR 1086 Berlin
Tel: 02 205 40

Director:
Egon Bischoff

Guest choreographer:
Peter Breuer

Ballet mistresses/masters:
Ingeborg Gerda Funke, Doris Topel,
Roland Gawlik, Bernd Dreyer

Teachers:
Erik Wolodin, Olga Ravlova, Alexei
Sakalinski

Principal dancers/soloists:
Monika Lubitz, Steffi Scherzer, Jorg Lucas,
Oliver Matz, Uwe Arnold, Torsten Handler,
Ines Dalchau, Korina Franke, Tatyana
Marinova-Ginkulow, Helga Schiele, Bettina
Thiele, Vladimir Ginkulow, Pedro
Hebenstreit, Raimondo Rebeck, Josef-
Hanus Sklenar, Hans Vogelreuther, Ralf
Stengel
Corps de ballet:
35 female, 22 male

Premières:

Don Juan/Faust, 11.11.89
Choreography: Peter Breuer
Music: Gluck, Liszt

Invitation to the Dance, 5.5.90

Les Sylphides
Choreography: Fokine
Music: Chopin

Le Spectre de la rose
Choreography: Fokine
Music: Weber

La Bayadère (Kingdom of the Shades)
Choreography: Petipa
Music: Minkus

Paquita grand pas
Choreography: Petipa
Music: Minkus

KOMISCHE OPER BERLIN/ TANZTHEATERENSEMBLE

Behrenstrasse 55
DDR 1080 Berlin
Tel: 02 220 2761

Artistic director and chief choreographer:
Professor Tom Schilling
Ballet director:
Dr Bernd Köllinger

Choreographers:
Harald Wandtke, Arila Siegert

Teachers:
Gisela Ambros, Frank Bey, Peter Steinbach,
Jack Theis, Barbara Voss-Kindt, Lothar
Wiebe (leader of Young Dancers' Group)

Principal dancers:
Hannelore Bey, Jutta Deutschland, Dieter
Hulse, Thomas Vollmet
Soloists:
Nadezda Tumowa, Katrin Dix, Andrea
Kollinger, Sigrid Kressman-Bruck, Angela
Reinhardt, Kremena Topola, Anke
Glasow, Angela Philipp, Gerald Binke,
Jurgen Hohmann, Thomas Kindt, Werner
Mente, Mario Perricone, Gregor Seyffert,
Jens-Peter Urbich
Corps de ballet:
30 female, 15 male

Premières:

Tanztheater-Forum VII, 24.3.90

American Quartet
Choreography: Pavel Smok

Alltägliche Apokalypse
Choreography: Carla Börner

Spectra
Choreography: Erwin Fritsche

Medea thimisu
Choreography: Dominique Efstratious

Keith
Choreography: Birgit Scherzer

Trilogy of Longing, 19.5.90
Choreography: Joachim Ahne

Der Wind
Music: Ravel

Les Noces
Music: Stravinsky

The House of Bernarda Alba
Music: Durco

STAATSOPER DRESDEN/SEMPEROPER

Theaterplatz 2
Dresden 8010
Tel: 48420

Director:
Dieter Losche
Artistic director/principal choreographer
Harald Wandtke

Guest choreographers:
Birgit Cullberg, Emöke Postényi, Hermann
Rudolph

Teachers:
Ingrid Czornik, Karin Frenzel, Roland
Giertz, Ludmila Safranowa

Principal dancers:
Evelin Beyer, Sonjarita Drescher,
Friederike Riedel, Carola Schwab, Carla
Spiewok, Kathrin Taube, Delia Hantiu, Ina
Meinhold, Thomas Hartmann, Reiner
Feistel, Calin-Eugen Hantiu, Hannes-Detlef
Vogel-Liebig
Corps de ballet:
38 female, 16 male

Premières:

Don Quixote's Dreams, 22.3.90
Choreography: Birgit Cullberg

La Valse, 22.3.90
Choreography: Hermann Rudolph
Music: Ravel

Bolero, 22.3.90
Choreography: Emöke Postényi
Music: Ravel

Kontraste IX (Kammertanz-Abend)

Improvisationen, 29.5.90

STÄDTISCHE THEATER LEIPZIG

Oper Grosses Haus
Karl-Marx-Platz
DDR-7010 Leipzig
Tel: 041 7641

Director:
Klaus Tews
Artistic director/chief choreographer:
Enno Markwart

Teachers:
Gisela Wehle, Siegfried Wende, Siegfried
Martin Wende

Principal dancers:
Marina Otto, Norbert Thiel
Soloists:
Christina Bruckner, Yvette Kagelmann,
Sibylle Schmidt, Christoph Böhm, Olaf
Gerbig, Mario Schroeder, Jorg Simon,
Werner Stiefel
Corps de ballet:
30 female, 20 male

Premières:

Kammertanz Abend, with choreography by
Enno Markwart, Dietmar Seyffert, Hannes-
Detlef Vogel-Liebig

Giselle
Choreography: Coralli and Perrot
Music: Adam

STAATLICHE BALLETTSCHULE BERLIN

Erich Weinert Strasse 103
DDR-1055 Berlin
Tel: 02 365 4021

Director:
Martin Puttke

Teachers:
Martin Puttke, Ursula Berndt, Stefan Lux,
and others

PALUCCA SCHULE DRESDEN
(Fachschule für Künsterlerische Tanz)

Basteiplatz 4
DDR-8020 Dresden
Tel: 051 239 1091

Senior study director:
Rainer Walther
Artistic director:
Thomas Hartmann

Teachers:
Gret Palucca (modern dance), Hans-
Joachim Metz, Karin Sandner (classical),
Bernhard Wunsch (dance folklore),
Wolfgang Zeibig (music), and others

FACHSCHULE FÜR TANZ LEIPZIG
(Staatliche Ballettschule)

Wilhelm Seyfferth Strasse 6
DDR-7010 Leipzig
Tel: 041 32 8034

Senior study director:
Heiner Muller
Artistic director:
Hans-Georg Uhlmann

236

Germany (West)

BERLIN

DEUTSCHE OPER BALLET

Richard Wagner Strasse 10
D-1000 Berlin 10
Tel: 3438 268

Director designate:
Peter Schaufuss (from August 1990)
Director:
Gert Reinholm

Ballet dramaturgy:
Dr Christiane Theobald
Ballet mistresses:
Gudrun Leben, Brigitte Thom

Principal teachers and choreographic assistants:
Cora Benador, Klaus Beelitz
Répétiteurs:
Gregory Gadzhiyev, Johann Kirschniok, Felix Mroczek, Jerzy Smoczynski
School director:
Prof. Tatjana Gsovsky

Principal dancers:
Charlotte Butler, Katalene Borsboom, Ronda Nychka, Raffaella Renzi, Maryvonne Robino, Silke Sense, Bart de Block, Yannick Bocquin, Iouri Borodine, Tomas Karlborg, Jenö Löscei, David Nixon, Marek Rozycki, Stefan Zeromski
Corps de ballet:
22 female, 13 male (and 6 apprentices)

New productions:

There is a Time, 11.11.89
Choreography: José Limón
Music: dello Joio

Land
Choreography: Christopher Bruce
Music: Arne Nordheim

Rooms
Choreography: Anna Sokolow
Music: Hopkins

Agon, 17.3.90
Choreography: Balanchine
Music: Stravinsky

Firebird
Choreography: Maurice Béjart
Music: Stravinsky

Le Sacre du printemps
Choreography: Maurice Béjart
Music: Stravinsky

Ring um den Ring, Berlin première, 7.3.90
(co-production with Béjart Ballet Lausanne)
Choreography: Maurice Béjart
Music: Wagner

Repertory:
Choreographers represented include John Cranko, Maurice Béjart, Oscar Araiz, Birgit Cullberg, John Neumeier, Paul Taylor, Hans van Manen, Tom Schilling, George Balanchine, Kurt Jooss, Roland Petit, Antony Tudor, Lucinda Childs, Vicente Nebrada, Jiří Kylián, Kenneth MacMillan, Valery Panov, László Seregi, Bournonville, Fokine, Petipa, etc.

Visiting companies at the Deutsche Oper:
Maly Theatre, Leningrad; Tokyo Ballet; Béjart Ballet Lausanne

Tours:
Amsterdam (December 1989); Marseille (January 1990); East Berlin (March 1990); Jerusalem (May 1990)

Number of performances:
57

DUSSELDORF/DUISBURG

DEUTSCHE OPER AM RHEIN

Heinrich-Heine-Allee 16a,
D-4000 Düsseldorf 1
Tel: (0) 211/8908340/8908341

Director:
Paolo Bortoluzzi
Administrative director:
Rainer von Camen

Choreographers:
Tom Schilling, Pierre Wyss

Principal company teachers:
Cristina Hamel, Andrzej Ziemski

Principal dancers and soloists:
Marie-Françoise Géry, Monique Janotta,
Inge Koch, Victoria Lahiguera, Alicia Olleta,
Danielle Fabre, Laurence Souc,
Emmanuelle Grizot, Martial Bockstaele,
Jean-François Boisnon, Paolo Bortoluzzi,
Falco Kapuste, Peter Mason, Jean-Jacques
Pomperski, Lazo Turozi, Irek Wisniewski,
Yves Haenni
Corps de ballet:
21 female, 19 male
Guest artists:
Almira Osmanovic, Gheorghe Iancu

Premières:

Wahlverwandschaften (Elective Affinities,
after Goethe's novel), Duisburg, 24.11.89
Choreography: Tom Schilling
Music: Schubert
Sets: Gerda Zientek
Costumes: Ingrid Rahaus

Cinderella, Duisburg, 15.4.90
Choreography: Pierre Wass
Music: Prokofiev
Sets and costumes: Andreas Reinhardt

Repertory:

Fantaisies
Choreography: Erich Walter
Music: Tchaikovsky
Sets: Heinrich Wendel
Costumes: Lieselotte Erler

Romeo and Juliet
Choreography: Erich Walter
Music: Prokofiev
Sets: Jorge Villareal
Costumes: Gerda Zientek

Aimer l'amour
Choreography: Paolo Bortoluzzi
Music: Schumann, Mendelssohn, Berlioz
Sets and costumes: Beni Montresor

Orchestersuite
Choreography: Istvan Herczog
Music: J.S. Bach
Sets and costumes: Istvan Herczog/Gerda
Zientek

Lieder ohne Worte
Choreography: Hans van Manen
Music: Mendelssohn
Staging: Mea Venema
Sets and costumes: Jean-Paul Vroom

Sonate und Kantate
Choreography: Maurice Béjart
Music: J.S. Bach
Staging: Bertrand d'At

Giselle
Choreography: Erich Walter/Ruzena
Mazalova
Music: Adam
Sets: Heinrich Wendel
Costumes: Jan Skalicky

Clair de lune
Choreography: Paolo Bortoluzzi
Music: Debussy

Le Sacre du printemps
Choreography: Erich Walter
Music: Stravinsky
Sets: Heinrich Wendel
Costumes: Günter Kappel

Der Nussknacker (Nutcracker)
Choreography: Heinz Spoerli
Music: Tchaikovsky
Sets and costumes: Andreas Reinhardt

Die vier Jahreszeiten (The Four Seasons)
Choreography: Paolo Bortoluzzi
Music: Verdi
Sets and costumes: Ramon Ivars

Arlésienne
Choreography: José de Udaeta
Music: Bizet
Sets and costumes: Ramon Ivars

Wagner
Choreography: Uwe Scholz
Music: Wagner
Sets and costumes: Ramon Ivars

Number of performances:
75

FRANKFURT

BALLETT FRANKFURT

Stadtische Bühnen Frankfurt
Untermainanlage 11
6000 Frankfurt am Main 1
Tel: 069/2562 319

238

Director:
William Forsythe
Superintendent and managing director:
Dr Martin Steinhoff

Choreographers:
William Forsythe, Amanda Miller

Teachers:
Urs Frey, Helga Heil, Barry Ingham,
Kathleen Fitzgerald

Principal dancers:
4 female, 4 male
Corps de ballet:
18 female, 14 male

Salary information:
Soloists: DM72,000 per year
Group dancers: DM 65,000 per year
(before taxes)

GELSENKIRCHEN

BALLET SCHINDOWSKI

Musiktheater im Revier Gelsenkirchen
Kennedyplatz
4650 Gelsenkirchen
Tel: 0209-4097138

Director and principal choreographer:
Bernd Schindowski
General manager:
Ludwig Baum
Assistants to choreographer:
Rianna Kuipers, Marta Nejm

Ballet conductor and musical assistant:
Salvador Caro

Principal company teachers:
Marta Nejm, Rianna Kuipers

Soloists:
Carmen Balochini, Rita Barretto, Ellen
Bucalo, Emma-Louise Jordan, Rianna
Kuipers, Marta Nejm, Scheyla Silva, Eden
Summers, Rubens Reis, Bernd
Schindowski, Cassio Vitaliano, Neng-Sheng
Yu
Corps de ballet:
10

Repertory:
(all choreography by Bernd Schindowski)

Erinnerung an das goldene Zeitalter, (Fading
Images of the Golden Age)
Music: Beethoven
Set: Manfred Dorra
Costumes: Bennie Voorhaar

Lied der Sonne (Song of the Sun)
Music: Steve Reich
Set: Erwin Zimmer
Costumes: Leonie Grimm

Nur wer die Sehnsucht kennt . . . (Those Who
Know Longing)
Music: Tchaikovsky
Set: Manfred Dorra
Costumes: Bennie Voorhaar

Reise nach Kythera (Journey to Kythera)
Music: Debussy
Set: Erwin Zimmer
Costumes: Leonie Grimm

Dr Coppelius – a ballet for children
Music: Delibes
Set: Manfred Dorra
Costumes: Bennie Voorhaar

Der Reigen
Music: Jean Françaix, Kurt Weill
Set: Erwin W. Zimmer
Costumes: Leonie Grimm

Feuerwerk
Music: Meredith Monk, John Adams
Set: Manfred Dorra
Costumes: Bennie Voorhaar

HAMBURG

THE HAMBURG BALLET

Ballettzentrum John Neumeier
Caspar-Voght-Strasse 54
2000 Hamburg 26
West Germany
Tel: (040) 21 11 88-0

Artistic director:
John Neumeier
Administrative director:
Christopher Albrecht

Principal choreographer:
John Neumeier
Ballet masters:
Ilse Wiedmann, Eduardo Bertini, Victor
Hughes, Roy Wierzbicki

Principal company teachers:
Ilse Wiedmann, Charles Mudry, Beatrice
Cordua, Denuk Laschan
Guest teachers:
Irina Jakobson, Giselle Roberge, Hans-
Joachim Metz, Sergiu Stefanschi

Benesh notators:
Susanne Menck, Patricia Tierney

Principal dancers:
Stefanie Arndt, Bettina Beckmann, Anna
Grabka, Gigi Hyatt, Chantal Lefèvre,
Colleen Scott, Gamal Gouda, Anders
Hellström, Jeffrey Kirk, François Klaus,
Jean Laban, Ivan Liška
Soloists:
Mette Bödtcher, Judith Carlson, Jessica
Funt, Jennifer Goubé, Eduardo Bertini, Ralf
Dörnen, Johannes Kritzinger, Janusz
Mazón, William Parton, Stephen Pier
Corps de ballet:
22 female, 14 male

Guest artists:
Noëlla Pontois, Vladimir Derevianko,
Benito Marcelino

Premières:

Des Knaben Wunderhorn, 10.12.89
Choreography: John Neumeier
Music: Mahler
Scenery and costumes: John Neumeier

Tristan, 12.5.90
Choreography: John Neumeier
Music: Henze
Set: John Neumeier
Costumes: Silvia Strahammer

Einhorn, 12.5.90
Choreography: John Neumeier
Music: Henze
Scenery and costumes: John Neumeier

Don Quixote, 12.5.90
Choreography: John Neumeier
Scenery and costumes: Marco Arturo
Marelli

Repertory:

Hommage à José Limón
Choreography: José Limón
Music: Schönberg, Purcell, Joio

Magnificat
Choreography: John Neumeier

Music: J. S. Bach
Scenery and costumes: John Neumeier

St Matthew Passion
Choreography: John Neumeier
Music: J. S. Bach
Scenery and costumes: John Neumeier

Othello
Choreography: John Neumeier
Music: Vasconcellos, Pärt, Schnittke
Scenery and costumes: John Neumeier

Peer Gynt
Choreography: John Neumeier
Music: Schnittke
Set and costumes: Jürgen Rose

Romeo and Juliet
Choreography: John Neumeier
Music: Prokofiev
Set and costumes: Jürgen Rose

A Midsummernight's Dream
Choreography: John Neumeier
Music: Mendelssohn and Ligeti
Set and costumes: Jürgen Rose

Ballettwerkstatt I–III
(additional workshops, introductions to
new productions, also a workshop for
young choreographers)

**Number of performances (August 1989 to
July 1990):**
105, including performances outside
Hamburg; in Copenhagen, Leningrad,
Ludwigshafen, Moscow, Paris, Stuttgart and
Taormina

Associated school

*Ballettschule der Hamburgischen
Staatsoper
Casper-Voght-Strasse 54
2000 Hamburg 26
West Germany*

Director:
John Neumeier
Faculty adviser:
Irina Jakobson

Teachers:
Brita Adam, Beatrice Cordua, Ann Drower,
Marianne Kruuse, Denuk Laschan, Charles
Mudry, Persephone Samaropoulo, Beatrice
Schickendantz-Giger, Eduardo Bertini,
Jeffrey Kirk

Guest teachers:
Sergiu Stefanschi, Hans-Joachim Metz, José de Udaeta

Organization:
Ursula Ziegler

Theoretical training:
Dr Frauke Hofert, Nils Jockel, Helmut Scheier

Boarding school:
Dorothea Igel

HEIDELBERG

HEIDELBERG BALLET

Friedrichstr. 5
D-6900 Heidelberg
Tel: (06221) 58 35 10

Director/principal choreographer:
Liz King

Assistant to choreographer:
Hartmut Stock

Principal company teacher:
Liz King

Dancers:
7 female, 7 male

New productions:

Die Gegeneinladung, 20.1.90
Choreography: Liz King
Music: Heinz Leonhardsberger
Design: Manfred Biskup

Was singt mir, in meinem Körper, das Lied?,
19.5.90
Choreography: Liz King
Music: Glenn Branca, Giorgy Ligeti
Design: Manfred Biskup

Touring:
Germany, Switzerland

Number of performances:
36

Salary information:
DM3,200 per month (equal rank)

MUNICH

TANZTENDENZ MÜNCHEN

Lindwurmstrasse 88
8000 München 2
Tel: 089/721 10 15
Tanztendenz represents the following five independent contemporary dance companies. Dancers' salaries (other than for rehearsal periods) depend on the fees paid by venues and dance festivals.

DANCE ENERGY e.V.

c/o Tanztendenz München
Lindwurmstr. 88
8000 Munich 2
Tel: 089/7211015

Artistic director:
Michael Purucker
Managing director:
Walter Heun

Dancers:
Sabine Glenz, Veronica Fischer, Christel Mayr, Max Schubert, Stefan Maria Marb, Anna-Carin Isacsson, and others

New productions:

Darwin Waltzes
Choreography: Michael Purucker
Music: Robert Merdzo
Design: Reiner Wiesemes

Katarakt
Choreography: Veronica Fischer, Stefan Maria Marb
Music: Robert Merdzo
Design: Christian Sedelmayer

IWANSON DANCE COMPANY

Hansastr. 12
8000 Munich 21
Tel: 089/571909

Artistic director:
Jessica Iwanson
Managing director:
Stefan Sixt

Dancers:
Karren Foster, Christer Reveny, Tommy Hakanson, Sabine Glenz, and others (total normally about 12 dancers)

New productions:

Ich fühle, also bin ich
Choreography: Jessica Iwanson
Music: Various composers
Design: Sabine Atzberger

TANZTHEATER NEGER

Karl-Theodor-Str. 48
8000 Munich 40
Tel: 089/334994

Artistic director:
Bonger Voges
Managing director:
Wolfgang Kreuzer

Dancers:
Claudia Weiss, Jutta Keller, Chester
Roberts, and others (total about 6–8
dancers)

New production:

Little Pleasant Alice
Choreography: Bonger Voges
Music: Stefan Massimo and Carl Hänggi
Set: Christoph Simons
Costumes: Branka Kokol

ARTGENOSSEN

Donnersbergerstrasse 9a
8000 München 19
Tel: 89/16 03 78

Artistic director/choreographer:
Angelika Meindl

Assistant choreographer:
Ruth Golic

Dancers:
Ruth Golic, Brigitta Jahn, Lesli Ann Carter,
Angelika Meindl

New production:

Time Gap
Choreography: Angelika Meindl
Music: Thomas Batoy, Richard Lewis,
Angelika Meindl, Gerhard Schedel, plus
live musicians
Design: Reiner Wiesemes

TANZPROJEKT MÜNCHEN

In residence at
Tanztheater der Städtischen Bühnen
Münster
Neubrücken str. 63
4400 Münster

Director:
Birgitta Trommler

Assistant to choreographer:
Waltraut Körver-Badji

Principal company teacher:
Pieter van der Sloot

Dancers:
Octavio A. Campos, Henry Daniel, Thomas
Langkau, Javier Picardo, Joaquim Sabate,
Patricia Schmid, Diane Sowter, Dörthe
Stöss, Patricia Vallis, Yoshiko Waki

New productions:

Stella, Tanztheater von Anne Rose Katz und
Birgitta Trommler, 20.9.89
Choreography: Birgitta Trommler
Music: Matthias Thurow
Set: Monika Ziefle
Costumes: Gudrun Schretzmeier

Jeder ist eine kleine Gesellschaft, 20.10.89
Staging: Birgitta Trommler
Music: Matthias Thurow
Set: Gudrun Schretzmeier

Ich möchte meinen Schatten fressen, 30.3.90
Staging: Birgitta Trommler
Set: Norbert Stück
Costumes: Gudrun Schretzmeier

STUTTGART

THE STUTTGART BALLET

Postfach 10 43 45
7000 Stuttgart 10
West-Germany
Tel: 0711 20321

Artistic director:
Marcia Haydée
Assistant director:
Alan Beale

242

Ballet masters:
Alan Beale, Alex Ursuliak, Kurt Speker,
Gabriel Popescu, Egon Madsen

Opera ballet master:
Angelika Bulfinski

Notator:
Georgette Tsinguirides

Principal dancers:
Marcia Haydée, Birgit Keil, Susanne Hanke,
Melinda Witham, Annie Mayet, Marion
Jäger, Ludmilla Bogart, Richard Cragun,
Vladimir Klos, Tamas Detrich, Stephen
Greenston, Randy Diamond, Wolfgang
Stollwitzer, Mark McClain, Benito
Marcelino, Hella Heim.
Soloists:
Sabine Bartels, Dominique Charlier,
Claudia Shinn, Eva Steinbrecher, Beatriz de
Almeida, Christian Fallanga, Thierry Sette,
Jean-Christophe Blavier
Corps de ballet:
23 female, 18 male

Guest artists during 1989/90:
Julio Bocca, Fernando Bujones, Gigi Hyatt,
Monique Loudières, John Neumeier

Number of performances:
135

Tours:
Hong Kong, Helsinki, Cairo, Singapore,
Vienna and Japan

New productions:

Giselle and the Wilis, 12.10.89
Choreography and direction: Marcia
Haydée
Music: Adam
Design: Elisabeth Dalton

Medea, 21.1.90
Choreography, designs and lighting: John
Neumeier
Music: Schnittke, Galasso, Bartók, J. S. Bach
and traditional music from Bulgaria and
Burundi

Wien, Wien, nur du allein, 24.3.90
Choreography: Maurice Béjart
Design: Nuno Côrte-Real

Beziehungen
Choreography: Marcia Haydée
Music: Stephen Micus

Costumes: Vladimir Klos

Repertory:

Adagio Hammerklavier
Choreography: Hans van Manen
Music: Beethoven
Design: Jean-Paul Vroom

Bolero
Choreography: Maurice Béjart
Music: Maurice Ravel

Brouillards
Choreography: John Cranko
Music: Debussy

The Chairs
Choreography: Maurice Béjart
Music: Wagner

ENAS
Choreography: Marcia Haydée
Music: Vangelis Papathanassiou

Gaieté Parisienne
Choreography: Maurice Béjart
Music: Jacques Offenbach
Design: Thierry Bosquet

Hommage au Bolshoi
Choreography: John Cranko
Music: Alexander Glazunov

In the Future
Choreography: Hans van Manen
Music: David Byrne
Design: Keso Dekker

Initials R.B.M.E.
Choreography: John Cranko
Music: Brahms
Set: Jürgen Rose

Isadoro
Choreography: Maurice Béjart
Music: Liszt, Chopin, Beethoven, Schubert,
Rouget de Lisle, Scriabin

Love Songs
Choreography: William Forsythe
Music: Bacharach, David, Ashford,
Simpson, Clarke, King, Wexler

Nuages
Choreography: Jiří Kylián
Music: Debussy
Set: William Katz

Onegin
Choreography: John Cranko
Music: Kurt-Heinz Stolze after Tchaikovsky
Design: Jürgen Rose

243

Opus 1
Choreography: John Cranko
Music: Webern

Poème de l'extase
Choreography: John Cranko
Music: Scriabin
Design: Jürgen Rose after Gustav Klimt

Requiem
Choreography: Kenneth MacMillan
Music: Fauré
Design: Yolanda Sonnabend

Return to the Strange Land
Choreography: Jiří Kylián
Music: Jánácek

Sarkasmen
Choreography: Hans van Manen
Music: Prokofiev

The Sleeping Beauty
Choreography and production: Marcia
Haydée after Marius Petipas
Music: Tchaikovsky
Design: Jürgen Rose

Song of a Wayfarer
Choreography: Maurice Béjart
Music: Mahler

Squares
Choreography: Hans van Manen
Music: Satie
Set: Bob Bonies
Costumes: Hans van Manen

Lighting: Jan Hofstra

A Streetcar Named Desire
Choreography and production: John
Neumeier
Music: Prokofiev and Schnittke
Design: John Neumeier

The Taming of the Shrew
Choreography: John Cranko
Music: Kurt-Heinz Stolze after Scarlatti
Design: Elisabeth Dalton

Three Pieces
Choreography: Hans van Manen
Music: Grazyna Basewicz
Design: Jan van der Wal

Troy Game
Choreography: Robert North
Music: Jon Keliehor and Bob Downes

ASSOCIATED SCHOOL

The John Cranko School
Staatliche Ballettakademie
Urbanstrasse 94
7000 Stuttgart I
Tel: (711) 203 2478

President:
Marcia Haydée
Director:
Heinz Claus

244

Hong Kong

HONG KONG BALLET

60 Blue Pool Road
Happy Valley, Hong Kong
Tel: 5-737398

General manager:
Antony Wraight
Artistic director:
Gary Trinder
Associate artist director:
Gary Harris

Guest teachers:
Cecilia Barrett, Peter Clegg, Victoria Simon,
Betsy Erickson

Number of dancers:
33

Premières:

Connotations, Lyric Theatre, Hong Kong,
16.5.90
Choreography: Val Caniparoli
Music: Benjamin Britten

Square Dance, Lyric Theatre, 16.5.90
Choreography: George Balanchine
Music: Vivaldi

Tarantella, 16.5.90
Choreography: Balanchine
Music: Gottschalk

Repertory:

Giselle
Choreography: Coralli, Perrot
Music: Adam
Production: Gary Trinder

Romeo and Juliet
Choreography: Andre Prokovsky
Music: Berlioz

The Nutcracker
Choreography: Peter Darrell
Music: Tchaikovsky

Three Dances to Japanese Music
Choreography: Jack Carter
Music: Kasahisa Kitada

**HONG KONG ACADEMY FOR THE
PERFORMING ARTS**

1 Gloucester Road
Wanchai, Hong Kong
Tel: (School of Dance): 5-823532

Dean of dance:
Carl Wolz

HONG KONG DANCE COMPANY

Sheung Wan Civic Centre
8th floor
Sheung Wan, Hong Kong
Tel: 5-8532604

General manager:
K.B. Chan
Artistic director:
Shu Qiao

Number of dancers:
36

Premières:

Dagger Society, Sheung Wan Civic Centre,
9.3.90
Choreography: recreation by Shu Qiao and
Bai Shu

The First Emperor of Qin, Hong Kong
Cultural Centre, 10.5.90
Choreography: Beijing choreographers

Revivals:

The Story of Zhou Xuan
Choreography: Leung Kwok-shing

The Love Story of Dalai VI
Choreography: Shu Qiao, Ying Eding

**CITY CONTEMPORARY DANCE
COMPANY**

110 Shatin Pass Road
Wong Tai Sin
Kowloon, Hong Kong
Tel: 3-268597

Founder director:
Willy Tsao
Artistic director
Helen Lai (on leave)

Number of dancers:
18

ZUNI ICOSAHEDRON

12th floor,
Rhenish Centre
248–250 Hennessy Road
Wanchai, Hong Kong
Tel: 5-8938419

Artistic director:
Danny Yung
Company manager:
Gabriel Yiu

Choreographers:
Kwan-sun Wong, Edward Lam

Number of dancers:
50

HONG KONG FESTIVALS

Hong Kong Arts Festival (Society Ltd)
Hong Kong Arts Centre
13th floor
Hong Kong
Tel: 5-295555
Fax: 5-279148

General manager:
Tseng Sun-man
Chairman:
Sir Run Run Shaw

Festival of Asian Arts
Urban Services Department
Hong Kong Cultural Centre
Administration Building
10 Salisbury Road
Tsimshatsui
Kowloon, Hong Kong
Tel: 3-7342804/2908
Fax: 3-7390066

International Festival of Dance Academies
and International Dance Conference
Hong Kong Academy for the Performing
Arts (School of Dance)
1 Gloucester Road
Wanchai, Hong Kong
Tel: 5-823500/532

Public relations:
Susanna Chan, tel: 5–823582

Hungary

HUNGARIAN NATIONAL BALLET

State Opera House
Budapest, VI
Népköztársaság utja 22
Pf.: 503
Tel: 1373

Director:
Gábor Keveházi
Artistic director:
Ildikó Pongor

Ballet manager:
Roland Bokor

Principal choreographer:
László Seregi
Resident choreographer:
Antal Fodor
Visiting choreographer:
Ferenc Barbay

246

Principal teachers:
Ágoston Balogh, Ildikó Kaszás, Tamás
Koren, Lilla Pártay, László Pethö, Viktor
Róna
Visiting teachers:
Maria Aradi, Simon Mottram, Martin
Puttke, Johanni Teresvouri

Principal dancers:
Regina Balaton, Katalin Hágai, Márta
Metzger, Ildikó Pongor, Edit Szabadi,
Katalin Volf, Tibor Eichner, Sándor Erdélyi,
Viktor Fülöp, Sándor Jezerniczky, Gábor
Keveházi, Tibor Kováts, Jenö Löcsei, Zoltán
Nagy Jr, Zoltán Solymosi, György Szakály
Soloists:
13 female, 7 male
Corps de ballet:
47 female, 30 male

Guest artists during 1989/90:
Pál Lovas, Kumiko Ochi

Length of season:
1 September 1989 to 23 June 1990

New productions:

Coppélia (revival), 16.2.90
Choreography: Gyula Harangozó
Music: Delibes
Decor: Zoltán Fülöp
Costumes: Tivadar Márk

Hommage à Milloss Aurél, 16.3.90
Variations
Choreography: Ferenc Barbay
Music: Rachmaninov
Scenery and costumes: Dorin Gál

Estri
Choreography: Aurél Milloss
Music: Petrassi
Staged by: Giancarlo Vantaggio

The Miraculous Mandarin
Choreography: Aurél Milloss
Music: Béla Bartók
Staging: Marga Nativo and Giancarlo
Vantaggio
Decor: Mátyás Varga
Costumes: Emanuele Luzzati

Mamma Maria, 2.6.90
Choreography: Birgit Cullberg
Music: J. S. Bach, arr. Inger Wikström
Designs: Miklós Borsa
Costumes: Judit Schäffer

A Midsummer Night's Dream, 22.12.89
Choreography: László Seregi
Music: Mendelssohn, arr. Gyula Jármai;
electronic sound effects by János Novák
Decor: Gábor Forray
Costumes: Nelly Vágó

Touring:
Seoul (September 1989), Spain (November
1989)

Number of performances:
108

Repertory:

Bhakti
Choreography: Maurice Béjart
Music: folk-music of India

Derby
Choreography: Péter László
Music: György Vukán
Decor: Gábor Forray
Costumes: Judit Schäffer

The Firebird
Choreography: Maurice Béjart
Music: Stravinsky
Costumes: Joëlle Roustan and Roger
Bernard

The Fountain of Bakhchisaray
Choreography: Vainonen
Music: Asafiev
Decor: Zoltán Fülöp
Costumes: Tivadar Márk

Giselle
Choreography: Adam, Perrot, Petipa and
Lavrovsky
Music: Adam
Decor: Zoltán Fülöp
Costumes: Tivadar Márk

The Miraculous Mandarin
Choreography: László Seregi
Music: Béla Bartók
Decor: Gábor Forray
Costumes: László Seregi

The Miraculous Mandarin
Choreography: Antal Fodor
Music: Béla Bartók
Decor: László Horváth
Costumes: Judit Szekulesz

The Nutcracker
Choreography: Vainonen
Music: Tchaikovsky
Designs: Gusztáv Oláh

247

Opus 5
Choreography: Maurice Béjart
Music: Webern

Próba (The Rehearsal)
Choreography: Antal Fodor
Music: J. S. Bach and Gábor Presser
Decor: Robert Wegenast
Costumes: Judit Schäffer

Romeo and Juliet
Choreography: László Seregi
Music: Prokofiev
Decor: Gábor Forray
Costumes: Nelly Vágó

The Rite of Spring
Choreography: Maurice Béjart
Music: Stravinsky
Costumes: Maurice Béjart
Lighting: Roger Bernard

Spartacus
Choreography: László Seregi
Music: Khachaturian
Decor: Gábor Forray
Costumes: Tivadar Márk

Swan Lake
Choreography: Petipa and Ivanov
Music: Tchaikovsky
Decor: Gábor Forray
Costumes: Gizella Seitz

Sylvia
Choreography: László Seregi
Music: Delibes
Decor: Gábor Forray
Costumes: Tivadar Márk

Variations on a Nursery Song
Choreography: László Seregi
Music: Dohnányi
Decor: Attila Csikós
Costumes: Judit Gombár

GYÖR BALLET

Kisfaludy Theatre
Györ, Czuczor G. u. 17
9022

Director and principal choreographer:
Ivan Markó

Principal dancers:
Éva Afonyi, Barbara Bombicz, Otto
Demcsák, János Kiss, Ivan Markó
Corps de ballet:
10 female, 9 male

Length of season:
1 September 1989 to 20 August 1990

New productions:

Anniversary, 2.11.89
Choreography: Ivan Markó
Music: arrangement
Design: Judit Gombár

Feast
Choreography: Ivan Markó
Music: Handel
Design: Judit Gombár

Touring:
London (November 1989), Italy, Germany
(April 1990)

Number of performances:
57

Repertory:
All choreography by Ivan Markó

The Chairs
Music: Schoenberg
Design: Judit Gombár

The Miraculous Mandarin
Music: Béla Bartók
Design: Judit Gombár

The Land of Promise
Music: Yehudi Menuhin and Ravi Shankar
Design: Judit Gombár

Those Loved by the Sun
Music: Orff
Decor: Gábor Forray
Costumes: Judit Gombár

Jesus, Son of Man
Music: Ferenc Liszt, Shostakovich, Xenakis
Design: Judit Gombár

Prospero
Music: Schubert
Design: Judit Gombár

The Samurai
Music: Japanese folk-music and László
Várady
Design: Judit Gombár

BALLET SOPIANAE (PÉCS BALLET)

National Theatre
Pécs, Pf.: 126
7601

Director:
Sándor Tóth
Artistic Director:
Imre Eck

Resident choreographers:
Sándor Tóth and Imre Eck
Visiting choreographer:
Antal Fodor

Principal teacher:
Zsuzsa Végvári
Visiting teacher:
Novkov Zivojin

Principal dancers:
Ildikó Baráth, Zsuzsa Kovács, Magdolna
Paronai, Gábor Hajzer, Lászlo Körmendy,
Pál Lovas, Pál Solymos
Corps de ballet:
10 female, 9 male
Guest artists during 1989/90:
Katalin Hágai, Angéla Kövessy, Márta
Molnár, Katalin Volf, Krisztina Végh

Length of season:
23 August 1989 to 18 June 1990

Premières:

Requiem for the Living, 2.3.90
Choreography: Antal Fodor
Music: Vivaldi, Schütz and Masayoshi
Sugiura
Decor: Lóránt Kézdi
Costumes: Judit Schäffer

Bolero, 2.3.90
Choreography: Antal Fodor
Music: Ravel
Decor: Lóránt Kézdi
Costumes: Judit Schäffer

Number of performances:
11

SZEGED BALLET

National Theatre
Szeged, Pf. 69
6701

Director:
György Krámer
Artistic director:
Zoltán Imre

Resident choreographers:
György Krámer and Zoltán Imre
Visiting choreographer:
Matthew Hawkins

Visiting teacher:
Nadezda Kostenko

Principal dancers:
Gizella Zarnóczai, Annamária Prepeliczay,
Ferenc Kuli
Corps de ballet:
10 female, 10 male

Length of season:
1 September 1989 to 30 May 1990

New productions: (current repertory):

Plays of the Underworld, 1.12.89
Choreography: Zoltán Imre
Music: Monteverdi, Scriabin, jazz
improvisations
Design: György Csik

Ballet '90, 28.4.90
The Fruits of Labour
Choreography: Matthew Hawkins
Music: Scottish folk-music and sound
effects
Design: György Csik

The Medium
Choreography: Zoltán Imre
Music: Berg and Schoenberg (arr.)
Design: György Csik

Exodus
Choreography: György Krámer
Music: Kylar
Design: György Csik

Number of performances:
32

STATE BALLET INSTITUTE

Budapest, VI
Népköztársaság utja 68
1062

Director:
Imre Dózsa

Salary information:
No details available but the average range
is between 8,000 Ft for *corps de ballet* and
20,000–30,000 Ft for principals.

Israel

BAT-DOR DANCE COMPANY

30, Ibn Gvirol St.
Tel Aviv 64078
Tel: 03-263175

Artistic director:
Jeannette Ordman

General manager:
Michael Cohen
Producer:
Batsheva de Rothschild

Assistants to artistic directors:
Ora Dror, David Shur, Ilana Soprun

Ballet masters:
Kenneth Mason, David Shur, Rosaline Subel-Kassel

Choreologist:
Ilana Soprun

Dancers:
12 female, 11 male

Premières:

Changing Wheels
Choreography: Rodney Griffin
Music: Kurt Weill

Autumn Phase
Choreography: Yair Vardi
Music: Ori Vidislavsky

Renascent
Choreography: Mauricio Wainrot
Music: Philip Glass

Symphonette
Choreography: Domy Reiter-Soffer
Music: Morton Gould

Quartet II
Choreography: Nils Christe
Music: Shostakovich

Aquelarre
Choreography: Oscar Araiz
Music: Paul Hindemith

Entangled Path
Choreography: Yair Vardi
Music: Ori Vidislavsky

Handel – Opus 6 No. 7
Choreography: Mark Haim
Music: Handel

Strolling
Choreography: Mauricio Wainrot
Music: Wim Mertens

Les Nuits d'été
Choreography: Domy Reiter-Soffer
Music: Berlioz

Tours abroad:
December 1989: Russia, Spain

BATSHEVA DANCE COMPANY

The Suzanne Dellal Centre for Dance and
Theatre
Neve Tzedek
6 Yechieli St.
Tel Aviv 65149
Tel: 03-651471-5

Artistic adviser:
Robert Cohan
Guest artistic director:
Ohad Naharin
Artistic director:
Shelley Sheer

Ballet master:
Jay Augen

General manager:
Mira Eidels

Batsheva II artistic director:
David Rapoport

Dancers:
13 female, 13 male

Premières:

Taken to Pieces
Choreography: Doug Varone
Music: Christopher Hyams-Hart

Cantata 78/Every Waking Hour
Choreography: Doug Varone
Music: Bach

Psycho Killer
Choreography: Daniel Ezralow, Jamey Hampton, Ashley Roland, Morleigh Steinberg
Music: Talking Heads

Eight Heads
Choreography: Daniel Ezralow
Music: Philip Glass

Rituals
Choreography: Robert North
Music: John Kayes, South African and Japanese music, Stephan Micus

Romantica
Choreography: Liat Dror, Nir Ben-Gal
Music: Blood, Sweat and Tears

Diluvium
Choreography: Doug Varone
Music: Stravinsky

Voix bulgare
Choreography: Doug Varone
Music: traditional Bulgarian folk-songs

Mariachi
Choreography: Peter Pucci
Music: traditional Mexican

In the Garden
Choreography: Peter Pucci
Music: Charles Ives

You Gotta Move
Choreography: Peter Pucci
Music: Gerry Murdas and Harmonicats

Tours:
France, Switzerland – March 1989; Poland – June 1989; Portugal – June 1989; Germany, Hungary – October 1989

INBAL DANCE THEATRE

6 Yehieli St.
Tel Aviv 65149
Tel: 03-653711

Founder and artistic director:
Sara Levi-Tanai
General managers:
Raffi Aharon, Shai Horev

Dancers:
7 female, 4 male

Repertory:

The Veil (Ra'alah)
Choreography: Sara Levi-Tanai, Ilana Cohen

The Well
Choreography: Sara Levi-Tanai
Music: Sara Levi-Tanai, Ovadia Tuvia

Rejoice, Poor One
Choreography: Sara Levi-Tanai
Music: Ovadia Tuvia

MOSHE EFRATI – KOL DEMAMA

Kol Demama House
61 Hayarkon St.
Tel Aviv 63432
Tel: 03-5102997

Artistic director:
Moshe Efrati

Artistic adviser:
Ester Nadler

Company manager:
Naama Koren

Company teachers:
Ester Nadler, Naama Koren, Avital Chen, Micky Homa

Dancers:
9 female, 6 male

Premières:

Out of the Box and the Apple
Choreography: Moshe Efrati

Dreams? (restaging)
Choreography: Anna Sokolow
Music: Bach, Webern

Tours abroad:
Portugal, Spain – November 1989

KIBBUTZ DANCE COMPANY

Kibbutz Ga'aton
Upper Gallilee, 251030
Tel: 04-858437 (studio)
8 Shaul Hamelech Blvd
POB 40014
Tel Aviv 61400
Tel: 03-5429011 (office)

Artistic director:
Yehudit Arnon
General manager:
Yeruham Cohen, Dan Rudolf (from Jan. 1990)

Resident choreographer, assistant to art director:
Rami Be'er

Administrator:
Zichri Dagan

Ballet masters:
Laverne Meyer, Ivan Kramer

Dancers:
8 female, 8 male

Premières:

Carousel
Choreography: Gertrud Kraus
Music: Stravinsky

Woman from a Soft Rock
Choreography: Anat Assoulin
Music: Wim Wenders

Gravity
Choreography: Ruth Ziv-Eyal
Music: Rafi Kadishsohn

The Sorcerer's Apprentice
Choreography: Rami Be'er
Music: Paul Dukas/collage

Reservist's Diary 1989
Choreography: Rami Be'er
Music: Bach

Soweto
Choreography: Mats Ek
Music: collage of contemporary pop

JERUSALEM TAMAR DANCE COMPANY

Gruss Community Centre
5 Zichron Ya'akov St.
Romema 94421 Jerusalem
Tel: 02-524711

Artistic director:
Amir Kolben
General director:
Meira Eliash-Chain

Dancers:
4 female, 5 male

Premières:

Requiem
Choreography: Amir Kolben
Music: collage

Show White
Choreography: Amir Kolben
Music: Ushiro Ikido

Three Roads
Choreography: Noa Dar
Music: Yas Kaz

T'nein
Choreography: Amos Pinchassi
Music: verses from the Qur'an

Azure
Choreography: Gall Alster
Music: Aviv Kurditz

Stones
Choreography: Noa Dar
Music: Purcell, George Crumb

As She Saw It
Choreography: Jeanette Stoner
Music: collage

Yes, Thank You, We Are Getting Used To It
Choreography: Amir Kolben
Music: Yello

The Window Project
Choreography: Neta Pulvermacher
Music: Astor Piazzolla

Adloyada
Choreography: Noa Dar
Music: Tzivia Sharett

Every Minute to Start Again
Choreography: Noa Dar
Music: Tzivia Sharett

THE ISRAEL BALLET

2 Kikar Hamedinah Hey Be'iyar
Tel Aviv 62093
Tel: 03-266610

(No information available)

OSHRA ELKAYAM MOTION THEATRE

119 Bar Kochva St.
Herzelia 46341
Tel: 052-544039

Artistic director:
Oshra Elkayam

YARON MARGOLIN DANCE COMPANY

106/15 Derech Beit Lechem
Jerusalem 93624
Tel: 02-716197

Artistic director:
Yaron Margolin
General manager:
Ora Gorali

Aesthetic adviser:
Naftali Ironi

Premières:

Davidsbündlertänze
Choreography: Yaron Margolin
Music: Schumann

TMU-NA DANCE THEATRE GROUP

28 De Haas St.
Tel Aviv 62667
Tel: 03-449878

Artistic director:
Nava Zukerman

Producers:
Ilan Rosenthal, Micky Zukerman

LIAT DROR – NIR BEN-GAL

11 Borochov St.
Tel Aviv 63263
Tel: 03-285957

Première:

Equus Asinus
Choreography: Liat Dror, Nir Ben-Gal
Music: Ori Vidislavski

RENA SCHENFELD DANCE THEATRE

14 Harav Friedman St.
Tel Aviv 62303
Tel: 03-446745

Artistic director:
Rena Schenfeld

Dancers:
Rena Schenfeld, Tamar Feigenbaum,
Ingeborg Sundby, Moshe Vardi

Guest dancer:
Mona Tzang

Premières:

Or Death
Choreography: Rena Schenfeld
Music: Brahms

Love Story
Choreography: Rena Schenfeld
Music: K. Numi

A Girl After the Revolution
Choreography: Mona Tzang
Music: A. de Silva

Silk
Choreography: Rena Schenfeld
Music: Menachem Zur

Water Mystery
Choreography: Mona Tzang
Music: Bruce Tovasky

AMNON RAVIV – ESTY POMERANZ DANCE THEATRE

54 Weitzman St.
Gevataim 53372
Tel: 03-5713259

Premières:

What a Wonderful World
Choreography: A. Raviv, E. Pomeranz
Music: collage

You Came to me One Weary Day
Choreography: A. Raviv, E. Pomeranz
Music: Ella Fitzgerald

In the Concert of Life Nobody Gets a Program
Choreography: E. Pomeranz, A. Raviv

Salary information:
Salaries are for 12 months, including
vacations. The figures do not include social
security, pension payments or insurance,
which are paid by the employer and which
amount to about 45 per cent of the salary.
  Salaries are generally low (often below
the official minimum wage) but most
companies allow dancers time in which to
teach and thereby increase their income.
The Kibbutz Dance Company does not pay
its members, whose kibbutzim provide
their livelihood.
  There are no distinctions of rank in

Israeli dance companies. Most dancers start as apprentices, and rise by seniority to higher rates of pay.

Salaries are given in Israeli New Shekels: Bat-Dor: 1,600–2,600

Batsheva: 800–1,700
Inbal Dance Theatre: 800–1,700
Tamar Dance Group: 700–1,200
Israel Ballet: 700–1,200
Kol Demama: 500–1,000

Italy

BALLET OF TEATRO ALLA SCALA, MILAN

Director:
Robert de Warren

Ballet master-teachers:
Vera Colombo, Olga Evreinoff, Grigore Vintila

Resident choreographer:
Robert de Warren
Visiting choreographers:
Micha van Hoecke, Ben Stevenson, Robert North, Wayne Eagling, Rudolf Nureyev

Guest teachers:
Sulamith Messerer, Lynn Wallis, Boris Akimov

Principal dancers:
Etoile, Oriella Dorella; Elisabetta Armiato, Ornella Costalonga, Giuliana Gaspari, Annamaria Grossi, Vera Karpenko, Maurizia Luceri, Anita Magyari, Vittoria Minucci, Bruna Radice, Isabel Seabra, Edoardo Colacrai, Tiziano Mietto, Paolo Podini, Francisco Sedeño, Biagio Tambone, Bruno Vescovo
Soloists:
Laura Caccialanza, Patrizia Canini, Marinella Carimati, Paola Maccaferri, Loredana Mapelli, Ornella Mariani, Claudia Papa, Piera Pedretti, Adriana Scameroni, Silvia Scrivano, Flavia Vallone, Patrizia Volpari, Francesco Aldrovandi, Giuseppe Arena, Marco Berrichillo, Matteo Buongiorno, Vittorio D'Amato, Luciano Peschini, Rosario Picco, Maurizio Vanadia, Michele Villanova
Corps de ballet:
23 women, 17 men

Guest artists:
Carla Fracci, Patrick Dupond, Andris Liepa, Gheorghe Iancu, Laurent Hilaire, Robert Hill, Li Cunxen, Oliver Matz

Resident lighting designer:
Vannio Vanni

Productions:
Ballet in Verdi's opera *I Vespri siciliani* (7.12.89 at La Scala, Milan)
Choreography: Micha van Hoecke

Giselle, 31.12.89
New production by Yvette Chauviré
Choreography: Coralli, Perrot
Music: Adam, revised by Michel Sasson (conductor)
Designs: based on those of Alexandre Benois

Workshop 90, at Teatro di Porta Romana 2.2.90
Works by young company members:

Colours of the Rainbow
Choreography: Rosario Picco
Music: Nicola Urru, Andrew Lloyd Webber
Costumes: Maurizio Tamellini

Moments
Choreography: Angelo Moretto
Music: Gustav Mahler
Costumes: Flavia Vallone

Dietro lo specchio (Behind the Mirror)
Devised by Simona Chiesa
Music: Purcell, Schumann, and others

Guardando sotto il lago (Looking under the Lake)
Choreography: Emilio Gritti
Music: Nicola Urru, Luca de Perini
Costumes: Francesco Giuseppe de Bronchetto

Cari colleghi . . . (senza offensa)
Devised by Biagio Tambone
Music: Walton, Saint-Saëns, Dvořák,
Mirageman

New Productions, Teatro Smeraldo, 17.2.90

Square Dance
Choreography: George Balanchine, staged
by Victoria Simon
Music: Antonio Vivaldi, Arcangelo Corelli

Tchaikovsky Pas de Deux
Choreography: George Balanchine

Three Preludes
Choreography: Ben Stevenson
Music: Sergei Rachmaninov

Troy Game
Choreography: Robert North
Music: Downes, Batacuda
Assistant in restaging: Sheri Cook
Costumes: Peter Farmer

A Midsummer Night's Dream, 26.4.90 (Teatro
Lirico)
Choreography: Robert de Warren (new
version)
Music: Mendelssohn
Designs: Nadine Baylis
Lighting: Tim Hunter

At the Teatro Nuovo, 17.4.90

Death and the Maiden
Choreography: Robert North
Music: Franz Schubert
(With Ben Stevenson's *Three Preludes* and
Les Sylphides, staged by Lynne Wallis)

. . . E Così Via (And So On), 12.5.90
Choreography: Paolo Bortoluzzi
Music: Jacques Charpentier
Scenery by the choreographer

Miss Julie (revival)
Choreography: Birgit Cullberg
Music: Ture Rangstrom

Participation in Tchaikovsky's opera *The
Queen of Spades*, 14.6.90 (co-production with
Los Angeles Opera)
Choreography: Wayne Eagling
Scenery: Ezio Frigerio
Costumes: Franca Squarciapino

MAGGIODANZA Resident company of the
Teatro Comunale (opera house), Florence

Director and principal choreographer:
Evgeny Polyakov

Other resident choreographer: (company
member):
Charles Vodoz

Ballet master:
Frédéric Jahn

Principal dancers:
Anna Berardi, Maria Grazia Nicosia, Rino
Pedrazzini, George Bodnarciuc
Soloists:
Franca Bellini, Camilla Pistilli, Massimo
Andaloro, Umberto De Luca, Orazio
Messina, Bruno Milo
Corps de ballet:
30 female, 21 male

New production:

Don Quixote, Teatro Verdi, 20.10.89
Choreography: Rudolf Nureyev, staged by
Richard Nowotny
Music: Minkus
Scenery: Raffaele Del Savio
Costumes: Anna Anni

At Teatro della Compagnia

Zoolook
Choreography: Charles Vodoz
Music: Jean-Michel Jarre
Scenery and costumes: Giuseppina
Messina

Contrastes
Choreography: Maguy Marin, restaged by
Elsa De Fanti
Music: Bartók

Apollo
Choreography: George Balanchine,
restaged by Rino Pedrazzini
Music: Stravinsky

France Dance (given as 'French Dance')
Choreography: William Forsythe, staged by
Elsa De Fanti
Music: J. S. Bach, William Forsythe
Costumes and lighting: William Forsythe

The Nutcracker (Teatro Comunale)
Choreography: Evgeny Polyakov
Music: Tchaikovsky

La Dame aux camélias, Teatro della
Compagnia

Choreography: Evgeny Polyakov
Music: Robert Schumann, John Field
Scenery and costumes: Vladimir Kara

Van Gogh, Teatro Olimpico, Vicenza
Choreography: Vicente Nebrada
Music: Gustav Mahler
Costumes: Annarosa Saracino

Sport, Roman Theatre, Fiesole, 28.6.90
Choreography: Gianfranco Paoluzi,
inspired by Luigi Manzotti's 1879 original
Music: Romualdo Marenco, arr. Gaetano
Gianni Luporini
Scenery: Giorgio Cristini

Costumes: Bonizza

Alternativa
Choreography: May Murdmaa
Music: Mirap Goghidze

Jeux
Choreography: Virgilio Sieni
Music: Debussy

Touring:
Tuscany

Salary information:
Not available

Japan

MATSUYAMA BALLET COMPANY

Minamiaoyama 3-10-16
Minato-Ku, Tokyo
Tel: 03-401-2548

Director:
M. Shimizu

Principal choreographer:
T. Shimizu

Principal teachers:
Y. Morishita, T. Shimizu, Y. Tonozaki

Principal dancers:
Y. Morishita, T. Shimizu, A. Yamakawa, H.
Kurata, K. Hiramoto, S. Sadamatsu

Number of artists:
45 female, 20 male

Current repertory:

*Mandala, Swan Lake, The Sleeping Beauty, Don
Quixote, Romeo and Juliet*

Matsuyama Ballet School:
Address and telephone as ballet company

Director:
M. Matsuyama

Teachers:
S. Ohko, T. Tanaka, K. Yamazaki, Y.
Tonozaki

Guest teacher:
M. Besobrasova

TOKYO BALLET COMPANY

Yakumo 5-1-20
Meguro-Ku
Tokyo
Tel: 03-723-2356

Director:
T. Sasaki

Principal choreographer:
S. Mizoshita
Visiting choreographers:
M. Béjart, J. Kylián, P. Lacotte, J. Neumeier

Principal teachers:
H. Tomoda, T. Suzuki, Y. Yasuda

Principal dancers:
S. Mizoshita, M. Tohdoh, Y. Saitoh, N.
Nishiwaki

Number of artists:
30 female, 24 male

256

Current repertory:
Kabuki, Tam Tam, The Sleeping Beauty,
Symphony in D, Swan Lake

Tokyo Ballet School
Address and telephone as Tokyo Ballet

Guest teacher:
M. Fredmann

MAKI ASAMI BALLET COMPANY

Nakano 6-27-13
Nakno-Ku, Tokyo
Tel: 03-366-8251

Director and principal choreographer:
A. Maki

Visiting choreographer:
A. Plisetsky

Principal teachers:
A. Maki, S. Ogura, K. Mitani, H. Imamura,
M. Toyokawa

Principal dancers:
K. Mitani, H. Imamura, Y. Kawaguchi, M.
Yuhki, N. Ohhara

Number of artists:
30 female, 24 male

Current repertory:
Swan Lake, Giselle, Raymonda, Don Quixote,
The Sleeping Beauty

Maki Asami Ballet School
Tomigaya 2-14-15
Shibuya-Ku, Tokyo
Tel: 03-460-9411

Director:
A. Maki

Teachers:
M. Toyokawa, H. Imamura, K. Mitani
Guest teachers:
A. Mahler, R. Orbach

TANI BALLET COMPANY

Nakane 2-21-27
Meguro-Ku, Tokyo
Tel: 03-717-7806

Director/principal choreographer:
M. Tani
Visiting choreographer:
B. Cullberg

Principal teachers:
K. Yashiro, S. Takada, Y. Takahashi, S.
Asami, Y. Ishida, K. Hirosa

Principal dancers:
Y. Omoto, N. Takaba, R. Ohtsuka, Y. Satoh,
K. Akagi, S. Sadamatsu

Number of artists:
20 female, 6 male

Current repertory:
Swan Lake, Giselle, La Fille mal gardée, Don
Quixote

Tani Ballet School:
Address and telephone as ballet company

TOKYO CITY BALLET COMPANY

Kozimacho 2-39-6
Chofu-shi, Tokyo
Tel: 0424 85-2915

Director:
G. Arima

Choreographers:
T. Ishida, K. Ishii, T. Kanai, N. Nakagima

Principal teachers:
K. Ishii, N. Hakajima, M. Aoyama
Guest teacher:
M. Fredmann

Principal dancers:
E. Adachi. M. Yoshizawa, N. Nakajima, N.
Ushijima

Number of artists:
20 female, 8 male

Korea (South)

THE NATIONAL THEATRE OF KOREA

SAN 14–67
Changchung-Dong 2ka
Chang-Ku
Seoul

The National Dance Company (address as above)

Director:
Song Bom

Number of dancers:
62

The National Ballet Company (address as above)

Director:
Lim Song-Nam

Number of dancers:
50

CHANG MU DANCE COMPANY

GPO Box 9511
Seoul, Korea
Tel: (02) 739 3577

Director:
Kim Maeja

Number of dancers:
50

The Netherlands

HET NATIONALE BALLET (DUTCH NATIONAL BALLET)

Postbus 16486
1001 RN Amsterdam
Waterlooplein 22
1011 PG Amsterdam
Tel: 020-5518911

Artistic director:
Rudi van Dantzig
Deputy artistic director:
Han Ebbelaar
Administrative director:
Anton Gerritsen
Deputy administrative director:
Dick Hendriks

Resident choreographer:
Toer van Schayk

Musical director:
Jac van Steen

Head artistic staff:
Reuven Voremberg

Ballet masters:
Maria Aradi, Robert Fischer, Sonja Marchiolli

First soloists:
Colleen Davis, Caroline Sayo Iura, Alexandra Radius, Karin Schnabel, Valerie Valentine, Jeanette Vondersaar, Joanne Zimmerman, Fred Berlips, Wim Broeckx, Clint Farha, Alan Land, Zoltán Solymosi
Second soloists:
Rachel Beaujean, Nathalie Caris, Jane Lord, Cathy Nussbaumer, Esther Protzman, Bruno Barat, Reinbert Martijn, Pierre Paradis
Artists:
22 female, 26 male
Elèves-aspirants:
16

Repertory:
Swan Lake, Sleeping Beauty; Ashton:
Symphonic Variations, The Dream;
Balanchine: *Prodigal Son, Serenade, Violin*
Concerto; Tchaikovsky Pas de Deux, Brahms
Schonberg Quartet; Van Dantzig (two new
works); Van Schayk (two new works); Van
Manen: *Corps*

NEDERLANDS DANS THEATER I

Postbus 15697
1502 BR Den Haag
Tel: 070–609931

Artistic director:
Jiři Kylián

Resident choreographers:
Hans van Manen, Nacho Duato

Administrative director:
Carel Birnie

Administration:
Peter Schreiber

Régisseur:
Hans Knill

Répétiteur:
Roslyn Anderson

Teacher:
Irena Milovan

Assistant artistic director:
Ulf Esser

Guest teachers:
Christine Anthony, Kathryn Bennets,
Benjamin Harkarvy, Jan Nuyts, Marian
Sarstadt

Dancers:
Catherine Allard, Simone Clifford, DeAnn
Duteil, Nancy Euverink, Karine Guizzo,
Jennifer Hanna, Karin Heijninck, Victoria
Jestyn, Cora Kroese, Marly Knoben, Sol
Leon, Fiona Lummis, Brigitte Martin, Joke
Martin, Pascale Mosselmans, France
Nguyen, Elke Schepers, Shaun Amyot,
Jean-Louis Cabané, Martin Corri, Patrick
Delcroix, Robert Dungey, Glenn Edgerton,
Jean Emile, Paul Lightfoot, Martin Muller,
Philip Taylor, James Vincent, Aryeh Weiner

NEDERLANDS DANS THEATER II
(same address)

Director:
Arlette van Boven

Assistants:
Hedda Twiehaus, Sabine Kupferberg,
Gerald Tibbs

Guest teacher:
Martinette Janmaat

Dancers:
Carolina Armenta, Ina Broeckx, Christina
Clark, Françoise Constant, Lisa Drake,
Cristina Hortiguela, Karina Silverio, Zane
Booker, Thomas Graham, Davide Luca,
Andrea Megarese, Keith Morino, Kirk
Ryder, Ivan Dubreuil

Repertory NDT I and II:
Kylián: *Soldiers Mass, Falling Angels, Nomads*
Van Manen: *Brainstorm, Shakerloops, Keep*
Going, Septet Extra, Black Cake, Fugitive
Visions, Duato: *Raptus, Na Floresta*
New works by Paul Lightfoot, Ohad
Naharin, Mats Ek, Lionel Hoche, Alida
Chase

SCAPINO BALLET ROTTERDAM

Luchtvaartstraat 2
1059 CA Amsterdam
Tel: 020–153916
Fax: 020–179206

Artistic directors:
Nils Christe, Armando Navarro
Administrative director:
Jan Schretzmeijer

Ballet mistress:
Anne van Tol

Répétiteur/coordination:
Annegien Sneep

Guest teacher:
Simon Mottram

Resident choreographers:
Nils Christe, Ed Wubbe

Dancers:
Jacqueline Brugman, Kirsten Debrock,

Sarah Duley, Victoria Edgar, Valerie Lecocq, Ilja Louwen, José de Nobel, Mariette Redel, Tamara Roso, Margaret Tappan, Maren Timm, Valerie Valentine, Marion Vijn, Paula Vink, Olivier Deguine, Matthias Eidmann, Wout Fransen, Par Isberg, Andreas Justrich, Hakan Larsson, Nico Marckmann, Waldo Oliveira, Keith Derrick Randolph, Jan de Schynkel, Rinus Sprong, Thomas Stuart, José Luis Viera, Michiel Verkoren, Anastassios Vitoros, Robin Woolmer

Repertory:
Choreography by Nils Christe, Ed Wubbe, Jan Linkens, Paula Vink, Tamara Roso, Armando Navarro

INTRODANS

Vijfzinnenstraat 80–82
6811 LN Arnhem
Tel: 085-512111

Artistic director:
Ton Wiggers
Administrative director:
Hans Focking

Resident choreographer:
Ed Wubbe

Répétiteur:
Nuria Castells

Guest teacher:
Anja Licher, Simon de Mowbray

Dancers:
Mariet Andringa, Charlotte Besijn, Mirjam Diedrich, Martin Freudenstein, Frank Holstein, Sandra Klijn, Hilde Machtelinckx, Diane Matla, Peter Rombouts, Dik Smits, Tony Vandecasteele, Elisabeth Veenendaal, Roel Voorintholt, Sjoerd Vreugdenhil, Marcel Wolfkamp, Kim van Savooyen (understudy)

Repertory:
Choreography by Ed Wubbe, Ton Wiggers, Graham Lustig, Nils Christe, Norbert Taatgen

ROTTERDAMSE DANSGROEP

's Gravendijkwal 58a
3014 EE Rotterdam
Tel: 010-4364511

Director:
Käthy Gosschalk
Deputy director administration:
Winne Consenheim

Répétiteur:
José Winkelman

Guest teachers:
Louise Frank, Nicolai de Lusignan, Ton Simons, Marian Sarstadt

Dancers:
Anne Affourtit, Gaby Allard, Anouk van Dijk, Caroline Harder, Felicia Sanders, Desirée Schneider, Marion Tolkamp, Charles Linehan, Rick Kam, Ruud van der Kooij, Matthijs Olieman, Tim Persent, Samuel Wursten

Repertory:
Choreography by Käthy Gosschalk, Amanda Miller, Stephen Petronio, Ton Simons, Shusaku Takeuchi, Gerrit Jan Vooren, Randy Warshaw

DANSGROEP REFLEX

Moesstraat 7
9717 JT Gronigen
Tel: 050-719888

Artistic director:
Yoka van Brummelem (until April 1990)

Direction assistant:
Erik van Raalte

Ballet master/répétiteur:
Henk Knaap

Teachers:
Henk Knaap, Nina Wiener, Norio Mamiya, Iwan Kramar, Pauline Daniels, Yoka van Brummelen

Dancers:
Diane Elshout, Marjolein Elsink, Josje Manuputty, Patrizia Tuerlings, Neel Verdoorn, Ney Branco, Timothy Calvin, Hein Hazenberg, Klaus Jurgens, Henley Smith

Repertory:
Choreography by Nina Wiener, Patrizia Tuerlings, Hans Tuerlings, Lucas Hoving, Pauline Daniels, Ted Brandsen, Piet Rogie

DANSGROEP KRISZTINA DE CHATEL

Plantage Muidergracht 155
1018 TT Amsterdam
Tel: 020-273970

Artistic director and choreographer:
Krisztina de Chatel
Administrative director:
Kees Korsman

Répétiteur:
Josje Neuman

Dancers:
Hans Beenhakker, Job Cornelissen, Janine Dijkmeijer, Oerm Matern, Dries van der Post, Paul Waarts (understudies: Henriette Koops, Patricia Nugteren)

STICHTING DANSPRODUKTIE

Plantage Kerklaan 61
1018 CX Amsterdam
Tel: 020-242166/253863

Artistic director:
Bianca van Dillen
Administration director:
Rob Mollée

Répétiteur:
Bob Foltz

Dancers:
Nanda Leenders, Gudio Severtien, Pink Niessen, Christopher Steel, Ilse van Dijk, Dietmar Janeck, Noortje Bijvoets

Repertory:
Choreography by Bianca van Dillen, Beppie Blankert

FOLKLORISTISCH DANSTHEATER

Postbus 16885
1001 RJ Amsterdam
Kloveniersburgwal 87–89
Tel: 020-239112

Director:
Ferdinand van Altena
Assistant artistic director:
Maurits van Geel
Teachers:
Silviu Ciuciumis, Ciga Despotovic, Ivonne Despotovic-Eschweiler, Tineke van Geel, Eddy Tijssen

Ballet master:
André Verdoner

Musicians:
Mike de Keijzer, Floor Minnaert, Willem Raadsveld, Roelof Rosendal, Monique Lansdorp

Dancers:
Ine van Alebeek, Geka Bleker, Marloes Hof, Therese Laurant, Marjan Mieremet, Susanna Millet, Daisy Rebel, Saskia Franke, Monique Le Belle, Miriam Kleppe, Andras Asboth, Armin Dorn, Peter Jakab, Hans Minnaert, Jeno Molnar, Junior van Rijn, Istvan Tanacs, André de Jong

For more information about other Dutch dance companies (listed below):

Nederlands Instituut voor de Dans (NID)

Herengracht 74
1016 BR Amsterdam
Tel: 020-237541

Publications:

Notes: edited by Ariejan Korteweg and Joost de Wolf; Amsterdam, NID 1989

Made in Holland: Promotion magazine on dance in the Netherlands; edited by the NID, 1989

Dansergids (Dutch and English editions): edited by the NID, Paul Bronkhorst; Amsterdam 1989–90

Dansjaarboek 1989/90: edited by the NID, Eva van Schaik; Amsterdam 1990 (September)

Companies: Cloud Chamber, Danstheater Nan Romijn, Dansstudio Pauline de Groot, Danscompagnie Limburg, Djazzex, Danserscollectief, Foltz + Company, Glashart, De Nieuwe Dansgroep, Nieuwe Danserije, Opus One, Pandora, Shusaku and Dormu Dance theatre, Villa Danthe, Vals Bloed/Het Concern, Zuil van Volta.

Salary information:
At the request of the dancers of the Dutch National Ballet, a Dutch research project has been started to investigate the salary levels of dancers around the world. All the Dutch subsidized companies, the artists' union (*Kunstenbond*) and the Netherlands

261

Dance Institute have united forces to secure a subsidy for this international research. Danielle Mol is the author of the report. (Further information from the Nederlands Instituut voor de Dans.)

New Zealand

THE ROYAL NEW ZEALAND BALLET

42 Vivian Street
PO Box 6682
Te Aro, Wellington
New Zealand
Tel: (04)843-668
Fax: (04)858-162

Artistic director:
Harry Haythorne

General manager:
Mark Keyworth

Principal company teachers:
Jacqui Trimmer, Peter Boyes, Harry Haythorne, Jon Trimmer

Principal dancers:
Kerry-Anne Gilberd, Brando Miranda, Lee Patrice, Jon Trimmer, Karin Wakefield
Soloists:
3 female, 5 male
Corps de ballet:
7 female, 6 male
Guest artists:
Evelyn Cisneros, Sherril Cooper (actress), Jean Guizerix, Marie Lindquist, Wilfride Piollet, Anthony Randazzo, Cecile Sicango, Jan-Erik Wikstrom

Première, Auckland, March 1990

Jean – The Ballet of Jean Batten
Choreography: Mary-Jane O'Reilly
Music: Jonathan Besser
Design: Kristian Fredrikson
Libretto: Philip and Mary-Jane O'Reilly
Lighting: Stephen Crowcroft

Repertory:
(all lighting designed by Stephen Crowcroft)

Le Beau Danube
Choreography: Leonide Massine
(reproduced by Harry Haythorne)
Music: Johann Strauss
Scenery: V. and E. Polunin
Costumes: Etienne de Beaumont

Carreau dans un Cercle
Choreography: Eugene Polyakov
Music: Chevalier de Saint Georges
Design: Eugene Polyakov

Coppélia
Choreography: Saint-Léon, staged by Cyril Johns and Leslie White after British productions by Nicholas Sergeyev
Production and new choreography: Harry Haythorne
Music: Delibes
Scenery: Kenneth Raynor
Costumes: Owen Anderson

Faust Divertissement
Choreography: Galina Samsova and André Prokovsky
Music: Charles Gounod
Design: Peter Farmer

A Servant of Two Masters
Choreography: Gray Veredon
Music: Vivaldi
Design: Kristian Fredrikson

Tell Me a Tale
Choreography: Gray Veredon
Music: Matthew Fisher
Design: Kristian Fredrikson
Various *pas de deux* danced by guest artists.

SOUTHERN BALLET AND DANCE THEATRE

PO Box 845
Christchurch, New Zealand

Director and principal choreographer:
Russell Kerr

Teachers:
Russell Kerr, Pamela Rathbone, Greer Robertson

Dancers:
Juliet Annan, Emma Bond, Renate Donovan, Yasuyo Fukui, Kathy Ferigo, Melanie Hamilton, Sharon Kuttner, Sarah March, Akemi Morisaki, Miki Norii, Melanie Peck, Mandy Weeks, Geordan Wilcox

Current repertory:

Mr Scrooge
Choreography: Russell Kerr

Concerto for 12
Choreography: Russell Kerr
Music: Scriabin

Inner Landscapes
Choreography: Russell Kerr
Music: Lilburn

Journey
Choreography: Russell Kerr
Music: Japanese folk music, Bach

Omage
Choreography: Russell Kerr
Music: Offenbach

Poems
Choreography: Patricia Rianne
Music: Carr

Ations
Choreography: Bull
Music: Davey

DANCE PACIFIC

101 Old Mill Road
Westmere, Auckland
Tel: 0 9 787958

Directors:
Cath Cardiff, Taiaroa Royal

Dancers:
Glen Birchall, Janine Burchett, Leonie Kaywood, Stephen Nunley, Ursula Robb, Taiaroa Royal, Susan Trainor

Current repertory:

Shaman of Visions
Choreography: Cath Cardiff
Music: van Teigham
Poetry text: Albert Wendt

Te Po/Night
Choreography: Taiaroa Royal
Music: Miles Davis and others

Thriving Decay
Choreography: Shona McCullagh
Music: Graham Humphreys

State of Mind (Greenpeace benefit performance)
Choreography: Cath Cardiff
Music: Vangelis

DOUGLAS WRIGHT & COMPANY

47 Clyde Street
Island Bay, Wellington
Tel: 0 4 835156

Director and choreographer:
Douglas Wright

Manager:
Susan Paterson

Dancers:
Mia Mason, Shona McCullagh, Glenn Mayo, Charles Neho, Kilda Northcott, Douglas Wright

Repertory:

Hey Paris, Quartet, Faun Variations, Ranterstantrum, Halcyon, How on Earth?, Passion Play

COMMOTION DANCE COMPANY

Tel: 0 4 829183

Director and choreographer:
Michael Parmenter

Manager:
Joanna Sylvester

Dancers:
Michelle Richecoeur, Alex Beasley, Janis Claxton, Claudia Kappenberg, Charles

THE STATISTICS OF DANCE COMPANIES

Neho, Anthony O'Flaherty, Helen Winchester, Michael Parmenter

Repertory:

Intimate Constellations
Choreography: Michael Parmenter
Music: Bach

Listeners at the Breathing Place
Choreography: Michael Parmenter
Music: Messiaen

JORDAN & PRESENT CO.

PO Box 9653
Wellington
New Zealand
Tel: (04) 758-285

Director/choreographer:
Susan Jordan
Administrative director:
Briony Ellis
Musical director:
Sue Alexander

Dancers:
Marie Gray, Holly Cooper, Kilda Northcott, Annaliese Forde, Robert Bree, Lisa Densem, Alex Beasley, Kathryn Mowat, Bill Jarman

Repertory:

Face Value, Old Bank of NZ Chamber, Wellington, 21.9.89
Music: Sue Alexander
Design: Susan Jordan, Alan McShane

Stone the Crow, Brierley Theatre, Wellington, 13.9.88
Music: various
Design: Susan Jordan, Simon Elson

Holy Women, Depot Theatre, Wellington, 23.7.87
Music: various
Design: Susan Jordan, Hanna von Randow

Against the Grain, Flying Kiwi Festival, Wellington, 19.3.86
Music: various
Design: Susan Jordan

Unknowing Steps, Old Depot Theatre, Wellington, 26.6.85
Music: various
Design: Susan Jordan, Paul McInnes

PAUL JENDEN & LOUIS SOLINO

42 Hollis Road
Paraparaumu Beach
Wellington

All choreography and design:
Paul Jenden

Repertory:

Public Figures
Music: Boccherini

Dead Ballerinas
Music: Chopin

Cheek to Cheek
Music: George Howard

Seven Deadly Sins
Music: Miles Medick

Intensive Care
Music: Peter Dasent

Hansel and Gretel
Music: collage

TAIAO

PO Box 5857
Wellesley St.
Auckland, New Zealand
Tel: 0 9 765792

Director:
Stephen Bradshaw

Administration:
Gail Richards, Carla van Zon

Teachers:
Stephen Bradshaw, Brigitte Te Whiti, Marianne Schultz

Dancers:
Hori Ahipene, Stephen Bradshaw, Cliff Curtis, Adrienne Gray, Corinna Hunziker, Norman Potts, Leichelle Tanoa, Pita Te Tau, Dorothy Waetford, Tracey Berghan

Repertory:

Assimilation
Choreography: Stephen Bradshaw
Music: Brian Eno, John Hassel

Hauora
Choreography: Moana Nepia

Music: Taura Eruera

Hoki ki te Timatanga
Choreography: Pita Te Tau, Dorothy
Waetford

Nga Wai Koropiro
Choreography: Rozeanne Worthington

Topu
Choreography: Suzanne Renner
Music: Adair Bruce

Salary information:
Not available

The Philippines

BALLET PHILIPPINES

Cultural Centre of the Philippines
Roxas Boulevard, Manila
Philippines
Tel: 832–3688

Artistic director:
Alice Reyes

Artistic associate:
Cecile Sicangco

Production director:
Salvador Bernal

Ballet master:
William Morgan

Resident choreographers:
Alice Reyes, Agnes Locsin, Edna Vida,
Denisa Reyes
Guest choreographers:
Norman Walker, Garth Welch, Alfredo
Rodriquez, Miro Zolan

Principal dancers:
Nonoy Froilan, Cecile Sicangco, Conrad
Dy-Liacco
Soloists:
Gina Katigbak, Tina Fargas, Melissa
Cuachon, Ramon Victoria, Perry Sevidal,
Sofia Zobel, Jun Mabaquiao, Ida Beltran,
Jinn Ibarrola
Number of artists:
15
Guest artists:
Yoko Morishita, Maniya Barredo, Christine
Walsh, Rey Dizon, Anna Villadolid,
Thomas Mayr, Lisa Macuja, Ricardo Ella,

Elizabeth Roxas, Toni Lopez Gonzalez,
Andre Reyes, Stephen Smith, Brando
Miranda

Repertory:

*Swan Lake, Cinderella, Paquita, Itim-Asu, Te
Deum, Carmen, Songs of a Wayfarer, Rama,
Hari, Variaciones Concertantes, Amada, Young
People's Pleasure, Vision of Fire, Carmina
Burana, Raymunda, Variations, Images, Ang
Sultan, Batique, Company, Dugso, Mga Babae,
Negro Spirituals*

Number of performances:
68

BALLET PHILIPPINES II

Cultural Centre of the Philippines
Roxas Boulevard, Manila
Philippines
Tel: 832–3675

Artistic director:
Agnes Locsin

Choreographers:
Agnes Locsin, Nonoy Froilan, Regine
Debuque, Conrad Dy-Liacco, Paul Ocampo

Number of artists:
18

Repertory:

*Igorot, Bagobo, Tatgubat, I, Judas, For Amparo,
Kabilang, Tinig, Konamiras, Vision of Fire, For
the Gods*

265

Number of performances:
11

PHILIPPINE BALLET THEATRE

PBT Studio, Meralco Building
Ortigas Avenue, Pasig
Metro Manila, Philippines
Tel: 631-2222

Artistic director:
Inday Gaston Manosa

Artistic council:
Julie Borromeo Roche, Gener Caringal,
Sony Lopez Gonzalez, Felicitas Radaic, Eric
Cruz, Vella Damian, Tony Fabella, Eddie
Elejar

Ballet mistress:
Vella Damian

Guest choreographer:
Robert Barnett

Number of artists:
23
Guest artists:
Lisa Macuja, Maiqui Manosa, Nicholas
Pacana, Rebecca Rodriguez, Manuel Molina

Repertory: for 1989 season:

*Coppélia, Serenade, Reflections, Tchaikovsky Pas
de Deux, A Bond, Rigodon, Vinta, Pinoy Talaga*

Number of performances:
21

BAYANIHAN PHILIPPINE DANCE COMPANY

Unlad Building
Taft Avenue
Manila
Tel: 583-187

Director/choreographer:
Lucrecia Reyes Urtula

Rehearsal masters:
Lito Valle Cruz, Annabelle Ramos, Bong
Jose

Number of artists:
90

Repertory:
Traditional and folk dances from the

Cordilleras and Mindanao, Spanish-
influenced dances, Lowland Christian
dances, ethnic/tribal dances

Number of performances:
395

RAMON OBUSAN FOLKLORIC GROUP

No. 4 Chapel Road
MIA Housing Area
Pasay City
Tel: 831-0894

Artistic director/choreographer:
Ramon Obusan

Rehearsal masters:
Cecile Obusan, Sergio Anlocutan, Lita
Obusan

Number of artists:
60

Repertory:
Traditional and folk dances from the
Cordilleras and Mindanao, Spanish-
influenced dances, Lowland Christian
dances, ethnic/tribal dances

Number of performances:
34

PHILIPPINE BARANGGAY FOLK DANCE TROUPE

131 Scout Fernandez Street
Quezon City
Tel: 951-275

Artistic director:
Dr Paz-Cielo A. Belmonte

Dance masters:
Ronaldo del Barrio, Gina Ante

Number of artists:
33

Repertory:

Traditional and folk dances from the
Cordilleras and Mindanao, Spanish-
influenced dances, Lowland Christian
dances, ethnic/tribal dances

Number of performances:
105

266

Singapore

SINGAPORE DANCE THEATRE LTD

101 Cecil Street
Tong Eng Building No. 20–08
Singapore 0106
Tel: 223-1511

Artistic directors:
Goh Soo Khim, Anthony Then

Number of dancers:
10 (4 apprentices)

Premières:

Coils of Silence
Choreographer: Christopher Bannerman
Music: Leo Bronwer

Gemini (Singapore première)
Choreography: Vicente Nebrada

Electric Sequences
Choreography: Vicente Nebrada

SINGAPORE FESTIVAL OF ARTS
Biennial: June–July 1990

Ministry of Community Development
MCD Building No. 15-00
512 Thomson Road
Singapore 1129
Tel: 258-9403

Spain

BALLET DEL TEATRO LIRICO NACIONAL LA ZARZUELA

Teatro Real
Plaza de Isabel II s/n
28013 Madrid
Tel: 1 542 55 98/33 76
Telex: 41493 TZM E
Fax: 429 71 57

Director: (From 1 June 1990):
Nacho Duato
Director:
Ray Barra

BALLET VICTOR ULLATE

Dr. Castelo 7
28009 Madrid
Tel: 1 275 03 85

Director:
Victor Ullate

DART COMPAÑÍA DE DANSA

Casp 108, 6c
08010 Barcelona
Tel: 3 246 5962

Director:
Guillermina Coll

BALLET DE EUSKADI

Henae 20
48009 Bilbao
Tel: 4 424 98 61

Directors:
Rafael Martí and Angeles Sautiño

BALLET CLÁSICO DE ZARAGOZA

Domingo Miral s/n
50005 Zaragoza
Tel: 76 23 63 32

Director:
Mauro Galindo

BALLET DEL ATLÁNTICO

Alameda de Colón 1
35002 Las Palmas de Gran Canaria
Tel: 28 36 86 87

Director:
Anatol Yanowsky

BALLET NACIONAL DE ESPAÑA

Teatro Real
Plaza de Isabel II s/n
28013 Madrid
Tel: 1 242 09 98

Director:
José Antonio

CUMBRE FLAMENCA

Corredera de Bayo 19
28004 Madrid
Tel: 531 68 70/522 49 73

Director:
Francisco Sanchez

BALLET ESPAÑOL DE MARÍA ROSA

Ayala 43
28001 Madrid
Tel: 1 276 72 38

Director:
María Rosa

BALLET DE ESPAÑA DE PACO ROMERO

Gutierrez de Cetina 16
28017 Madrid
Tel: 1 407 57 91

Director:
Paco Romero

Manager:
Nacho Sánchez
Barquillo 32 1° Izq.
28004 Madrid
Tel: 1 522 24 94/531 21 29

LUISILLO MUSICA Y DANZA

Felipe Ill 4, 1° Izq.
28012 Madrid
Tel: 1 265 84 04

MARIO MAYA

Centro de Actividades Flamencas
Pasaje Mayol 20
41003 Sevilla
Tel: 54 41 52 09

CARMEN CORTÉS

Costanilla de los Desemparados 10
28014 Madrid
Tel: 1 429 45 10/228 40 82

BLANCA DEL REY

Morería 17
28005 Madrid
Tel: 1 265 10 46

LA TATI

Del Prado 7
28014 Madrid
Tel: 1 429 34 54/462 96 65

Agent/contact:
Leo Alonso

BALLET CONTEMPORANI DE BARCELONA

Guitard 41 Baixos
08014 Barcelona
Tel: 3 419 2738/322 10 37/490 88 96/
490 72 73

Direction:
Amelia Boluda and Anselm García

COMPAÑÍA GELABERT/AZZOPARDI

Torrent de l'Olla 146
08012 Barcelona
Tel: 3 416 00 68

Direction:
Cesc Gelabert and Lydia Azzopardi

LANÓNIMA IMPERIAL

Diputació 377 4 art.
08013 Barcelona
Tel: 3 245 27 43

Director:
Juan Carlos García

Contact:
Dietrich Grosse

MUDANCES

Domenec 9 5°
08012 Barcelona
Tel: 3 217 66 49

Director:
Angels Margarit

METROS

Torrent de l'Ollaropral. 1a
08012 Barcelona
Tel: 3 258 08 16

Director:
Ramón Oller

DAMAC DANZA

Apdo. Correos 9388
08080 Barcelona
Tel: 3 242 75 83/210 53 60

Direction:
Sabine Dahrendorf and Alfonso Ordóñez

AVELINA ARQÜELLES

Benet Mateu 60 entlos.
08034 Barcelona
Tel: 3 203 21 87

MAL PELO – MARÍA MUÑOZ Y PEP RAMIS

Aribau 45 Atico
08011 Barcelona
Tel: 3 254 90 89

MARÍA ANTONIA OLIVER

Carrer del Carme 30-32
08001 Barcelona
Tel: 3 302 54 90

TRANSIT

Carrer San Bru 9
08301 Mataro, Barcelona
Tel: 3 790 40 31

Director:
María Rovira

ANANDA DANZA

Padre Rico 8 B Izq.
46008 Valencia
Tel: 6 326 22 22

Direction:
Edison Valls and Rosangeles Valls

VIANANTS

Calamocha 3 pta. 24 A
46007 Valencia
Tel: 6 357 13 58

Direction:
Gracel Meneu

Agent:
David Poliakoff Management
Marqués de Sotelo 5
Pasaje Rex B 7° 19° B
46002 Valencia
Tel: 6 351 16 82

CARMEN SENRA

Apolonio Morales 3
28036 Madrid
Tel: 1 458 16 51/254 78 43

10 Y 10

Arturo Soria 241
28033 Madrid
Tel: 1 457 61 41/742 26 57

Administrative director:
Monica Runde

Choreographers:
Pedro Berdayes and Monica Runde

Agent:
Nacho Sánchez (see Ballet de España de Paco Romero)

ZIRADANZA

San Bernado 119 7° Izq.
28015 Madrid
Tel: 1 448 98 97

Director:
Denise Perdikidis

COMPANIA BLANCA CALVO

Julio Danvila 12
28033 Madrid
Tel: 1 475 72 22

Director:
Blanca Calvo

MARÍA JOSÉ RIBOT

Nicolas Usera 64
28026 Madrid
Tel: 1 475 49 22

FRANCESC BRAVO

Marqués de Santa Ana 10 3° Dcha.
28015 Madrid
Tel: 1 523 05 47

PABLO VENTURA

Conde Duque 24 4°
28015 Madrid
Tel: 1 248 96 92

ANTONIA ANDREU

Santos Cosme y Damian 3
28012 Madrid
Tel: 1 228 27 69

MÓNICA VALENCIANO

Zurita 20 3° Pta. 2
28012 Madrid
Tel: 1 230 40 27

HIDRA DANZA

Luis Montoto 147 3° D
41007 Sevilla
Tel: 5 457 91 45

MÁLAGA DANZA TEATRO

Huerta 3
29014 Málaga
Tel: 52 26 55 89

Director:
Josep Mitjans

YAUZKARI DANZA CONTEMPORÁNEA

Urzainki 7
31014 Pamplona (Navarra)
Tel: 48 12 87 33

Director:
José Láinez

FESTIVALS

Festival Internacional de Danza Itálica,
held June–July

Organized by the Diputación Provincial de Sevilla
Fundación Luis Cernuda
Avda. Constitución, 24 Pasaje de los Seises
6°
41001 Seville
Tel: 5 421 32 22, 5 421 40 24

Director:
Juan Antonio Maesso

Madrid en Danza – month-long international festival held in May, organized as a collaborative effort between the following institutions:

Centro Cultural de la Villa de Madrid
Jardines del Descubrimiento
Plaza de Colón, s/n
28001 Madrid
Tel: 1 576 64 51

Director:
Antonio Guirau

Centro Nacional de Nuevas Tendencias
Escénicas
Sala Olimpia
Plaza de Lavapiés, s/n
28012 Madrid
Tel: 1 227 46 22

Director:
Guillermo Heras

C.E. y A.C.
Consejería de Cultura
Comunidad de Madrid
Plaza de España, 8 3°
28008 Madrid
Tel: 1 580 26 78

INAEM
Ministerio de Cultura
Plaza del Rey, 4 3°
28004 Madrid
Tel: 1 532 00 93

Festival Internacional de Teatro, held in
May, includes dance
Ayuntamiento de Granada
Gabinete de Teatro
Palacio de la Madraza
Oficios, 14
18001 Granada
Tel: 58 22 84 03

Director:
Manuel Llanes

*Festival Internacional de Música y Danza
de Granada*, held mid-June
Corral del Carbón
Mariana Pineda
Apartado de Correos, 64
18080 Granada
Tel: 58 22 80 51

Director:
Maria del Carmen Palma

Feria de Teatro de Huesca, held in May,
includes dance
*Dept. de Cultura de la Diputación General
de Aragón*
P° María Agustín, s/n
Edificio Pignatelli
50004 Zaragoza
Tel: 76 43 95 00, ext. 2409/00/17

*Festival Internacional de Teatro, Música y
Danza de Zaragoza*, held in May
San Jorge, 1
50001 Zaragoza
Tel: 76 39 09 29

Coordinator:
Pilar Ariza

Festival Internacional de Santander, held
in August
Avenida Calvo Sotelo, 15 5°

39002 Santander
Tel: 42 21 05 08, 42 31 48 19

Festival Internacional de Segovia, held in
July–August, includes dance
Ayuntamiento de Segovia
Plaza Mayor, 1
40001 Segovia
Tel: 11 35 04 99, 11 43 36 11

Festival de Tardor, held October–
November
Olimpiada Cultural, SA
Rambla de Caputxins, 74
08002 Barcelona
Tel: 3 317 00 24, 3 317 00 93

Director:
Mario Gas

Grec, held June–August
Palau de la Virreina
Ramblas, 99
08022 Barcelona
Tel: 3 301 61 00, 3 318 25 25

Director:
Elena Posa

Sitges Teatro Internacional, held April–
May
Plaça de L'Ajuntament, 18
08870 Sitges
Tel: 3 894 45 61, 3 894 46 61

Director:
Toni Cots

Festival de Otoño, held October–November
Paseo de la Castellana, 101 1°
28046 Madrid
Tel: 1 546 24 40, 1 524 24 12

Glaucia del Burgo
Centro Cultural Villa de Móstoles
Antonio Hernández, s/n
28931 Móstoles (Madrid)
Tel: 1 618 30 14, 1 618 30 44

Veranos de la Villa, held July–September,
includes dance
Organized by Concejalía de Cultura
Ayuntamiento de Madrid
Mayor, 83
28013 Madrid
Tel: 1 247 30 51, 1 247 25 57

271

Festivales de Navarra, held in August
Organized by Departamento de Educación
y Cultura del Gobierno de Navarra
Ansoleaga, 10
31001 Pamplona
Tel: 48 22 73 00

Dansa a València, held in February
Servicio de Teatro de la Generalitat
Valenciana
Avda. del Campanar, 32
46015 Valencia
Tel: 6 386 65 00

Director:
Toni Pastor

Jornadas de Danza Contemporánea, held in
May
Servicio de Promoción y Difusión Cultural,
Diputación Foral de Guipúzcoa
Plaza de Guipúzcoa, s/n 20004 San
Sebastián
Tel: 43 42 35 11

Sweden

ROYAL SWEDISH BALLET

Opera House
PO 16 094
103 22 Stockholm, Sweden
Tel: 08–791 43 00

Artistic director:
Nil-Åke Häggbom

Guest choreographers:
Per Jonsson, Regina Beck-Friis

Principal teachers:
Janek Schergen, Konstantin Damianov,
Björn Holmgren, Mariane Orlando-Jönsson

Notators:
Alison Goodwin, Agneta Stjernlöf-Valcu

Principal dancers:
Anneli Alhanko-Skoglund, Johanna
Björnson, Kerstin Lidström, Margareta
Lidström, Madeleine Onne, Ann-Berit
Sörensen, Weit Carlsson, Niklas Ek, Pär
Isberg, Per Arthur Segerström, Mats
Wegman
Soloists:
8 female, 6 male
Artists:
36 female, 25 male
Guest artists:
Faroukh Rouzimatov, Zhanna Ayupova

Premières:

Opportunity Makes the Thief, 26.8.89
Choreography: Regina Beck-Friis
Music: 18th-century music, arr. John
Lanchbery
Design: David Walker

Soliman II or The Three Sultanas, 26.8.89
(comedy with song and dance in three
acts)
Choreography: Ivo Cramér
Music: Joseph Martin Kraus

Heze, 22.2.90
Choreography: Per Jonsson
Music: Per Jonsson with Leif Elggren and
Kent Tankred
Design: Per Jonsson

Repertory:

Sleeping Beauty
Choreography: Nicolai Sergeyev after
Petipa, additions by Dame Beryl Grey
Music: Tchaikovsky
Designs: David Walker

Before Nightfall
Choreography: Nils Christe
Music: Martinu
Designs: Keso Dekker

The Moor's Pavane
Choreography: José Limón

272

Music: Purcell
Costumes: Pauline Lawrence

Les Sylphides
Choreography: Mikhail Fokine
Music: Chopin

Le Sacre du printemps
Choreography: Maurice Béjart
Music: Stravinsky
Design and lighting: John van der Heyden

La Bayadère
Choreography: Natalia Makarova after Petipa
Music: Minkus, arr. John Lanchbery
Set design: Pier Luigi Samaritani
Costumes: Theoni Aldredge

La Fille mal gardée
Choreography: Frederick Ashton
Music: Hérold, arr. John Lanchbery
Set design: Osbert Lancaster

The Eleventh Dawn
Choreography: Per Jonsson
Music: Sven-David Sandström
Design: Per Jonsson, Lena Thyrell and Leif Elggren

Swan Lake
Choreography: Natalia Conus after Petipa
Music: Tchaikovsky
Set design: Henry Bardon
Costumes: David Walker

Onegin
Choreography: John Cranko
Music: Tchaikovsky, arr. Stolze

Sinfonietta
Choreography: Jiři Kylián
Music: Leos Janáček
Designs: Walter Nobbe

Number of performances:
About 90 (the Opera House was rebuilt during the autumn).

Foreign tours:
October, Spain; November, Northern Ireland (Belfast)

Swedish Ballet School

Director:
Gösta Svalberg

Teachers:
Bessie Arovén, Conny Borg, Cecilia Edelman, Elise Englund, Marianne Fröijd,

Birgit Grefveberg, Donald Kirkpatrick, Laszlo Meszaros, Mariane Orlando, Åsa Scharp, Astrid Strüwer, Vasil Tinterov (all classical ballet); Britt Håkansson (jazz), Regina Beck-Friis, Kerstin Lidström (historical dances), Siv Ander (free dance), Birgit Ljungberg (free dance, improvisation, acrobatics), Gun Larsson (free dance, improvisation, classical ballet), Pierre de Olivo (character and acrobatics) Per Thunman (acrobatics)

THE CULLBERG BALLET

Riksteatern
145 83 Norsborg, Sweden

Artistic director:
Mats Ek

Guest choreographers:
Jean Gaudin, Christopher Bruce, Nacho Duato, Jiři Kylián, William Forsythe

Principal teachers:
Istvan Kisch, Sighilt Pahl, Peter Stamm, Alexander Ursuliak, Victor Valcu

Répétitrice:
Lena Wennergren

Ballet master:
Jens Graff

Dancers:
Yvan Auzely, Bernard Cauchard, Boaz Cohen, Anna Diehl, George Elkin, Jorma Elo, Gunilla Hammar, Saila Korhonen, Patrick King, Kristin Kåge, Ana Laguna, Gaetan Massé, Vanessa McIntosh, Monica Mengarelli, Livia Patrizi, Veli-Pekka Peltokallio, Pompea Santoro, Jacek Solecki, Allyson Way

Premières:

Old Children, Stockholm, 28.11.89
Choreography: Mats Ek
Music: collage

The Vile Parody of Address, Lund, Sweden, 20.2.90
Choreography: William Forsythe
Music: Bach
Design: William Forsythe

Rassemblement, Örebro, Sweden, 27.2.90
Choreography: Nacho Duato
Music: Toto Bissainthe, electronic music by
Walter Kallup
Set design: Walter Nobbe
Costumes: Nacho Duato

Repertory:

*The Ascetic of San Clemente and the Virgin
Mary*
Choreography: Jean Gaudin
Music: Rossini and John Lurie
Design: Groupe Sirene

Ghost Dances
Choreography: Christopher Bruce
Music: Inti Illimani
Set design: Christopher Bruce
Costumes: Belinda Scarlett

Giselle
Choreography: Mats Ek
Music: Adam
Design: Marie-Louise Ekman

Grass
Choreography: Mats Ek
Music: Rachmaninov
Design: Karin Ek

Jardi Tancat
Choreography: Nacho Duato
Music: Catalan songs sung by Marie del
Mar Bonet
Designs: Nacho Duato

Overgrown Path
Choreography: Jiři Kylián
Music: Leoš Janáček
Design: Walter Nobbe

Up North
Choreography: Mats Ek
Music: J. P. Nyströms
Design: Karin Ek

Like Antigone
Choreography: Mats Ek
Music: Manos Hadjidakis and Greek Folk
music
Design: Marie-Louise Ekman

Swan Lake
Choreography: Mats Ek
Music: Tchaikovsky
Designs: Marie-Louise Ekman, Peder Freij

Number of performances:
About 80

Foreign tours:
June, Seville; September, Melbourne;
October, Barcelona

GOTHENBURG BALLET

Stora Teaterns Balett
Stora Teatern
Parkgatan 2
411 38 Gothenburg, Sweden
Tel: 031-17 47 45

Director:
Juhani Teräsvuori

Visiting choreographers:
Tiit Härm, Jorma Uotinen, Robert North,
Marjo Kuusela

Guest teachers:
Marina Stavitskaja, Viktor Rona, Tiit Härm,
Valentina Savina

Répétitrice:
Helen Sjöstedt

Soloists:
Liselott Berg, Nancy Clery, Helle Fritz-
Petersen, Eileen Jones, Lillemor Jonsson,
Vaclav Havlik, Ivor Howard, Istvan Nagy
Artists:
19 female, 14 male

Premières:

In the Garden of Memories, 3.11.89
Choreography: Jorma Uotinen
Music: Serge Aubry
Design: Jorma Uotinen

Troy Game, 11.1.90
Choreography: Robert North
Music: collage
Designs: Peter Farmer

Ronja, the Robber's Daughter
Choreography: Marjo Kuusela
Music: Jukka Linkola
Designs: Michael Forssén

Repertory:

Giselle
Choreography: Tiit Härm after Coralli,
Perrot and Petipa
Music: Adam
Designs: Michael Forssén

Entre Dos Aguas
Choreography: Robert North
Music: Simon Rogers and Paco de Lucia
Designs: Andrew Storer

Seven Japanese Prints
Choreography: Ulf Gadd
Music: Vivaldi, played by Koto New
Ensemble
Costumes: Svenerik Goude

Number of performances:
About 90

Gothenburg Ballet School

Director:
Margrethe Schultz

MALMÖ BALLET

Malmö Stadsteater
PO 17 520 Malmö, Sweden
Tel: 040-20 84 00

Director:
Jonas Kåge

Number of dancers:
30

Premières:

The Nutcracker
Choreography: André Prokovsky
Music: Tchaikovsky
Design: Abelardo Gonzales

The Four Temperaments
Choreography: Balanchine
Music: Hindemith
Costumes: Bart Cook

The Fight for the Royal Crown
Choreography: Birgit Cullberg
Music: Björn Hallman
Set: Adèle Änggård
Costumes: Börje Edla

Number of performances:
26

Malmö Ballet School

Director:
Barbara Gray

NORRKÖPING BALLET

Östgötateatern
Box 3114, 600, 03 Norrköping, Sweden
Tel: 011-10 62 80

Director:
Vlado Juras

Number of dancers:
11

**MODERNA DANS THEATER
(MODERN DANCE THEATRE)**

Skemppsholmens hus 103
111 49 Stockholm
Tel: 08-20 14 56

Resident dance group:
Pyramiderna (The Pyramids)

Artistic director:
Margaretha Åsberg

THE GLASS HOUSE (GLASHUSET)

Wollmar Yxkullsgatan 13
PO 17 011
104 62 Stockholm
Tel: 08-44 78 03

Resident dance group:
Vindhäxor (Wind Witches)

Artistic director:
Eva Lundqvist

FESTSALEN (BANQUET HALL)

161 04 Bromma, Sweden
Tel: 08-87 87 20

Resident dance group:
Efva Lilja Dansproduktion

Artistic director:
Efva Lilja

HOUSE OF DANCE

Wallingatan 21
111 24 Stockholm
Sweden
Tel: 08-796 49 40

275

Artistic director:
Jan Zetterberg

UNGA ATALANTE

Övre Husargatan 1
411 22 Göteborg

Sweden
Tel: 031–11 82 00

Resident dance group:
Rubicon

Switzerland

BALLET OF THE ZÜRICH OPERA HOUSE

Schillerstrasse 1
8001 Zürich
Tel: (01) 251 69 20

Director and chief choreographer:
Uwe Scholz

BALLET DU GRAND THÉÂTRE DE GENÈVE

11, bd du Théâtre
1211 Genève
Tel: (022) 21 23 18

Artistic director:
Gradimir Pankow

BASEL BALLET (BASLER BALLETT)

Basel Theatre
4010 Basel
Tel: (061) 22 11 30

Artistic director and chief choreographer:
Heinz Spoerli

BÉJART BALLET LAUSANNE

Palais de Beaulieu
Avenue des Bergiers

CH-1000 Lausanne 22
Tel: (21) 452400

Artistic director and chief choreographer:
Maurice Béjart

STADTTEATER LUZERN BALLET COMPANY

Stadtteater Luzern
Theaterstrasse 2
6002 Luzern
Tel: (041) 23 33 63

Artistic director:
Ben van Cauwenbergh

STADTTEATER BERN BALLET COMPANY

Nägeligasse 20
3000 Bern 7
Tel: (031) 21 17 11

STADTTEATER ST GALLEN BALLET COMPANY

Museumstrasse 24
9004 St Gallen
Tel: 25 24 11

Artistic director:
Marianne Fuchs

United Kingdom

ENGLISH NATIONAL BALLET (formerly London Festival Ballet)

Markova House
39 Jay Mews
London SW7 2ES
Tel: 071 581 1245

President:
Dame Alicia Markova, DBE

Artistic director (to January 1990):
Peter Schaufuss
Acting artistic director, formerly assistant artistic director:
Elizabeth Anderton
Artistic director designate (taking up post in September 1990):
Ivan Nagy

General administrator:
Richard Jarman (to April 1990):
Carole McPhee (from April 1990)

Music director:
Graham Bond

Teachers:
Johnny Eliasen, Woytek Lowski, Anne Manger, Adrienne Matheson

Notators:
Marilyn Vella-Gatt, Mark Kay, Michele Braban

Principal dancers:
Tim Almaas, Patrick Armand, Leanne Benjamin, Christine Camillo, Paul Chalmer, Laura Contardi, Johnny Eliasen, Eva Evdokimova, Alexander Grant, Andria Hall, Martin James, Nicholas Johnson, Alessandro Molin, Janette Mulligan, Koen Onzia, Niels Bjorn Larsen, Pablo Savoye, Peter Schaufuss, Trinidad Sevillano, Lynn Seymour, Matz Skoog, Alexander Sombart, Lucia Truglia
Guest artists (for 40th Anniversary Gala only):
Reid Anderson, Patrice Bart, Fernando Bujones, Richard Cragun, Michael Clark, Flemming Flindt, Carla Fracci, Denys

Ganio, Sylvie Guillem, Marcia Haydée, Dominique Khalfouni, Andris Liepa, Yulia Makhalina, Ekaterina Maximova, André Prokovsky, Maya Plisetskaya, Vladimir Vasiliev

Premières:

Symphony in Three Movements, Bristol Hippodrome, 27.11.89
Choreography: Christopher Bruce
Music: Stravinsky
Designs: Nadine Baylis

The Moor's Pavane, College Theatre, Athens, 1.12.89
Choreography: José Limón
Music: Purcell, arr. Simon Sadoff
Staging and reconstructions: Jennifer Scanlon
Costumes: Pauline Lawrence

Revival:

Echoing of Trumpets, Palace Theatre, Manchester, 28.5.90
Choreography: Antony Tudor
Music: Martinu
Staging: Viveka Ljung
Designs: Birger Berling

Repertory:

Anastasia
Choreography: Kenneth MacMillan
Music: Martinu
Design supervision: Kenneth MacMillan, Anna Watkins

Apollo
Choreography: George Balanchine
Music: Stravinsky

Aureole
Choreography: Paul Taylor
Music: Handel
Design: Tacit

Bolero
Choreography: Maurice Béjart
Music: Ravel

Coppélia
Choreography: Ronald Hynd after Petipa/
Cecchetti
Music: Delibes
Design: Desmond Heeley

Etudes
Choreography: Harald Lander
Music: Riisager after Czerny
Design: after Rolf Gerard

Flower Festival at Genzano (pas de deux)
Choreography: Peter Schaufuss after
August Bournonville
Music: Edvard Helsted
Costumes: David Walker

Land
Choreography: Christopher Bruce
Music: Arne Nordheim, folk-song
Design: Walter Nobbe

Napoli
Choreography: Peter Schaufuss after
August Bournonville
Music: Gade, Helsted, Paulli, Lumbye
Design: David Walker

The Nutcracker
Choreography: Peter Schaufuss
Music: Tchaikovsky
Design: David Walker

Onegin
Choreography: John Cranko
Music: Tchaikovsky, arr. Kurt-Heinz Stolze
Design: after Jürgen Rose

Romeo and Juliet
Choreography: Frederick Ashton
Music: Prokofiev
Design: Peter Rice

Song of a Wayfarer
Choreography: Maurice Béjart
Music: Mahler

Swan Lake
Choreography: Natalia Makarova after
Petipa and Ivanov, with additions by
Frederick Ashton
Music: Tchaikovsky
Design: Gunther Schnieder Siemsson &
Dietmar Solt

Swansong
Choreography: Christopher Bruce
Music: Philip Chambon

La Sylphide
Choreography: Peter Schaufuss after
August Bournonville
Music: Herman Løvenskjold

Design: David Walker

Three Preludes
Choreography: Ben Stevenson
Music: Rachmaninov
Costumes: Peter Farmer

Number of performances:
228

Foreign tours:
USA, July–August 1989; Athens, December
1989; Vienna, March 1990; Netherlands,
June 1990

English National Ballet School
Markova House
39 Jay Mews
London SW7 2ES
Tel: 071-581 1245

Principal:
Lucia Truglia

Administrator:
David Rees

Teachers:
Wojtek Lowski, Lynn Seymour, Andria
Hall, Adrienne Mattheson, Christine
Camillo, Nicholas Johnson, Craig
Randolph, Phillipe Arrona
Guest teachers:
Dinna Bjorn, Tatiana Legat, Kevin Hagen

Contemporary:
Gayrie MacSween
Jazz:
Christopher Hall, Arlene Erb
Character:
Zinna Mamamedova
Character and mime:
Nina Finburgh, Adam Darius

Salary information:

Corps de ballet 1st year, £184 per week; 2nd
year, £186.50; 3rd year, £189; 4th year,
£194; 5th year, £197. Coryphée, £206;
junior soloist, £217; soloist, £235; senior
soloist, £265; principal, £318; senior
principal, £380.50 (more by agreement).
Touring allowances are in addition at a
minimum of £152 per week.

278

LONDON CITY BALLET

London Studio Centre
42–50 York Way
London N1 9AB
Tel: 071 837 3133

Patron:
HRH The Princess of Wales

Artistic director:
Harold King
Assistant artistic director:
Marian St Claire
Rehearsal director:
Michael Beare

Ballet master:
Jaakko Helkavaara

Administrative director:
Heather Knight
Musical director and principal conductor:
Chris Nicolls

Guest répétitrice:
Julie Lincoln

Guest teachers:
Anna de Boisson, Chinko Raffique, Gerard Sibritt

Prima ballerina:
Marian St Claire
Principals:
Beverly Jane Fry, Kim Miller, Edwin Mota, Jane Sanig, Stanislav Tchassov, Andrei Ustinov
Guest character principals:
Terry Hayworth, Michael Hogan, Simon Horrill
Junior principals:
Mandy Brak, Nicola Lawson, Jack Wyngaard
Senior artists:
Tracey Newham Alvey, Lawrence Beazley, Lucinda Garner, Ayumi Hikasa, Joss Urch
Soloist:
Stefan Umhey
Artists:
8 female, 7 male
Guest artists:
Derek Deane, Matz Skoog, Kader Belarbi and Marie-Claude Pietragalla on Summer 1989 Japanese Tour

Premières:

La Traviata, Gordon Graig Theatre, Stevenage, 11.11.89
Choreography: André Prokovsky
Music: Verdi, arr. Guy Woolfenden
Orchestrations: Guy Woolfenden, Stephen Hancock
Design: Peter Farmer

Aurora's Wedding, (from *The Sleeping Beauty*), Churchill Theatre, Bromley, 20.11.89
Choreography: Marius Petipa
Music: Tchaikovsky, arr. Chris Nicolls
Producer: Jaakko Helkavaara
Costume design: Shirley Lawrenson

Dances from Napoli, Marina Theatre, Lowestoft, 14.4.90
Choreography: after August Bournonville
Music: Eduard Helsted
Producer: Harold King

Revivals:

Giocosa Variations (Istvan Herczog), *Graduation Ball* (David Lichine), *Transfigured Night* (Frank Staff), *Three Dances to Japanese Music* (Jack Carter)

Touring:
October 1989 to July 1990, throughout the UK (including small tour of gala performances to five venues in Northern Ireland)

Number of performances:
October 1989 to July 1990, UK: 201

Salary information:
Not available

LONDON CONTEMPORARY DANCE THEATRE

The Place
17 Duke's Road
London WC1
Tel: 071 387 0324

Artistic director:
Dan Wagoner
Associate director:
Jonathan Lunn

Principal choreographers:
Dan Wagoner, Darshan Singh Bhuller, Jonathan Lunn

Visiting choreographers:
Kim Brandstrup, Aletta Collins, Jo Ann Fregalette Jansen

Principal teachers:
Dan Wagoner and Robert Masarachi plus Gill Clarke, Jo Ann Fregalette Jansen, Joan Norvelle with ballet from Terry Etheridge and Ivan Kramer

Dancers:
Helen Beatty, Darshan Singh Bhuller, Aletta Collins, Kate Coyne, Peter Dunleavy, Tracey Fitzgerald, Patrick Harding-Irmer, David Hughes, Paul Liburd, Jonathan Lunn, Julian Moss (on leave), Isabel Mortimer, Leesa Phillips, Andrew Robinson, Isabel Tamen, Kenneth Tharp, Anne Went, Sharon Wray

Premières:

To Comfort Ghosts, (1988), company première, 4.10.89, Mayflower Theatre, Southampton
Choreography: Dan Wagoner
Music: Shostakovich
Design: William Ivey Long

Orfeo, 4.10.89, Mayflower Theatre, Southampton
Choreography: Kim Brandstrup
Music: Ian Dearden
Design: Craig Givens

Turtles All the Way Down, 18.10.89, Theatre Royal, Plymouth
Choreography: Dan Wagoner
Music: Aaron Copland
Design: Kit Reading

Ace of Spades, 18.10.89, Theatre Royal, Plymouth
Choreography: Darshan Singh Bhuller
Music: Samuel Barber, Barrington Pheloung
Design and lighting: Robert Cohan
Costumes: Darshan Singh Bhuller

Goes Without Saying, 24.10.89, University of Warwick, Coventry
Choreography: Jonathan Lunn
Music: Orlando Gough
Design and lighting: Peter Mumford

Doppelgänger, 26.10.89, University of Warwick, Coventry
Choreography: Johathan Lunn
Music: Philip Glass

It's Gonna Rain, 18.4.90, The Place, London
Choreography: Aletta Collins
Music: Steve Reich
Design: Tom Cairns

The Dybbuk (1988), company première, 18.4.90, The Place, London
Choreography: Kim Brandstrup
Music: Ian Dearden
Design: Brothers Quay
Costumes: Craig Givens

Noon Talk on Millionth Street, 18.4.90, The Place, London
Choreography: Jo Ann Fregalette Jansen
Music: Scott Johnson
Conceptual design: James Welty
Costumes: Byron Suber

Repertory:

Arden Court (1981)
Choreography: Paul Taylor
Music: William Boyce
Design: Gene Moore

Metamorphoses (1989)
Choreography: Robert Cohan
Music: Benjamin Britten
Design: Peter Farmer
Photography: Anthony Crickmay

Tour:
Southampton, Plymouth, Coventry, Bristol, Leeds, Cardiff, Liverpool, London (Sadler's Wells and The Place Theatre), Brussels (Belgium), Palma (Majorca), Terrassa, Reus (Spain), Northampton, Hexham, Oxford, Newcastle, Glasgow, Canterbury, Kiev (USSR)

Associated school:

London Contemporary Dance School
The Place
16 Flaxman Terrace
London WC1H 9AT
Tel: 071 387 0152

Principal:
Rev. Dr Richard Ralph

Teachers:
Jane Dudley, Juliet Fisher, Jayne Lee, Janet Smith, Julie Blackman, Mary Evelyn, Clover Roope, Maggie White, Ronald Emblen, Brenda Last, Tony Wright, Ingegard Lonnroth, Anca Frankenhauser, Kate Harrison, Sonia Noonan, Iris Tomlinson,

Jenny Henry, Jeremy Barlow, Gerda
Geddes, Joan Scanlon, Karen Burgin,
Belinda Quirey
Guest teachers:
Eileen Cropley, Victoria Marks, Gillian
Hurst

Easter course teachers:
Maggie White, Lynn Earnshaw, Karen
Burgin
Guest teachers:
Catherine Kerr, Robert Small, Gillian
Hurst, Angela Robinson, Sonia Noonan,
Howard Haigh

Salary information:
Above Equity minimum – between £200
and £250 per week, subject to negotiation
plus touring allowances.

NORTHERN BALLET THEATRE

Spring Hall
Huddersfield Road
Halifax
HX3 0AQ
Tel: 0442 380 420

Artistic director:
Christopher Gable
Assistant artistic director:
Michael Pink

Administrator:
Stephen Revell

Ballet mistress:
Jacquelin Barrett

Guest teachers:
Mollie Guilfoyle, Nancy Kilgour, Deirdra
Lovell

Principal dancer:
Graciela Kaplan
Leading artists:
Duncan de Gruchy, Antony Harith, Jeremy
Kerridge, Victoria Westall
Soloists:
3 female, 2 male
Artists:
14 female, 8 male
Number of dancers:
32
Guest artists:
Patrick Armand, Elaine McDonald,
Trinidad Sevillano

Premières:

Liaisons amoureuses, 26.11.89, Palace
Theatre, Manchester
Choreography: Ronald Hynd
Music: Offenbach, arr. Carl Davis
Production design: Peter Docherty

Strange Meeting, 26.11.89, Palace Theatre,
Manchester
Choreography: Michael Pink
Music: Philip Feeney
Production design: Lez Brotherston

Lipizzaner, 26.11.89, Palace Theatre,
Manchester
Choreography: Gillian Lynne
Music: Carl Davis
Production design: Tim Goodchild

Giselle, 6.2.90, Sheffield City Hall
Choreography: Jean Coralli, Jules Perrot
Music: Adolphe Adam
Production design: Roger Butlin
Lighting design: Robert Ornbo

Number of performances:
180

Tour:
England, Scotland, Wales

Length of season:
February–July, October– November

Touring weeks:
26

Associated school:

Central School of Ballet
10 Herbal Hill
Clerkenwell Road
London EC1R 5EJ
Tel: 071 837 6332

Artistic director:
Christopher Gable
Administrative director:
Ann Stannard

Principal teachers:
Christine Carter, Christopher Gable, Carole
Gable, Murray Kilgour, Nancy Kilgour,
Deirdra Lovell

Music:
Karin Greenhead

RAMBERT DANCE COMPANY

94 Chiswick High Road
London W4 1SH
Tel: 081 995 4246

Director:
Richard Alston
Administrative director:
Roger Taylor
Associate choreographer:
Siobhan Davies
Musical director:
Roger Heaton

Dancers:
Mark Baldwin, Lucy Bethune, Lee Boggess, Steven Brett, Amanda Britton, Christopher Carney (to July 1989), Alexandra Dyer, David Greenall (from August 1989), Sue Hawksley, Michael Hodges (to July 1989), Jeremy James, Gary Lambert, Sara Matthews, Elizabeth Old, Paul Old, Colin Poole (from August 1989), Cathrine Price, Marishka van Loon (from August 1989), Glenn Wilkinson

Notators:
Merrilee Macourt (rehearsal director), Kate Russell

Guest teachers:
Christine Anthony, Nancy Kilgour, Paul Melis, Simon de Mowbray, Sally Nichols, Gary Sherwood, Yacov Slivkin

Premières:

Sounding, Nottingham, 12.5.89
Choreography: Siobhan Davies
Music: Giacinto Scelsi
Lighting: Peter Mumford
Costumes: Trevor Collins

Pulau Dewata, London, 21.6.89
Choreography: Richard Alston
Music: Claude Vivier
Design: Antony McDonald
Lighting: Peter Mumford

Calm, London, 21.6.89
Choreography: Mary Evelyn
Music: Morton Subotnick
Design: Stephen Buckley
Lighting: Peter Mumford

Currulao, Mold, 9.2.90 (Frederick Ashton Memorial Commission)

Choreography: Ashley Page
Music: Orlando Gough
Costumes: John Galliano, Steven Robinson
Lighting: Peter Mumford

Dealing with Shadows, London, 14.3.90
Choreography: Richard Alston
Music: Mozart
Costumes: English Eccentrics

Longevity, London, 21.3.90
Choreography: Gary Lambert
Text: Martin Luther King

Major revivals/new versions:

Mythologies, London, 21.6.89
Choreography: Richard Alston
Music: Nigel Osborne
Set design and lighting: Peter Mumford
Costumes: Candida Cook

Embrace Tiger and Return to Mountain, Oxford, 24.11.89
Choreography: Glen Tetley
Music: Morton Subotnick
Design: Nadine Baylis
Lighting: John B. Read

Company première:

Doubles, Birmingham, 30.1.90
Choreography: Merce Cunningham
Music: Takehisa Kosugi
Design and lighting: Mark Lancaster

Repertory:

Carmen Arcadiae, Cinema, Dark Elegies, Embarque, Hymnos, Opal Loop, Septet, Soda Lake, Soldat, Strong Language

Total number of performances:
99 (excl. educational residencies, etc.)

Films:
Soldat

Touring:
England, Wales, Scotland, Ireland, France, Holland, Spain

Ballet Rambert School
West London Institute for Higher Education
300, St Margaret's Road
Twickenham, Middlesex
Tel: 081-891 0121

Artistic director:
Ross McKim

Artistic adviser:
Richard Alston

THE ROYAL BALLET

Royal Opera House
Covent Garden
London WC2E 9DD
Tel: 071-240 1200 (administration)

Director:
Anthony Dowell
Administrative director:
Anthony Russell-Roberts
Music director:
Isaiah Jackson

Principal choreographer:
Kenneth MacMillan
Resident choreographer:
David Bintley

Ballet master:
Christopher Newton
Ballet mistress:
Rosalind Eyre

Principal répétiteurs:
Monica Mason, Donald MacLeary

Principal company teachers:
Gerd Larsen, Brian Shaw

Notators:
Grant Coyle, Monica Parker, Douglas
Steuart, Faith Worth

Principal dancers:
Maria Almeida, David Bintley, Bryony
Brind, Phillip Broomhead, Fiona Chadwick,
Lesley Collier, Jonathan Cope, Antony
Dowson, Viviana Durante, Wayne Eagling,
Wendy Ellis, Stephen Jefferies, Jay Jolley,
Irek Mukhamedov (from August 1990),
Ashley Page, Karen Paisey, Bruce Sansom,
Mark Silver, Ravenna Tucker
Principal character artists:
Michael Coleman, Sandra Conley, David
Drew, Leslie Edwards, Derek Rencher
Soloists:
7 female, 7 male
First artists (coryphées):
12 female, 8 male

Artists (corps de ballet):
14 female, 7 male
Guest artists:
Altynai Asylmuratova, Deanne Bergsma,
Julio Bocca, Sylvie Guillem, Laurent
Hilaire, Robert Hill, Derek Jacobi (speaking
role), Wayne Sleep, Konstantin Zaklinsky

Length of season:
29 September 1989 to 4 August 1990

Premières:

The Prince of the Pagodas, Royal Opera
House, 7.12.89
Choreography: Kenneth MacMillan
Music: Benjamin Britten
Design: Nicholas Georgiadis

Laurentia – pas de six, Royal Opera House,
16.1.90
Choreography: Vachtang Chabukiani,
reproduced by Rudolf Nureyev
Music: Alexander Krein orch. John
Lanchbery
Design: Nicholas Georgiadis

Repertory:

La Bayadère
Choreography: Natalia Makarova after
Marius Petipa
Music: Minkus orch. John Lanchbery
Design: Pier Luigi Samaratini (scenery),
Yolanda Sonnabend (costumes)

Capriccio for Piano and Orchestra (Rubies)
Choreography: George Balanchine
Music: Stravinsky
Design: André Levasseur

Cinderella
Choreography: Frederick Ashton
Music: Prokofiev
Design: David Walker

La Fille mal gardée
Choreography: Frederick Ashton
Music: Ferdinand Herold, arr. John
Lanchbery
Design: Osbert Lancaster

Frankenstein, the Modern Prometheus
Choreography: Wayne Eagling
Music: Vangelis
Design: Emanuel

Galanteries
Choreography: David Bintley
Music: Mozart
Design: Jan Blake

283

Giselle
Choreography: Petipa after Coralli, Perrot
Music: Adam
Production: Peter Wright
Design: John MacFarlane

Gloria
Choreography: Kenneth MacMillan
Music: Poulenc
Design: Andy Klunder

Grand Pas classique
Choreography: Victor Gsovsky
Music: Auber

A Month in the Country
Choreography: Frederick Ashton
Music: Chopin, arr. John Lanchbery
Design: Julia Trevelyan Oman

My Brother, My Sisters
Choreography: Kenneth MacMillan
Music: Schoenberg, Webern
Design: Yolanda Sonnabend

Other Dances (company première, 6.11.89)
Choreography: Jerome Robbins
Music: Chopin
Costumes: Santo Loquasto

Piano
Choreography: Ashley Page
Music: Beethoven
Design: Howard Hodgkin

Pursuit
Choreography: Ashley Page
Music: Colin Matthews
Design: Jack Smith

Requiem
Choreography: Kenneth MacMillan
Music: Fauré
Design: Yolanda Sonnabend

Romeo and Juliet
Choreography: Kenneth MacMillan
Music: Prokofiev
Design: Nicholas Georgiadis

Song of the Earth
Choreography: Kenneth MacMillan
Music: Mahler
Design: Nicholas Georgiadis

'Still Life' at the Penguin Café
Choreography: David Bintley
Music: Simon Jeffes
Design: Hayden Griffin

Swan Lake
Choreography: Petipa, Ivanov
Music: Tchaikovsky

Production: Anthony Dowell
Design: Yolanda Sonnabend

A Wedding Bouquet
Choreography: Frederick Ashton
Music: Lord Berners
Design: Lord Berners

Number of performances:
121 (including 16 at the Hippodrome,
Birmingham and the Palace Theatre,
Manchester) and 2 school matinées

Salary information:
Corps de ballet 1st year, £193.18 per week;
2nd year, £206.06; 3rd year, £224.09; 4th
year, £239.55; 5th year, £257.58. First artist,
£283.34; junior soloist, £340.00; senior
soloist, £373.49; first soloist, £412.11;
principal, £450.77; senior principal,
£592.42 (more by agreement). Touring
allowances are in addition at a minimum of
£152 per week.

SADLER'S WELLS ROYAL BALLET
(from August 1990, **THE BIRMINGHAM
ROYAL BALLET**)

Royal Opera House
Covent Garden
London WC2E 9DD
Tel: 071-240 1200 (administration)
From August 1990:
Birmingham Hippodrome
Thorp Street
Birmingham B5 4AV (administration)

Director:
Peter Wright
Administrator (administrative director):
Christopher Nourse

Assistant to the director and ballet master:
Desmond Kelly

General manager:
Derek Purnell

Régisseur:
Ronald Plaisted

Ballet mistress:
Anita Landa

Teacher:
Galina Samsova

284

Senior répétiteur:
Alain Dubreuil

Notators:
Denis Bonner, Amanda Eyles

Principal dancers:
Mireille Bourgeois, Joseph Cipolla, Karen Donovan, Sherilyn Kennedy, Sandra Madgwick, Kevin O'Hare, Michael O'Hare, Mark Silver, Marion Tait, Ravenna Tucker, Miyako Yoshida, David Yow
Guest artists:
Margaret Barbieri, Cynthia Harvey, Petter Jacobsson, Roland Price, Yannick Stephant
Principal character artists:
June Highwood, David Morse, Stephen Wicks
First soloists and soloists:
7 female, 5 male
First artists and artists:
15 female, 12 male
Number of dancers:
60

Premières:

Meridian of Youth
Choreography: Vincent Redmon
Music: Béla Bartók
Design: Claudia Mayer

Game
Choreography: William Tuckett
Music: Debussy
Design: Stephen Meaha

Inscape
Choreography: Graham Lustig
Music: Peter McGowan
Design: Henk Schut

Repertory:

Auras
Choreography: Vincent Redmon
Music: Poulenc
Design: Malcolm Steed

Allegri Diversi
Choreography: David Bintley
Music: Rossini
Design: Terry Bartlett

Danses Concertantes
Choreography: Kenneth MacMillan
Music: Stravinsky
Design: Nicholas Georgiadis

Divertimento No. 15 (company première)
Choreography: George Balanchine, staged by Victoria Simon
Music: Mozart
Design: Peter Farmer

Don Quixote pas de deux
Choreography: Marius Petipa
Music: Ludwig Minkus, orch. Robert Irving
Design: André Levasseur

The Dream
Choreography: Frederick Ashton
Music: Mendelssohn
Design: Peter Farmer

Elite Syncopations
Choreography: Kenneth MacMillan
Music: Scott Joplin, and others
Design: Ian Spurling

Façade
Choreography: Frederick Ashton
Music: William Walton
Design: John Armstrong

La Fille mal gardée
Choreography: Frederick Ashton
Music: Ferdinand Herold, arr. John Lanchbery
Design: Osbert Lancaster

Flowers of the Forest
Choreography: David Bintley
Music: Malcolm Arnold, Benjamin Britten
Design: Jan Blake

Las Hermanas
Choreography: Kenneth MacMillan
Music: Frank Martin
Design: Nicholas Georgiadis

Hobson's Choice
Choreography: David Bintley
Music: Paul Reade
Design: Hayden Griffin

Paramour
Choreography: Graham Lustig
Music: Poulenc
Design: Nadine Baylis

Solitaire
Choreography: Kenneth MacMillan
Music: Malcolm Arnold
Design: Desmond Heeley

Swan Lake
Choreography: Petipa/Ivanov/Peter Wright
Music: Tchaikovsky
Production: Peter Wright/Galina Samsova
Design: Philip Prowse

Les Sylphides
Choreography: Fokine
Music: Chopin
Design: Alexandre Benois

Tchaikovsky pas de deux
Choreography: George Balanchine

Those Unheard
Choreography: William Tuckett
Music: Benjamin Britten
Design: Stephen Meaha

The Two Pigeons
Choreography: Frederick Ashton
Music: André Messager, arr. John
Lanchbery
Design: Jacques Dupont

Valses nobles et sentimentales
Choreography: Frederick Ashton
Music: Ravel
Design: Sophie Fedorovitch

Foreign tour:
New Zealand

Number of performances:
184

Salary information:
see Royal Ballet

SCOTTISH BALLET

261 West Princes Street
Glasgow
G4 9EE
Tel: 041-331 2931

Chief executive:
Peter Kyle

Guest artistic directors:
Nanette Glushak (August 1989 to June
1990), Galina Samsova (July to December
1990)

Visiting choreographers:
Oleg Vinogradov, Massimo Moricone,
Michel Rahn, Amanda Miller, Jack Carter

Principal teacher:
Paul Tyers
Guest teachers:
Yelena Vinogradova, Nanette Glushak

Choreologist:
Kristin Johnson

Principal dancers:
Vincent Hantam, Noriko O'Hara, Robert
Hampton, Linda Packer, Judy Mohekey,
Clare French, Kenny Burke
Soloists:
5 female, 4 male
Coryphées:
4 female, 4 male
Corps de ballet:
8 female, 8 male

Premières:
Royal Gala Performance for Glasgow
European City of Culture 1990–92: March,
Theatre Royal, Glasgow. British première
of:

Scotch Symphony
Choreography: George Balanchine
Music: Mendelssohn
Staging: Nanette Glushak, Michel Rahn

Who Cares? Theatre Royal, Glasgow, 6.3.90
Choreography: George Balanchine
Music: George Gershwin
Staging: Nanette Glushak, Michel Rahn

Paquita grand pas, Theatre Royal, Glasgow,
6.3.90
Choreography: Marius Petipa
Music: Minkus
Staging: Oleg Vinogradov, Yelena
Vinogradova

Aquarelle, Tramway Theatre, Glasgow,
17.5.90
Choreography: Michel Rahn
Music: Bach, arr. Leopold Stokowski
Production and costume design: Michel
Rahn

Zwei Gesänge, Tramway Theatre, Glasgow,
17.5.90
Choreography: Massimo Moricone
Music: Brahms
Costumes: Massimo Moricone

Sun and Steel, Tramway Theatre, Glasgow,
17.5.90
Choreography: Massimo Moricone
Music: Guy Hamilton
Design: Massimo Moricone

Pretty Ugly, Tramway Theatre, Glasgow,
17.5.90
Choreography: Amanda Miller
Music: Peter Scherer, Arto Lindsay
Costume and lighting design: Amanda
Miller

Kirov divertissements, Theatre Royal, October 1989
Staging: Oleg Vinogradov, Yelena Vinogradova
Design: Oleg Vinogradov

Paquita pas de trois
Choreography: Petipa
Music: Minkus

La Esmeralda pas de six
Choreography: Petipa
Music: Pugni, Drigo

The Fairy Doll pas de trois
Choreography: Legat
Music: Bayer

La Vivandière pas de six
Choreography: St Léon (reconstructed by Lacotte)
Music: Pugni

Grand pas de fiancées (Scottish première)
Choreography: Jack Carter
Music: Tchaikovsky
Design: Norman McDowell

Current repertory:

The Nutcracker
Choreography: Ivanov/Darrell
Music: Prokofiev
Design: Philip Prowse

Peter Pan
Choreography: Graham Lustig
Music: Edward McGuire
Design: Margaret Woznica

Petrushka
Choreography: Oleg Vinogradov
Music: Stravinsky
Design: Vyatislav Okunev, Irina Press

Chéri
Choreography: Peter Darrell
Music: David Earl
Design: Philip Prowse

Three Dances to Japanese Music
Choreography: Jack Carter
Music: Kisahisa Kitada
Design: Norman McDowell

Symphony in D
Choreography: Jiri Kylián
Music: Haydn
Design: Tom Schenk

La Sylphide
Choreography: Bournonville (staged by Hans Brenaa)

Music: Løvenskjold
Design: Peter Cazalet

The Prisoners
Choreography: Peter Darrell
Music: Bartók
Design: Barry Kay

Number of performances:
210

Foreign tours:
Japan, Hong Kong, Taiwan

Associated school:

The Dance School of Scotland
Knightswood Secondary School and
261 West Princes Street
Glasgow

Artistic director:
David Long
Administrative director:
Rosemary Denny

Salary information:
£200 to £418 per week with additional fees by arrangement

SMALL BRITISH DANCE COMPANIES

ADVENTURES IN MOTION PICTURES

Katharine Doré
Sadlers Wells Theatre
Rosebery Avenue
London EC1R 4TN
Tel: 071-278 6563

Artistic director:
Matthew Bourne

Choreographers:
Matthew Bourne, Jacob Marley

Dancers:
Carrollynne Antoun, Keith Brazil, Matthew Bourne, Bill Eldridge, Susan Lewis, Catherine White

Premières:
Arnolfini Theatre, Bristol, March 1990

I Surrender, Dear (1990)
Choreography: Marley

Music: Duncan Scott, Henry Mancini, Mozart, Bing Crosby and others
Design: Simon Vincenzi

Repertory:

The Infernal Galop (1989)
Choreography: Bourne
Music: Mistinguette, Charles Trenet, P. and F. Boyer, Piaf, Emile Prud'homme, Offenbach
Set design: Clive Mitchell
Costumes: David Manners

Touring:
UK

Salary information:
Equity rates

Awards:
Barclay's New Stages Award

THE CHOLMONDELEYS

Roz Powell
The Place Theatre
17 Dukes Road
London WC1H 9AB
Tel: 071-380 1268

Director and choreographer:
Lea Anderson

Dancers:
Lea Anderson, Teresa Barker, Gaynor Coward, Emma Gladstone

Repertory:

Flag (1988)
Choreography: Anderson
Music: Drosten Madden, Steve Blake, performed by The Pointy Birds
Text: Carl Smith
Design: Sandy Powell, Pam Downe
Dancers: The Cholmondeleys and The Featherstonehaughs

Flesh and Blood (1989)
Choreography: Anderson
Music: Steve Blake, performed by The Pointy Birds
Costumes: Sandy Powell
Dancers: The Cholmondeleys plus Alex Reynolds, Marisa Zanotti and Sonia Bucci

Touring:
Flesh and Blood: UK, Belgium, Switzerland

Salary information:
Equity minimum rate (£144 per week plus allowances)

Awards:
Digital Dance Award

DIVAS

Liz Aggiss
92 Centurion Road
Brighton BN1 3LN
Tel: 0273-27894

Artistic directors:
Liz Aggiss (choreographer), Billie Cowie (composer)

Dancers:
Liz Aggiss, Maria Burton, Ellie Curtis, Ginny Farman, Ralph Saunders, Sian Thomas

Premières:
New double bill including *Love Duets* (Created by Eurodanse 1990 in Mulhouse)

Repertory:

Dorothy and Klaus
Choreography, music, text: Aggiss, Cowie
Design: Chris Ure
Machine construction: Ralfee

Die Orchidee im Plastik-Karton
Choreography: Aggiss
Music: Cowie
Design: Chris Ure
Text: from BBC *Kontakte* German Language Course

Touring:
Covent Garden Festival, Holland, Germany, UK, France

Awards:
Brighton Festival Zap Dance Award

Salary information:
An average of £50.00 per performance plus expenses

DV8 PHYSICAL THEATRE

Deborah Chadbourne
Arts Admin Ltd
295 Kentish Town Road
London NW5
Tel: 071-482 3631

Artistic director:
Lloyd Newson

Dancers:
On a project-by-project basis. Core include:
Lloyd Newson, Nigel Charnock, Michelle
Richecoeur, Liz Ranken, Russell Maliphant,
Douglas Wright

Premières:

If Only Rouen, France, June 1990
Devised: Mark Foley, Lloyd Newson

Repertory:

Dead Dreams of Monochrome Men
Collectively devised and performed by
Lloyd Newson, Russell Maliphant, Nigel
Charnock, Douglas Wright
Original music: Sally Herbert
Lighting design: Tom Donnellan

Touring:
If Only: Rouen, Montpellier, UK, Europe;
Melbourne Festival of Arts

Salary information:
Due to the size of the *If Only* project and
of the planned international tour, the
company hopes to pay £200.00 per week
for the rehearsal and touring period

EXTEMPORARY DANCE THEATRE

Joe Clift
Extemporary Dance Theatre
The Drill Hall
16 Chenies Street
London WC1
Tel: 071-631 5109

Artistic director:
Sean Walsh

Dancers:
On a project-by-project basis. Dancers for
the new season to be announced

Premières:

A Flaming Desire
Choreography: Walsh
Music: Jeremy Sams

Salary information:
Above Equity minimum (£200 per week
plus allowances)

MOTIONHOUSE

Belinda Reggio
Chisenhale Dance Space
64–84 Chisenhale Road
London E3 5QY
Tel: 081-981 3093

Artistic directors:
Louise Richards, Kevin Finnan

Performers:
Louise Richards, Kevin Finnan, Joanna
Walker, Shaun Powell, Harry Dawes, Ray
Lee

Premières:

The Ticking Man (1990) Prema Arts Centre,
Gloucestershire, 27.1.90
Choreography: Richards, Finnan
Music: Ray Lee, Harry Dawes

Repertory:

Dancing Inside (1989)
Choreography: Richards/Finnan

A Curious Day (1989)
Choreography: Richards/Finnan
Music: Harry Dawes, Simon Prince

Touring:
UK, Egypt and Israel (workshops on new
work)

Salary information:
Equity minimum rate (£144 per week plus
allowances)

ROSEMARY BUTCHER DANCE COMPANY

The Dance Gallery
179 Blythe Road
London W14 0HL
Tel: 071-603 6819

Director:
Rosemary Butcher (choreographer)

Dancers:
On a project-by-project basis. Currently:
Maxine Braham, Rosemary Butcher, Gill
Clarke, Dennis Greenwood, Michael
Hodges, Lauren Potter, Catherine Tucker,
Fin Walker

289

THE STATISTICS OF DANCE COMPANIES

Premières:

d. 2, Spitalfields Church, London, 29.5.90
Choreography: Rosemary Butcher
Music: Jim Fulkerson
Design: John Lyall

3-d (commissioned by Glasgow 1990
Festival)
Choreography: Rosemary Butcher
Music: Jim Fulkerson
Design: John Lyall

Repertory:

d. 1 (1989), presented at Royal Festival
Hall, September 1989 and toured to
galleries in UK January–March 1990
Choreography: Rosemary Butcher
Music: Jim Fulkerson
Design: Zaha Hadid
(First part of a three-part work)

SECOND STRIDE

Lucy Mason
Dance Umbrella Ltd
Riverside Studios
Crisp Road
Hammersmith
London W6 9RL
Tel: 081-741 9358

Director:
Ian Spink (choreographer)
Associate director:
Antony McDonald (designer)

Performers:
Engaged on a project-by-project basis. For
Heaven Ablaze: Catherine Burge,
Christopher Carney, Frances Carty,
Andrew Gallacher, Stephen Goff, Justin
Joseph, Jackie Horner, Martin Lindsay,
Frances Lynch, Josephine McNally,
Gabrielle McNaughton, Sally Owen,
Michael Popper, Michele Smith

Repertory:

Heaven Ablaze In His Breast, Towngate
Theatre, Basildon, 5.10.89
Choreography: Spink
Music: Judith Weir
Design: Antony MacDonald

Touring:
UK, France, Netherlands

Awards:
Digital Dance Award

Salary information:
Equity rates (£144 per week minimum plus
allowances)

SIOBHAN DAVIES COMPANY

Dance Umbrella Ltd
Riverside Studios
Hammersmith
London W6 9RL
Tel: 081-741 9358

Director:
Siobhan Davies (choreographer)

Performers:
Gill Clarke, Scott Clark, Paul Douglas,
Michael Fulwell, Cathy Quinn, Lauren
Potter, Lizie Saunderson

Repertory:

White Man Sleeps (1988)
Choreography: Davies
Music: Kevin Volans
Design: David Buckland

Cover Him With Grass (1989)
Choreography: Davies
Music: Kevin Volans
Lighting design: Peter Mumford

Drawn Breath (1989)
Choreography: Davies
Music: Andrew Poppy
Design: Hugh O'Donnell

Awards:
Digital Dance Award

Salary information:
Equity rates (£144 per week minimum plus
allowances)

PHOENIX DANCE COMPANY

Yorkshire Dance Centre
3 St Peter's Buildings
St Peter's Square
Leeds LS9 8AH
Tel: 0532-423486

Artistic director:
Neville Campbell

Administrator:
Pauline Fitzmaurice

Choreographers:
Members of the company
Guest choreographers:
Aletta Collins, Michael Clark, Phillip
Taylor, Darshan Singh Bhuller, Tom Jobe,
Simon Rice, Emilyn Claid

Dancers:
Edward Lynch, Donald Edwards, Douglas
Thorpe, Stephen Derrick, Booker T. Lewis,
Ricky Holgate, Chantal Donaldson, Dawn
Donaldson, Pam Johnson, Seline Thomas

Awards:
Bagnolet Prize for Dance Theatre (Aletta
Collins's choreography)

USA

The following were the only companies to respond to our request for information.

AMERICAN BALLET THEATRE

890 Broadway
New York, New York 10003
Tel: (212) 477 3030

Directors:
Jane Hermann, Oliver Smith
Assistant to the directors:
Ross Stretton

Ballet mistresses:
Elena Tchernichova, Georgina Parkinson,
Wendy Walker, Shelley Washington
Ballet masters:
Jurgen Schneider, Terrence S. Orr, David
Richardson, Alexander Minz

Lighting consultant:
Jennifer Tipton

Régisseur:
Susan Jones

Principal dancers:
Victor Barbee, Julio Bocca, Leslie Browne,
Ricardo Bustamente, Wes Chapman,
Christine Dunham, Alessandra Ferri,
Guillaume Graffin, Cynthia Gregory,
Cynthia Harvey, Susan Jaffe, Kevin
McKenzie, Amanda McKerrow, Michael
Owen, Danilo Radojevic, Johan Renvall,
Faruk Ruzimatov, Ross Stretton, Marianna
Tcherkassky, Clark Tippet, Martine van
Hamel, Cheryl Yeager
Soloists:
6 female, 6 male

Corps de ballet:
35 female, 24 male
Guest artists:
Fernando Bujones, Serge Lavoie

Premières:

Brief Fling, War Memorial Opera House,
San Francisco, 28.2.90
Choreography: Twyla Tharp
Music: Michel Colombier, Percy Grainger
Costumes: Isaac Mizrahi

Birthday Offering, Houston (company
première), 25.10.89
Choreography: Frederick Ashton
Music: Glazunov, arr. Robert Irving
Staging: Faith Worth
Costumes: André Levasseur

Elegy pas de deux
Choreography: Vasiliev

Touring:
To celebrate its 50th anniversary during
the 1989–90 season, ABT toured to Japan
and London, in addition to its regular
American tours, with a special anniversary
visit to Minneapolis, St Louis and Houston.

American Ballet Theatre's School of
Classical Ballet closed at the start of 1990.

Number of performances:
168

Salary information:
As per AGMA agreement (see San
Francisco Ballet)

THE STATISTICS OF DANCE COMPANIES

NEW YORK CITY BALLET

New York State Theatre
Lincoln Centre Plaza
New York, NY 10023
Tel: (212) 877 4700

General director emeritus:
Lincoln Kirstein

Ballet master in chief:
Peter Martins
Ballet mistress:
Rosemary Dunleavy
Assistant ballet masters:
Sara Leland, Bart Cook, Susan Hendl,
Christine Redpath

Dancers:
Helène Alexopoulos, Ib Andersen, Merrill
Ashley, Peter Boal, Maria Calegari, Bart
Cook, Lindsay Fischer, Peter Frame, Judith
Fugate, Robert Hill, Nichol Hlinka, Gen
Horiuchi, Darci Kistler, Leonid Kozlov,
Valentina Kozlova, Robert LaFosse,
Lourdes Lopez, Adam Lüders, Kyra
Nichols, Melinda Roy, Stephanie Saland,
Jock Soto, Heather Watts, Damian Woetzel,
Jukka Aromaa, Michael Byars, Stacy
Caddell, Kelly Cass, Victor Castelli, Jeffrey
Edwards, Jean-Pierre Frohlich, Lauren
Hauser, Kipling Houston, Ben Huys,
Katrina Killian, Carlo Merlo, Jeppe
Mydtskov, Otto Neubert, Shaun O'Brien,
Simone Schumacher, Roma Sosenko,
Margaret Tracey, Wendy Whelan, Diana
White
Other dancers:
61

Repertory:
Extensive repertory of works by Balanchine
and Robbins (including a Jerome Robbins
Festival in June 1990 of 26 of his ballets)
and by Peter Martins

Associated school:

School of American Ballet
144 West 66th St.
New York, NY 10023
Tel: (212) 877 0600

SAN FRANCISCO BALLET

455 Franklin Street
San Francisco
California CA 94102
Tel: (415) 861 5600

Artistic director:
Helgi Tomasson
Artistic director emeritus:
Willam Christensen

President:
W. McNeil Lowry
Vice-president and general manager:
Joyce A. Moffat

Ballet mistress and assistant to the artistic director:
Bonita Bourne
Ballet mistress:
Virginia Johnson

Principal dancers:
Sabina Allemann, Joanna Berman,
Christopher Boatwright, Evelyn Cisneros,
Laurie Cowden, Cynthia Drayer, Timothy
Fox, Ludmila Lopukhova, Muriel Maffre,
David McNaughton, Mikko Nissinen,
Gregory Osborne, Lawrence Pech,
Anthony Randazzo, André Reyes, Jim
Sohm, Wendy van Dyck, Jamie
Zimmerman
Principal character dancers:
Val Caniparoli, Anita Paciotti, Tomm Rudd
Soloists:
Alaina Albertson, Jean-Baptiste Bello Porty,
Antonio Castilla, Pascale Leroy, Shannon
Lilly, Elizabeth Loscavio, Kathleen Mitchell,
Christopher Stowell, Ashley Wheater, Yuri
Zhukov, Alexi Zubiria
Corps de ballet:
21 female, 11 male, 4 apprentices

Premières:

The Sleeping Beauty, War Memorial Opera
House, San Francisco, 13.3.90
Choreography: Helgi Tomasson after
Petipa
Music: Tchaikovsky
Design: Jens-Jacob Worsaae

Pas de cinq, 27.1.90
Choreography: Helgi Tomasson
Music: Granados

292

Pas de deux, 27.1.90
Choreography: Helgi Tomasson
Music: Drigo

Harvest Moon, 27.1.90
Choreography: Lisa de Ribère
Music: Wagner
Design: Theoni Aldredge

The 'Wanderer' Fantasy, 8.2.90
Choreography: David Bintley
Music: Schubert, Liszt
Design: Terry Bartlett

Krazy Kat, 30.1.90
Choreography: Brenda Way
Music: Jelly Roll Morton, Charles Roberts,
William Bolcom
Design: Wayne Thibaud
Costumes: Wayne Thibaud and Sandra
Woodall

Rodin, US première, 11.4.90
Choreography: Leonid Jakobson
Music: Debussy, Berg

La Sylphide, new production 13.4.90
Choreography: Bournonville
Music: Løvenskjold
Staging: Tomasson
Design: José Varona

Repertory:

Serenade
Choreography: Balanchine
Music: Tchaikovsky

Ballo della Regina
Choreography: Balanchine
Music: Verdi

Symphony in C
Choreography: Balanchine
Music: Bizet

Variations de Ballet
Choreography: Balanchine, Christensen
Music: Glazunov

Menuetto
Choreography: Tomasson
Music: Mozart

The Comfort Zone
Choreography: James Kudelka
Music: Beethoven

In the middle somewhat elevated
Choreography: William Forsythe
Music: Tom Willems

Interplay
Choreography: Jerome Robbins
Music: Morton Gould

Connotations
Choreography: Val Caniparoli
Music: Benjamin Britten

Rodeo
Choreography: Agnes de Mille
Music: Aaron Copland

Il distratto
Choreography: Lew Christensen
Music: Haydn

Handel – a Celebration
Choreography: Tomasson
Music: Handel

Forgotten Land
Choreography: Jiři Kylián
Music: Benjamin Britten

The Nutcracker
Choreography: Lew Christensen
Music: Tchaikovsky
Staging: Willam Christensen, Helgi
Tomasson
Design: José Varona
Costumes: Sandra Woodall

Salary information:
American Guild of Musical Artists
(AGMA) specified minimum fees for
contracted dancers as follows: new dancers,
$445.00 per week; *corps* dancers, $523.00;
soloists $570.00; principals, $619.00; plus
payments for overtime, touring, etc.

Associated school:

San Francisco Ballet School

Director:
Helgi Tomasson

School director:
Nancy Johnson Carter

School administrator:
Jane LeComte

Faculty:
Henry Berg, Christine Bering, David Boyet,
Leslie Crockett, Irina Jacobson, Daniel
Simmons, Larisa Sklyanskaya, Jocelyn
Vollmar, Jonathan Watts, Mary Wood

Coordinator and teacher, Dance-in-Schools:
Charles McNeal
Musician, Dance-in-Schools:
David Frazier

OBERLIN DANCE COMPANY/SAN FRANCISCO

3153–17th Street
San Francisco
California 94132
Tel: (415) 863 6606

Founder and artistic director:
Brenda Way
Co-artistic director:
K. T. Nelson

Associate choreographer:
Kimi Okada
Assistant to choreographer:
Arturo Fernandez

Dancers:
Mae Chesney, Frank Everett, Arturo
Fernandez, Ney Fonseca, Robert Henry
Johnson, Julie Kanter, Lizanne McAdams,
K. T. Nelson, Lisa Willgren
Guest artists:
Richard Chen See, Jeff Friedman, Robert
Moses

Premières:

Krazy Kat (commissioned and performed by
the San Francisco ballet)
Choreography: Brenda Way
Music: Jelly Roll Morton, Charles L.
Roberts, William Bolcom
Costumes: Wayne Thiebaud, Sandra
Woodall
Design: Wayne Thiebaud

Secret House (commissioned by University
of California, Berkeley's Cal Performances)
Choreography: Brenda Way
Sound score: Paul Dresher, Jay Cloidt
Text: Rinde Eckert
Design: John Woodall

Bold Sally, Herbst Theatre, San Francisco,
10–13.5.90
Choreography: Brenda Way
Music: Vivaldi
Costumes: Brenda Way

Repertory:
Choreography by Brenda Way unless
otherwise stated

Force of Circumstance
Music: Paul Dresher

Yellow Wallpaper
Music: Paul Dresher

Loose the Thread
Music: Paul Dresher

Laundry Cycle
Music: The Bobs

Constant Reminders
Music: Scott Johnson

Natural Causes
Music: Rhiannon

Second Wind
Music: Ry Cooder

No Secrets
Choreography: K. T. Nelson
Music: Jamie Kibben

The Velveteen Rabbit (for children)
Choreography: K. T. Nelson
Music: Benjamin Britten

Tours:
Soviet Union and American cities

Salary information:
$16,000–20,500 per year, according to
seniority. Benefits include health insurance,
life insurance and paid vacation.

**MERCE CUNNINGHAM DANCE
COMPANY**

463 West Street
New York, New York 10014
Tel: (212) 255 8240

Director/choreographer:
Merce Cunningham

Assistant to choreographer:
Chris Komar

Principal company teacher:
Merce Cunningham

Dancers:
Helen Barrow, Kimberly Bartosik, Michael
Cole, Merce Cunningham, Emma Diamond,
Victoria Finlayson, Alan Good, Chris
Komar, David Kulick, Patricia Lent, Larissa
McGoldrick, Randall Sanderson, Robert
Swinston, Carol Teitelbaum, Jenifer
Weaver, Robert Wood

Premières:

August Pace, University of California,
Berkeley, 22.9.89
Choreography: Merce Cunningham
Music: Michael Pugliese
Design: Sergei Bugaev (Afrika)

Inventions, University of California,
Berkeley, 23.9.89
Choreography: Merce Cunningham
Music: John Cage
Design: Carl Kielblock
A preview without Carl Kielblock's designs
was given at the Théâtre Antique, Arles,
France, 23.7.89

Polarity, City Centre Theatre, New York,
20.3.90
Choreography: Merce Cunningham
Music: David Tudor
Design: Merce Cunningham (scenery),
William Anastasi (costumes), Carl
Kielblock (lighting)

Repertory:
All choreography by Merce Cunningham

Cargo X
Music: Takehisa Kosugi
Design: Dove Bradshaw

Carousal
Music: Takehisa Kosugi
Design: Dove Bradshaw

Eleven
Music: Robert Ashley
Design: William Anastasi

Events
Music: Takehisa Kosugi, Michael Pugliese,
David Tudor

Fabrications
Music: Emanuel de Melo Pimenta
Design: Dove Bradshaw

Field and Figures
Music: Ivan Tcherepnin
Design: Kristin Jones, Andrew Ginzel

Five Stone Wind
Music: John Cage, Takehisa Kosugi, David
Tudor
Design: Mark Lancaster

Native Green
Music: John King
Design: William Anastasi, Dove Bradshaw

Pictures
Music: David Behrman
Design: Mark Lancaster

Points in Space
Music: John Cage
Design: William Anastasi, Dove Bradshaw

Quartet
Music: David Tudor
Design: Mark Lancaster

Rainforest
Music: David Tudor
Design: Andy Warhol

Shards
Music: David Tudor
Design: William Anastasi

Trails
Music: John Cage
Design: Mark Lancaster

Touring:
Italy, France, USA, Britain, Germany,
Holland, Canary Islands

Number of performances:
66

Associated school:

Merce Cunningham Studio
55 Bethune Street
New York NY 10014
Tel: (212) 691 9751

Artistic director:
Merce Cunningham

Administrator:
Alice Helpern

Technique classes:
Merce Cunningham and others

Salary information:
The dancers are not on a yearly contract;
they sign contracts for work periods during
which they are paid weekly. Salaries are
the same for rehearsal weeks as for
performance weeks. On tour they receive a
per diem for living expenses, which varies
according to the city and country. The
dancers are members of AGMA (American
Guild of Musical Artists) and weekly
salaries vary from $445 (AGMA minimum)

to $771. (This scale is for the fiscal year, 1989–90)

GARTH FAGAN DANCE

50 Chestnut Street
Rochester, New York 14604
Tel: (716) 454-3260

Founder/artistic director:
Garth Fagan

Assistant to Mr Fagan:
Norwood Pennewell

Principal company teacher:
Garth Fagan

Dancers:
Steve Humphrey, Norwood Pennewell, Bit Knighton, A. Roger Smith, Valentina Alexander, Mark Luther, Richard Boydston, Juel Bedford, Rebecca Gose, Natalie Rogers, Sharon Skepple, Bill Ferguson, Lavert Benefield

New productions:

Telling a Story, Joyce Theatre, New York, 14.11.89

Part I: *A Short Hand of Sensation**

Part II: *A Précis of Privilege**
Choreography: Garth Fagan
Music: Miles Davis
Costumes: Zinda Williams
*These parts are sometimes performed independently, as self-contained works.

Repertory:
All choreography by Garth Fagan

Eastern Freeway Processional
Music: Philip Glass
Costumes: Tony Alaura

From Before
Music: Ralph MacDonald
Costumes: Garth Fagan

Landscape for 10
Music: Brahms
Costumes: Garth Fagan

Mask Mix Masque
Music: Grace Jones, Trevor Horn
Costumes: Garth Fagan, Zinda Williams

Never top 40 (Juke Box)
Music: various
Costumes: Garth Fagan, Zinda Williams

Oatka Trail
Music: Dvořák
Costumes: Garth Fagan

Of Night, Light and Melanin
Music: Keith Jarrett
Costumes: Garth Fagan
Sculpture: Susan Ferrari Rowley

Passion Distanced
Music: Ärvo Part
Costumes: Garth Fagan, executed by Zinda Williams

Prelude
Music: Dollar Brand, Max Roach
Costumes: Zinda Williams

Time After before Place
Music: Art Ensemble of Chicago
Costumes: Garth Fagan

Touring Jubilee 1924 (Professional)
Music: Preservation Hall Jazz Band
Costumes: Garth Fagan

Traipsing through the Hay
Music: Vivaldi
Costumes: Garth Fagan, executed by Zinda Williams

Touring:
Italy, USA, New Zealand

Number of performances:
74

Associated school:

Garth Fagan School of Dance
50 Chestnut Street
Rochester, NY 14604
Tel: (716) 45-3260

Artistic director:
Garth Fagan

Administrator:
Deborah Lattime

Technique classes:
Garth Fagan and others

USSR

BOLSHOI BALLET

Sverdlov Square, 2
Moscow, USSR
Tel: Moscow 292-9986

Chief choreographer:
Yuri Grigorovich

Ballet master/administrator:
Vladimir Nikonov

Répétiteurs and teachers:
Boris Akimov, Vera Boccadoro, Nikolai Fadeyechev, Rimma Karelskaya, Marina Kondratieva, Tatiana Krasina, Asaf Messerer, Vladimir Nikonov, Regina Nikiforova, Galina Petrova, Marina Semenova, Nikolai Simachev, German Sitnikov, Raisa Struchkova, Galina Ulanova, Shamil Yagudin

Principal dancers:
Nina Ananiashvili, Alla Artilushkina-Khaniashvili, Natalia Arkhipova, Yelena Akhulkova, Natalia Bessmertnova, Tatiana Bessmertnova, Yelena Bobrova, Maria Bylova, Yulia Volodina, Tatiana Golikova, Marina Karnaukhova, Marina Kotova, Yulia Levina, Marina Leonova, Erica Luzina, Yekaterina Maximova, Alla Mikalchenko, Irina Nesterova, Marina Nudga, Nadezhda Pavlova, Maya Plisetskaya, Irina Piatkina, Irina Prokofieva, Yelena Radchenko, Ludmila Romanovskaya, Ludmila Semeniaka, Nina Semisorova, Nina Speranskaya (28 female)
Boris Akimov, Valery Anisimov, Vitaly Artiushkin, Victor Barykin, Alexandr Bogatyriov, Andrei Buravtzev, Nikolai Dorokhov, Alexi Fadeyechev, Nicolai Fedorov, Viacheslav Gordeyev, Alexei Lazarev, Irek Mukhamedov, (to June 1990) Leonid Nikonov, Mikhail Sharkov, Andrei Smirnov, Sergei Soloviev, Gedeminas Taranda, Alexandr Valuyev, Vladimir Vasiliev, Yuri Vasyuchenko, Alexandr Vetrov, Yuri Vetrov, Boris Yefimov, Viacheslav Yelagin (25 male)
Artists:
107 female, 90 male

Total:
250
Guest artists:
Michael Shannon, Rika Tanaka, Manuel Legris, Florence Clerc, Charles Jude

Premières:
None this season

Repertory:

Aniuta
Choreography: Vasiliev
Music: Gavrilin

Chopiniana
Choreography: trad.
Music: Chopin

Cyrano de Bergerac
Choreography: Petit
Music: Constant

Don Quixote
Choreography: Gorsky
Music: Minkus

Esquisses
Choreography: Petrov
Music: Schnittke

Giselle
Choreography: trad./Grigorovich
Music: Adam

The Golden Age
Choreography: Grigorovich
Music: Shostakovich

Ivan the Terrible
Choreography: Grigorovich
Music: Prokofiev/Chulaki

The Lady and the Lapdog
Choreography: Plisetskaya
Music: Shchedrin

Legend of Love
Choreography: Grigorovich
Music: Melikov

Love for Love
Choreography: Boccadoro
Music: Khrennikov

297

Mozart and Salieri
Choreography: Boccadoro
Music: Mozart/Salieri

The Naiad and the Fisherman pas de deux from
Ondine
Choreography: Perrot
Music: Pugni

The Nutcracker
Choreography: Grigorovich
Music: Tchaikovsky

La Rose Mourante pas de deux
Choreography: Petit
Music: Mahler

Romeo and Juliet
Choreography: Grigorovich
Music: Prokofiev

The Seagull
Choreography: Plisetskaya
Music: Shchedrin

The Sleeping Beauty
Choreography: trad./Grigorovich
Music: Tchaikovsky

Spartacus
Choreography: Grigorovich
Music: Khachaturian

Swan Lake
Choreography: trad./Grigorovich
Music: Tchaikovsky

KIROV BALLET

*Leningrad Academic Theatre for Opera and
Ballet
Theatre Square, 1
Leningrad, USSR
Tel: Leningrad 216-4441*

Chief choreographer:
Oleg Vinogradov

Ballet master:
Gennady Schreiber

Répétiteurs:
Irina Kolpakova, Takhir Baltacheyev,
Gabriela Komleva, Galina Kekisheva,
Ninella Kurgapkina, Olga Moiseyeva,
Vladilen Semenov, Gennady Selyutsky

Teachers:
Iraida Utretzkaya, Sergei Berezhnoi

Principal dancers:
Altynai Asylmuratova, Zhanna
Ayupova,Tatiana Berezhnaya, Natalia
Bolshakova, Olga Chenchikova, Irina
Chistiakova, Vasira Gannibalova, Annelina
Kashirina, Margarita Kulik, Lubov
Kunakova, Olga Likhovskaya, Yulia
Makhalina, Galina Mesentzeva, Yelena
Pankova, Yelena Sherstynyova, Olga
Vtorushina, Svetlana Yefremova, Yelena
Yevteyeva (18 female)
Eldar Aliyev, Ravil Bagautdinov, Sergei
Berezhnoi, Boris Blankov, Marat Daukayev,
Andrey Garbuz, Vadim Guliayev, Yuri
Gumba, Vladimir Kolesnikov, Nikolai
Kovmir, Alexander Kurtov, Evgeny Neff,
Gennady Selyutsky, Alexandr Stepkin,
Makharbet Vaziyev, Sergei Vikharev,
Sergei Vikulov, Valery Yemetz, Konstantin
Zaklinsky, Vitaly Zvetkov (21 male)
Artists:
78 female, 59 male
Total:
176
Guest artists:
Sylvie Guillem, Susan Hogard, Rudolf
Nureyev, Natalia Makarova, Peter
Schaufuss

Premières:
None this season

Repertory:

Giselle
Choreography: trad.
Music: Adam

Le Corsaire
Choreography: trad., Gusev
Music: Adam, Delibes, Drigo

Swan Lake
Choreography: trad., Sergeyev
Music: Tchaikovsky

The Sleeping Beauty
Choreography: Petipa, Sergeyev
Music: Tchaikovsky

La Bayadère
Choreography: Petipa, Chabukiani,
Ponomariov
Music: Minkus

La Sylphide
Choreography: Bournonville, von Rosen
Music: Løvenskjold

Don Quixote
Choreography: Gorsky
Music: Minkus

Nutcracker
Choreography: Vainonen
Music: Tchaikovsky

The Fountain of Bakhchisaray
Choreography: Zakharov
Music: Asafiev

Cinderella
Choreography: Sergeyev
Music: Prokofiev

The Stone Flower
Choreography: Grigorovich
Music: Prokofiev

Spartacus
Choreography: Yakobson
Music: Khachaturian

Leningrad Symphony
Choreography: Belsky
Music: Shostakovich

Notre Dame de Paris
Choreography: Petit
Music: Jarre

Creation of the World
Choreography: Kasatkina, Vasiliov
Music: Petrov

Asiyat
Choreography: Vinogradov
Music: Kajlayev

The Knight in the Tiger's Skin
Choreography: Vinogradov
Music: Machavariani

The Battleship Potemkin
Choreography: Vinogradov
Music: Tchaikovsky

Proba
Choreography: Antal Fodor
Music: Bach, Presser
Designs: T. Murvanidse

Theme and Variations, Scotch Symphony
Choreography: Balanchine
Music: Tchaikovsky, Mendelssohn
Costumes: G. Solovieva

Kirov Ballet School

Artistic director:
Konstantin Sergeyev

Principal teachers:
Natalia Dudinskaya, Ninella Kurgapkina,
Inna Zubkovskaya, Irina Trofimova,
Vladilen Semenov, Gennady Selyutsky,
Constantin Shatalov, Boris Bregvadse,
Anatoly Nisnevich, Nikolai Kovmir, Oleg
Sokolov, Nikolai Serebrennikov, Irina
Gensler, Tatiana Shymrova, Yuri Umrikhin,
Ludmila Safonova, Ludmila Morkovina,
Valentina Rumiantzeva

Choreographer:
Voldemar Korneyev

TIBILISI BALLET

Theatre for Opera and Ballet
Tibilisi
Georgia

Chief choreographer:
Georgy Alexidse
Choreographer:
Zurab Kikaleishvili

Administrator/ballet master:
Igor Podgorsky

Répétiteurs/teachers:
Revaz Magalashvili, Maria Bauer, Anna
Tzereteli, Liliana Mitaishvili, Irina
Djandieri, Irakly Tushishvili, Guram
Kukuladse, Vera Tzignadse, Chekertma
Gudiashvili, Lev Asauliak

Principals:
Natela Arobelidse, Maria Alexidse, Svetlana
Cochiashvili, Yamse Dolarberidse, Alla
Abasedse, Ludmila Gaganina, Liya
Bakhtadse, Irina Danelia, Angelina
Masepchik, Irma Nioradse, Irina
Abulashvili (11 female)
Zakhary Amonashvili, Vladimir
Djukhaladse, Nugzar Magalashvili, Nugzar
Makhateli, Tamaz Vashakidse, Valery
Masepchik, Mikhail Gelovani, Oleg
Manukovsky, Gocha Meloyan (9 male)
Artists:
45 female, 23 male

Repertory:

Brilliant Divertissement
Choreography: Georgy Alexidse
Music: Mikhail Glinka
Designs: Ushangi Imerishvili

Pirosmani
Choreography: Georgy Alexidse
Music: Sulkhan Nasidse
Régisseur: Guram Meliva
Designs: Ushangi Imerishvili

The Swan of Tuonela
Choreography: Georgy Alexidse
Music: Sibelius
Régisseur: Guram Meliva
Designs: Ushangi Imerishvili

Francesca da Rimini
Choreography: Georgy Alexidse
Music: Tchaikovsky
Régisseur: Guram Meliva
Designs: Ushangi Imerishvili

Demon
Choreography: Georgy Alexidse
Music: Giya Kancheli
Régisseur: Guram Meliva
Designs: Ushangi Imerishvili

La Fille mal gardée
Choreography: Kikaleishvili
Music: Hertel

Giselle
Choreography: trad.
Music: Adam

Swan Lake
Choreography: trad.
Music: Tchaikovsky

Don Quixote
Choreography: trad.
Music: Minkus

Chopiniana
Choreography: Fokine
Music: Chopin

Serenade
Choreography: Balanchine
Music: Tchaikovsky

The Moor's Pavane
Choreography: Limón
Music: Purcell

Gorda
Choreography: Tchabukiani
Music: Toradse

Gayaneh
Choreography: Galstian
Music: Khachaturian

Carmen Suite
Choreography: A. Alonso
Music: Bizet, Shchedrin

Porgy & Bess
Choreography: Mikhail Lavrovsky
Music: Gershwin

Cinderella
Choreography: Alexidse
Music: Prokofiev

The Prodigal Son
Choreography: Alexidse
Music: Prokofiev

The Seasons
Choreography: Alexidse
Music: Vivaldi

School:

Tibilisi Ballet School
Tibilisi
Georgia

Director:
Baram Baramidse
Artistic director:
Gregory Alexidse

Consultant:
Vakhtang Tchabukiani

STANISLAVSKI AND NEMIROVICH-DANCHENKO MUSIC THEATRE BALLET,
generally referred to as:

Stanislavsky Ballet
Music Theatre
Pushkin Street 17
Moscow
Tel: Moscow 229 28-35

Chief choreographer:
Dmitry Briantzev

Ballet master/administrator:
Zurab Sakhoniya

Teachers/répétiteurs:
Tatiana Legat, Nina Chkalova, Nina
Dorenskaya, Yuri Trepykhalin, Arkady
Nikolayev

Principal dancers:
Margarita Drosdova, Galina Krapivina,
Margarita Levina, Ludmila Ryzhova,
Svetlana Smirnova, Natalia Trubnikova,
Tatiana Trankvelitzkaya, Svetlana Tzoi,

Tatiana Chernobrovkina, Galina
Stepanenko, (10 female)
Vladimir Kirillov, Mikhail Krapivin, Vadim
Tedeyev, Timur Fayziyev, Valery Lantratov,
Viacheslav Sarkisov, Vladimir Petrunin,
Vadim Bondar, Alexandr Dubinin (9 male)
Artists:
64 female, 44 male

Repertory:

Swan Lake
Choreography: trad., Bourmeister
Music: Tchaikovsky

Snow White
Choreography: Bourmeister
Music: Tchaikovsky

Esmeralda
Choreography: Bourmeister
Music: Pugni, Glière, Vasilenko

Doctor Oh it Hurts!
Choreography: Kholfin
Music: Mosrozov

Cinderella
Choreography: Chichinadse
Music: Prokofiev

Don Quixote
Choreography: trad., Chichinadse
Music: Minkus

Straussiana
Choreography: Bourmeister
Music: J. Strauss

Evening Dances
Choreography: Schilling
Music: Schubert

Francesca da Rimini
Choreography: Chichinadse
Music: Tchaikovsky

The Little Hump-backed Horse
Choreography: Briantzev
Music: Shchedrin

La Sylphide
Choreography: Bournonville, Vinogradov
Music: Løvenskjold

Bravo, Figaro!
Choreography: Briantzev
Music: Rossini, Cohen

Nine Tangos and Bach
Choreography: Briantzev
Music: Bach, Piazzolla

Evening of Modern Choreography
Choreography: Briantzev, Béjart, Schilling
Music: various composers

Evening of Classical Choreography
Choreography: Petipa, Gorsky, Fokine
Music: Minkus, Chopin and others

*Ballet . . . ballet . . . ballet (Les Scythes, The
Swan Song, The Cowboys)*
Choreography: Briantzev
Music: Prokofiev, Chausson, Gershwin

Le Corsaire
Choreography: Dmitry Briantzev (original
new choreography)
Music: Adolph Adam
Designs: Vladimir Arefiev

**MODEST MUSSORGSKY THEATRE OF
OPERA AND BALLET**

*191011, ploschchad Iskusstv, 1
(Square of the Arts)
Leningrad, USSR
Tel: Leningrad 2103717*

Artistic director and chief choreographer:
Nikolay Boyarchikov

Choreographer:
Leonid Lebedev

Ballet master:
Anatoly Sidorov

Teachers/répétiteurs:
Larisa Klimova, Svetlana Sheina, Yekaterina
Pavlova, Anatoly Nisnevich, Nikolay
Tagunov, Yadvega Kuks

Soloists:
Yelena Alkanova, Tatiana Fesenko, Tatiana
Goryshina, Natalia Kirichek, Irina
Kirsanova, Angelika Kondrashova,
Margarita Kurshakova, Regina Kuzmicheva,
Anna Linnik, Natalia Lobachkova, Alla
Malysheva, Tatiana Podkopayeva, Irina
Shapchitz, Tamara Statkun (14 female)
Vladimir Adjamov, Vladimir Korobkov,
Serguei Kosadayev, Konstantin Novoselov,
Vassily Ostrovsky, Yuri Petukhov, Gennady
Sudakov, Oleg Ujinsky, Yury Vasilkov,
Rafik Zaripov, Mikhail Zavialov (11 male)
Artists:
50 female, 25 male
Total in company:
100 dancers

Repertory:

Macbeth
Choreography: Boyarchikov, Tagunov
Music: Kallos

The Brigands
Choreography: Boyarchikov
Music: Zhurbin

Tzar Boris
Choreography: Boyarchikov
Music: Prokofiev, Martynov

The Ugly Duckling
Choreography: Lebedev
Music: Tzeslukova, Mikita, Petrova

Coppélia
Choreography: Vinogradov
Music: Delibes

Fadette
Choreography: Boyarchikov
Music: Delibes

The Little Hump-backed Horse
Choreography: Belsky
Music: Shchedrin

The Nutcracker
Choreography: Belsky
Music: Tchaikovsky

The Cranes are Flying
Choreography: Petukhov
Music: Uspensky

La Sylphide
Choreography: Bournonville, von Rosen
Music: Løvenskjold

Giselle
Choreography: trad.
Music: Adam

Swan Lake
Choreography: trad., Boyarchikov
Music: Tchaikovsky

Esmeralda
Choreography: trad., Gusev, Vecheslova
Music: Pugni and others

Petrushka
Choreography: Fokine
Music: Stravinsky

Le Sacre du printemps
Choreography: Kasatkina, Vasiliov
Music: Stravinsky

La Fille mal gardée
Choreography: Vinogradov
Music: Hérold

Evening of Petipa:
Les Millions d'Arlequin, La Halte de Cavalerie, Paquita (grand pas)
Music: Drigo, Arnsheimer, Minkus

Evening of Balanchine:
Serenade, Theme and Variations, Pas de deux
Music: Tchaikovsky